MODERN HUNGARY

MODERN HUNGARY

Readings from *The New Hungarian Quarterly*

Edited by Denis Sinor

INDIANA UNIVERSITY PRESS
BLOOMINGTON & LONDON

Manufactured in the United States of America

Library of Congress Cataloging in Publication Data

Main entry under title:

Modern Hungary.

   1. Hungary—History—1945–   —Addresses,
essays, lectures. I. Sinor, Denis. II. The
New Hungarian quarterly.
DB956.M57 1977 943.9'05   77–74441
ISBN 0–253–33862–X   1 2 3 4 5 81 80 79 78 77

CONTENTS

CONTENTS

PREFACE

This book, conceived as a reader for college courses on Hungary or East-Central Europe, could not have been produced without the understanding help of the editorial staff of *The New Hungarian Quarterly*. I am deeply indebted to Iván Boldizsár and Miklós Vajda, editor and literary editor of this fine periodical, respectively, for having understood the importance of the project and for having provided clean copies of the articles. They were also instrumental in securing the necessary copyright permissions. The authors of the selections have graciously waived royalties. Ágnes Széchy, editorial assistant of the *NHQ*, was of constant help in ironing out technical difficulties and in gathering information for the biographical sketches. My friend Miklós Szántó gave me some sound advice concerning the selection of the articles. I am grateful to all and hope that the product of our common labors will be well received and deemed useful by my colleagues in American higher education.

The first volume of *The New Hungarian Quarterly* appeared in September 1960. In his opening statement editor Iván Boldizsár paid tribute to the memory of József Balogh, editor of a *Hungarian Quarterly* published in the interwar years, who was murdered by the Nazis in 1944. I, for one, greatly appreciated this linking with the past, the acceptance of a heritage. However revolutionary the changes in a country's history may be, the present remains a continuation of the past, and our own lives affect but a small part of the material and spiritual inventory of the nation.

Bloomington, Indiana   DENIS SINOR

EDITOR'S INTRODUCTION

The purpose of this book is to provide in an easily accessible format some information about contemporary Hungary. Scores of courses are taught in the colleges and universities of the English-speaking world, particularly in the United States, which should and often do incorporate some material about modern Hungary. Unfortunately, the teachers and students of such courses are often hampered by the lack of up-to-date, balanced materials. To be sure, there is no dearth of information concerning the events of 1956, but undue emphasis on that era does not provide an objective approach for those who seek facts about contemporary Hungary. Much has changed in Hungary in the past twenty years. By providing some firsthand information on various aspects of Hungarian life in recent years, this anthology of articles from *The New Hungarian Quarterly*, a sophisticated periodical published in Budapest, attempts to remedy a serious lack.

The aim of *The New Hungarian Quarterly*, founded in September 1960 and edited since then by the eminent Hungarian writer Iván Boldizsár, is to acquaint the English-speaking world with current political, social, economic, and cultural developments in Hungary. Almost all the articles published in the *Quarterly* and reprinted in this volume were originally written by Hungarians in Hungarian and were published initially in Hungarian periodicals, for internal consumption. Many of the authors hold or have held official positions in Hungary, and thus their writings tend to reflect the thinking of the current political, economic, and cultural leadership. The reader may well disagree with some or even most of the opinions held, he or she may even wish to contest certain of the facts presented, but one cannot deny that a study of the positions represented here is essential to an understanding of Hungarian reality.

This book is concerned with the period following 1956, although all the articles selected were originally published between 1966 and 1976. It does not attempt to sketch the history of those two decades, or of the events of the last ten years; rather it aims at presenting in a series of "stills" the nature and evolution of Hungarian life in its diverse aspects during this period. I have tried to select articles dealing with various facets of the Hungarian scene, from pictures of the everyday life of the average Hungarian to philosophical problems of Marxism and the views of some of Hungary's leaders. As I see it, there is only one major omission in this coverage: nothing is said about the relations between church and state, a topic of great importance and one that commands wide interest outside Hungary. Few aspects of Hungary's internal structure, if any, have been more seriously misunderstood; none has received more hostile criticism. I was genuinely sorry that I could find no material in the *NHQ* relevant to this issue.

No East-Central European people is less known and perhaps less accurately represented to the English-reading world than the Hungarians. There are a number of reasons for this state of affairs and it may be of use to mention some of them briefly. In the first place, the Hungarian language is inaccessible to most non-Hungarians. Secondly, Hungary has often been interpreted to the Western world by writers holding an anti-Hungarian point of view. Historical Hungary—and I refer to the country as it existed from about 900 to 1920—incorporated peoples of several nationalities who, quite understandably, would have preferred to live in their own countries or to be united with their ethnic brethren across the border. In the aftermath of the settlement imposed by the Entente powers in East-Central Europe after World War I, the newly created states of the Versailles system incorporated large Hungarian populations. Writings emanating from these countries were frequently hostile to Hungary.

A third reason for the distorted views prevalent about Hungary must rest with the Hungarians themselves. The fact is that many of the emerging writings on Hungary since 1920 have been by Hungarian émigrés who have attempted to discredit the regime that they left. This is true of persons who left Hungary after World Wars I and II and to some degree of the post-1956 émigrés as well. The aftermath of the Communist revolution of 1919 in Hungary—an event that was not received with much sympathy in Western countries—produced a crop of émigrés, for the most part intellectuals, who carried their grievances abroad and did their best to discredit the Horthy regime. On the other hand, many of the writings of Hungarians in Hungary during the interwar period were directed toward the revision of the Treaty of Trianon, a respectable and logical aim; one could hardly expect less from citizens of a country that had lost two-thirds of its territory and population. But as a result, Hungarian writing, particularly historical writing, assumed the character of passionate pleading, addressed in vain to international justice. The post-World War II years saw a new wave of emigration which included, among many people genuinely frightened by the Soviet occupation, a fair number of ex-Nazis. Unsuccessful politicians of the first group to rule after World War II were soon to join their ranks. In their memoirs, members of this

group tended to claim that they alone, in the long line of politicians who pre-
ceded and followed them, were right and honest. Their writings, which received considerable attention in Western countries, although often of value for
the study of the period, could not help but perpetuate the distorted view of
Hungary that had been inherited from the Horthy epoch.

This situation has been rectified somewhat in the period since the explosion
of 1956 when, among those who left Hungary, scores of intelligent, open-
minded men and women seized the opportunity to breath fresh air. The
intellectuals in this wave of emigration included many capable of objectivity,
if not toward Hungary's present, then at least toward its past. Working
in the field of historiography outside Hungary during the past two decades,
these scholars have produced more and better books about Hungary's past
than were written in English between the two wars. An enlightened
policy of the Hungarian government—political amnesty came in 1963—has
allowed most of these historians or political scientists to return to Hungary
and make use of archival materials there as well as of secondary sources
needed for their work. After half a century of neglect, the study of Hungarian history flourishes outside the borders of that country to an extent unprecedented in the historiography of Central Europe. To be sure, this change
for the better is less noticeable in the treatment of the period since World
War I, or in writings dealing with contemporary events. As background to
the present volume, therefore, the following outline may be helpful for understanding the principal events that occurred in Hungary between the end
of World War II and the beginning of the period during which these articles
from *The New Hungarian Quarterly* first appeared.

The collapse of Germany followed barely one month after Soviet troops
completed the liberation of Hungary on April 4, 1945. Hungary, an increasingly reluctant ally of Germany (with which it had shared in the beginning the desire to bring about a revision of the treaties signed under duress
at the end of World War I), had been occupied by German forces on March
17, 1944. Horthy, the aged regent, found himself faced with a problem
similar to the one that had confronted the monarchs of Norway, Denmark,
Holland, and Belgium in the early stages of the German conquest in 1940.
But Horthy was deprived of the choice open, for instance, to Queen Wil-
helmina of the Netherlands when her country was invaded, for there was no
place where he could have taken refuge. So he remained where he was,
hoping, like Leopold III, king of the Belgians, to be of some service to his
country, and to limit the baleful consequences of foreign occupation. In this
he probably succeeded to a limited extent, but at the price of confusing the
issues, as Pétain had done in France in the summer of 1940.

But the Germans of 1944–1945—leaders as well as soldiers—were very different from the fresh, optimistic victors of five years earlier. By August 1944 they were aware of fighting a losing battle, with only a dim hope that a split among the Allies might produce a change in alignments. Harassed and demoralized as is the wont of retreating troops, they showed little regard for anyone, least of all for their useless allies. Here and there, the isolated action of a civilized soldier or administrator saved lives, or spared a city such as Paris, but the major part of the German army continued to perform the task for which it had been forged, namely to fight, disregarding the internal problems of the countries in which it was operating. But as the war was engulfing Hungary—the first Soviet troops crossed her borders on September 23—it became plain that German and Hungarian interests were diametrically opposed. For the Germans, not only was fighting on Hungarian soil a duty, but it also meant protecting their own territory. For the Hungarians, it meant the destruction of their land for the sake of aliens who were basically indifferent to the welfare and even the survival of the population. Belatedly, Horthy, who had always hoped that by temporizing he might secure an Anglo-American occupation of Hungary instead of a Soviet one, sent his emissaries to Moscow, where, on October 1, they requested an armistice. Horthy's attempt to detach Hungary from the agonized Third Reich on October 15 was thwarted, and he was arrested and transported to Germany. Hungary, now the theatre of a war of annihilation, came under the control of the Hungarian Nazi leader Szálasi.

The nightmare of the following months left an indelible trace on the minds of all who were lucky enough to survive them. The further development of Hungarian society, and the change in outlook after the watershed of 1945, cannot be understood without taking into account this traumatic experience. The liberation of Hungary was accomplished by Soviet occupation forces, and the reception of foreign soldiers engaged in fighting is never a pleasant experience. Over 140,000 Soviet soldiers lost their lives in Hungary, yet those who put the word "liberation" in inverted commas should be reminded of the thousands who had been murdered by the Hungarian Nazis, and of the inferno of the siege of Budapest, which lasted from December 24, 1944, to February 13, 1945. It is probably true that for the very great majority of Hungarians, except for those guilty of atrocities, the arrival of the Soviet forces was indeed a personal liberation.

The clearing away of the physical and spiritual rubble left by more than six months of fighting (which, it should be remembered, engaged Hungarians on both sides) began in various places at various times, as the fighting ceased. Physically, Hungary had lost about forty percent of her national wealth, but while the destroyed factories, houses, and railroads could be rebuilt, it was clear to anyone with a minimum of perspicacity that the political superstructure of the interwar years could not and should not be restored. It must be borne in mind that Horthy's rule spanned only a quarter of a century. The dissolution of the Habsburg empire had left Hungary mutilated, a kingdom without a king—a country which, like Austria, had to adjust to a new way of life resulting from and demanded by complete independence. Horthy's authority, although exercised in strictly constitutional ways, had been very much dependent on his own personality; the choice of his successor would have caused problems even in a time of peace. The end of the Horthy intermezzo, which in fact had been a continuation of the Austro-Hungarian way of life, marked the necessary beginning of a new Hungarian era, which, for better or for worse, was definitely weaned from lingering Habsburg polities. The kingdom without a king became a republic on February 1, 1946.

The proclamation of the republic was the culmination of a political process that had begun with liberation from the Nazi nightmare. Hungarian tradition called for a multi-party system, but the nascent and renascent parties agreed on the necessity of adopting a basic, common platform that would enable them to cope with the towering problems presented by the political and economic situation. On December 3, 1944, in Szeged, representatives of five political parties agreed on the creation of the Hungarian National Independence Front to pursue a basic political and social policy; and they took the first preliminary steps leading to the formation of a provisional government. Under the premiership of Béla Dálnoki Miklós, this government began its work on December 21. Almost a year later, on November 4, 1945, the whole country went to the polls for an election in which, to the surprise of many political pundits, the party of the Independent Smallholders—a remnant of the prewar years—won a sweeping victory by obtaining 57.03 percent of the votes, an absolute majority. The Hungarian Communist Party, emerging from its prewar illegality, and the Social Democrats each obtained 17 percent of the votes cast. A coalition government was formed, headed by Zoltán Tildy, a Smallholder, who on February 1, 1946, became the president of the republic.

Cooperation within the coalition was less than harmonious. On March 5, 1946, a so-called Leftist Bloc uniting Communists, Social Democrats, and some smaller groups was formed, pressing for increased and accelerated socialization of the country's shaky economy. The prewar currency lost just about all its value—banknotes of one billion were in current use—and everyone welcomed the introduction on August 1 of a new stable currency, the forint. The release by the United States of some Hungarian goods that had been taken to Germany, including gold worth $32 million, was a factor of importance in the monetary stabilization, which was further helped by an American credit of $10 million for the purchase of American Surplus Property and by substantial contributions from UNRRA. Credit for the Improvement in living standards was claimed by the Leftist Bloc, which adroitly exploited the reluctance of most politicians to accept a "rightist" label. The time-honored political adage *divide et impera* was put into practice with the gradual assimilation or elimination of opponents by intimidating or discrediting them. This "salami tactics" was masterminded by Matthias Rákosi, who since February 1945 had been secretary general of the Communist Party.

Rákosi (1892–1971)—a Communist since World War I when he was a prisoner of war in Russia—was a founding member of the Hungarian Communist Party of 1919. After the fall of the Hungarian Soviet Republic (July 31, 1919), he fled and between 1921 and 1924 served as a secretary of the Communist International. At the end of 1924 he returned illegally to Hungary, where he was arrested in September of the following year. He was to spend some fifteen years in prison until, in 1940, he was allowed to go to the Soviet Union, whence he returned in January 1945. Thus during more than a quarter of a century, Rákosi spent only some nine months as a free man in Hungary, a circumstance that may partially explain his obvious lack of understanding of Hungary's specific problems and of the Hungarian mentality. A man of many talents, he was an ardent practitioner of Communism of the Stalinist brand, and he guided with much skill and total unscrupulousness the destinies of the revived party, for which he had made such great personal sacrifices. To him, unrepentant even in his Soviet exile after 1956, "revolutionary legality" was a contradiction in terms, and the imprisonment and internment of thousands was only a "natural" phenomenon in a revolution which, by definition, was "above the law."

The year 1947 and the first half of 1948 are usually referred to as "the year of change." In one respect at least, the appellation is misleading. The peace treaty that Hungary had to sign in Paris on February 10, 1947, reestablished the Trianon frontiers, with the added penalty of ceding to Czechoslovakia a bridgehead on the right bank of the Danube opposite Bratislava. On the matters of Hungary's territorial integrity and the destinies of the Hungarian populations living in neighboring states, the new leadership, however democratic, had received no more consideration than its predecessor. The treaty (and this is probably the only argument that can be made in its favor) did prevent the expulsion of some two hundred thousand Hungarians from Czechoslovakia. Relations between that country and Hungary remained strained, however, and the tensions, with dire consequences for many individuals, diminished only with the increasing influence of the Communist parties of the two lands.

The Hungarian public, appalled by the territorial provisions of the peace settlement, had little opportunity to express its feelings; public attention was soon claimed by the momentous internal changes of this period. August 1, 1947, was to be the starting point of a Three-Year Plan whose aim was to attain the living standard of prewar Hungary by increasing the industrial output by 27 percent; the bourgeois classes were to carry the heaviest economic burden. The elections held August 31, 1947, brought about the virtual collapse of the Independent Smallholders (15.1 percent of the votes). The Social Democrats just about held their own (15.1 percent), while the Communists slightly increased their electorate (22 percent). However, as these and other parties had entered into a coalition, they could together claim over 60 percent of the votes cast, whereas the rightist opposition parties—the Democratic People's Party and the Hungarian Independence Party led by István Barankovics and Zoltán Pfeiffer, respectively—obtained only 16 percent and 14 percent of the votes. By the end of the year both had been suppressed by a government led by Lajos Dinnyés, in which Rákosi was minister of state and László Rajk, minister of the interior. The government accelerated the nationalization of a variety of financial and industrial enterprises, a process begun in 1946.

On June 12, 1948, the two "workers' parties"—the Communists and the Social Democrats—declared their fusion into the new Hungarian Workers' Party (Magyar Dolgozók Pártja, MDP). This was in fact tantamount to the latter's absorption by the former. Secularization of the schools, strongly resented by important segments of the population, was decreed on June 16, and this elicited vituperous attacks from Cardinal Mindszenty, head of the Catholic Church in Hungary. Tempers were frayed, and Tito's expulsion from the Cominform (June 1948) had baneful consequences for the internal equilibrium of the Hungarian Communist leadership. Rákosi's hysterical denunciations of the Yugoslav leader and his policies carried ominous warnings for external as well as internal affairs. The year ended with the arrest of Mindszenty.

By spring 1949 the MDP and the remaining skeleton parties—deprived of or abandoned by their leaders—were clustered in an all-embracing Hungarian Independent Popular Front (Magyar Függetlenségi Népfront), which, not surprisingly, collected 95.6 percent of the votes cast at the election held on May 15, 1949. In Hungary, the unification of all political parties is normally regarded as a positive achievement, and it is conceded that many of Rákosi's actions in the years immediately following the liberation of the country deserve credit. Yet barely four years after the end of the fighting, the great hopes of decent men of all persuasions had been dashed, for Rákosi's heavy-handed, dogmatic rule crushed not only dissent but also any constructive ideas that did not originate with him.

The spring of 1949 brought the arrest of such reliable Communists as László Rajk and György Pálffy, among others, who were tried on fabricated charges and executed in the fall of that year. The trial of Mindszenty in February 1949 had given the public some indication of the working of the judiciary, but at the same time the intransigence of the accused seemed to lend it a measure of credibility. The accusations leveled at Rajk and his companions—and later, in the early fifties, at Communists and Social Democrats such as János Kádár, Gyula Kállai, György Marosán, Árpád Szakasits, and many others—were sheer fabrications. It seemed indeed incredible that numbers of men who had made great personal sacrifices to advance the cause of socialism should now freely confess that they had worked for the establishment of a fascist regime or that they were guilty of espionage. When a great man falls, ordinary citizens with whom he has had little contact may be led to accept the notion of his guilt, but when thousands are arrested without apparent rhyme or reason, their families, friends, and colleagues who are directly affected by their plight form an important segment of the population; by statistical necessity, this group must include a high proportion of individuals reluctant to believe in the spontaneity of self-inculpating confessions made by people well known to them. It is implausible that thousands of peaceful, apolitical citizens should suddenly reveal themselves as artful plotters, scheming to overthrow the regime; but to the closer circle of such a victim his guilt is not merely improbable, it is inconceivable. And as the number of those accused as "enemies" grows, so does the number of those who begin to realize that Kronos swallows his children not for fear of being overthrown by them, but simply to satisfy his appetite. Doubt led to disbelief, and only fear of the unknown cowed a population demoralized by the drabness of daily existence as much as by the apparent triumph of evil.

On August 20, 1949, a new constitution transforming Hungary into a People's Republic became effective. Although it declared that "the highest organ of state exercising all rights deriving from the sovereignty of the people" was the National Assembly, it was evident to all that power was in the hands not even of the MDP but of Rákosi and his closest circle, known as the "troika" and comprising, beside himself, Ernö Gerö and Mihály Farkas, minister of defense from September 1948 to July 1953, under whose de facto authority stood the dreaded political police (AVH). The Central Committee of the Party, and even the Politburo, were seldom consulted. Their members assembled mainly to applaud and approve the measures or ideas proposed by one of the troika, or, on occasion, by someone else in the innermost circle, such as József Révai, who played an important role in the ideological indoctrination of the Hungarian people.

Fear for life and liberty was but one aspect of an increasingly dissatisfying daily life. Some basically sound ideas, such as the need to expand the country's heavy industry, were marred by association with totally unrealistic timetables. And while production was hailed as the supreme good, a neglected agriculture, paralyzed by the erratic persecution of some of the most productive elements of the peasant population, could not lift itself even to its prewar level. As countless hours were wasted on the rites of the personality cult, the living standards of the population as a whole were actually regressing. Those were hard years indeed, and they left an indelible mark, not only on those who suffered torture, imprisonment, deportation, and countless personal indignities, but also on those who enjoyed privileges, modest in scope and clearly insecure. The random quality of Rákosi's terror—and this was its aim —did not allow anyone, however close to the seat of power, to harbor the illusion of safety, while the material rewards for hard work, blind loyalty, or spineless sycophancy could be judged only minimal by all who had seen or experienced higher living standards.

The radical transformation of the Hungarian economy and social structure during the years of Rákosi's rule may or may not be considered a positive achievement, but that it took place is undeniable. It is of lesser importance, and less well known, that Rákosi also exerted a lasting influence on the development of Hungarian advanced research in the natural as well as the social sciences and humanities. World opinion, usually highly sensitive to any real or imaginary injury inflicted on writers or artists, has little understanding for the needs of scholarship. While the oppressive atmosphere of the 1950s was most uncongenial for the flourishing of the fine arts or literature, the reorganization of the Hungarian Academy of Sciences in 1949 proved to be of immense benefit for the development of scholarship in the humanities and social sciences. To be sure, many of the products of the period bore the stamp of the personality cult, but in some cases it was merely a sycophantic footnote or other acknowledgment. In any event, on the foundations laid in 1949, the Academy—a venerable institution established in 1825—acquired financial resources which can be envied by many Western states, and it has developed into one of the most respected and efficient places of learning in Europe.

The universities were less favorably affected by the changing pattern of Hungarian society. Many distinguished professors were dismissed on account of their political views or their bourgeois origins. They were replaced either by men of lesser intellectual ability or by young scholars who, at that time, had not yet proved their worth but were acceptable in the party. Forced ideological indoctrination was, in many instances, counterproductive, and the universities' admission policy was strongly biased against the children of the former middle classes. Not talent but social background determined who should be admitted and who not. As a result of such "affirmative action" the student body contained a sizeable segment of those who neither could nor really wanted to cope with the burden that a higher education is bound to impose on those who receive it. Since failing a student of "popular origin" might have had dire consequences for the instructor, the standards had to be lowered. During those years the universities produced a fair-sized crop of graduates who held diplomas of little worth and were discontented by the realization that the fulfilment of expectations depended on their abilities rather than on the easy obtaining of a degree. Many of those who owed everything to the regime of the early 1950s became its most vociferous enemies in 1956.

The death of Stalin in March 1953, with the consequent changes in Soviet leadership, could not but affect the destinies of his diligent emulator Rákosi, who in August 1952 had added to his party post that of prime minister. At the end of June 1953, at a plenary session of the Central Committee—to the astonishment of all—Rákosi indulged in a bout of self-criticism: he accused himself of having abandoned the practice of collective leadership and pleaded guilty to charges of personality cult and of mistaken policies resulting from a lack of proper consultation. Gerö, Farkas, and Révai followed his example. Breaches of socialist legality were also admitted, but the monstrosity of the fake trials was not revealed. Farkas and Révai had to relinquish their seats in the Politburo, of which Rákosi and Gerö remained members. Imre Nagy became prime minister. He rescinded some of Rákosi's most oppressive measures and changed several of his most objectionable policies. A serious effort was made to improve the supply of consumer goods and to increase real wages. Of even greater consequences was the release of many political prisoners. The psychological effect of the reappearance of men whose destinies had been unknown, and many of whom had been considered dead, produced general elation, and resulted in the lifting of the fear that had lain so oppressively over the country. It was possible—so it now appeared—to survive the horror; there was no finality in the ordeal, and hope returned triumphant.

Nagy's premiership was of short duration and carried in itself the germs of tragic conflicts. Having gone through what he no doubt considered the mere formality of self-criticism, Rákosi made no real changes in his own political game. Within a short time Farkas was back in the Politburo, and the old leadership did not attempt to put into practice the policies that would logically have resulted from the revelations made in June 1953. But the clock could not be set back. In October 1954, serious misgivings were voiced at a meeting of the Central Committee on account of Rákosi's procrastination. The meeting also revealed an increasing polarization between the sectarian faction of Rákosi and the revisionist elements within the party grouped around Nagy. The tug of war ended with Rákosi's temporary victory. In April 1955 Nagy lost his seat in the Politburo and was also relieved of his post as prime minister. In November of the same year, accused of rightist deviation, he was expelled from the party.

Rákosi's victory proved to be shortlived. Once more he fell victim to a deus ex machina, in this case Khrushchev and his revelations to the Twentieth Congress of the Communist Party of the Soviet Union. The ghost of Rajk returned to haunt the man responsible not only for his murder but also for the temporary discredit brought upon his name. Rajk had too many friends and comrades convinced of his innocence to give respite to Rákosi. Reluctant though he was to admit his personal guilt in the matter, he conceded that Rajk (and others) had been tried on fabricated evidence. The posthumous rehabilitation of Rajk followed, a bitter pill for Rákosi and other unrepentant Stalinists. A disoriented party was unable to cope with an increasingly restive public. On July 18, 1956, Rákosi was relieved of his post of first secretary of the MDP and he lost his seat in the Politburo. Unfortunately for Hungary, Ernö Gerö became his successor, a man perhaps less tainted with the blood of the purge victims but still a collaborator, and a stubborn individual who lacked Rákosi's adaptability and cunning.

Ordinarily revolutions do not occur when things are at their worst. Explosions depend not only on the pressure built up within a container but also on the resistance of its walls. Remedial actions taken by a leadership that had lost confidence in itself could not placate a population that had lost confidence in the moral justification for the power wielded by its government. Rákosi's disgrace was interpreted as a weakness in the party, a concession to outside influences rather than a genuine attempt to right wrongs. The explosion did not occur because seething discontent created unprecedented pressures, it came about because a hesitant, unsure leadership was unable to control, let alone direct, political forces carrying along (rather than led by) self-appointed tribunes intoxicated by the discovery or rediscovery of their own voices. The late summer and early fall of 1956 was not a time of quiet counsel, but one of claims and counterclaims, outbreaks of lofty idealism and of sordid self-interest. Pent-up bitterness and hopes of bettering their daily lives were driving people to seek paths to self-fulfillment, people who were bewildered or enchanted by delusive roadsigns pointing to an El Dorado, erected by men who ought to have known, and very often did know, better. At the end of the road there was no El Dorado, but an insurrection that broke out on October 23 and ended, after the intervention of Soviet troops, on November 4 with the creation of a new government led by János Kádár, and with the reorganization of the party under a new name: Hungarian Socialist Workers' Party (Magyar Szocialista Munkáspárt).

Almost sixteen years later, speaking informally on the occasion of his sixtieth birthday, Kádár recalled those terrible days: "In 1956 a grave and critical situation arose which is called counterrevolution by historians. We know this is the learned definition of what happened in 1956. But there is also another name for it that we all can accept: it was a national tragedy. A tragedy for the party, for the working class, for the people as a whole and for individuals as well. It was a wrong turning, and this resulted in tragedy. And if now we are past it—and we can safely say we are—it is a very great thing indeed." (See below, p. 40.)

MODERN HUNGARY

SIXTY

This is the 60th issue of THE NEW HUNGARIAN QUAR-
TERLY. Fifteen years. The editor may well reflect that the magazine
took him from maturity into approaching old age. He was in his
late forties when he started the paper; and he could almost be
said to be in his mid-sixties now, writing Sixty at the head of these
prefatory notes. Never in his life has he held the same job for so long, and
that is worth thinking about as well. In early youth he had taken Reinhardt's
advice to heart: never stay put longer than five or six years if you wanted
to get anywhere, thus making a virtue of necessity. His frequent change
of jobs, loss of employment, to put it plainly, was the work of politics
and war. In the past fifteen years neither politics nor its continuation by
other means sacked the editor, or put an end to the paper. The real
reason is part of history. These fifteen years have been one of the quietest,
when development was smoothest, in the history of the Hungarian nation.
It has given the editorial staff and all contributors great intellectual satisfaction to keep track of this progress, pausing at the points, expressing
the results in a variety of ways: factual report and fiction, scholarly report
and higher journalism, never forgetting the difficulties along the way, the
sins of commission and omission, and all that remains to be done; en-
deavouring to make it all accessible to the great English-reading public.

But have we succeeded? Have we attained the aim we set ourselves in
the very first issue in September 1960: "Could a more attractive task be
conceived of than to afford English-speaking readers an insight into the
life and thinking of a small but much-talked-about, and so often mis-
represented nation?"

It is up to the reader to answer. The staff of THE NEW HUNGARIAN
QUARTERLY feel that, given the scope of a quarterly review, they have
done all they could to present, in words and pictures, today's Hungary,

socialist society, the traditions of the past, the political objectives, economic changes and achievements, literature and the arts, thus improving relations between nations, helping to dispatch the Cold War back where it belongs, into the ice-age of humanity. Though to tell the truth we also feel that our work has nowhere near attained the result we had hoped for, and still hope for. Our reputation and image change more slowly than the real place and role of Hungary in international life. The misconceptions of the Cold War survive in public opinion and in people's minds.

The staff of THE NEW HUNGARIAN QUARTERLY think they can best mark the appearance of No. 60 by examining what Hungary's image in the world is, and the rate at which it changed, even though they are well aware at the start that the tempo is a mere *andante*.

Image has only recently become fashionable in British and American journalese, French, German, Dutch and other writers following suit. In Hungary it can look back to a reputable past. Not the word, but the notion. "Our reputation in the world" has become a conventional expression, often recurring in newspaper and periodical headings, frequently as the name of a regular feature. As an editor I myself have employed it twice to head such a regular feature: first in the weekly *Új Magyarország* during the years immediately following the Liberation, and then in the daily *Magyar Nemzet*, in the early 'fifties. Recalling this allows me to show how uneven changes have been. In 1945 and the years that followed I was able to report almost week by week how much Hungary's reputation was improving, how the facts and results of Liberation, reconstruction, self-awareness were effacing the negative image of the Horthy era, and of Hungary's participation in the war. In the early 'fifties it was already more difficult to edit. Music and football were just about the only fields where good things were being done for the Hungarian image at the time. "Our reputation in the world" actually owes its birth to an essay by Gyula Illyés of that title published in the 'thirties; but being a small nation, the Hungarians have always been interested in what the world is saying about them.

Of course, the term "image" itself has been naturalized in the Hungarian language (and this small fact helps to disprove a frequently stressed negative aspect of it—that we are cut off from all information supplied by the Western world and from the free flow of ideas. . . .) There is still some difference between the two terms—good name or reputation on the one hand, and image, on the other—due not only to image being of more recent origin. It means more.

"Our reputation in the world" was born at a time before this earth shrunk thanks to mass travel and the mass media. It referred at the time only to what appeared about Hungary in the press and an occasional book. Image is a more complex notion, it has a visual reference as well, which springs from two sources. One is bilateral travel. Never before have so many citizens of other countries come to Hungary with peaceful intent, nor have as many Hungarians gone abroad, as in the past fifteen years. (At the Helsinki Conference on Security and Cooperation in Europe, János Kádár pointed out that last year more than eight million foreigners visited Hungary and three million Hungarians travelled abroad. To this one may add that of these three million about 300–400,000 went to Western or other capitalist countries.)

Image thus means not only that indirect notion obtained by public opinion in another country from the press, but the impressions, right and misleading alike, derived from direct personal experience. This image derived from personal contact is intensified many times over by television, since even those who have never crossed the frontiers of their country can see foreign cities, countries and people on the small screen. This is a two-way truth: not only Hungarians know, or think they know, the world since they travel and watch television (in about half of the country's area the Vienna, Graz, Zagreb, Ljubljana, Belgrade and Bratislava programmes can be received as well) but the foreign visitor and television viewer also have a wider view of Hungary and the Hungarians than they had before.

There is one more factor which further broadens the concept of image, and this is that the time of the "we are on our own" slogan fashionable in the Horthy era is over, we Hungarians are not on our own, neither in the way we look at ourselves, nor in the way the world sees us. What I have in mind is that the Western half of the world applies what it sees in Hungary, to the other people's democracies and the whole of the socialist community as such. This is a very important but insufficiently considered aspect of the way the West sees Hungary and the Hungarians.

One cannot even today, after sixty issues and fifteen years, disregard in this connection a characteristic, almost conventional position taken up in the West, that is thinking in terms of an Iron Curtain or rather, being obsessed by it, something that goes with the misconception of looking on the socialist countries as a monolith. I might put it in this way: the term Iron Curtain cannot be weeded out or eradicated from Western public opinion largely because the media find the expression Iron Curtain countries more convenient than that of socialist countries, using it even in reports that argue that they did not meet with an Iron Curtain. This is a survival, in the minds of the Western public, of the period of Cold War and the personality cult. Neither those who provide the information nor those for whom it is meant take into account that the socialist countries do have a common denominator, and that is the building of socialism, but a common denominator and an identical pattern are not the same thing. Looking even more closely at this attitude, it becomes clear that this concept is not simply monolithic but a negatively monolithic one. It is worth bearing this in mind at all times. If something is observed in any of the socialist countries that looks favourable and points to progress, no general conclusion applying to the others is drawn, but if anything negative is found in one— whether it is really there or not—it is readily applied to all.

Few reports appear of Hungarian political, economic or cultural developments when they are really taking place and palpably becoming part of the scene, but if there is any faltering or setback, or if the run of things can be interpreted to suggest one, attention is concentrated on it immediately. I have, on a number of occasions,* told that no report of Hungarian tourist passports has ever appeared in the Western press, nor have Western newspapers found the hundreds of thousands of Hungarians travelling abroad every year worth a story. Should one young man however of the half million Hungarians every year who take their holidays in Yugoslavia, swim across to the Italian shore, this is immediately reported so that a Western reader must perforce reach the conclusion that there is a permanent shuttle-service across the bays of the Adriatic shore. He is what is more likely to infer that obviously no one in Hungary is allowed to take a trip to the West, although if he himself looks around in his own town, he may well see cars with Hungarian registration numbers by their hundreds during the summer months. But the image of a foreign country and its system contains the paradox that people are more willing to trust the press, the radio, or television than their own eyes.

Three factors go to make up the current image of Hungary. There is a traditional one; a half-new one which is however, really obsolete and out-of-date; and there is a new one, but this is ambivalent.

The first, traditional, is not even bad, it is only false, and only—this time I mean "only" in quotation marks—humiliating. The traditional image is traditional also because it belongs to the days of Horthy and even to those of Francis Joseph. These are notions that serve to tickle the palates of the customers of travel agencies. I mention them since responsibility for such survivals and their proliferation rests on the shoulders of the tourist trade. According to them Budapest is the setting of an operetta and Hungary is a *puszta* peopled by wild cowboys in folk-costumes, eating *gulyás* and drinking Tokay. Hungary, they proclaim, is a romantic country where

* See e.g. No. 52: "A Day at Edmund Wilson's."

natives and visitors have fun to the tune of Gypsy violins and everyone is friendly and amiable, but should not really be taken seriously. Does this sound funny? I cannot tell it otherwise, it certainly is not a joke. Such ideas essentially camouflage Hungarian reality.

Half-new but already absolute ideas are diametrically opposed to these appetizing, traditional images, but often emerge at the same time in the consciousness of the same sort of person, what is more, of the same person. Since Hungary is a socialist country, they imagine life is grim and gloomy by order, everyday life is dull, people go in fear of one another, culture is monotonous, censorship is ruthless, and theatres present nothing but plays about enthusiastic tractor drivers and the loves of millgirls who keep on increasing their productivity. There is no need to explain that this image is a remnant of the long years of the Cold War and, in part, of the period of the personality cult.

The new but ambivalent ideas spring from the realization that, in the past fifteen years, everything in Hungarian has changed. Even though belatedly, with reservations, and high-handedly, the Western press, and media generally, nevertheless publish this, after all, millions of Western visitors have come to Hungary in recent years and they go about with their eyes open. People keep talking about life in Hungary having changed and improved, but they simply cannot imagine what it is like. In the Western world they already take it for granted that to use their terminology Stalinism is no more, but they cannot imagine what a socialist country can be like where the ruling norms are not those of the personality cult. This is why they are still suspicious.

How deeply this ambivalent image is rooted in men's minds can be illustrated by anyone who is in touch with people from other countries. Cold War propaganda has been so profoundly imprinted on the consciousness even of sympathizers, as well as socialists, and Communists that, in spite of their ways of thinking, intentions, and better knowledge, they are still prone to fall into its traps. This summer a young Party secretary, from a working-class suburb in the environs of Paris with a Communist majority, and his wife, were the guests of a friend of mine. They came to see me at the Balatonfüred heart sanatorium, and there the French guest was suddenly taken ill; appendicitis was suspected and we took him to a hospital in Veszprém. On the way there he felt a bit better and we talked. Although he knew that medical services in Hungary are free for everybody, they are a civil right, he asked nevertheless, how much I paid in the heart sanatorium where I was being treated. Although he was familiar with the statistics of household farms in Hungary, yet he asked whether cooperative peasants really owned household plots. Although he had read that the government in Hungary granted long-term loans to support home-building, when we came to the outskirts of Veszprém, he did not believe that a row of pretty new houses there were the homes of workers as well. Taking the risk that his appendix might play up, we went into five of those ten houses, and found four of them to be the homes of workers. He was operated on in Veszprém. When I called for him a week later, he asked me to get the surgical registrar to sign a paper attesting that his parents were still peasant members of the cooperative farm in a neighbouring village with the fine-sounding name Királyszentistván.

These three kinds of attitude are to be found in every Western country, in all classes, and they pervade public opinion. Or don't they?

I have ventured on the risky undertaking of talking about public opinion in general. If I restrict the scope of the Hungarian image, limiting it to culture, to intellectual development, to literature in the first place, one more paradox confronts us. The people with whom I would argue abroad (I am, of course, speaking of the Western world) are mostly members of the public, listening to lectures or attending similar functions. Their majority have a close relationship to literature, and to humanities. Time and time again I experienced that while cooperating on certain concrete projects, engaging in joint intellectual ventures, preparing and carrying out programmes, the ideas such people entertain about Hungary and the Hungarians, about literature and the arts in Hungary, about the state of development of socialism in the country, tally with the real facts. At such times they know that the Hungarians are equal partners, generally hard working, sometimes even (if a little bragging be permitted once in sixty issues) more enterprising than their own. But as soon as we come to speak of things outside their art, or discipline, their profession, or speciality, they immediately withdraw and become ordinary laymen, average newspaper readers, who put hair-raisingly naive questions and are surprised—if they have not yet seen it—by the table of contents of The New Hungarian Quarterly.

By way of example and proof let me here enumerate four international organizations whose discussions, symposia and round-table conferences I have frequently—according to my good friends, much to frequently—attended these past fifteen years. The four are: Unesco, International PEN, *Société Européenne de Culture*, and the World Peace Council. All that I have so far said about our reputation and image does not hold good in these four organizations. Their executives and staff, the officials and permanent representatives of various national commissions, centres, clubs and councils are fully aware of the actual state and development of Hungarian society and culture today, and many of them are familiar also with details of the country's economic development. All this, however, does not mean that, in this general picture, Hungarian literature holds the same place as it does in Hungary, and it is worth pausing at this point.

Literature in Hungary is part and parcel of the national consciousness. The same is true of the Poles and the Russians, to a smaller extent also of the Germans, but there are Western nations, for example the French, the English, the Spaniards or the Italians, whose literatures are considered great for good reasons, but they do not shape to that degree the national consciousness, or make history, as Hungarian literature does. That is why it is natural that even those foreign friends and other interested persons who have a sound image of socialist Hungary are not really aware of the importance of literature within it.

This is my answer to the often raised question why prose, verse and sometimes drama as well take up so much room in THE NEW HUNGARIAN QUARTERLY. It is unusual that a general review should devote so much space to literature itself and not only to writings on literature. We have felt ever since the paper was started and now, having in fifty-nine issues already discussed a great many social, political, and economic issues, and dealt with subjects in history, technology and many other fields, we feel even more that Hungarian reality cannot be properly presented if literature is not given its due place. In many cases it is precisely through short stories and poems that we can express what is most difficult to demonstrate: what is different, what is new, and what is socialist in today's Hungary.

While this number goes to press, we are basking under the summery climate of cooperation and *détente*, living in the days of the signing of the document of Security and Cooperation in Europe. Therefore, after this far from flattering drawing up of the balance sheet, we can rightly hope that, in the next sixty issues of this periodical, we shall be able to speak of Hungary to Europe and to the whole world with greater effect. These few words are all that appears on the Helsinki events, or the document there signed, in the present issue. The time it takes to translate, set up, print, and bind a paper like ours makes real comment impossible at such an early stage.

Earlier in this preface I used the word "virtue". It could be that this rare word has a familiar ring in the ears of our oldest and most faithful readers. The introduction to the first issue used it as well. Allow me to quote:

"It is quite an undertaking for Hungarians to edit and publish in Budapest an English-language periodical intended to be read in the English-speaking world. In the audacity and difficulty of this task—and it is not only the linguistic difficulty we have in mind—there is something that the Hungarian language denotes by the word *virtus*. This term is not identical with the Latin *virtus*, from which it derives, and is only a remote relative of the English *virtue*. *Virtus* is an undertaking which at first sight surpasses the strength of a person or of a group, but in itself or in its aims is too significant and attractive for its challenge to be resisted."

The international climate today is more favourable, and what was only a pious wish in our first issue—mutual knowledge and understanding between countries and between peoples,—is making some progress, bringing out an English-language periodical about Hungary, a socialist country, however is still today as a part of the humanism of the twentieth century a virtuous undertaking.

IVÁN BOLDIZSÁR

TEACHING "HUNGARY"

(Hungarian studies as an academic subject)

by

DENIS SINOR

For more years than I care to count I have been trying to convey to French, British or American students an understanding of what I like to call the Hungarian reality.* On and off I have taught Hungarian language, literature, and history, and in doing so, I have become increasingly aware of the difficulties encountered by such a fragmentary presentation. It is possible to learn the language or even the history, the art, the music of a given people, but the sum of the knowledge so obtained will amount to little else than at best, a lopsided, at worst, a distorted picture of the true characteristics of the daily life, the patterns of thought, the working habits, in short, of everything that really matters when we wish to understand a people.

Words mean different things to different people and they are notoriously inadequate for the purposes of visual description. Anna Karenina will appear differently to each and everyone, and the mental picture of Monsieur Swann will vary from reader to reader, notwithstanding the constancy of Proust's text. How much nearer we come to the understanding of such novels if we have a direct experience of the place and of the epoch in which they are situated. Even a picture of the Champs Élysées will be of immense help and a visit to present-day Paris will further enhance the understanding we can gain of those places, avenues, parks which, according to Proust, are not less transient than time itself.

The problem, then, to convey the reality of one country to someone bred in another is always great. And yet by the time a British or an American student reaches the university he will have heard a great deal about, say, France. With some luck he might even have some knowledge of French; he must have seen innumerable pictures, some films; perhaps, indeed, he might even have travelled to France. But ask an average American under-

---

* Since I have taught for almost a decade in the United States, most of the examples given and many of the problems touched upon should be set against the present-day American background.

graduate to tell you everything he knows about Hungary: a few sentences will exhaust his store of knowledge and it is very likely that some of those will contain gross inaccuracies. But there is also a positive side to the question. Experience has shown—and there is no cause for surprise in this—that most students who wish to learn something about Hungary have an *a priori* interest in the country or in a related subject. This is fortunate for the teacher. He faces highly motivated students who do not come to the course because it is compulsory, but because they wish to learn something about a topic in which they are interested. But given this basic interest, and perhaps a little factual knowledge acquired through reading, the fact remains that the understanding of Hungary presents a greater challenge to the British and American student than does that of most other European countries.

Among the accidental reasons, unfamiliarity with Hungarian literature and the absence of Hungarian films are probably the most important. Many facets of Spanish, French, Italian, etc. life have become familiar through literary media even to those not particularly well-read or interested in foreign countries. But there is a deep-lying reason which makes the interpretation of Hungarian civilization to American, and, to a lesser degree, to British students, particularly difficult: the originality of Hungarian culture. The fact that the Hungarian language is totally unrelated to those of the neighbouring countries can be taken as its symbol. Even some of the aspects of Hungarian civilization and life which are very similar if not completely identical with those to be found in other Central European countries are totally alien to a British and, *a fortiori*, to an American student. The difficulties are further compounded by the political system of Hungary of which most American students have a completely distorted view. The majority of these students will be surprised to find out such obvious things as the fact that one can own property in Hungary, that travel within the country is free, that churches are open and attended, that denominational schools not only function but are supported by the state. On a more sophisticated level, they still have some mistaken concepts about the role the Party is playing in Hungarian life. They tend to visualize it as rather shady, working behind the scenes in a way different pressure groups or lobbies work in American life.

There is a marked difference between British and American students with regard to their direct experience of state-run enterprises and services. A British student will show no surprise when he learns about the Hungarian equivalent of the National Health Service which, even today, to many Americans, will appear as a useless and even dangerous infringement on the individual's right to suffer and perhaps to die according to his means.

It is because of such differences in basic attitudes which are very likely to appear among his students, that the teacher should avoid praise or blame and should present Hungary simply as it is.

The word "partial" has a double meaning in English. If we do not present the whole of a subject, then we are partial, i.e. we select the good or the bad according to our judgment. Let me take a delicate example to show the complexity and the pitfalls an incomplete presentation of a citizen's daily life may present. A Hungarian citizen moving his home two blocks down the same street must report this change to the police. This may or may not be a useful or commendable practice, but cries of "communist police state" would certainly be out of place. The duty of a citizen to report his change of address to the police is general in Central Europe and has a long tradition. There is nothing new, nothing specifically Hungarian and nothing communist in it. Registration was compulsory also for the subjects of Francis Joseph or Wilhelm II. If such police control seems distasteful to a British or American citizen, the former would take for granted and the latter would probably envy the amount of police protection every Hungarian citizen receives. Budapest with its two million inhabitants is a big city even by American standards and yet it has no unsafe districts and a lady may walk safely through its streets, through any street, by day or by night. Pleasant though such a state of affairs may be, neither is it specifically Hungarian; indeed, one has to live outside Europe to learn to appreciate it.

So when we try to present Hungary, it is essential to point out again and again the features that are general to Europe or to Central Europe and set against their background our explanations of what is specifically Hungarian.

To understand the average Hungarian it is important to bear in mind that he has probably experienced a more than ordinary share of the horrors in which our century has been so rich. The simple survival of our imaginary Hungarian, now, say, seventy years of age, may be bordering on the miraculous. He and his family may have gone through two World Wars with periods of hunger, destruction, and lack of fuel in their wake. He may have learned to hide in periods of unbridled terror; he may have lost his kin at the hands of German or Hungarian Nazis. Perhaps he knows the horror of political imprisonment or deportation which he might have suffered more than once, a victim of men claiming to follow different political ideologies. He may have lost all his belongings, his fortune, more than once, and never of his own fault. Into what a horror-strip most Hungarian lives could easily be converted. This is a basic fact that has to be brought near, made plausible, to students to whom all these happenings are not only distant but also unrealistic.

A man who has never suffered physical pain finds it difficult to understand its true nature. The moral agonies of countless Hungarian generations have been difficult to translate in terms of American optimism. In this respect it is amazing to find the metamorphosis that American—and, to a lesser extent, also Western European—youth has undergone in the last five years. While the most ferocious "police brutality" in the U.S. is a velvet-handed caress compared with Nazi terror, while the horror of the Vietnamese war is—in its effect on the daily life of the people of the U.S.—a small skirmish when set against the terrible bloodbaths of World War I or II; the dissatisfaction with a war that cannot be won, the prolonged absence of prisoners of war, the steadily worsening situation of the economy strained by and geared to an unpopular war are realities that can effectively be compared with some of the more recent Hungarian experiences. And one feels, sometimes, a little ashamed to be congratulated on the apparent wisdom and foresight that went into some "prophecies" uttered some years ago, when these were but the projection into the American future of some past Hungarian experiences. I vividly remember the difficulty encountered in explaining to an incredulous class on medieval Hungarian history that the disappearance of silver from U.S. coinage was just as bad a sign for American economy as was the debasing of the silver coin for 12th century Hungary. Familiar with two inflations in 20th century Hungary, it was not too difficult three years ago to foretell that prices will continue to rise in the U.S.

In my own teaching career most of my students have belonged to an affluent society and more than once I have found it wellnigh impossible to convey to them the difficulties and problems of Hungarian life in the 20th century while, at the same time, counteracting their tendency to impute these difficulties to the inaptitude of the leaders, if not of the whole people. Probably I would have found an audience more sympathetic to these woes in the generation that grew up during the depression years.

Natural selection in its crudest form has put its stamp on most Hungarian characters and accounts for the extraordinary toughness of Hungarian life. "There are too many Eskimos and not enough seals"—a saying by the Hungarian writer Madách—sums up well the insoluble Hungarian problem, that of a small country with few natural resources, in which an unusually high percentage of relatively gifted people have to earn a living. There are more skilled or highly skilled men in Hungary, more intellectuals, more good scholars and gifted artists than can be provided for by the economic means of the country on, say, the American level of material standard of living.

Ernő Osvát, a figure central to the Hungarian literary renewal of the first decades of this century, found poignant words to describe what he thought to be the destiny of the Hungarian genius:

"More talented people come to a miserable end in Hungary than anywhere else in the world. They do not go down working, feverish, in the deadly tussle of energies. They succumb with their virile arms rested, ere they could have left the dark alleys of evolution, traceless, noticed but by the few, as if they had been born to become mere sketches. Hungary is, as it were, a sketchbook of nature. It is a splendid, great, marble mountain range covered with reliefs; protruding heads, arms, fractions of man, à la Rodin, unable to liberate their trunks. The pressure of circumstances and a numbing bewitchment keeps them spellbound. And Time comes and under its footsteps, the marvelous human visages are worn out."

When writing these lines, Osvát thought—as most idealists do—that remedy was near at hand, that a change in the social structure of Hungary would breathe life into the half-detached limbs. Nearly half a century later, in a restructured Hungary, many of the problems that beset Osvát and his friends have remained, though in a less acute and somewhat different form. The great difference is that today more people know that many of these problems and, more specifically, the problem presented by a relatively limited field of opportunity for the most talented or the most highly skilled, are common to all small, highly civilized and relatively densely populated countries. Or, to put it in other terms, to countries where the gross national product in intellects is greater than the local demand for this commodity. The "brain drain" of the early sixties from Great Britain to the United States can be quoted here as a good example not only of the accuracy of this statement but also for the relativity of the adjective "small."

Since World War II, the USA has generally been considered the most prosperous nation in the world. This is not the place to agree or to disagree with such a statement but it is a fact that any "teacher of Hungary" in the USA has to take into account when speaking about his subject. The great majority of his students—and until very recently almost their totality—is convinced of the superiority of their own country's ways and means over that of any other country in the world. He who has the task of conveying to an academic audience the reality of a foreign culture must always be prepared to show the existence of another scale of intrinsic values than that which is used in its own country. The further apart the two countries are, the more difficult the task becomes. Living standards can be measured according to different scales and—it is my conviction—that many of us are victims of the conformity imposed upon us by lazy economists who find it more convenient to reckon with uniform measures. But just as much as it is futile to calculate the monthly average income of a Pakistani railway-porter in US dollars, it is equally, though less obviously, mistaken to judge the living standards of one country solely in terms of the *material* aspects of another country's civilization. The sordid life of an inhabitant of a Cleveland ghetto compares very unfavorably with the *dolce far niente* of a Sicilian peasant, though the former possesses more material goods than are ever dreamt of by the latter. There is, however, no need to seek examples so extreme.

It is possible, nay desirable, not to limit the assessment of the living standards of a given country to, say, durable consumer goods. While one can measure the living standards with the number of automobiles, refrigerators, television sets per capita, it is, I submit, equally valid to take for standards the number of opera-performances, live entertainment occasions, or number of trees per year, per capita or per square mile. And how does an ever-increasing crime rate tally with an ever increasing standard of living? What is the ratio of murders committed every year to the number of the population?

All these are countable facts and, therefore, relatively easy to handle, but it is much more meaningful—though much more difficult—to compare seemingly heterogeneous elements of human life. There is unanimity in considering "crowded living conditions" inherently unpleasant but I know of no statistics setting side by side the number of square feet available per capita for private accomodation and those available for public use. And in the latter category I would not include ordinary streets, elevated highways or dumping grounds.

Let us follow up this example. Everyone familiar with Hungarian living conditions would agree that the greatest single headache of an ordinary Hungarian citizen is the general inadequacy of lodgings, particularly in the big cities. By Western European or American standards most of them are over-crowded. It is quite easy to provide statistics on the number of living rooms of bathrooms available per person in the country but the truth they objectively mirror will not really convey the degree of convenience they represent in the life of the citizen. Without condoning the lack of adequate lodging (has anyone ever defined what "adequate" means?), one has to point out the compensatory aspects of Hungarian life, such as the numberless clean, neat and cheap "espressos" where one can spend a delightful afternoon or evening totally undisturbed by anyone. It is sometimes difficult to convey to my American students what public swimming pools or even *safe* public parks and gardens mean to their Hungarian colleagues. Not to stay at home does not mean in Budapest lingering on street-corners surrounded by flying litter, sitting in run-down hang-outs situated in streets where it is unwise to walk in the evenings, or even the necessity of having to drive somewhere. The nearest espresso, the nearest park is probably within a walking distance of ten minutes.

The case is similar with automobile statistics. It is obviously a "good thing" to own a car—which has the value of a fetish to most Hungarians—but to give a true meaning to car statistics from the point of view of human life, one has to investigate whether there are other means of transportation. Thousands of well-to-do New Yorkers living in Manhattan do not use, or do not even have, a car, because it is more comfortable to use public transportation. One can delve even deeper into differences in living-patterns and public amenities. In the charming university town in which I am living there are many elegant neighbourhoods studded with houses which, to an average Hungarian, would look like dream-homes but which have no sidewalks—a public facility universal in any mud-bound, Hungarian village street. So the somewhat paradoxical situation arises, that the "rich" American mother has to ferry her children in her "rich" American car to three different, perhaps even nearby schools, because it is unsafe to let the small children go alone on the streets devoid of sidewalks; whereas the "poor" Hungarian mother who cannot even afford dreaming of a car may set her children safely on a sidewalk, pat them on their heads and return to her own work.

Clearly, the ideal solution is to have cars and sidewalks, as the two are not mutually exclusive. However, my task is not to draft a political platform or to make suggestions for improvement, but simply that of showing that reality is multi-faceted and that it is completely misleading not to recognize the built-in compensations each system has for its own shortcomings.

One does not have to agree with Gandhi's very un-American principle that the renunciation of wants, not a multiplicity of wants, is the true criterion of civilization, to point out that wants may be of a very different nature. The hardest task the "teacher of Hungary" has to face is to point out the very existence of commodities, often uncountable in their character, totally unknown by his audience. It is very difficult to explain what good French cooking is to someone who measures the quality of his meal by the number of ounces his steak weighs. Value preferences exist only when several values are known and the most important task—and at the same time the hardest— is to show those values of Hungarian life which American life does not, or no longer, or not yet possesses. Justice as well as tact and expediency demand that this should not be done by a rather easy debunking of local shortcomings, a way of action which may assure some hilarity in a public meeting but would be improper for a scholar and out of place in a classroom.

Naturally, the best method is to proceed from the known to the unknown, beginning by the comparison of kindred phenomena existing both in Hungary and in the United States. Within a greater framework more specific problems can be dealt with in a way which not only commands attention but which, on a research level, may lead to new insights. I will quote two such examples.

The first is the much-abused history of the treatment of national minorities in pre-World War I Hungary. Up to a few years ago most of the students—and not a few among specialist scholars—were content with parroting the old accusations of the unjustifiable oppression of these minorities. While it is certainly possible to level criticism on this account against old Hungary, and against the whole of the Habsburg Empire, a much better understanding and a more lenient view can now be gained by drawing comparisons with the destinies of the not-yet assimilated minority groups of the United States.

A difficult subject—but one that always commands attention—is the comparison in aims, techniques, and achievements of the Hungarian and American systems of secondary and higher education. To an audience composed of undergraduate or graduate students the topic has an immediacy which no other can match, since going to school is about the only experience certainly common to the members of the class. In this sector of public life it is interesting to examine the contemporary and burning issue of opening up the universities to the children of the under-privileged classes. The problem was tackled in the first decade after World War II by the socialist government of Hungary in a manner not vastly dissimilar to the methods advocated and followed at present by a great number of American universities. At first sight the centralized, state-controlled educational system of Hungary—and let me add that to the best of my knowledge educational systems are state-controlled everywhere in continental Europe—bears little resemblance to the highly variegated and individualistic American system. Yet, just as millions of individuals may knowingly or unknowingly follow identical trends, those followed by institutions of higher learning in the United States tend to develop along more or less the same lines. The present nation-wide effort to open up the universities to Negroes and other under-privileged ethnic groups by lowering university requirements resembles in more than one point early, socialist Hungarian educational policies. My own, private crystal ball shows me that in a decade or so these American educational policies will bear fruits similar to those picked in Hungary a decade or so after the new educational system was put into practice.

Analogies remain just that; to be effective they should not be pushed too far. The size, the resources, the traditions of the U.S. are so vastly different from those of Hungary that the experiences and practices of one country cannot help the politicians of the other. It is the egghead's privilege to see the shape of things to come without being able to influence them. Indeed, if he could influence them he would act counter to his own predictions.

As I said before, the essential prerequisite to "teaching Hungary" is the bridging of the gap that separates the culture of the student-body from that of Hungary. To do this a spirit of understanding has to be created, prejudices have to be shed to allow objective enquiry. Once these preconditions are met, the teacher can present his subject *sine ira et studio*, without advocacy or criticism.

During the decade it has been my privilege to teach subjects related to Hungary—and head a department which gives high priority to them—I noticed a marked change in the attitude of the students toward Hungary, or, for that matter, toward most foreign cultures. Much has been written and more said on world-wide student unrest and its causes and I do not wish to join the debate. From the point of view of the study of foreign cultures in general and Hungary in particular, the recent increase in the political awareness of many American students has to be welcomed though, as will be seen, not without some reservations.

In these last years the students have become more receptive to world problems because, in all likelihood, these seem to have an increasing effect on their daily lives. And while it would be wild exaggeration to state that whatever happens in Hungary would materially affect the daily life of my students, the possibility of such influences is no longer regarded as entirely absurd. There is more interest in, and more understanding for, the problems of a country like Hungary, and more sympathy for the difficulties the country has to contend with in this century. There is also an increased "feel" for some aspects of socialism. Ten years ago it took some pains to explain and even to justify the care taken in Hungary of the sick. Today, with Medicare being part of American life, even students disapproving of it have a basis for comparison.

As can only be expected, such sympathy is rather uncommon in the ranks of what is called the "new left". From their own point of view this is regrettable because much could be learned from the experiences of various Hungarian left-wing movements of the past divorced—as the "new left" is—from the working classes. There are many other relevant lessons to be drawn from other events of the last half century of Hungarian history but this is not the place to enter into such details. From the point of view of the academic future of Hungarian studies the essential and welcome fact is the increased interest among students in matters Hungarian. There are more, many more, students attending such classes than were in the academic year 1956–57 when Hungary was very much in the news.

Interest breeds understanding and knowledge which, in their turn, motivate human actions. To illustrate the effects of ignorance on mental attitudes and on actions inasmuch as Hungary is concerned, I should like to close on a little, personal story.

In November 1957 I was asked to resign my presidency of the Cambridge University Hungarian Society because I had publicly expressed my opinion that the Kádár regime was to remain in power for some time to come. The students who asked that I should resign laboured under the same illusions as had the Foreign Office official ten months earlier who disbelieved a similar statement made to him. In fact, this was the last time I have ever been consulted by the Foreign Office.

Perhaps I am overly optimistic but I like to think that ignorance as abysmal as that displayed by the students and the Foreign Office would no longer be shown in the same circles. And if this is so, it may be partly due to the efforts of some of us who have been "teaching Hungary" as an academic subject. But all our efforts would have remained vain had it not been for a change in the general attitude of the student body. It seems to me that only the "gauchiste" radicals, the pastiche-revolutionaries of the well-to-do middle classes, have not learned the lessons of recent American history; the great majority of the students have. When all things are reduced to the great common denominator of the human condition, suffering, then the basic brotherhood and interrelatedness of mankind becomes manifest. Distant Hungary can become so alive in the American Middle West that even the munching of chewing gum may stop in the classroom. And, when all is said and done, who could ask for more?

L'UNITÀ INTERVIEWS
JÁNOS KÁDÁR

János Kádár, First Secretary of the Central Committee of the Hungarian Socialist Workers' Party, received Mr. Giuseppe Boffa, special correspondent of L'Unità, the central organ of the Italian Communist Party. This is the full text of the interview which was published in the December 1st, 1969 number of L'Unità and also in Népszabadság.

Historic experiences

QUESTION: In view of the 50th anniversary of the Council Republic, you drew up in Hungary a balance-sheet of the long road covered by the Hungarian Communist Party from the period of Béla Kun to that of Rákosi and on to the present. In the light of this half-century, what do you consider the most important experiences in the history of your party, and which are the negative moments which you criticize bearing in mind their lessons for the future?

ANSWER: As far as the first question is concerned, on the 50th anniversary of the proclamation of the 1919 Council Republic which was commemorated recently, we indeed surveyed the road which we have covered and took stock of the experiences which we gathered. I'd like to note that we name the various periods in the fight carried on by the party in a manner which expresses their social essence, and do not consider them "periods" belonging to one or the other leader. The road covered has been arduous, the fifty years have been eventful, often stormy. In consequence, our party has collected many kinds, and important experiences, and it is making use of these today in a wide range of its activities. Therefore, the policy as a whole of the Hungarian Socialist Workers' Party provides the full answer to your question.

I would nevertheless emphasize, as especially important experiences in the fight carried on by the party, a policy guided by principles, the unity of the party, oneness with the masses, and internationalism. It may be stated that the party was successful when it maintained the principles of Marxism–Leninism in their purity, and applied them in a constructive way, and was condemned to failure when it yielded to revisionism or dogmatism in ideology, to rightist opportunism or "leftist" sectarianism in politics. The strength of the party was redoubled when it was united ideologically, politically and organizationally, but it became powerless when it was split by factions and groups. It was able to fight and to work successfully when it enjoyed the full and active support of the toiling masses; it became isolated and unable to fulfill its mission when it became separated from the masses. The strength of the party was multiplied when it maintained clearly the idea of proletarian internationalism, when it correctly reconciled the national and international interests of the revolutionary struggle; it was weakened when it violated the principles of internationalism, or when its ties with the forces of socialism, with the international labour movement were weakened for any reason.

Our Italian friends know very well that Hungarian Communists fought through hard battles in the recent past. They know that at the end of the forties and the beginning of the fifties the dogmatism and sectarian policies of the Rákosi-leadership, the revisionism and class-treason of the Imre Nagy group, the struggle between these two cliques on the one hand, the machinations and open attacks of the class enemy, of the imperialists, on the other, led to a long crisis in the party and in our society. All this led up to the 1956 counterrevolutionary uprising in Hungary.

Fighting on two fronts

The progress achieved since then proves that our party has taken historic experiences seriously. One of the principal lessons of those critical times has been that we always have to face reality and not what we would like to see; that we have to get rid of every sort of subjectivism and have to follow a realist policy.

Realism, the facing of reality, the realization of the difficulties and their earnest consideration are a command, a necessity, for the Communist Party, and for Communists in general. Of this, Gramsci wrote so expressively: "It is characteristic of the weak that they become lost in the plays of the imagination, that they dream with open eyes that their desires have the power of reality and that everything happens in accordance with their wishes... In reality then, wherever such people get to work, they will find that the difficulties are extremely grave, because they have never thought of them concretely."

I have spoken of difficult struggles, of crises successfully overcome by principled policies. We are, nevertheless, of the opinion that we have to continue to work unabated, day after day, for the purity of our guiding principles, for the agreement and support of the masses, for the unity of the party, for the socialist unity of our society. These tasks can never be considered solved "once and for all." Domestic and international developments continuously raise new questions which have to be answered by the party in due course. Consequently, Marxism–Leninism has to be defended against distortions, but also against becoming rigid. We fight against the revisionist views appearing again and again in new questions raised by new situations, just as we do against a dogmatic treatment of questions. This is what we call the "two front" struggle. We are convinced that it is needed if our party is to apply Marxism–Leninism in a really constructive way.

National and international interests

In touching on the experiences of history, we have to emphasize that in the course of a fight that has now gone on for fifty years it has always been a powerful source of strength for us that our party has fought and laboured during the whole time of its existence as a militant part of the international Communist movement. The historic experience of our party is evidence of the invincible and irreplaceable power and validity of proletarian internationalism. In our ideological and practical work we endeavour to make use of the experiences of all fraternal parties in addition to our own. Among the fraternal parties, we value especially highly, and hold indispensable, the experiences of the Communist Party of the Soviet Union. It was this party that carried to victory the first socialist revolution in the world, and the Soviet Union has always been the main support of the struggle fought for progress on a world-wide scale.

In the international Communist movement in general, and especially in the countries of the socialist world system, the correct reconciliation of national and international interests is an important task of the Communist and Workers' Parties. In our experience, the disregarding of national characteristics, particularities and interests is harmful, and at the same time, no assumed or real separate national interests can be asserted at the expense of the international interests of progress and socialism. If we violate the interests of the international Communist movement of the community of socialist countries this will, in the last resort, damage also the national interest.

I am able to say that one of the important factors of the strength of the Hungarian Socialist Workers' Party is that it was able to be national and international at the same time throughout its entire existence. This prevailed in the day to day work of the party, including the most critical periods at the time of the first and of the second world war, most recently in the calamitous days of the 1956 counter-revolution, and always when the reconciliation of national and international interests had an especially great importance. This has made of the party of the Hungarian Communists, in the course of its history, one of the firmest internationalist sections of the international Communist movement, and at the same time, the leading party of the nation.

"Who is not against us, is with us"

Q.: After the 1956 crisis you sought as wide as possible support in the country for the policies of the party and for socialist construction on the basis of the slogan "who is not against us, is with us." Do you consider the balance of this effort positive, and to what extent do you hold this slogan to be still valid?

A.: I have already said that the Hungarian party considers it particularly important that the broad masses understand and support the policies of the party, that it should lead the masses—not by commands but by convincing them—, and that the party should fight and work united with them in mutual trust. The winning of the support of the masses has demanded a radical break with all erroneous conceptions and prejudices and a return to the correct Leninist style of work.

The struggle for winning the support of the masses had to be begun at the end of 1956 after grave mistakes and a heavy defeat, in the midst of stirred-up nationalism, anarchy, and ideological confusion. In addition to all this, an attempt was made to whip up ignoble passions and to use psychological and moral terror to turn the people against us Communists, as Comrade Togliatti showed so well at the time in his article written on the *Irodalmi Újság* ("Literary Gazette"). Even in that difficult situation, when first dogmatism and then revisionist treason had destroyed the party's ties with the masses and created immeasurable ideological confusion, the principal strength of us Communists was the purity and power of our Marxist–Leninist ideas, and our unshaken confidence in the masses of workers, peasants and intellectuals. Our aim was first of all the restoration and strengthening of trust in the Party, loyalty to our regime, belief in socialism, in internationalism, and in fraternal friendship with the Soviet Union and other socialist countries.

In such a situation the first task was of course to put the Communists, and all those who believed in socialism, back on their feet and to unite them. But we laid no less stress on separating from the real enemies of socialism and leading back to the right path, those who had been misled, whose number was not small. This policy rested on Marxist–Leninist principles, was sincere, communist, and hence humanist. We publicized our policies without pause and worked to win over the masses, but never made any concessions to anti-socialist views, to nationalism, or to anti-Sovietism. We laboured for the unity of our working class, for the strengthening of the worker-peasant alliance, for a broad national rallying of forces —but strove to achieve all this while openly declaring our objectives, and on the foundation of socialist principles.

The statement quoted in your question, which has in a certain sense become a slogan, "who is not against us, is with us," is an expression of this policy. It was not by chance that this slogan was coined at a free exchange of views between Communists and non-party people, at a meeting of the National Council of the Patriotic People's Front.

Socialism is the cause of the entire people

We still consider this slogan adequate and valid today. We emphasize and try to assert in the proper way the leading role of our party in the life and activities of society. We also emphasize at the same time that the socialist society is not only being built for the Communists, but for all working men and women, for the people. It is obvious that Communists cannot construct socialism on their own, this can only be achieved as the common work of the whole people. For this very reason, we consistently endeavour in the Hungarian People's Republic to draw every honest man, all creative forces of the people, of the nation, into the construction of a socialist society, and thus turn the construction of a socialist society into a national cause. We try to get the Communists respected and followed by non-party people because of the work done by them for society. We declare at the same time that the same rights and esteem are due to everybody who participates in the work of socialist construction and does a proper job, irrespective of party membership, ideology, origin or occupation.

These ideas determine our relationship not only to the masses of workers and peasants, but also to the creative intellectuals. Our scientists and artists, whether they are or are not members of the party, are not simply "given tasks", but participate actively in the development of the arts and sciences and in the elaboration of solutions for the problems of our society. The country provides all possible requisites for the creative work of Hungarian scientists and artists. This is in keeping with their sense of vocation and with the responsibility which they feel to the people. The result has been lively and rich intellectual activity, and harmonious cooperation between the party and the intellectuals. We strive for a relationship in which the intellectuals share with the party and the state the responsibility for the present and the future of the country. Many things are needed for the formation of this sense of responsibility, including sincere trust as well as the thorough discussion of divergent views. But we are convinced that if we are able to achieve this—and we are succeeding to an increasing extent—, this is a much more efficient safeguard of the interests of our people in the construction of socialism, than any petty guardianship or officiousness. The struggle, the work to achieve this cooperation has not been easy, it did not occur from one day to the next, and it is not yet completed. But its fruits are already here, and we are convinced that this apparently longer road is in fact the shorter and more effective one.

As far as the slogan "who is not against us, is with us" is concerned in practice it has to be said openly that its aim has been to induce those honest citizens whose ideology is not identical with ours or who are perhaps quite removed from us Communists to take part with even greater devotion in the work of socialist construction. This is not some sort of compromise or unprincipled "enticement". It is of course not indifferent to us to what extent the socialist consciousness of Hungarian citizens, their identification with socialism, grows. It is clear to us that the spreading and strengthening of socialist ideas in both the masses and in individuals is a process which interacts with the material construction of a socialist society and with the daily work done by individual men and women.

It is the duty of our party, of the Communists, to do everything to further the material construction of a socialist society as well as to spread and to deepen socialist thought and to draw individual men and women into both. In answer to your question I am pleased to repeat what was said a good number of years ago: in our socialist conditions, those who are not engaged in a plot against the regime, in destructive activity, but do socially useful work in any domain, participate in the work of socialist construction. In other words: who is not against us, is with us!

The Hungarian economic reform

Q.: Two years ago a reform was introduced in Hungary which affected all aspects of the economy and of planning. Are you satisfied with the results, and do you consider that further steps will be necessary in the same direction?

A.: So much information, explanation and even misinterpretation circulates abroad about the Hungarian economic reform introduced on 1st January 1968, that saying a few words about its essence is unavoidable.

I must first of all stress that this was not a general reform, but a reform of the mechanism of economic management, the further development of the system of the guidance of the socialist economy. The principal characteristic of our economy continues to be that it is a socialist planned economy.

It is an essential element of the reform that it wishes to ensure the realization of the national economic plans not through concrete plan directives sent to plants, but through economic levers resting on the laws of commodity-, money-, market- and value relations which are valid also in a socialist economy. The managers of plants were given considerable independence and, with the guiding figures of the national plans in view, and aware of economic levers, they make their own plans in accordance with the interest of the plant in more efficient and more profitable production.

The conclusions that may be drawn from the first two years of the reform are satisfactory. In spite of essential changes in the method of central management, there has been no hitch in production and in consumption which in itself should be considered a success in such a vast reorganization. It has of course not been possible to achieve the fundamental objectives of the reform within such a short time, but experiences so far are encouraging. The faithfulness to plan of production has not diminished, but has even somewhat improved. The ratio of sales to production has improved, imports and exports have increased—the latter to a greater extent—, hence, the balance of payments has improved. The fundamental objective of the reform is the increase of the economic efficiency of labour. Although this has not yet occurred in all areas, and we can only speak of initial results, the importance of these is very great. These, in short, are the conclusions that may thus far be drawn from the reform.

The process of observing and analysing the result continues and the various economic levers are continuously being adjusted. The better and more efficient effectiveness of the principles of the reform, and through this the adequate development of the fundamental factors of the economy, of productivity and of the growth of production remain a permanent task.

Experience shows that there is no need to modify the fundamental principles of our system of management. It is obvious that such a vast measure which affects all areas of the economy may only be carried out gradually and that its introduction is no free of problems. Consequently further measures will follow those which have already been taken. But these will not affect the essential traits of the system which has been introduced but will serve their more efficient realization. I am certain that the full development of the reform of economic management will be in the service of a vigorous continuation of the work of construction and the great goal of the building of a socialist society.

The development of socialist democracy

Q.: Do you think that reforms introduced in economic activity—an important aspect of life in the country—must be followed by reforms in other domains, especially in the sphere of political activity?

A.: We are aware that there is a lot of guessing concerning this question, and certain imperialist circles and "theoreticians" even hope and predict that as a result of the economic reform our society will be "loosened up" somehow. These are vain hopes. On the contrary, we are sure that as a result of the increasing efficiency in the economy, our state, our regime and the power of the working class will be strengthened further and confirmed.

There are no plans for and there will not be any change in our political structure, in the structure of the party, in the practice of the principle of democratic centralism, or in the basic institutions, in the essential characteristics of our social system as an effect of the introduction of the economic reform.

The elaboration and introduction of the reform were never, for us, simply an economic question. We have always seen clearly that this is a complex sociopolitical question. It has always been clear to us that there is a close connection between the political life and the economy, that these two important sectors of social life are in constant interaction. In accordance with our ideas there will be and there has already begun a certain change in policial activity in our country in concrete connection with the economic reform. What are these changes? The party and the government strive continuously to further develop socialist democracy within our regime. These ideas played a role also in the elaboration of the economic reform.

These are the concrete changes in policy and economic policy: 1. In proportion with the increased independence of the managers of plants, the role and weight of party branches, trade unions and other social associations within plants are enhanced. 2. The direct interestedness of the collectives of industrial plants and agricultural producers' cooperatives and other independent economic units increases the interest and active participation of working people in public affairs. 3. The sphere of activity, independence and responsibility of the basic institutions of our state, the local councils, also increases and this will cause an increase in the interest taken by the population and in their activity within local government. Similarly in the factories the questions of production and other questions affecting the entire collective are not decided behind closed doors either, but with the wide participation of working men and women and with due regard for their views.

It is obvious that as a result of all this social activity and socialist thinking by working people, by the broad masses of the population, will grow further, socialist democracy will increase and the policial strength of the party, and our regime will grow with it.

Q.: To what extent do you consider socialist the society that has been built in Hungary in the last twenty years? In your view, what is necessary for it to be completely socialist?

A.: The social process which began in Hungary following liberation was transformed into a socialist revolution from 1948 on, when the working class conquered political power. The 8th Party Congress held at the end of 1962 was justified in stating that with the socialist reorganization of agriculture the laying of the foundations of a socialist society was completed in our country.

I consider that our society is fundamentally socialist in character. Power is in the hands of the working class, of the working people. The means of production are—with few exceptions—in socialist common ownership; there is no exploiting class in our country. The exploitation of man by man has ceased in the Hungarian People's Republic.

The limits of an interview do not allow me to explain in detail and to define scientifically what is still needed for us to be able to declare in our country: the building of a socialist society has been completed. But I am well aware that in Hungary our people has in 25 years overcome the backwardness of centuries. In the place of an agrarian country burdened with the survivals of feudalism, a fundamentally socialist, advanced industrial-agrarian country was born. The economic level of the country has risen fast, starvation and privation have ceased, compared to the past the standard of

living of working men and women has become high and secure. Great
revolutionary changes have occured in the domain of education and culture.

At the same time I know that there are still sections that are in a difficult
situation, who do not earn enough and are not adequately provided for; that
the housing problem is not yet satisfactorily solved; that some of the young
have to solve difficult questions at the beginning of their lives on their own.
I believe that for the completion of the building of socialism substantially
more advanced means of production and a higher level of scientific work,
of public education and culture are needed as well as the achievement of
a higher standard of living.

We also know full well that socialism does not mean only a larger loaf
of bread, better housing, a refrigerator and maybe a car, but primarily new
social relationships and new human ties. The building of socialism is not
only an economic task but has to ensure the development of a full human
life, in the true sense of the word, the harmonious relationship and evolution
of the individual and of society. We have achievements to our credit in this
domain also. Beyond the internationally acknowledged achievements of the
revolution in culture I am thinking here for instance of the consciousness-
forming social activity by the socialist brigade movement, which developed
spontaneously in plants and was initiated by the masses, or of cooperative
democracy in the villages. The socialist brigade movement, which embraces
large masses, with its slogan "to live, study and work in a socialist way"
and internal democracy in the agricultural producers' cooperatives, and
other new, young but important achievements of our public life, serve not
only production but culture as well, and implied in the latter the socialist
way of life, the shaping of men by the community.

Although we still face many tasks, we are on the road towards the realization in our society of Lenin's great dream, turning the thousands of years
old culture of mankind into the common treasure of the masses. In addition
we endeavour not only to maintain this heritage but to continue and to
renew it, to develop a socialist culture and arts. Socialism has not made life
gray; like so many other hostile prophecies, this one has not come true
either, on the contrary, it is well-known that the atmosphere prevalent in
the advanced capitalist countries "alienates" the individual and the masses
and standardizes them. The alternative offered by socialism is not simply
more human, but is the sole possible prospect for mankind.

We are not able to tell today when the building of socialism will be
completed and communism will be created. Our task is not to foretell and
to promise, but to work and to fight. Our party does not lose sight of
historic objectives. We are certain that the party of the Hungarian Com-

munists, the Hungarian working class, the Hungarian people will not stop half-way. They advance, and every step brings them nearer to the great goal, the creation of a socialist Hungary, and they are going to reach this goal.

The strengthening of the unity of the international communist movement

Q.: Do you consider progress in the unity of the international communist movement possible after the Moscow Conference, in view of the differences of opinion which were manifest both among those present and as regards the parties that were absent?

A.: I am fully confident that we are in the midst of the process of the strengthening of the international Communist movement, and within this of the unity and cooperation of the socialist countries.

My confidence rests—among other things—on the extremely important and successful Moscow Conference. True, there were differences of opinion among the parties present and such differences were also manifest in relation to the parties which were absent. However, there were not only differences of opinion in Moscow, but what is much more important, a unity and a striving for unity, which were much stronger than the differences of opinion, were also shown. It is sufficient to point out that the more than seventy parties present were unanimous in their appraisal of the international situation, and of the most important questions of the struggle against imperialism. The Conference was unanimous in showing proletarian internationalist solidarity with the struggle of the people of Vietnam. Unity was similarly expressed in solidarity with the Arab peoples and in numerous other, unanimously adopted, solidarity declarations.

I'd also like to refer to the differences of opinion as regards the principal document, between the great majority of the parties on the one hand and a few fraternal parties on the other. It is well known that at the 1960 Moscow Conference a resolution was unanimously adopted and published. It is also well known that in 1961, only a few months after the conclusion of the Conference—unfortunately—grave signs of the dissolution of unity appeared in the international Communist and labour movement. There were some who disregarded the common resolution adopted and signed by them, and set out on a road of dissent. Now the resolution was not entirely unanimous, we are nevertheless justified in stating that the Conference indeed strengthened unity and the striving for unity, and since the conference heartening facts connected with efforts corresponding to the spirit of the agreements have been evident. These included the successful World Congress of Trade Unions, which was held in Budapest recently, and the common efforts made by the European socialist countries in the interest of the peace and security of the Continent, which have had an increasing echo especially since the Prague declaration.

The representatives of not a single Communist and workers' party could have left the 1969 Moscow Conference with the feeling that anybody wanted to restrict them in the free explanation of the views of their party or wanted to put moral pressure on them to sign anything that did not agree with their convictions. The openness, democratic preparation and conduct of the Conference as a whole gave me the impression that it was a genuinely free and comradely exchange of views which strengthened our unity. The comradely atmosphere, democratic method and internationalist spirit of the whole Conference enabled and prompted those fraternal parties which dissented at the Conference to compare and consider their views now after the Conference with those represented by the others, and to bring their own standpoint closer to the latter. The decision of the Conference to send its resolutions to those parties which were not present at the Conference and to call on them to join in the common struggle against imperialism, was also truly internationalist.

I repeat, I am optimistic, the unity of the international Communist movement will become stronger, the more so, as the differences of opinion are transient, while the interests of the international working class, of the peoples represented by our parties are not transient and are common, such as the fundamental questions of Marxism–Leninism, as well as socialism and of peace. International imperialism is our common enemy, and against it we can fight more effectively only if we strengthen our unity.

The Budapest Appeal

Q.: The well-known Call of the Warsaw Pact countries concerning the European collective security system was issued in Budapest. In your view, what are the prospects today of this initiative, especially in the light of the outcome of the elections held in the German Federal Republic on the 28th September and the formation of the Brandt government?

A.: The Budapest Call of the Warsaw Pact countries, which proposes a meeting of the representatives of the European states, and the negotiation of a collective security system is very important and its prospects are promising. I am basing this opinion on many things.

In the stage of evolution that can be foreseen today, European peoples living in countries with different social orders—unless they wish to become annihilated in a destructive war—have no other alternative for a more peaceful period than the creation of a collective security system on the continent. A readiness for this exists in the Soviet Union and in the European socialist countries, as evidenced by the Budapest Call and by the declaration issued by the conference of foreign ministers held in Prague.

The countries of Europe have not forgotten the horrors of the Second World War, and they are well aware that the most powerful military forces that exist in the world today are here, on our continent, at an arm's length from each other. If we do not somehow arrange elementary security questions, this can lead to nothing good. The echo of the Appeal, the fact that more than two thirds of the countries of Europe have reacted positively, is also encouraging. The memorandum of the Finnish Government and the personal efforts of President Kekkonen deserve special mention, as these are a great contribution to the successful preparation of the conference. It would favourably influence the common cause of the peoples of Europe if every government of the continent—including the Italian Government— were to give a positive answer to the Budapest Appeal and to the declaration issued by the meeting of the foreign ministers of the Warsaw Pact countries.

We believe that the conditions for the convocation of a European security conference are ripening, and it would be heartening if a decisive step were taken in 1970.

There are forces acting as a brake which do not dare to obstruct the initiative in the open, but are very busy behind the scenes. As is known, in the declaration issued by the Prague conference of foreign ministers, the Warsaw Pact countries proposed a date and two items for the agenda. They also declared that they were ready to examine any other proposal as well. The opponents of the conference now say that the date is too early, and that we have not proposed any "genuine" questions, etc. And those who are inclined to pessimism believe them. We are convinced that we, the Warsaw Pact countries, have made propositions which can be accepted by anybody. We proposed a free exchange of views, a conference, and a solution. It any government has something better to offer, we look forward to its proposals, and our governments are ready to examine them.

As far as the elections held in the German Federal Republic and what is called the *Kleine Koalition* government led by Chancellor Brandt are concerned, I consider this, from the aspect of the prospects of European security something that may turn out to be a positive factor. The positive feature of this change is primarily that the CDU–CSU Christian Democratic party alliance, which has dominated the German Federal Republic since its foundation, the policies of which had led to a growth in strength of revanchist, military forces, which did not recognize the European frontiers brought about by the Second World War, which unlawfully claimed sole representation and opposed the German Democratic Republic, was defeated.

In the appraisal of the new West German Government, its actions will of course be decisive. One thing is certain: we shall not reject any initiative that will be progressive and will genuinely serve European peace and security.

This was what I could answer to your questions. In conclusion, I take this opportunity of sending through *L' Unità* my cordial greetings and best wishes to our Italian comrades and friends, and to the working people of Italy. I wish them lots of success in their endeavours and efforts for their own future and for friendship and understanding between nations.

JÁNOS KÁDÁR:
REFLECTIONS AT SIXTY

On May 25, 1972, the Central Committee of the Hungarian Socialist Workers' Party gave a luncheon party, in one of the reception rooms of Parliament, in honour of János Kádár, First Secretary of the Central Committee, on the occasion of his sixtieth birthday. Attending the luncheon were members of the Central Committee of the Party, and personalities prominent in Hungary's political, social and cultural life. At the luncheon Béla Biszku, member of the Political Bureau of the Hungarian Socialist Workers' Party and Secretary of the Central Committee, congratulated János Kádár on the occasion, and presented him with the Central Committee's letter of congratulation.

We publish here János Kádár's reply to the greetings.

Dear comrades, my dear friends:

Comrade Biszku's address has made it clear to all, including me, that this is an official function, a luncheon arranged by the Central Committee and attended by other guests as well on, as it were, a People's Front basis. Comrades had already told me earlier they were planning such a get-together. I had only one thing to ask of them at the time: Do it if you think it is a good thing to do, but don't urge anyone to attend.

In the kind of atmosphere prevailing here I can allow myself to say something simply and not officially, the way one does among friends. On such an occasion I have to say something, though it is not very easy to talk at such a time.

First of all I'd like to tell you that my early circumstances were such, that in the family where I was brought up it was not the custom to celebrate wedding anniversaries, or birthdays, or name-days. That was how I grew up. It was only in the last ten to twenty years that I first realized that it is a good thing to celebrate such things both officially and unofficially. I want to say that it is right to celebrate the great events of family life. Only I had no share in such things, I wasn't used to them and it is only lately I have begun to become accustomed to them. The reason I say so, comrades, is to let you understand that I feel a kind of uneasiness about this anniversary and these celebrations, they worry me, I am even embarrassed. Bearing this in mind—and I beg you to—I should still like to say a few words.

First I want to thank everyone present for honouring me by coming here today for us to spend an hour or two with one another.

As I said, birthday celebrations as a family affair are right and proper, and are in fact traditional among our people. I am only sorry I had no share in them at an age when, you might say, one is growing up both physically and mentally.

But it's a different matter when such a family event, for instance, a birthday, is transformed into a public or political affair. The way I feel about it is that I understand and in fact I think it perfectly acceptable, in certain cases and within proper limits, that an obviously private matter—a birthday—becomes a political, a public affair. I understand, and approve it, on two conditions: that it is kept within proper limits and that it is not about me. Once it is about me, well, I repeat what I've already said—it makes me uneasy, I feel embarrassed, I have simply never been used to it.

I am supposed to be—I can even see the number before me on the table—sixty years old, according to the papers, so it certainly must be true. Even by the most modern expectations of life this is regarded as an age by which, they say, one ought to have formulated a philosophy of life. If it is a question of a philosophy of life the letter of the Central Committee, I think, has expressed it better than anything I could say about it. Nonetheless I would like to make a couple of personal remarks.

What is the course of a man's life? I think that if what a man has in mind is not merely his biological life, but human life in the finer sense of the word, then the first thing he has to do is to understand that it is not as an individual that he has, as it were, to get on and fight his way in life, he has to realize, to see, that as a human being happiness is not achieved alone, only together with others.

The letter of the Central Committee speaks about *my* course of life, about *my* merits. Let me say that the individual can only claim merit for certain things. For instance—and I think this is a kind of merit—when someone, at some stage of his life, realizes that he is no leopard or tiger—not even a hamster—that if he wants to live he must live honestly together with the working people; and that if he wants to live better he must live better together with them. I consider myself fortunate that, at a crucial stage in my life—at the ages of seventeen, eighteen, nineteen—I came to understand that man alone can be neither human nor happy. The individual can fairly take merit to himself for realizing this: he makes the choice himself, which way he intends to go from there.

Another such merit which can fairly be credited to the individual is the effort he makes. The effort he makes, after he recognizes an idea, to live in conformity with it. I consider myself fortunate to have encountered the idea of socialism, of Marxism–Leninism. I familiarized myself with this idea, and it fascinated me. And—do not get me wrong, this is not boasting on my part—in that critical stage of my life, though not without help, I managed to understand that if I wanted to be human, happy and free, a man free in mind, I could not be it alone. I could be it only together with the working class, with my class companions, and only if I tried to understand this already recognized idea and ideology still better and if I lived accordingly, as well as I could. So much can be claimed as personal merit. Everything else, I want to stress, depends on other things, not on the personal resolution of the individual.

Man individually and as a social being cannot live a human life without ideas, without ideals. There are those indeed who live without ideas and ideals, but that is not a human life. At least that is what I think. I am a Marxist and declare myself a Communist, but I can understand somebody who is not a Marxist and a Communist, provided that he possesses some general human idea that dictates his actions and prompts him somehow to serve the community.

Without ideas and ideals, I think, neither man nor society can exist. A society that has no great guiding idea is doomed. I'm going to make a little digression here; I want to emphasize that our working class, our peasantry, our intelligentsia and, I think I may say our people as a whole, have identified themselves with the socialist world of ideas. I don't want to go into the details of how far and how much—it isn't even what counts—but generally speaking one can say that they have identified themselves with it, and since they have ideas and ideals, they have a future and will prosper.

I know of other countries which have greater material wealth and live better than we do, yet their social system has no future, because it has no guiding idea that could lead them forward. So I think one is fortunate to have an idea and to be able to work for it.

When it is a birthday, and when on top of it the family gathering becomes a political affair, one is inevitably bound to draw up a balance sheet: one has to pause for a moment and think of what one has done thus far and how one looks ahead. I tell you frankly I am glad I became a worker, a worker for society and a Communist, and that looking at the balance sheet one can say that some results have been achieved.

As I told you, comrades, if I look at it from my personal angle, life has not particularly spoilt me. I was brought up and lived under difficult circumstances, and later I came up against the world as it was in those days and suffered all the consequences. Those present today know that not even after Liberation was my individual path exactly smooth going. But when nevertheless I try to strike a balance I can honestly say to you: that in all my conscious life I have lived and acted according to my convictions. If something was against my convictions, I refused to do it and suffered the consequences.

Where do these qualities come from? No one has them at birth, no one gets them in the cradle, or even in the family. I can affirm that these qualities, which can be useful to society, can only be acquired by the Party member from the Party, by the worker from the working class—from the people. They are not things acquired on one's own. As far as I am concerned, it has been the Party, the working class movement, the toiling masses that have made me into what I am. I have a pretty good memory, and I know what I was like when I found my way into the movement, and whatever is here, so to say, of use, or which can be turned to use for the community, has all been given me entirely by the movement, by our working class and our people. And if this life of mine we are talking about here today has yielded any results, I think it has to be viewed like this.

The next thing I want to say is that one does not work alone. There are still private artisans today—it may be that they work alone; in working for society one does not. And if you are saying that good results have sprung from the work I have done—I do not wish either to evaluate or discuss it here—then I want to say I have never worked alone. Ever since I was seventeen I have belonged to the working class movement, to the progressive movement of our people, and for this I am indebted to those who at that time spared no trouble on my behalf, and who have guided me here. If you, comrades, say that I am doing my work satisfactorily, then my thoughts instantly turn to the Political Bureau, the Central Committee, our Government, the Presidential Council, the National Council of the Patriotic People's Front. These results could only be achieved because these collective bodies have worked together in agreement, and for the same goal. And incidentally, of course, there are other colleagues who are generally not mentioned on such occasions—the members of the administrative and technical staffs. One cannot do without them either. They are necessary for the organization of all our work.

The need of a certain background has also been mentioned. I always say that a life companion endowed with very much patience and with good nerves, and an appropriate home background are needed if one is to be able to live and work. In this respect as well I consider myself fortunate. A small circle of my colleagues have complimented me today and expressed gratitude for my humanity. Why, yes, you may be human after all in the office, but you are not always so at home. For you have to relax a little somewhere. So our political collaborators, the strength of the collective, our allies, our friends, our administrative colleagues and our individual home background— are all needed for us to be able to work and produce good results.

Now I come specifically to the experience and philosophy of life. Well, yes, in my life and my work for society I have certainly acquired a philosophy, which I don't want to recount in detail, though I would like to stress one or two aspects, since we are here together in a company where it may be worth while talking about them. There are here today people of different ages, some quite young and some even older than I am. You all know how one feels about one's age. The twenty-year-olds seem old to those of ten, the thirty-year-olds to those of twenty, the forty-year-olds to those of thirty, the fifty-years-old to those of forty, and so on up to the furthest limit of human life. The truth of the matter is that, however old you are, anybody ten years your senior is an old man—and everybody knows this. All the same, some-how or other one is bound to acquire a certain amount of experience. One has to learn a lot of things. I have acquired some experience of life, or some-thing that might be called the wisdom of life, but I want to make it clear that none of it is any discovery of mine, or my own innovation or invention. It had all been discovered by many before me, only every single man must also discover it for himself, if he is to profit by such wisdom.

I should also like to say a word about our scientific ideology—Marx-ism–Leninism, the ideology of socialism, of communism. In my child-hood I used to live in the country, later I came up to town and became an industrial worker and a Communist. There is a certain wisdom which already at the age of five you learn from older people, who say that something that is very important is human common sense. I think this is true. As I said, an idea and an ideal is needed to guide one, for otherwise one cannot proceed in a socially useful way. It may well be that somebody accepts Christianity or some other belief as his ideal. I am biased: I hold Marxism–Leninism to be the best system of ideas. An idea is therefore needed. What is needed in addition are human commonsense and a sense of reality. I don't want to quote examples, but if we only keep our eyes on the final goal, and disregard the given situation and given possibilities, ignoring how and to what extent people understand what we are trying to do—then the final goal can only be harmed. Consequently there is need for both an idea and a sense of reality in order to see how much of the idea can be realized at the time, so that we can come nearer to the final goal. I may be allowed to let slip—for we also have older people among us here—that life is nevertheless in many respects a compromise. Nothing is realized the way one first envisages it. In the old world I also dreamt of liberation, socialism, communism, and even though it was doubtful whether I would live to see the day of Liberation, there was no doubt in my mind that when the day came all that was needed were a few sensible ordinances and socialism would become a reality. That was over a quarter of a century ago, and it has since become clear that things do not get done quite that way. In short, life forces us to some extent to compromise, but compromise in the good sense of the word. The compromise that we need is not one which retards us; what we need are decisions which take the real situation into account, decisions which lead us onwards towards our ideals and goals.

Our Marxist–Leninist ideology is a scientific system of ideas directing the life of our society. But it cannot be against human common sense. Our theory has to be more than plain human understanding taken in its everyday sense, but it must not conflict with it, for if it does it is not, in my opinion, Marxism–Leninism or communist doctrine any longer, and there is something wrong with it. Thus we have a system of ideas, which we call dialectical materialism, according to which the social life of society, and nature as well, have their own dialectics. Everyone knows those dialectics. Everyone knows that dialectics are something more than logic. But, one of the conclusions derived from my philosophy of life, if I may say so, is that dialectics cannot be inconsistent with logic, they also have to be logical, because if they are not, they are not dialectical.

I could go on talking about a few more discoveries like that, but I want to mention only one. Marxism–Leninism as a science, and communism as an idea are, I am convinced, the humanism of our age. And therefore they mean humanity and a humane attitude. It is also their aim to improve the lot of the working people. I sometimes say that the connection between Marxism–Leninism, socialism, communism, the Hungarian working class and the Hungarian people is not that we have an excellent theory and that we test it on some ten million experimental subjects. And that if the theory is good it has to work. I think of it in the reverse: the reason why Marxism–Leninism and the whole system of communist ideas exists is to ensure that these ten million Hungarians are better off. For if this was not the reason for its existence, and if there were something wrong in this respect, then we would not be doing our work properly. I am very glad that this realization is growing stronger steadily amongst us, that those representing the

Marxist–Leninist ideology are increasingly inspired with a sense of reality and humanity, with respect and esteem for non-Communists, and with the realization that we can only progress all together.

Another aspect of this development is that there is a growing realization in the minds of non-Communists that, irrespective of the ideology or beliefs they hold, socialism paves the way for the prosperity of our working class, our peasantry, our intelligentsia, the people as a whole. In this way we can prosper, work in a good spirit together for the common cause, argue about what is to be argued about, and move forward together.

In our days it is inevitable that we should argue. That in Hungary we have a system of people's democracy which embodies the power of the working class, of which the goal is socialism, is a settled issue. That is settled once and for all. We can affirm this with a firm conviction because conditions at home and in the world are such that the process cannot be reversed. But a big question remains. How shall we proceed, what should be the rate of advance, the pace of revolution? This is an open question, both in the world of ideas and in action.

In so far as the world of ideas is concerned we might well say, let's get together and take a vote as to whether there is a God or not. For some think there isn't, others insist there is. But we won't vote. Because we take people's feelings into account, and respect them. We leave it to the passage of time to solve the question; it's something for scientific conferences and scientific journals to do. Nonetheless we can still work peacefully together and find ways and means for believers and non-believers to work in unity for the common socialist goal.

An important question concerning the pace of revolution is how much we can use today and how much we should invest for the future. And this is not a simple question at all, because to one and the same person it looks one way this moment and another the next. If somebody looks at the question purely objectively, he wants to have as much as possible today; but if one looks at it as a patriot and Communist, or a socially responsible man, then one comprehends that it is unjustifiable to use up everything today, that investments should also be made for the future. For we have to create a socialist country, a socialist nation has to live here, and it has to live a beautiful and good life, and this makes demands on the present-day generation. We have to wage a battle with ourselves over what can be distributed now and what should be squeezed out for tomorrow, for the day after tomorrow, for the future.

I mention all this only by way of example—I won't go any further—to demonstrate that most of man's wisdom is of the kind that needs no special discovery, it has already been discovered, only we have to discover it afresh for ourselves and take it into account in our actions.

This is how I live, this is how I work. The letter of the Central Committee also refers to the last fifteen years, which has of course been a decisive stage in our development, and in which, of course, I have also been an active participant. It gives me a special pleasure that one becomes so absorbed in things that I have great difficulty in distinguishing between what I myself have done and what I have not, what we all have done together.

In 1956 a grave and critical situation arose which is called counter-revolution by historians. We know this is the learned definition of what happened in 1956. But there is also another name for it that we all can accept: it was a national tragedy. A tragedy for the Party, for the working class, for the people as a whole and for individuals as well. It was a wrong turning, and this resulted in tragedy. And if now we are past it—and we can safely say we are—it is a very great thing indeed.

I have been working as an organized Communist since 1931, and I had already taken part in the working-class movement a couple of years earlier. I have been working ever since that time, because it is the rule for man to work. Yet I feel that, if you have nothing else to say for yourself except that in 1956, in a critical period, and in the following few years, you were of some use—you can say you have not lived in vain.

Now this is a family gathering, isn't it? Since it is about me, I cannot describe this birthday as a political celebration. On such an occasion, of course, one is bound to think of what one must do, how one must continue. Nobody can change his skin, and I think the most essential thing is that the political process itself should continue, and everyone should help the way they can. Everyone without exception. In the result the efforts of the 100-member Central Committee, the 200-member National Council of the Patriotic People's Front and that of the millions of Hungarian citizens is also included. So what we have achieved is the result of the work of our whole active working society. This process must continue in every way possible. It is the duty of all to help in it as far as they can. And this also, of course, applies to me.

There may be a few birthday meditations, but the way I feel about it is that this morning as usual I asked to be given my mail, in order to see what's going on. The calendar says today is a weekday, and whatever we may arrange, life does not stop, it continues on its way.

That's the way one philosophizes and meditates. As an individual I have had to renounce a great deal in private life in the course of these last forty years. I have even had a few things to suffer. Before Liberation they were physical; after they were pains of the soul—the others did not matter. For it's a pain for the soul when men ask, as with me, whether one is an honest man or not. It makes no difference that a man spent a week or five years in jail, that is not what counts, but that anyone could say he is not an honest man, although he has been one all his life. I am talking about this only for you to understand that, all things considered, I look on myself as a fortunate man, even a happy one, in the sense that in all circumstances I have lived up to my convictions and I have been able to work and fight for a cause which I have always had at heart, doing what my mind and heart told me to do.

There are situations when one has to do something which few people understand at the given moment, yet still one has to do it in the hope that it will be understood later. I also consider myself happy that I have lived to see that very many people, hundreds of thousands and millions, have understood what we had had to do in certain given situations which few understood at the time. And I am happy that this has come about not through force, not by pressure, but by discussion, by persuasion.

I wish the Central Committee, as I also wish myself, to continue working in this spirit and to spare neither trouble nor patience where the work of of persuasion has to be done, because the way that looks shortest is not always the shortest in the end. On occasion one has to stop and argue, to listen patiently to the other party. That is also part of a philosophy of life, if you like, not to go on singing our own tune, but to listen to others as well, and then think about what was said and why. Opinions should be reconciled to show what we all have to do.

Forgive me this philosophizing, but since I am here talking to you I felt I ought to disclose a few of my thoughts and feelings, among friends. We have often discussed and argued together, and on the whole with good results so far. I would like to conclude my remarks by stressing that I feel a sincere and profound gratitude, that I offer my warm thanks to the Central Committee, the Government, the Presidential Council and the National Council of the Patriotic People's Front for this mark of attention, and for the honour you have all done me on the occasion of my sixtieth birthday. I am grateful to you both for the distinction you have awarded me and for this social gathering.

I think we all know each other more or less. Today is just a day in the calendar, tomorrow will be the twenty-sixth, after that the twenty-seventh, life will go on, and there will always be work to do. I will not change any more. Last week I was the same as I am today, and next week and after I shall be the same as I have been up to now. If I am allowed to interpret your words—and I refer now not only to members of the Central Committee but to everyone present—as meaning that nothing will change the common determination that has brought us thus far and has also brought us together at this table today, and that we shall go on working untiringly together for the same goal, in the same spirit—then I can say that I have had a happy birthday.

I thank you, comrades, and propose that now all of us, Party members and our non-Party friends and allies here present, raise our glasses to our Central Committee, our Party, our working class, our peasantry, our intelligentsia, to the Hungarian people and their prosperity—and I do so especially to your own personal health.

THE NEXT TWENTY-FIVE YEARS

by

JENŐ FOCK

A historic event, the 25th anniversary of Hungary's liberation from fascism will be celebrated throughout the Hungarian People's Republic in April 1970. It gives me much pleasure to address the readers of *The New Hungarian Quarterly* on this festive occasion. I shall use this opportunity to outline what these twenty-five years have meant to the Hungarian people, and with what sort of expectations Hungarians face the coming years.

All those familiar with the history of this area know that the Hungarian state has existed for more than a thousand years; they can rightly ask therefore whether it is proper to give so much emphasis to the anniversary of 1945; twenty-five years are a comparatively short period in the history of a nation with such a long and distinguished past. However it is a historic fact that the Hungarian nation and the Hungarian people were not always identical. We Hungarians are proud of our past, of the many battles fought by the people, but not even this pride can conceal the truth. A true turning-point was only reached on April 4, 1945. The Soviet Union took on the decisive role in the destruction of fascism, and in the liberation of the Hungarian people. It allowed the people to make the country truly theirs, and finally established a real and unreserved identity between the political nation and the working people. This is the reason why of all national holidays, we rightly specially honour this anniversary. The nation, the people—making use of the opportunities offered, realizing the dreams and plans of the centuries and the objectives of the nation's best—made significant progress in these twenty-five years.

An attempt to summarize all that happened to Hungarians since 1945 would not fit into the framework of a short article. Nor will I try to outline a detailed programme for the time which lies ahead. Instead, I offer a few thoughts in the spirit of this anniversary which we, the workers, peasants, intellectuals, and responsible officials of Hungary who continuously work for our common cause, have together formulated, learning from achievements and mistakes, concentrating our attention primarily on the future.

The country's liberation brought much-desired peace and the chance for social progress. The economic position was catastrophic. The Second World War cost more than half a million Hungarian lives. This is a staggering figure for a people of barely ten million. Hundreds of thousands had lost their homes, and the losses suffered by the economy amounted to the total national income of five pre-war years. The withdrawing Nazi hordes acted like vandals destroying and pillaging. Transport was paralysed, they carried off entire factories and plants, they drove off most of our livestock, and took our valuables, including the entire gold reserves of the National Bank.

STARTING FROM SCRATCH

We had to start from scratch twenty-five years ago. In the summer of 1945, a member of parliament belonging to a major political party announced without any hesitation that there would be no reconstruction, nor any national rebirth possible in this country within the next forty years, unless Hungary was granted a large dollar loan. Such a loan could not be expected without political strings, and what is more, instead of help the West at that time offered Hungary the artificial division of Europe, and a whole chain of acts of economic discrimination which were part of the cold war. And yet it did not take forty years to climb out of the trough. In roughly five years the damage caused by the war was repaired, the country was rebuilt, industrial output and national income reached the pre-war level. This concretely expressed the whole strength, will and creative force of working people in Hungary. The social system, which set out to build socialism, liberated the energies latent in the people, and enlisted them in the service of overall development. But we could not have done without the disinterested help of those friendly nations who share our aims and principles. These twenty-five free years are evidence that the world communist movement and the progressive movements which include the major part of the humanity, support the existence and the growth of the Hungarian People's Republic. Hungary's membership of the community of socialist nations, of their joint defensive system and their organization of economic co-operation is a pledge of the country's progress. These factors mean that the basic international conditions of the present, past and future progress of the country are secure. Such ties linking up the community must therefore be nursed and developed.

Neither the political, nor the economic development of Hungary can be regarded as an uninterrupted, rising straight line. There were times of great impetus, but there were also breaks. Since the defeat of the counter-revolutionary attempt of 1956, the country's progress can be said to have been uninterrupted. One may state with a certain satisfaction that working-class rule which was threatened was successfully reinforced and made firm, that the peasantry was persuaded to move in the direction of agricultural co-operatives, and that a period of faster and more efficient economic growth was initiated. In carrying out all three of these objectives the country could count on the active participation, approval and support of the working masses, and it was entitled to do so. This creative impetus, the unity of people and nation, which is the driving force of development, must be emphasized on the occasion of this anniversary.

PER CAPITA NATIONAL INCOME

Twenty-five years of hard work by the Hungarian people produced a seven and a half fold increase in industrial output, a three and a half fold increase in national income, compared with the pre-war position, in fact a present per capita annual income of approximately $7–800. This is the basis of a continuing systematic rise in the standard of living, and of the establishment of a socialist Hungary possessing a fully developed industry, and a fully industrialized, large-scale agriculture.

I should like to say a few words about Hungary's educational system, cultural life, social welfare, and health service. Before the war, even the six years of compulsory primary education were not completed by all children, nowadays every child, almost without exception, passes through the eight-year course of basic general education introduced in 1945. It is enough to say of the increase in higher education that the number of university students has risen from 11,747 in 1937–38 to 78,727 in 1968–69. This is a secure foundation for advanced scientific development.

Following thorough preparation and discussion by a wide circle of specialists and others interested in the matter certain ideas for the further encouragement of scientific research work were worked out.

I should like to emphasise at this stage that the Hungarian government favours freedom of scientific research, and that this is a basic feature of our ideas on the subject. We encourage and support activity that discovers scientific truths. The discovery of truths serves the public interest, the realisation of the aims of socialism and the progress of the people. We ensure that scientists can argue their opinions in the appropriate places. They must on the other hand bear the resources of the country in mind, and also know the demands of society.

The role of scientific bodies, in the first place that of the Hungarian Academy of Sciences will be strengthened. We emphatically wish to support all international scientific relationships that are not in conflict with the national interest, and we wish to widen the scope of exchanges with other countries, as regards intellectual products. All this will certainly speed up and widen the progress of research in Hungary.

LITERATURE, THEATRE, AND THE ARTS

The rising level of cultural life can likewise be indicated by statistical evidence. Several times as many books are published as before the war. According to 1964 UN figures, Hungary leads among European countries with 52 publications a year for every 100,000 inhabitants. The numbers of those attending theatrical performances or visiting museums is increasing all the time parallel with the rapid spread of radio and television.

The far from commonplace talent and creativity of the Hungarian people was indicated even before liberation by great figures such as Bartók, Kodály and Gyula Derkovits; or Ady, Babits, Móricz, Attila József and Radnóti in literature. One may say without inmodesty that their importance was not circumscribed by the country's boundaries. However, this culture did not reach those for whom it was primarily intended. Today, we can talk of a genuine mass-culture in Hungary. The number of those who enjoy art and literature has grown to many times its earlier size.

Interest in the classics is particularly high. In the last twenty-five years, the works of Dickens, Balzac, Tolstoy and Thomas Mann have appeared in such large editions, the plays of Shakespeare and Molière have been performed so frequently, that, bearing in mind the country's population, the figures compare favourably with the writers' own countries. I read in *The Times* that Shakespeare has always been one of the greatest Hungarian playwrights. *The Times* was right: since 1945 there have been 4,012 performances of the immortal bard's works and more than 2 million people were able to see them. In the atmosphere of this heightened interest on the part of mass-audiences, the creative energy of artists has also increased and is still growing.

There has been a revolutionary change in public health. Before the war, tuberculosis was a widely spread and serious illness in Hungary: it was even called "morbus hungaricus." Today, it is virtually extinct. Medical care is assured for every Hungarian citizen. All medical services are free for those who work and their families and for pensioners. The number of doctors per head of population is one of the highest in Europe. In addition to social welfare, everybody who works is entitled to a pension—peasants working in co-operatives are included. By such means, socialism in Hungary has contributed a great deal to lightening the cares of the old and the ill.

The Reform of the Economic Mechanism

Life is becoming more complex, primarily owing to technological progress; in present Hungarian circumstances it cannot be considered right to make central decisions in matters concerning day-to-day details of economic life, or to direct from above each phase of the work of factories and other economic units. This is linked with a natural requirement of progress, socialist democracy must be continuously strengthened and widened. It is in the interest of the management and the workers in each plant, as well as of the whole of society, to make sure that they participate as directly as possible in making decisions which affect their work. Circumstances have made it necessary, and the high degree of development of productive forces has made it possible, to change methods employed in previous years in directing a progressively growing planned economy.

The recognition of this state of affairs led to those reforms in the system of management of the economy which were introduced on January 1, 1968, and which we have been applied ever since.

The new economic mechanism is in the first place meant to serve a sound scientific perfection of economic planning, it is not based purely and simply on commodity and money relations, i.e. on economic regulators. But subjective factors also have great significance, such as rational activity by executives on various levels and in different areas and their greater political and economic responsibility. Without this, the advantages of the reform cannot make themselves felt to the desired extent or at the desired rate, nor could technological progress or the tapping of the reserves made available by modernization, or for that matter profitable management that is to the advantage of the economy as a whole, shape adequately.

The functioning and development of the new system of directing the economy are kept under close observation. It is essential that all those concerned with economic affairs should quickly and effectively change the way they think and act. Independence and initiative must be increased, as must the efficiency of industrial organization. The energy latent in democracy ought to be exploited.

It is understandable that in the first year of the new economic mechanism, while earlier economic directives had not yet lost their effect, those responsible proceeded with caution. They were still trying to find out how the new regulators worked, they concentrated their efforts on solving problems that were inherent in the change-over. Experience is available now which allows a system of management to take shape which is appropriate to the spirit of the new economic mechanism.

A free Hungary embarking on the second quarter century of its history engaged in constructing socialism aims to continue systematically what was begun twenty-five years ago. The state must be strengthened further, therefore democratic ways must be given more room in every field, economic policy must be systematically made effective in the first place, in order to raise the standard of living of all those who work; and progress in the direction of complete socialism must be confident and at a rate consistent with the realities.

SOCIALIST DEMOCRACY IN PRACTICE

The meaning of democracy is discussed all over the world. Politicians, philosophers and economists all contribute their opinions. The people of Hungary demand a socialist democracy in their own free country. This means that Hungary does not look on democracy as an aim in itself, but as something that is in the interests of the community of those who work. In practice this shows itself in the participation of public opinion in the widest sense in solving all important questions. This is what happened during 1966–67 in laying the groundwork for the economic reform; more recently, a large number of scientists and others concerned with the organization of research were engaged in preparing a new policy for the sciences. All those involved have the right to say their piece when the affairs of a working or social collective unit are discussed and every decision ripens in the heat of debate. But when a decision is finally born in harmony with the interests of a society engaged in building socialism, every citizen conscious of his position must do his best in the interests of the common aim.

Two major tasks await us on the threshold of the coming period. The first is to draw up the fourth, 1971–75 five-year plan. Its guide-lines have already been established following complex analytical and synthetizing work. Parallel with this, long-range economic forecasts for the years 1971–85 are being worked out. Governmental institutions will have reached a position by the late 1970s where they can assess the proposed plan for each five-year period in terms of long-range developmental notions.

HOUSING AND URBANIZATION

The aim of the fourth five-year plan is to raise the standard of living of the population, and to further increase raising real wages and real incomes. The most important factor in improving living conditions is the construction of housing. Everything is done to increase the rate of building. This is a most serious problem which in spite of determined efforts can only be solved partially by the end of the period of the five-year plan. By then the one million new dwellings which make up the fifteen-year building pro-gramme (1961–75) will be built. Although this is a very impressive number in view of the circumstances, the housing shortage will, according to present calculations, continue nevertheless. In the first place, the standard demanded is rising, and secondly urbanization is proceeding faster than had been expected. Circumstances demand that the capacity for building 80–90,000 dwellings a year should be available as soon as possible. This will very likely be the case after about 1975.

Urbanization is leaving its ineradicable mark on the society of the future. This process is a natural consequence of the speedy growth of the forces of production and of the structural changes in the economy. During the past twenty-five years the number of those employed in agriculture has dropped from 2 million to 1.4 million, while the number of those engaged in industry has risen from about 670,000 to 1,750,000. This is the main reason why the population of towns and cities has increased by one million between 1949 and 1969. Before the Second World War, less than a third, while today roughly half the country's population live in towns.

The process of urbanization is taken into account by the national econo-my's long-range plans for regional development. It takes into account the fact that the structural changes which can be expected to take place in the economy will further reduce the numbers of those employed in agriculture and exploitative industries, and that at the same time the development of secondary industries and services will be speeded up.

The Application of Variants in Planning

A variety of schemes of improving the rate of development of the economy and for improving the efficiency of production are being examined. It is desirable that the rate of economic development should be realistically fast, stable and free of fluctuations and that the quantity of accumulation should correspond to the rate of increase of the national income. Final decisions and details of the plan will be worked out in full knowledge of the variants. The state will determine certain general index numbers that will ensure and direct planned development, but the only ones approved and given the force of law are those which provide the barest necessary direction to executive instrumentalities when working out their own plans.

When working out the broad outlines of the 1971–85 long-range plan, in the course of elaborating a number of working hypotheses, it became more and more obvious that all those economic, technical, social and natural processes which are part of economic life had to be analysed in a novel and scientific manner. A number of variants are worked out for the long-range plan also, and the final choice will be made after complex and detailed analysis.

Long-range Planning Notions

A number of most important questions must be borne in mind. One is the proportion of national income devoted to accumulation (investment). Some consider this too high, others are of the contrary opinion. In my view the current 25 per cent is desirable and conforms to the conditions prevailing in the country. It is true that a high rate of accumulation generally produces faster economic growth. But a high rate of accumulation is neither the only, nor a necessary factor of speedy growth. Concentrated well-timed investment activity can lead to a speeded up growth of production, distribution and exchange, and to a considerable increase in the quantity of goods necessary for economic activity and an improvement in the conditions of life.

In many cases, a most efficient use of existing equipment could achieve better results even with smaller investment. The only way is first to improve the effectiveness of investment, and secondly to better exploit existing equipment.

The objectives sketched above must be achieved in such a way that by the end of the fourth five-year plan technological development and the increase of productivity can be just about the only source of economic growth in the country. After all, one of the major factors in improving living standards should be the further shortening of working hours which means that the hours of work at the disposal of the economy cannot increase fast in spite of the growth of the numbers employed. Gradually the agricultural reserves of labour will become exhausted, while the employment of women otherwise engaged in housework is also a gradually decreasing source. The need for speeding up development in fields outside industry, especially in services and in social welfare, draws attention to the fact that to develop the most dynamic industrial sources of economic growth, a level of technology is needed which is considerably higher than the present one.

PEACE AND SECURITY

Twenty-five years ago Hungary was a backward country, today it is a moderately developed one which is making up for the effect of hundreds of years of neglect. I am convinced that in the coming period every working Hungarian will concentrate his efforts so that this socialist country will be reckoned among the highly developed ones. This naturally cannot be done without world peace.

The people and the government of the Hungarian People's Republic do not merely desire peace but are prepared to do everything within their power to bring it about and secure it. Hungary is particularly concerned in European affairs. For this reason we consistently work for the realization of the ideas published as the "Budapest Appeal" in the interest of European peace and security. The strengthening of our alliance with the Soviet Union and with other socialist countries is a determining factor of our foreign policy, which fights for peace among men and for the peaceful co-existence of nations living under differing social systems. The further development of economic co-operation between socialist countries, and the raising of socialist integration to a higher level both help to establish even more varied relations with all countries which serve the interests of peace in as many different ways as possible.

THIRTY YEARS
OF HUNGARIAN FOREIGN POLICY

by

FRIGYES PUJA

The most important date in Hungary's recent history is April 4, 1945. On that day, thirty years ago now, the Red Army drove the remnants of the defeated German armies out of the country and the entire territory was liberated from Hitlerite fascism and its Hungarian allies. The time had come when the Hungarian people could become the masters of their own destiny, taking over power and setting a new course for the development of their country.

At that time this was not as natural as it appears today. Hungary was still shrouded in the shadow of her past. The supporters of the overthrown régime had not yet given up the struggle and whispered rumours purposefully spread, frightening gullible people that a comeback of the old masters was threatened. Of all the parties of the Hungarian National Independence Front only the Hungarian Communist Party had a clear, consistently popular democratic programme. The parties of the coalition disagreed on fundamental questions of home policy. The Hungarian Communist Party and the left wing of the Social Democratic and National Peasant Parties alone consistently stood for a clear break with the past. The leaders of the Independent Smallholders' Party, a few prominent politicians excepted, wanted to steer the country towards bourgeois democracy. This was the main reason why, soon after Liberation, the domestic situation became so tense. The parliamentary elections of 1947 and events of the subsequent months, the programme of the new coalition government and then the historic fusion of the two workers' parties, the Hungarian Communist Party and the Social Democratic Party, clearly showed that the Hungarian working class, the toiling peasantry and progressive professional people, that is to say, the overwhelming majority of the country's population, wished to take the road to socialism.

Thirty years are a short period as history goes but it proved enough to change life in Hungary down to the roots. An underdeveloped country acquired a developed industry and large-scale socialist agriculture and a cultural revolution in the Leninist sense was carried through successfully. Industrial production has risen tenfold and agricultural output, in spite of war damage, has increased by 61 per cent compared to the 1934–1938 average. The standard of living of Hungarians has reached unprecedented levels. There is no stopping, progress continues along the charted course. The Party Programme, adopted by the 11th Congress, opening up a wealth of prospects for the future, declares: "That great principle of human equality *From everyone according to his ability, to everyone according to his needs* is coming true thanks to our work and struggle. That is how our people comes closer to that universal human goal, communism, a new world free from all oppression and exploitation, where nations dwell together in peace and prosperity, and humanity finally enters the realm of freedom."[1]

I

The liberated country had to decide its foreign policy orientation just as it did the guidelines of its home policies. Without a firm and well-established foreign policy, and favourable international conditions, the Hungarian people would not have been in a position to reconstruct the country and to lay the foundations for a new life. The government of free Hungary had to get rid of the dismal heritage of the past, to launder out the stains which the country's participation in the Second World War had left on the honour of the Hungarian people; to arrange for the signing of a treaty of peace; to build and develop relations with all those countries which were ready for them; and, first of all, to acquire friends who could be depended on, friends who would help Hungary realize her lofty and far from easy objectives.

Hungary had taken part in the Second World War as an ally of the fascist powers. Miklós Horthy's anti-democratic system and later, after October 15, 1944, Szálasi's arrow-cross "government" had given all-out support to the German war machine. This policy plunged Hungary, which had not really maintained a network of relationships before the war either, into complete international isolation. Before the end of the Second World War, Hungary had diplomatic relations with only a few countries; political contacts, commercial, cultural and other ties existed only with the Axis

[1] *A Magyar Szocialista Munkáspárt XI. kongresszusa* (The 11th Congress of the Hungarian Socialist Workers' Party) Kossuth, 1975. p. 223.

powers and a limited number of neutral states. A serious effort had to be made to change this situation.

A major task confronting Hungary was thwarting unceasing attempts by the imperialist powers to interfere in the country's affairs. The imperialists did not favour Hungary seeing herself as a people's democracy. In their view the country's home and foreign policies ought to have been given a capitalist orientation and Hungary was meant to act as a sort of *cordon sanitaire* between the Soviet Union and the Western powers. The governments of the imperialist countries adopted a double-faced policy in the hope that Hungary's line would move in a direction to their liking. They established diplomatic relations, stressing their readiness to develop inter-state relationships, and even promised to grant economic aid and credits as well. Making use of such contacts, they engaged in organized subversion designed to slow down and handicap the growth of a people's democracy in Hungary. They conspired with the enemies of the people, with reactionary Horthyist elements, who found refuge in political parties, social organizations and government bodies, and with bourgeois forces in order to effect a swing to the right, if need be, by the use of force. They addressed notes, protests and warnings couched in sharp terms and "well-meaning" appeals to the Hungarian government applying sanctions thereby to embolden and support their accomplices inside the country.

Differences of opinion between parties of the National Independence Front making up the government existed also regarding foreign policy, although on the surface they appeared to differ from divergencies on issues of domestic policy.

The pivot of the coalition government, the Hungarian Communist Party, took up a clear and unambiguous position. It indicated as the most important point in foreign policy the development of close co-operation with the Soviet Union and the democratic countries. To quote the draft programme published by the Central Committee of the party in November 30, 1944: "The democratic transformation of Hungary is inseparable from a democratic foreign policy... There is need for a radical break with a policy hostile to the Soviet Union, a policy that has followed only and exclusively from the anti-democratic policy of the Hungarian reaction, brought the country to ruin and turned progressive humanity against us, being diametrically opposed to the Hungarian national interest... We have to create good neighbourly relations and sincere co-operation with all surrounding countries, first of all with the new Yugoslavia and democratic Czechoslovakia, furthermore with Great Britain and the United States, and close friendship with the defender of the freedom and independence of peoples, the powerful Soviet Union, which helps us shake off the German yoke."[2] Close co-operation with the Soviet Union and the countries desirous to become people's democracies was essential; it was a requirement of the internationalism of the communist movement; there were common aims and common enemies; we were equally interested in safeguarding a lasting peace; and only such a line could further the realization of specific national aspirations both in domestic and in foreign politics. Common experiences stimulated us to become good neighbours and to join forces. From the outset we had been aware that we would be able to lead Hungary on the road of socialism only if we relied on the first socialist state in the world, the Soviet Union, with its immense strength and great international prestige, together with the countries with similar systems. On the other hand, close co-operation with the Soviet Union and the people's democracies was indispensable also in order to repel imperialist interference in home affairs.

The picture was nowhere near as clear in the other parties of the National Independence Front. The masses of the Social Democratic and National Peasant Parties shared the ideas of the Communists also regarding foreign policy, but different views came to the fore among the leaders. In both parties there were men who wished to lean on the imperialist forces, the Anglo-Saxon powers in the first place. The leadership of the Independent Smallholders' Party, apart from a few leftists, inclined to the Western powers. The same forces which wanted to lead Hungary on the road to bourgeois democracy supported an Anglo-Saxon orientation in foreign policies.

In spite of this, right after the Liberation, none of the parties openly questioned the importance and necessity of co-operation with the Soviet Union though their reasons varied. The foreign policy proposals of the November 30, 1944 draft programme of the Hungarian Communist Party were accepted by all the parties of the National Independence Front. They were included in the programme of the Front issued on December 3, 1944. In public, even politicians who could hardly be described as democrats, argued in favour of good relations with the Soviet Union. They had no alternative, the will of the masses was manifest. In secret, they nevertheless conspired against such ideas and endeavoured to tie Hungary to the leash of the Western powers.

After the 1947 elections and the formation of the new government, developments were accelerated in foreign policy as well. Hungary strengthened relations with the Soviet Union and other democratic countries. In 1948 treaties of friendship and mutual assistance were signed with the

[2] Resolutions of the Hungarian Communist and Social Democratic Parties, 1944–1948. Kossuth Könyvkiadó, 1967, p. 40. (In Hungarian.)

Soviet Union, Poland and Rumania, in 1949 with Bulgaria and Czechoslovakia. In 1949 the country helped to establish the Council of Mutual Economic Assistance. Hungary was among the first to recognize the People's Republic of China following the victory of the Chinese revolution. Solidarity was expressed with the Democratic People's Republic of Korea in its battle with imperialism. The government took part in a number of multilateral actions by the socialist countries intended to strengthen international peace and security. In 1955 Hungary was one of the signatories to the Warsaw Pact. Faced with the preparations for war of the imperialist powers, it was indispensable to organize more efficiently the common defence of the socialist countries.

Bilateral relations were built up with a number of developed capitalist countries. A start was made on settling problems outstanding between Hungary and capitalist countries, such as questions concerning property rights. In the years 1950 to 1955 our relations with most of the European capitalist states were developing appreciably.

The Hungarian People's Republic strove to establish relations with developing countries that had recently won independence as soon as this became possible. Diplomatic relations with Egypt were established in 1947, with the Republic of India in 1948, after they became independent.

An important event was the signing of the treaty of peace in February 1947. Although diplomatic relations with Western powers were established earlier, with the United States, e.g., in 1945 and with France in 1946, their signatures on the treaty of peace confirmed once again that they recognized Hungary as a sovereign and independent state, though soon after they nevertheless asserted the contrary. Eventually, however, they had to agree to the Hungarian People's Republic being admitted to membership in the United Nations in 1955.

Between 1945 and 1956 Hungary had to contend with many difficulties of a foreign policy nature. In 1945–46, the position of the country did not permit extensive diplomatic activity, later the Western powers had started the Cold War. The socialist countries, Hungary among them, had to make great effort to counteract imperialist machinations designed to disrupt peace. At that time every small result required great exertion on the part of the socialist countries. In 1953–54 the ice of Cold War began to thaw, and Hungarian foreign policy activities, following the example of the Soviet Union and the other socialist countries, also began to liven up. There was every sign that the process would favour the expansion of relations between Hungary and other countries. This promising development was interrupted by the 1956 counter-revolution.

2

The party and government of Hungary had to work very hard to overcome the effects abroad of the counter-revolution, which wanted to change Hungary's foreign policy cutting off the country from the community of socialist states and withdrawing it from the Warsaw Treaty Organization.

The governments of the imperialist powers meant to demonstrate that —though maintaining diplomatic relations with the Hungarian People's Republic—they refused to accord "full recognition" to the Revolutionary Workers' and Peasants' Government of Hungary. They did not appoint new ambassadors, nor did they consent to visits on a ministerial or higher level. Except for trade relations, they slowed down the development of bilateral contacts; they did nothing at all in the area of cultural relations; in some respects they even organized cultural boycotts against Hungary. They managed, in the United Nations, to have the credentials of the Hungarian delegation suspended, requesting that the Hungarian government make it possible for the "Committee of Five" of the United Nations to function in Hungary. They used the forum of the United Nations to stir up feelings against the Hungarian People's Republic and took every opportunity to keep an anti-Hungarian propaganda campaign going.

The party leadership and the government of the Hungarian People's Republic did not allow themselves to be influenced by the fierce attacks of Western propaganda and the political steps of the imperialist governments. They made every effort to do away with the consequences of the counter-revolutionary revolt and to establish the future of the country on a solid basis. Thanks to this, a few months only after the defeat of the counter-revolution, life in Hungary was back to normal, industrial and agricultural production was growing rapidly and transport and commerce functioned satisfactorily. National economic plans were successfully fulfilled year after year. The most difficult task of socialist construction, the socialist reorganization of agriculture, was accomplished without difficulties in 1964.

The major results achieved in home politics and in economic affairs affected also the international position of Hungary. Public opinion in the Western countries became increasingly convinced that their politicians and news media had misled them with false and tendentious reports on the situation in Hungary. The moment came when the governments of the capitalist countries had to change their minds and abandon the policy of forcible isolation. The "Hungarian question" was taken off the agenda of the United Nations in 1962. In October 1964 the Foreign Minister of Austria was the first Western politician, after a long gap, to pay an official visit to Hungary.

The change for the better that took place in the international position of Hungary in the late fifties and early sixties was thus essentially a consequence of successes at home. The picture would not be right, however, if one failed to mention the great and very effective help which the Soviet Union and other socialist countries rendered Hungary. One should not forget the successful efforts of Hungarian diplomacy either. Hungarian diplomacy played a part in finally breaking the capitalist diplomatic and cultural blockade, ensuring that relations with capitalist countries expanded on the basis of full equality and mutual advantage. In that period Hungary established diplomatic relations with many developing countries.

As a result of all this, in the mid-sixties, the Hungarian People's Republic entertained diplomatic and other relations with far more countries, and enjoyed considerably greater prestige in international life than in 1955.

3

In the time that elapsed between the mid-sixties and the present the foreign policy of the Hungarian People's Republic has carried out its national and international duties in every respect. Foreign policy has become more active, increasingly taking the initiative and making good use of the possibilities for promoting the aims of the Hungarian people and the socialist community.

Looking back at the road traversed, one can rightly say that Hungary's position has radically changed on the international scene. Today the Hungarian People's Republic is an honoured member of the socialist community and, given the results it has achieved and its consistent foreign policy, it has secured the respect of the non-socialist world as well. The extension of its international relations is shown by the fact that it maintains diplomatic relations with a hundred and four countries, including fifty-nine embassies and seven consulates general as well as four missions accredited to international organizations.

In the course of thirty years of international activity the Hungarian People's Republic has accumulated much experience that it uses and applies in the handling of foreign affairs.

(a) Developments in the world situation show, first, starting in the mid-sixties in a fluctuating manner, later more steadily, a lessening in international tension and a gradual spread of détente. Today one already talks about a major change having taken place. The Declaration of the 11th Congress of the Hungarian Socialist Workers' Party rightly say: "At present, under the aegis of the peaceful coexistence of states with different social systems, a turn is taking place in the international situation from a period of cold war towards political as well as mutually advantageous economic, scientific, technological and cultural co-operation."

The chances are that, in accordance with the shift in international power relations in favour of socialism, of progress and peace, détente will continue to spread and ultimately become irreversible. This, however, is no smooth, automatic process, for the enemies of détente will try over and over again to slow down and halt détente and, what is more, even to bring back a fresh version of the cold war. In the present situation such efforts cannot really succeed.

(b) On the basis of the experience gained in international activity spread over thirty years, in co-operation with the socialist countries, Hungary has established the main lines of foreign policy. These can be described as follows.

—Shaping favourable international conditions for the building of socialism; a fight against aggression and against imperialist efforts made to disrupt peace and to subject other nations.

—Strengthening the unity and cohesion of the socialist countries, increasing their political, economic and military weight.

—Solidarity with the popular forces fighting for democratic liberties, for peace and progress in the capitalist countries; support for the national liberation movements in their struggle against colonialism, neo-colonialism, imperialist oppression and aggression.

—Fostering many-sided co-operation with the developing countries.

—Fighting for the realization of peaceful coexistence of countries with different social systems, for the consistent safeguarding of the principles of peaceful coexistence.

We know from experience that the most favourable condition for the building of socialism is lasting, stable and secure peace. The Hungarian aim is to contribute, as far as the country's moderate means extend, to the fulfilment of this central task.

(c) Based on the main line of foreign policy, Hungarian international activity has considerable scope. I shall list a number of aspects.

Hungarian foreign policy attaches the greatest importance to relation with the Soviet Union. It does so for reasons of principle and practice. Hungarian Communists have always looked on relations with the Soviet Union as a criterion of internationalism. They have always held the view that progress in this age, and the successful building of socialism, are inconceivable without, or in opposition to, the Soviet Union. Whoever wants socialism has to go with the Soviet Union. In the spirit of internationalism the Soviet Union has always selflessly assisted, as it still does, the socialist countries in their difficult struggle. The history of free Hungary offers eloquent proof that the Soviet Union has always stood by her. The Soviet leadership has made its wealth of experiences in the building of socialism available to the Hungarian people, it has given them assistance in the economic reconstruction of a country devastated and looted by German fascists, and in the development of industrial and agricultural production. The alliance with the Soviet Union has saved Hungary from the imperialist powers' attempts to interfere. It was with Soviet help that the counter-revolution was crushed and that its consequences were done away with. Hungarians protect their own national interests when they strive for still closer, still more intimate and still more harmonious co-operation with the Soviet Union. These endeavours were well served by the talks held in Moscow when the Hungarian party and government delegation headed by János Kádár journeyed there in September 1974. The significance of that visit was given its due by the meeting of the Central Committee held on November 20, 1974. "A political event of outstanding importance for our country," the communiqué issued after the Central Committee's meeting stated, "was the visit to the Soviet Union by the Hungarian party and government delegation in September. The visit has made it clear that fraternal relations and co-operation between the Hungarian People's Republic and the Soviet Union develop all the time and serve the interests of both countries, of the socialist community and of the progressive forces of the world. It has demonstrated the total unity of principle and policy between the Hungarian Socialist Workers' Party and the Communist Party of the Soviet Union, the Hungarian and the Soviet government, and the two nations. The Central Committee has set high value on the results of the talks. It establishes that the party and government delegation has completely fulfilled its mission, and has continued to strengthen indissoluble Hungarian–Soviet friendship."[3]

The Hungarian People's Republic takes an active part in the work of the common organizations of the socialist countries. Hungary endorses the proposals which serve to strengthen these organizations, improving their work. A Hungarian delegation, headed by János Kádár, participated in the meeting of the Political Consultative Committee of the Warsaw Treaty,

[3] Communiqué on the November 20 meeting of the Central Committee of the Hungarian Socialist Workers' Party. *Népszabadság.* November 21, 1974.

held in Warsaw in April 1974, which effected a thorough analysis of the international situation and defined the common foreign policy tasks of member countries for the future. The Warsaw Treaty member states celebrated the twentieth anniversary of the organization, emphasizing the enormous significance of the organization from the point of view of safeguarding peace and thwarting the machinations of imperialism. A Hungarian government delegation headed by Jenő Fock attended the anniversary session of the Council of Mutual Economic Assistance held in Sofia in June 1974. That was a good opportunity for the representatives of the CMEA countries to appraise twenty-five years of activity of the organization and to define the tasks needed for the consistent carrying out of the Complex Programme. The 29th Session of CMEA held in Budapest in June 1975 approved the coordinated plan of integrational measures for the 1976–1980 period taken by member states. Important resolutions were also passed concerning long-term cooperation among member states stretching as far as 1990.

In the recent past great successes have been scored by national liberation movements. As a result of the positive turn of events in Portugal, independence has come within reach of the former Portuguese colonies. Guinea-Bissau and Mozambique have already become independent and the proclamation of the independence of the Cape Verde Islands is expected in the near future. It is to be hoped that the issue will soon be decided in Angola as well, and that these countries will also achieve independence. New independent countries, presumably with progressive policies, will thus appear on the political map of the world. The socialist countries, including Hungary, will obviously strive to build extensive relations with these countries.

The Hungarian government makes great efforts to expand relations between Hungary and the Arab countries. This is only natural. Progressive trends worthy of support are manifest in the Arab world. The Arabs fight a just cause, to put an end to Israeli aggression and its consequences. The events taking place in the Middle East have a direct effect also on developments of the situation in Europe. Hungarian political and economic interests alike require closer co-operation. Hungary maintains traditionally good relations with the vast majority of Arab countries. The visits made by Prime Minister Jalloud to several socialist states in February 1974 bear witness to the fact that Libya also wishes to improve relations with the socialist countries. Over and above political and economic ties Hungary is taking steps to broaden cultural contacts as well. A pledge of this was the inauguration of the Hungarian Scientific and Cultural Center in Cairo last autumn.

The Hungarian People's Republic strengthens its relations with the developing countries of Asia as well. This objective was served by the visits of Jenő Fock to India and Burma. Hungary has also begun to build relations with Asian countries with which contacts so far have been only occasional or non-existent. Signs of this were the visits to Hungary last year by the Foreign Ministers of Singapore, the Philippines and Indonesia, by the Deputy Foreign Minister of Thailand and by a government delegation from Laos.

Hungary strives to build extensive relations with the developed capitalist countries on the principle of the peaceful coexistence of countries with different social systems. Among these attention is focussed on the capitalist countries of Europe. This is natural since Hungary is a European state.

The intimacy of our relations with neutral Finland was well demonstrated by János Kádár's visit to Finland in September 1973, and the visit by Prime Minister Kalevi Sorsa of Finland to Hungary last year. Good neighbourly relations with Austria have expanded in practically every field. Important new agreements which will be signed in the near future have been initialled. A new stage in the relations between Hungary and Norway was marked by the visit of the Norwegian Prime Minister, Trygve Bratteli, to Hungary last year. Relationships between Hungary and major capitalist countries have likewise developed, although faster progress would also be conceivable in some respects. For the first time in the history of the Hungarian People's Republic and the Federal Republic of Germany, official —and successful—negotiations took place between the Foreign Ministers of the two countries. Subsequently the Hungarian foreign minister visited the Federal Republic of Germany during which he conferred with the Foreign Minister and was received by the Federal Chancellor. The visit to Hungary by Aldo Moro, the then Italian Foreign Minister, has shown that the Italian government is interested in developing bilateral relations. It is hoped that a new impulse can be given also to Hungarian–French and Hungarian–British relations in the near future.

One cannot be fully satisfied with relations between Hungary and the United States. In spite of Hungarian intentions all questions could not be settled as yet.

The recent democratic change in Portugal confronts Hungary with the task of establishing extensive relations with that country. Hungary wishes to intensify relations with Greece as well, where a positive change has occurred.

In keeping with its strength and capacity, the Hungarian People's Republic takes a hand also in the solution of a number of international problems.

Allow me to refer first to the European conference on security. Hungarian politicians and leading officials of the Ministry of Foreign Affairs, in order to ensure that the security conference be convened and later in the interest of this successful work, held comprehensive consultations and exchanges of views with leading politicians of the developed capitalist countries and put forward the agreed ideas and proposals of the socialist community. It is hoped that, as a result of the joint efforts of the socialist and other peace-loving countries, the second stage of the security conference will soon be concluded, and the third stage will be convened at the highest level.

Hungary collaborates with the Warsaw Treaty countries in the interests of the success of negotiations on the reduction of armed forces and armaments in Central Europe. Unfortunately, the NATO countries' desire to secure unilateral advantages has so far hindered progress at the Vienna talks.

Hungarian representatives are active in negotiations promoting the limitation of the arms race and the cause of disarmament. They take part in the work of the Committee on Disarmament in Geneva. The country co-operates in finding solutions to problems of detail concerning disarmament in the United Nations, as well as in other international organizations.

The government of the Hungarian People's Republic has resolutely opposed the schemes of the Greek military junta and aggressive NATO circles who threatened the independence of Cyprus. The situation in Cyprus still overshadows the improving situation in Europe. A just settlement of the conflict is needed, based on the restoration of, and respect for, the independence and sovereignty of the Republic of Cyprus. The Hungarian government supports the relevant proposal of the Soviet Union.

The government of Hungary continues to think it indispensable that the Middle East crisis be settled peacefully by implementing the resolutions of the Security Council. Israel must withdraw her forces from occupied Arab territories and recognize the Palestinians' right to self-determination and statehood. Recently the situation in the Middle East has again become more critical. Increasing American support has buttressed Israeli self-confidence; the Israeli leaders refuse to discuss the withdrawal of their armed forces from all occupied Arab territories; they organize armed provocations against Arab countries and decline to recognize the Palestine Liberation Organization, showing reluctance to negotiate with its representatives. They are opposed to the resumption of the Geneva conference. The responsibility for the unsettled Middle East situation and for any new armed conflict in the area is Israel's and that of its foreign backers.

A major event of our times is the victory of the people of Vietnam over Imperialism and its satellites, following a long and self-sacrificing strug-

gle. The Hungarian people, showing all the admiration and recognition
due, supported this heroic struggle in the spirit of active solidarity. It was
a fight waged for the implementation of the Paris agreement, for the freedom and independence, unity and social advancement of their country,
fought by the patriots of South Vietnam under the immediate direction of
the National Liberation Front of South Vietnam and the Provisional Revolutionary Government of the Republic of South Vietnam and in collaboration with their northern brothers. Now, when after a victory won at the
expense of great sacrifices, the tasks of reconstruction and of the creation
of a democratic society are given first priority in this much suffering country, the Hungarian people will continue to support the people of Vietnam
in the spirit of fraternal internationalist cooperation.

The Chilean military junta carried out their coup a year and a half ago.
It has not been able to consolidate its position. The opposition of the Chilean
people is mounting, and the bloody military junta must sooner or later
disappear from the scene.

The government of the Hungarian People's Republic categorically con-
demns the Chilean fascists and demands that the will of the Chilean
people be enforced.

4

During the thirty years of its foreign affairs activity, the Hungarian
People's Republic has experienced much of general validity. Most of the
socialist countries have reached the same conclusions and this strengthens
the Hungarian position. Such experience is taken into consideration in
international activities.

(a) The Marxist-Leninist view that the foreign policy of a socialist
country is most closely connected with its home policy appears to be justified. The other side of this connection is also important: the foreign
policy of a socialist country exerts an effect on domestic policy, even though
this connection is not as direct as the other one. A country's striving towards
socialism cannot be enduring if, in its foreign policy, it fails to incline
towards the community of the socialist countries, that is towards the Soviet
Union. If the leaders of a socialist country fail to take this into account,
if they isolate themselves from the socialist community, if they pursue
a different foreign policy, this will sooner or later have a negative effect
upon their domestic policy and will ultimately jeopardize the building of
socialism in their country. The most telling example of this is the foreign
policy of the Maoist leaders of the People's Republic of China.

(b) Experience shows that a country building socialism, or any other progressive country, cannot adopt a position half-way between the socialist community and the imperialist camp, it cannot manoeuvre between them with the idea of being able to take advantage of both sides for its own good. If the leaders of a country really choose the road leading to socialism, they must dissociate themselves from the aspirations of imperialism and must oppose them; they must of necessity come closer to the international objectives of the socialist community. If this is not taken into account in foreign policy this is proof that a socialist orientation is not seriously desired, or, at the very best, that in the maelstrom of international events the wrong path was chosen.

(c) Experience in foreign policy shows that a *sine qua non* of the successful international activity of socialist countries is close alliance and co-operation with the Soviet Union. This increases the possibilities of the socialist countries in the field of foreign affairs and enhances their international standing. That the present-day international position of the Hungarian People's Republic cannot even be compared to that of prewar Hungary is largely due to close co-operation with the Soviet Union. It is a mistake to believe that the loosening of co-operation with the Soviet Union in foreign affairs can be to the advantage of any socialist country. This kind of attitude is apt only to diminish the effectiveness of the foreign policy of the socialist community.

(d) Experience shows that closer co-operation of the international activities of the socialist countries is an indispensable requirement of our times. The socialist countries have to co-ordinate virtually all of their major tactical steps, since only in this way can they struggle effectively against the ideas of the imperialists and their allies. This conclusion is convincingly justified by international negotiations in recent years, the European security conference being a particularly good example. Besides joint services to common aims and to the cause of the international proletariat, besides the more effective protection of our own national interests, we are obliged to this also by the "unification" efforts of capitalist monopolies, by the fact that the leaders of capitalist countries take a joint stand on many questions in which they oppose the socialist countries. Passing over such phenomena out of narrow-minded egoism would be tantamount to political blindness.

(e) From the point of view of promoting the cause of peace and security, of improving on a larger scale the relations of socialist and capitalist countries, of settling controversial international problems, of curbing and then halting the arms race, the government of the Hungarian People's Republic attaches paramount importance to the development of Soviet–U.S. relations, to the already regular meetings between the General Secretary of the Communist Party of the Soviet Union and the President of the United States of America. Hungary welcomes the talks and agreements between representatives of the two major world powers. At the same time Hungary opposes all those who on this account foster mistrust of the Soviet Union. The results attained thus far demonstrate beyond question that the Soviet leaders, in their talks with American leaders, always start from the vital common interest of the socialist countries.

(f) Experience justifies the Marxist-Leninist view that the priority of politics is valid in foreign affairs as well. The socialist countries subordinate their economic objectives to their international political aims. At the same time they cannot neglect international economic interests which are important for the life of their peoples. There are stages in the building of socialism when international economic interests come particularly into focus and when the socialist countries increasingly strive to expand their international economic relations.

At the present time it seems proper to make use of the possibilities inherent in the expansion of economic relations with the developed capitalist countries. The ruling circles of capitalist countries appear to have a greater inclination than before for more extensive economic cooperation with the socialist countries. But those Western circles which think that the socialist countries will make political concessions in exchange for broader economic contacts with capitalist countries, are mistaken. It would be well for them to bear in mind that the expansion of economic relations is important not only for the socialist countries but also for them, and that this is not a matter of one-way advantages. They also cannot expect to be able to obstruct the progress of socialist construction by weakening the economic contacts between their respective countries and the socialist ones. The failure of the economic blockade and discrimination employed against the countries of the socialist community during the Cold War years has shown that there is no way in which the imperialist powers can halt the successful march of the building of socialism.

(g) The history of socialist foreign policy shows that the socialist countries can achieve their foreign policy objectives only through an active struggle against imperialism. Substantially, imperialism has still not given up its plans to contain the advance of socialism and undermine its positions, and to restore capitalism the world over. To this "programme" we oppose the objectives of socialism, of progress, of a foreign policy that guarantees that in proportion to the shift in international power relations socialism is gradually gaining ground everywhere in the world.

Some pseudo-leftist "revolutionaries" maintain that talking to representatives of the leading capitalist countries and co-operating with them on certain matters is incompatible with the anti-imperialist struggle. These people evidently do not understand the dialectic of peaceful coexistence, the fact that peaceful coexistence means both co-operation and struggle at the same time. They do understand what compromises with the imperialist countries mean. They tend to forget that Marxism-Leninism has never been against compromises as such, that it has opposed only compromises entailing concessions on matters of principle. If, however, the compromises promote the cause of socialism and of progress, they are right and necessary.

(h) While active in the international sphere, Hungary has reached the conclusion that contacts between party leaders are of increasing importance for the relations between countries. In the case of socialist countries this is self-evident: the leading organs of their communist parties are responsible also for the conduct of foreign policy, and their consultations and agreements exercise a decisive influence on bilateral relations between their respective countries. This is to a certain extent valid also for relations between socialist countries and those developing countries that are governed in terms of a progressive system. In recent years contacts have been established between the leaders of the communist parties of the socialist countries and those of the social democratic parties of Western Europe. Although the social democratic parties, in the spirit of their traditions, try to keep party relations apart from interstate relations, their talks and agreements with leaders of socialist countries in practice exert en effect on interstate relations as well.

In my view the few characteristics of the international activity of the Hungarian People's Republic here described give a true picture of these thirty years of Hungarian foreign policy.

WHAT HAPPENED
TO THE REVOLUTION?

by

PÉTER RÉNYI

The "New Left", at least a considerable part of it, accepts as an axiom in need of no proof that power in the socialist countries is held by conservative, non-revolutionary forces, that social movements are governed by a hardened apparatus, a bureaucracy defending its privileges, a new bourgeoisie that has nothing to do with the revolution, or with the revolutionary development that helped it to become dominant. This view just about tallies with the anticommunist propaganda of the capitalist world which, pointing to the hypothetical "new bourgeoisie" of the opposite side, has long been taking pains to justify the existence of the old—that is, its own existence. The conventional bourgeois argument runs something like this: "It is not better there; or rather it is worse there, for we at least have experience..." Sceptical as the New Left is in general, it here sings the same tune as those organs which it usually unmasks (and most often rightly so) as unscrupulous manipulators misinforming public opinion. The present short essay, or whatever I might call it, is intended to confront those views, rooted probably not only in prejudices but in something like ignorance, with a few Hungarian experiences of the era of socialism. Nothing would seem to demonstrate this better than the fact that these movements exert but very little influence in the socialist countries, Hungary among them. Even though there are young people who are discontented, trying to find their places, they see and judge our society in a much more differentiated manner.

*

The problem—what becomes of revolution once it has triumphed?—is as old as revolution itself. After the victorious bourgeois revolutions it was almost normal for disillusioned revolutionaries to rise in bitter revolt against their own creature, the power they had achieved. But let us not be afraid to speak out: this is the most natural thing in the world. An abstract model of revolution also makes it evident that this must inevitably be so.

What then is revolution? Revolutionaries are prone to talk about it as if, for progressives who want what is new and good, there were no other condition worthy of man—they think all that is progressive, is revolutionary in the strict sense of the word. But is this really so? Social revolution is a peculiar determinate stage in the process of history, a leap by which quantitative changes accumulated in the social order are transformed into a new quality, establishing the new order of the rising class. So much is revolution, neither less nor more. To speak of the permanence of revolution is even logically an absurdity, revolution can occur only as a result of preceding evolution, it simply cannot come about without it. A permanent process, namely one which remains homogeneous over a long time, cannot be called revolution unless we are playing with words.

But if this is so, then it is understandable also just for psychological reasons that a part—and no small part even—of the generation carrying out the revolution is dissatisfied with the accomplished revolution and demands its continuation. And this for the much too simple reason that one who sacrified years and tens of years to the preparation of the revolution, who before and during the fighting staked his life on its victory, who—as the saying goes—was burning with revolutionary ardour is for the most part hardly capable of appreciating the new situation created by the accession to power of the revolutionary forces and the ensuing new requirements. Total concentration upon the struggle, destruction of the old—a necessary, and even imperative, requirement of revolution—inevitably lead to a point where the ideologically unprepared revolutionary "absolutizes" the revolution, sees it as a unique way of life, not only as a unique form of motion of society. This false consciousness became the tragedy of more than one group of revolutionaries. Let us think, for example, of the doctrinaire avant-gardists of the Russian revolution, or the many representatives of "proletarian culture" who failed already in the early twenties, in the period of the switch-over to peaceful construction. One could say that this is the most dangerous period in the lasting victory of revolution—more critical than that of the conflict with the class enemy. I have in mind the period when the revolution has to consolidate its gains, change over to peacetime arrangements under new conditions, in other words it has to abandon itself, itself that is as it was fought on the barricades, in the civil war, or by militant mass movements.

This is a bitter test for any power born in revolution, if only because this is where it appears whether, emerging from the state of spiritual dependence, the new class has grown independent in revolutionary consciousness, and whether it is possessed by something different and more than mere revolt against past oppression, more than the feeling that it does not any longer want to live the way it lived before. This is the "ideological" test that decides whether the new class has positive, really progressive ideas about a future society; this is where it is proved whether the new class has carried out only a spontaneous insurrection which—morally superb as the performance may be in itself—may even point back to the past, or whether it has indeed been a revolution which points in the direction of general human progress. We often seem to forget that, besides the several dozen proper evolutions known to mankind, there have been hundreds or maybe thousands of abortive, bloodily suppressed revolts whose memory even is buried in oblivion. This must be discussed in a clear-cut manner; in this case any kind of dialectically sounding 'on the one hand, on the other' is specially harmful, since it gives a head start to revolutionary demagogues who loudly proclaim their own ideas. He who, when the time has come, is unable to change over from the open or armed revolutionary struggle to the consolidation of the positions attained, to the shaping of a new social and state order appropriate to the objectives and interests of the revolution, has failed to recognize the essence of revolution. He may have been the most sublime hero at the time of the trying major conflicts; if he does not understand that conditions undergo a radical change with victory, he becomes a Don Quixote, or possibly a clown, of the revolution, if not—for this is also possible—a downright enemy of it, as happened, for example after 1917, to a few fearless revolutionaries who eventually joined the anarchists, the bands of adventurers like Machno and others.

*

Let me try to demonstrate from some actual typical examples from the Hungarian people's democratic "revolution" (more precisely, revolutionary transformation) what is the outcome of a situation in which revolutionaries are unable to recognize the cardinal changes following on victory.

The most instructive period of this process in Hungary was the "year of change" which fell at the turn of the years 1947 and 1948. Early in 1948 plants and enterprises employing more than a hundred workers were nationalized; in early summer the two workers' parties merged; and in early autumn the new definition of the established power was laid down, stating that the Hungarian people's democracy essentially fulfils the functions of a proletarian dictatorship. In other words, the socialist revolution has been victorious. The principal slogan now came to be "The country is yours, you build it for yourself!" replacing the former one devised as far back as 1946 which said, "We build the country for the people, not for the capitalists". How we reached the latter slogan starting with the former, how socialism could triumph though there was no revolution in the conventional, everyday sense of the word, all that took place were mass actions, electoral campaigns, negotiations for a coalition, various crises in and outside Parliament, in the course of which the Communist Party and its allies managed to outmanoeuvre the adversary who lost his positions, one after another and became more and more paralyzed, until action was controlled entirely by the left-wing forces, is a different question. But I will not go into this matter, what is essential to our subject is only the fact that sharp and resounding clashes were followed by the change, the aforementioned "trying" new situation, in which revolutionary consciousness, political and public attitude should have changed.

The afore-cited slogan—"The country is yours, you build it for yourself!" —was a terse expression of the changed situation, and this was underscored also by the term "year of change". But revolutionary conservatism—if I may use this formula (in the sense defined above)—reappeared. What is more, it broke out with particular vehemence, and even this could not have been by chance. As early as 1945, right after Soviet troops had entered Hungarian territory the belief showed itself (especially among the surviving participants of the 1919 revolution) spontaneously at first, sporadically and naively, that Hungary must at once switch over to a dictatorship of the proletariat, by which they meant also that there must be a violent reckoning with the class enemy. This was prevented by the leadership of the Communist Party, and by the Soviet army command. It was evident that naked force was needed only where the adversary also used force, under the circumstances at the war front, since the active forces of Hungarian reaction were fighting on the side of the Germans. But since that fight (in which smaller Hungarian units also took part on the side of the Soviet Union, as part of the antifascist coalition) had broken down the resistance of the enemy, continued struggle by force of arms on the domestic front would have been tantamount to provoking a civil war. With the end of the fighting the only "armed" task, if I may say so, was to keep public order, to apprehend the fascist perpetrators of occasional acts of sabotage, and to call war criminals to account; the occupying powers even made this latter task a special obligation of the organs of the new Hungarian state.

This was then the first "delaying" action, the curbing of tempers which, allowed to have their way, could have been nothing else in practice than outbursts of vengeance. But there was "delaying" practice also in the next few years when the conscious revolutionary forces embraced the people's front policy, urging the union of all forces which were ready to take joint action against fascism and the vestiges of the feudal system. Such action called for a special kind of tactical sense, a well-considered conduct of policy which, as far as possible, always reduced the chances of conflict to a minimum. Those specializing in the period call this "salami tactics", not without a certain irony, using a term invented by western journalists. To be sure, anyone who sizes up the essence of the matter has to admit that until the change this was the way demanding the least sacrifice in the interest of the victory of socialism; it is utter shortsightedness to regard that course of action as cheap manipulation, a sort of cat-and-mouse game, or political playacting; what depended on these "salami tactics" was nothing less than the question whether socialism would triumph without a civil war in Hungary. Even if that was not the only possible way and cannot be set up as an example for others, what took place in this country between 1945 and 1948 is called, in Hungarian terminology today, the "peaceful road to socialism" which, as is well known, is right to this day one of the most attractive alternatives, one of the hopes of social progress.

*

But the strange thing happened that afterwards, when victory had been won, there arose a sort of revolutionist acting, if I may call it so, which, in spite of so much "delaying" or, on the contrary, just because of the success of delaying over so many years, could burst the dams of rationalism: as long as the fight was on—and often it went on fiercely indeed—we could confine the ultra-radical fighting spirit within limits, when the fight was over we could not check it any longer. I know that many kinds of explanations for the events that followed were given (the personality cult, the sham trials, other illegal actions which replaced persuasion by orders from above, the proliferation of violations of the Leninist norms in the party, the gradual suppression of democratic authorities, etc.), and these certainly had momentous causes and interrelations on the international plane, too. But I do not believe that it would be fair to ascribe a greater role to external causes than to internal conditions, all the more so because, as far as the international process was concerned, Rákosi and his associates did not always play an inferior role, in important matters they even took the initiative, and the motives of this are to be found only in the peculiarities of internal Hungarian development. As if that period, becoming more and more tragic, had been overshadowed by the thought that the revolution simply could not win without violent conflicts, though the enemy was compelled to surrender his power anyway, though things worked out so peacefully that all we had to tackle was a number of not too significant attempted plots, a few sabotage attempts and street clashes. Very much in tune with that pseudo-revolutionary logic, although not as a direct consequence of that strange "feeling of want", were the sham trials which were expected to prove that behold! there was a much more dangerous conspiracy after all in the party leadership itself, there were those who prepared treacherous attempts against the general staff of our people's democracy, and who wanted to take the country over into the camp of imperialism, etc., etc.

That is how that danger of a civil war—after we had happily avoided it in reality—emerged as a legend, as an artificial illusion. So it became possible to implement measures based on the assumption that the situation was coming to a head. This turned things so much inside out that one is unwilling to believe it today, but it was true. After the declared and real victory of socialism the fear of a civil war in Hungary was growing much stronger than ever before, and the measures taken to avert it increased a hundredfold. There is no more painful example of a misunderstanding of the new situation that arose with the victory of revolution, and of what was required as a result.

What appeared in this world turned upside down? In essence, nothing else than what we still today see as the source of every sectarian-dogmatic distortion: disbelief in the idea of socialism, always related to mistrust and contempt for the masses, this most dangerous distortion of revolutionary avant-gardism. What did they disbelieve in—those who after 1948 tightened control in every respect? They disbelieved in the force of attraction and cohesion of a policy of plans for a new social order, which by then had won the minds and sympathies of millions of people. A current explanation in the West was of course just the opposite: anticommunism alleged that the extensive application of forcible methods was logical and necessary, because, quoth they, no change had occurred in the consciousness of the masses, people invariably rejected the idea of socialism, they regarded it as a phalanstery that had been forced upon them and was alien to them. (Here again, as almost always, a striking similarity existed between the ultra-Left and that of the right wing. Even if they differed in their judgment, both started from the assumption that the masses were opposed to the new social order.)

That process is still worth remembering since western New Leftism is loath to associate itself with these distortions, it pretends that its ideas can in principle have nothing to do with the political mistakes and crimes committed around the turn of the forties and fifties. On the contrary, it poses as the most determined opponent of antidemocratic distortions of this kind. Any one of its representatives whom you may call upon argues that those distortions resulted from the bureaucratization of authority, from excessive consolidation, from the group interest of those in direct possession of power. They claim to be in favour of the opposite way, namely that of keeping the masses in permanent motion, attacking ceaselessly the positions of the bureaucracy, preventing consolidation—because consolidation, in their view, is the root of all evil. Permanent revolution, revolution within the revolution—is the only policy for revolutionaries, they say.

Whichever way we may look at the events of that time, we cannot with the best of intentions explain them as an exaggeration of the efforts to produce consolidation. They were the very opposite of consolidation, an artificial instigation of class warfare which was then subsiding. Not even their chief promoters and representatives resembled bureaucrats in the traditional sense of the word, who were known to be characterized not by intentional transgression of the law but by perverse adherence to its letter. The New Left of western Europe wishes to erect something like the Great Wall of China—in both senses of the word—between the bureaucratic "Leftism" of that time and its own "Leftism", to make the lessons appear as if they were conflicting with one another. But the facts show that the differences lie primarily in methods—partly also in the character of individual intentions—but in essential matters they are alike.

What are the differences? As regards the intentions, it must be conceded to the "leftists" of today, if not always but in a considerable number of cases, that their acts and their ideas are determined by inexperience, naiveté and immaturity. This cannot be an excuse for the leading "leftists" of the personality cult era, at least as far as democracy in society is concerned. Those were experienced men, who cannot claim to have known no alternative. This is evidenced, among other things, by the fact that between 1945 and 1948 they had gone a different way themselves; what turned their heads were the successes which the forces of socialism had obtained just when proceeding along that other way. They were veritable masters of a policy which knew how to avoid sharpening the class war; and now they were busy professing the principle formulated by Stalin that under the conditions of socialism the class struggle is intensifying incessantly and from day to day, the class enemy of necessity penetrates into the party and occupies the key positions of socialism.

The methods, if I look at their formal side, were bureaucratic. They had recourse to police, state security and judicial authorities and made use of the organs of administration; unlawful proceedings were made to appear (wherever possible) in the guise of strict legality; the handling of affairs was not left to organized mass action. Outwardly, the picture was really not one of anarchy, it indicated stern discipline. But in reality there was unscrupulous adventurism, a sort of gambling with devices of an inconceivably anarchical nature. To call this breakneck game consolidation, in any sense whatever, would be a play on words. This practice could exist only in a mentality which, somewhere deep inside, was related to the conspiracy obsession and rude anarchism of the revolutionary movements of earlier times and those of today not yet grown to maturity; the thoughts possessing minds were similar to those entertained at the time when ostentatious attempts and individual terror were expected to substitute for the political persuasion of the masses. No, to erect a Wall of China between these forms of "Leftism"—however different the intentions may be—is impossible. We in Hungary have had to learn this at the cost of hard experience.

*

An often quoted saying is that revolution, any revolution, devours its children. Let us suppose, for the sake of an imaginary experiment, that this is so. Then, according to the notion here discussed, the reason for it is that the adherents of consolidation forcibly repress those who wish to continue on the way of revolution. We might as well say that consolidation devours the revolutionaries, it betrays the revolution. Even for this there is a classical precedent: that of the Great French Revolution, in which the bourgeoisie, after achieving power, liquidated the radicals of the proto-proletariat among the plebeians and the petty-bourgeois. The question, however, is whether this analogy is applicable to the socialist revolution and to the occurrence which disturbed development in a few countries after the revolutionary change, whether it is really typical of such events that the "moderates" settle accounts with the "radicals" as Brumaire did with the Left?

The converse applies better (though not even precisely): the "radicals" —I mean those who fail to understand that the victory must open up a new stage of the revolutionary process—square accounts with those who are proclaimed moderates, opportunists collaborating with the enemy. They create a strained revolutionary situation when this is already outdated and when it is necessary to concentrate upon constructive action. Naturally what I am sketching here is a model-like simplification of the picture, which was in reality much more complex even at that time. For in the meantime, in both the concrete and the figurative sense of the word, the construction of socialism continued, and it did so with great intensity; the negative processes intermingled in a complicated way, so that nothing appeared clearly and unambiguously. That is why everything was so difficult to discern, recognize and evaluate. But we cannot undertake here to present a complex history of that period, I have picked out merely one of the characteristic aspects of the conflicts of that time.

*

I would like to say a few more words about other overheated manifestations of "revolutionism". Until the change of 1948 the revolutionary movement had as a natural and indispensable corollary the policy and propaganda of raising living standards. No kind of ascetic radicalism, no kind of idealistic shyness muzzled this objective of the left-wing forces and of the Communist Party. Time and again the opponents called the communists "spud politicians", but these proudly accepted the nickname intended as a defamation. Only after the change did the propaganda of the Party and the movement adopt a terminology that consistently described as "materialistic" the most natural and by no means unrealistic demands of the masses, talking—as Rákosi did—about hens laying golden eggs which it would be unreasonable to kill. This was the period of the domestic antecedents of the irony which regards the socialist efforts to raise the standards of living as a deformation of socialism, as a form of its inactivity, and which speaks, in the mocking tone used in Hungary, about "refrigerator-socialism".

Also curiously in harmony with the conception of the "leftists" of today is the utopianism of the economic policy of those days. There was a "big leap" in Hungary, too, even if the slogan was different. According to a notorious dictum of Rákosi—"the star-studded sky is the limit". Anyone who can remember all this (the younger generation, unfortunately, knows little about it) is hardly willing to regard the ultra-radicalism of today and that of those times as at opposite poles, and is more likely to see the likeness. He sees the similarity in the way the youngsters committed to the cause respond and are made use of. True, we had no "Red Guardsmen" in our country, nor did we get secondary-school pupils to raid the party branches, but there certainly was a fanning of emotions bordering on hysteria, and there was indeed a "realization" that it was easy to involve less experienced young people in the immaturities of pseudo-Leftism.

Accordingly, we already had relatively rich experiences of our own when the wave of "Leftism" appeared in Europe as new. If I may say so, it seemed rather as if we were facing our own past—in both the good and the bad sense of the word (even though this, like historical analogies in general, is only partially to the point). The ambivalence of our emotions also reflected this. Sympathy for the progressive ambitions of the young, for their critical spirit and militant determination on the one hand and, on the other, anxieties about mixing up supposed and actual enemies, antagonizing those who ought to be won over, sometimes confusing revolutionary ideas and revolutionary phraseology, revolutionary action and empty, merely symbolic revolutionary gestures, content and form. Oh, how familiar many, many things were! And just because they were familiar, it was so uncanny for us, for in our nerves and bones we still carry the memory of those tragic conflicts which ultraradicalism provoked in this country. We cannot forget our realization that what contradicts common sense and realistic stock-taking, even if it has the most revolutionary ring, cannot serve the cause of working men, of the workers, of the people. If somebody seeks an answer to the question of why the negative influence of the "New Left" in Hungary was only minimal—while we made an objective appraisal of its positive aspects—he has to look for the explanation in the experiences of those who have been through 1949, 1953 and 1956, and are unwilling to forget the bitter lessons they then learnt.

*

The fact that the adult generation possesses the experience does not, of course, relieve us of the obligation to answer the question which the young do not cease to ask: where should they look for their own revolutionary tasks today? At the beginning of these thoughts I stated that revolution, once it has won, must complete itself. Let me now add the following: It is quite true that, after the victory of the political revolution (namely after the process in which the rising class takes over power, the state apparatus and the basic means of production), the revolution in this sense cannot go on. Any change in the possession of state power and the means of production subsequently can mean only one thing: counter-revolution (of which we had enough in 1956), which leads to the restoration of the original (or renewed) form of the old system. Consequently, if I use the word revolution in the above sense, I have to speak out plainly: there is no "revolution in the revolution". Compared with the capture of power every task following the revolution is of an evolutionary character, it is not explosion-like, it cannot be performed by means of cavalry charges, campaigns, hasty actions of a military, militant nature. In all fields of the economy, culture and even politics, methodical, assiduous, patient, systematic activity is needed for a long time to come.

In this sense today's rising generation, which we try to educate in a revolutionary spirit (thereby adding to the revolutionary impatience normal at its age), is in a particularly difficult situation. They feel that we, their parents, have stolen the revolution from them, together with its rich, colourful and vivid experiences; all we have left to them is everyday work and study, they are doomed to a drab, philistine existence to the end of their lives. Many even if not all of them, feel this way and they are entitled to an answer, all the more so as most of them reject ultra-leftist solutions as false ones, as blind alleys leading nowhere. But do they have to reconcile themselves to the fact that what is in store for them, the first post-revolutionary generation, is only the execution of their duties and a monotonous life, "deeds" actualized in school marks or routine bonuses? This is not so. One can show this also by the aforementioned simplified model of revolution.

The victory of the socialist revolution, as the taking over of state power and the securing of control over the means of production, is a single act that is concluded at a determinable point; upon its conclusion other tasks come into the foreground. However, the socialist revolution differs from the bourgeois and other revolutions also in that it does not consummate the transformation of society as political revolutions do in general, it only begins the process. After a bourgeois revolution every kind of progressive movement necessarily turns against the existing order. After the definitive completion of the bourgeois transformation of society the bourgeoisie had only one slogan left: "Enrichissez-vous". Therefore, after the victory had been won, torpor and with it the decadence of the entire system (phenomena which are not so conspicuous today because the wrestling with socialism galvanized capitalism into fresh activity) are inevitable and natural, the revolution had to stop in all respects, because "the task" was completed; for want of new ideas there was no other objective, and the creative forces of the system had nothing else before them than accommodation and self-adaptation to the regime, the building up of positions and the application of the achievements.

The victory of socialism in this respect, let me say this, means *less*. With its revolution it creates only a new state power, even this just in a most elementary form, everything else begins only thereafter. The establishment of a new society, of the forms of a new democracy, the development of a new economic system, of a new culture, etc., etc. That is why Lenin could call socialism a transitional social structure of the kind which is revolutionary throughout the entire period of its existence.

Right at the outset this society comes into existence as a contradictory structure, as a society of peculiar contradictions, and it continues to be that, though decreasingly, until it transcends itself, when one can begin to speak about communism. Of course, here we have to emphasize strongly the peculiar character of the contradictions, lest we might give rise to the impression that the question is about a sort of contradictoriness similar or related to that of capitalism. The specific contradictions of socialism are not the opposition of oppressor and oppressed, not of exploiters and exploited, not of expropriators and expropriated, but—in the most general way—the opposition of the individual and the community, the tension following from the reconciliation of individual and collective interests: in this sense socialism is a preeminently contradictory system; nay, it is in this sense more contradictory than any other structure. The fact is that the contradictions of socialism, unlike the fundamental contradictions of previous societies, cannot be suppressed, force can here function only as a regulator protecting the foundation. But as soon as it transgresses these bounds, as soon as it assumes a bigger function, it disturbs what is the essence of the transition, the rapprochement between individual and collective interests, their integration, which is the essence of communism. Socialist society, as I have already mentioned, is a determinate undertaking, it realizes conscious purposes, but from this point of view it is at the same time in a state of constant manoeuvre, of continuous compromise. This is not its fault, but its natural state.

To be sure, it is an oversimplification when I reduce the formula to the opposition of the individual and the community, for what is involved here is also the interplay of many class and group interests, a whole conglomerate of different interests, whose complex equilibrium makes up the equilibrium of the system. On the one hand there is a circle of elementary and common interests which link together the various elements, these are the frequently mentioned foundations of socialism. Their cohesion determines the stability of the system, e.g. its ability to resist hostile, antisocialist attacks, attempts at penetration and loosening up. On the other hand, there is a field, a sphere, in which interests diverge and even conflict now and then. To come back to the notions applied to the previous train of thought, I would say: in the first field the revolution has already won, in the second the revolutionary struggle is still going on. This latter is difficult to discern. This is the source of all our difficulties in clarifying the revolutionary tasks of our days.

And what do the young see? It is that in this latter field individualistic, egoistic ambitions alien to the small or the large community, ambitions which (for this is precisely what upsets them) we do not crush by force and do not stifle, as we smashed the strongholds of capital at the time, occur. This is roughly where their dilemma starts, they still feel that there are considerable contradictions here, that a struggle is on concerning questions of principle, that great forces are in competition. But the front line where this revolutionary struggle is waged cannot be drawn on the map, it is not fighting troops taken in the original sense that are facing each other. If I may refer to an already classical literary work, Robert Musil's *The Man without Qualities,* I would say that their dilemma very much reminds me of the scene in which an old general of the Imperial Austrian army sets forth his complaint: he has been commissioned (the story is set at the beginning of this century) to draft an account of the spiritual, ideological struggles of his time; the old gentleman, who has worked with the general staff, can of course see no other way than to have a map drafted of the theatre of operations, the support lines, the positions of the fighting forces. And he cannot avoid noting that "in this civilian mess," where no one obeys military orders, everything is topsy-turvy: it sometimes happens that a unit gets reinforcements from the enemy lines. Let there be no mistake about it, I do not refer to this example in order to question whether a struggle is on. There is one indeed, but not of the earlier kind.

Let us take but one example, the Hungarian reform of the system of economic management. To the outsider it seems as if the whole reform were built on the automatism of economic interests, on a wise system of wages, subsidies and bonuses, on economic laws of the most peaceful kind. Where can the role of an advancing avant-garde be, where can individual will, unselfishness and devotion be put to the test? Much of it looks like something we have copied from the practice of the modern capitalist economy. But, in fact, it is not an automatic process and not even a reform in the conventional sense, the question is not about changes by which society adapts itself subsequently to the practical requirements of life. Not at all. These reforms (and let us not forget that we are as yet at the beginning) do not belong to the sphere of phenomena of which Marx said: the past dominates the present, i.e. the present answers the insufficiencies of the past. It is more and more the present and the future with its prospects that dominate the past. Or we may well try this formulation: the ideas of the construction of socialism determine action in an increasingly sovereign manner, not shortages and insufficiencies enforce decisions, but a revolutionary plan regulates the course of action.

Nobody in Hungary wants to make himself believe this in its entirety and in every detail. There are still many half-solutions, necessities resulting from the insufficiency of material means, compromises dictated by the given limits. But just the same, and for this very reason, we can live in the awareness that the aim and the direction are set by our own will, the revolutionary idea. If this were not so, if spontaneous economic development were to decide everything, there could really be no answer to the question, "what happened to the revolution?" If it were not so we ought to say that we stopped halfway, that we established the power of socialism but failed to use it for what it is destined to carry out, the construction of a socialist society, which can only be a product of conscious activity. (That this is so is demonstrated among other things by the fact that we do not want to suppress the querying attitude of part of today's youth, their conscious search for objectives. We want to mould it into social energy.)

At its meeting in February 1970 the Central Committee of the Hungarian Socialist Workers' Party emphasized with good reason that to clarify the task, place and role of the young generation is in this sense a preliminary condition of further progress. There can be no future for a society which is not backed by the young, and which cannot open up prospects for the revolutionary reform plans of youth. This must be done, and it is up to the mature to make clear what revolutionary objectives and revolutionary conduct mean in the given situation. The objectives of our period will not resemble revolution on the surface. We might as well accept that where this "invisible revolution" looks like revolution, it very likely is a fake, an *ersatz* of no merit, a sort of pseudo-revolutionism which, whatever it may sound like, is the flesh and blood of revolutionary phrase-mongering. The less symbolic and spectacular the manifestations of this revolutionary attitude will become, and the sooner it will get past the level of "general mobilization" and become realized in actual deeds, in political and economic and cultural acts, the closer we will come to genuine solutions.

Of course, by these "different" revolutionary deeds—let us hasten to add—we should in no way mean restricted professional or educational requirements, whose successsful satisfaction is always and everywhere desired. What I mean are attitudes and deeds which directly serve the revolutionary transformation in the transition period. Obviously that "revolutionary" element in question cannot be a minor or major routine task, the simple execution of duties: the point at issue can only be the tackling of problems, test of behaviour, which help to promote development in the political or ideological or moral sense and speed up the solution of the social contradictions of the transition; in other words, activity and, let us say it straight, fight in the public arena. This fight may and does take place against bureaucratism, against all manners of conservatism, against old and new privileges, against manifestations of injustice, against anarchist and asocial elements, against the spirit of intellectual laziness, cosiness and indifference, against egotism, against the extreme forms of individualism. The furtherance of this struggle, as a matter of course, requires the development and broadening of socialist democracy, for only in democratic movements in society is it possible to activate and render effective the forces which must be made to join the struggle to shape man and society. But the importance of democracy does not reside in itself in this either; what we have in mind are not debates for debates' sake, but open forums where, with administrative interference confined to the defence of socialist laws, the ideas of socialism can freely compete with the ideas of people who think differently, where an open struggle is waged over very substantial questions, ranging from ideology to morality, from politics to economics.

Hungarian ideological life is already going this way, but, as I have already stated, we are still at the beginning, since these first "rounds" in the discussion have only taken place among some sections of the intelligentsia. With the broadening of socialist democracy it will become possible and necessary to mobilize many more people. The struggles will not be easy, nor are they so now; they involve all that puts individual will, character and knowledge to the test and requires perseverance and stamina; the critical situations jarring the nerves and intellect are part of them just as the periods of picking up strength, of preparation and study.

Even when there will be no identifiable "foes" opposed to each other, because for the most part debates and conflicts will be between men professing identical political views, I think those who will take part in them, fighting for new truths of socialism, of Marxism, will ask less frequently: where is that revolution, where should it be fought?

FATHERLAND
AND NATION IN CENTRAL EUROPE—
AN IDEOLOGICAL DISCUSSION

by

BÉLA KÖPECZI

'**M**en are the producers of their conceptions, ideas, etc.—real, active men, as they are conditioned by a definite development of their productive forces and of the intercourse corresponding to these, up to its furthest forms. Consciousness can never be anything else than conscious existence, and the existence of men is their actual life-process. If in all ideology men and their circumstances appear upside-down as in a *camera obscura*, this phenomenon arises just as much from their historical life-process as the inversion of objects on the retina does from their physical life-process."[1]

This is how *The German Ideology* defined the relations between existence and consciousness.

The historic notion, which forms part of the social consciousness, is determined by historiography, by the teaching of history, by literature inspired by history, by scientific vulgarization, as well as by ancient views and sentiments which the family, the group and the class have transplanted into everyday consciousness.

In Hungary, in the nineteenth and at the beginning of the twentieth century, the ruling class disseminated, through all the means at its disposal, a nationalist view of history, many elements of which survive in everyday consciousness, although several decades have now passed since the fall of the capitalist system.

Marxist historiography[2] achieved sound results before and, mainly, after the Liberation in the critique of nationalism and in the propagation of a new view of history. József Révai[3] and others conducted an efficient struggle

---

[1] Marx–Engels: *Die Deutsche Ideologie*, Berlin 1953 Dietz Verlag, p. 22. (Karl Marx and Friedrich Engels: Selected Works in three volumes. Progress Publishers, Moscow, 1969. Volume 1, p. 25. See: Marx/Engels/Werke. Band 3. p. 26. Dietz Verlag, Berlin, 1958.)

[2] See Zs. P. Pach: *L'historiographie hongroise au cours du dernier quart de siècle*. Nouvelles Études Hongroises, 1972, pp. 110–130.

[3] See *"Études historiques" (Historic Studies)*, Budapest, 1955. Akadémiai Kiadó, p. 168.

against the nationalist policies and historiography of the Horthy regime. It was their great merit to introduce the concept of the class struggle into Hungarian historiography without separating it from the fight for independence.

This sound view was denied by a dogmatist and arbitrary policy which had a strong effect on Hungarian historiography. The latter policy simplified the contradictions of the Hungarian past, neglected to analyse the social conflicts in the wars of independence, and was not able to present the struggles of the Hungarian working class—and notably the Republic of Councils—in their true light. In its fight against these oversimplifications, revisionism proclaimed a false national unity of the past and of the present, and led to the resuscitation of reformist trends in the working-class movement.

After 1956, debates centred on topics such as nation, fatherland, patriotism, independence, progress and internationalism, contributed to a large extent to the condemnation of these deformations and helped to throw light on the fundamental problems of Hungarian history.[4]

These discussions have shown that it is wrong to generalize and to extend the idea of the bourgeois nation to the whole of the history of the Hungarians as well as the impossibility of simplifying relations between the struggles for independence and social progress, since—in the given case—independence and social progress may be in agreement but also in opposition to each other. They indicated the need of examining more carefully the relations that exist between the history of Hungarians and that of neighbouring nations.

As far as the working-class movement is concerned, they proved the importance of analysing relations between the class struggle and the national problem and of a detailed evaluation of the policies of the working-class parties.

That these discussions took place and that they achieved the results mentioned, is due first of all to the late Erik Molnár, to his impassioned desire to see clearly, to his tenacity in the search for the truth, and to his great and international experience.[5]

While recognizing the great value of what was done, it has to be admitted that, concerning certain points, the argument reached a state of polarization

4 See: Nouvelles études historiques (New Historic Studies). Vol. 1–2. Budapest, 1965. Akadémiai Kiadó.
5 A number of Erik Molnár's works were published in languages other than Hungarian: Les fondements économiques et sociaux de l'absolutisme. Budapest, 1965. Akadémiai Kiadó. — Das Problem des Zusammenhanges zwischen nationaler Unabhängigkeit und gesellschaftlichem Fortschritt. Budapest, 1961. Akadémiai Kiadó. — "Le rôle historique de la République Hongroise des Conseils." Acta Historica (1959), T. VII, No. 1–2. — La politique d'alliances du marxisme (1848–1889). Budapest, 1967. Akadémiai Kiadó, p. 440.

which is not very convincing from the scholarly point of view. It was clearly recognized that the objective of these discussions was to analyse the consequences of the huge nationalist wave which rolled over the country in 1956, and the work of clarification was greeted with a certain satisfaction. Nevertheless, certain doubts arose in the case of Marxists and non-Marxists alike concerning the soundness of the foundation of certain theses concerning the problems of the coming into being of the nation and the role of nationalism. These differences of opinion received further emphasis in consequence of those that arose in the international working-class movement concerning the problems of the nation, of independence and of sovereignty.

A certain "plebeian" view of history, which derives from "populism", refuses to accept conclusions which reduce the importance of the wars of independence and of phenomena which are attached to the idea of an "eternal nation". On the other hand, the supporters of "desideologizing" forged their arguments from "hyper-critical" judgements passed on the Hungarian past to prop up a certain cosmopolitanism of poor quality.

The Marxists ask themselves questions like the following: what is the relation between the class struggle and national evolution? Did popular patriotism really exist? What was the importance of the struggles for independence from the point of view of social progress?

Let us examine some of the problems which have been raised and which, in my view, are of importance not only for Hungarian historiography and ways of thinking, but also for international discussions of ideological questions.

Popular Patriotism

Erik Molnár opened the debate on the question of the development of the nation in 1960 by asserting that Hungarian Marxist historiography had made concessions to bourgeois views by extending the notion of "fatherland" and "nation" to all social formations. On the other hand, this historiography had simplified the history of the wars of independence by confronting the manifold treasons committed by the nobility with the patriotism of the serfs. According to him, the notions of fatherland and of nation are products of capitalist evolution, and a particular "patriotism" of the serfs did not exist; if something like that occurred, this must be explained as the influence of the ideology of the ruling class.

Molnár was right as far as the formation of the nation was concerned; as regards fatherland and patriotism one may well question his argument.

Lenin's view that the ideology of the ruling class is the ruling ideology of the given period is known. This does not, however, mean in the least that other ideologies do not exist as well. The exploited class also develops its own ideology which reflects its situation and serves its interests, even if it contains elements of the ruling ideology. This argument is in agreement with Lenin's views on the two cultures.

The characteristics of popular patriotism are: attachment to the place where one lives, to where one was born and the defence of working and living conditions, efforts to improve these conditions within the given geographic, linguistic and cultural framework.[6]

Let me add that the ideology of the oppressed could be made conscious primarily by intellectuals of noble, bourgeois or peasant origin, first of all by priests and ministers of religion, by schoolmasters, by teachers and students who were more or less close to the exploited class. These intellectuals, while in most cases disseminating the ideology of the ruling class, were also able, in critical times, to express the demands and the needs of the oppressed. The Hungarian protestant ministers of the second half of the seventeenth century, for instance, or the students participating in Ferenc Rákóczi II's War of Independence (1703–1711) were not spokesmen for the nobility only, but also representatives of the popular movement of the *Kuruc* (a word derived from *Cruciatus*, "Crusader").[7] The Hungarian Jacobins[8] did not only represent Josephinism as the ideology of enlightened absolutism, but they also recognized the importance of the liberation of the serfs. Petőfi and the plebeian democrats of 1848 certainly supported Kossuth's programme of national independence, but they were also intransigent partisans of social reform in the interest of all nations that lived in Hungary.[9]

---

[6] Zs. P. Pach drew attention to this point early on in the debate: "In any event, this notion of 'fatherland' always includes and implies the idea of the place of birth and of the native land, and therefore reflects a genuine relationship. I believe that I am not wrong in my conviction that this real element plays a great role in the beginning and later as well, and that its importance is much greater when it concerns 'fatherland' ideas of the oppressed, as against that of the lords. It reflects the conditions of work and of the real existence of the serfs—miserable as they may be—and the attachment of the serf and of the peasant to the land on which he works, to his small fortune, to his working tools." *Századok*, 1962. p. 396. (In Hungarian)

[7] See Ágnes Várkonyi: *Hapsburg Absolutism and Serfdom* in Hungary at the Turn of the XVII and XVIII Centuries. Budapest, 1965. Akadémiai Kiadó. (In English) — Béla Köpeczi: *La France et la Hongrie au début du XVIIIᵉ siècle*. Étude d'histoire des relations diplomatiques et d'histoire des idées. Budapest, 1971. Akadémiai Kiadó, 624 pp.

[8] K. Benda: *Probleme des Josephinismus und des Jakobinertums in der Habsburgischen Monarchie*. Munich, 1966. Oldenbourg.

[9] J. Révai: *Le contradizzioni interne della rivoluzione ungherese del 1848/49*. Rome, 1948. — P. Hanák: *The Nationalities of the Austrian Empire and the Hungarian Revolution of 1848/49*. Budapest, 1953. Akadémiai Kiadó p. 80. (In Russian) — I. Z. Tóth: *Kossuth and the National Question in 1848–1849*. Budapest, 1954. Akadémiai Kiadó p. 122. (In Russian)

It is important to underline that there is a continuity in the ideology representing the interests of the oppressed. It is the national ideal of the ministers of religion, of the Jacobins, of the plebeian democrats of the Reform Period and of the War of Independence which led to the poet Ady and to the radicals of the beginning of the twentieth century, and also to the patriotism, at first democratic then socialist, of the working class.

When Lenin spoke of the national pride of the Great Russians, he drew the revolutionary line which in Russia led right up to the Bolsheviks, a chain of which Raditchev, the Dekabrists, the Rasnotchinetz revolutionaries of the 70s and the workers of the 1905 revolution were the links. The fact that, in Russia, the "social" tendencies were more homogeneous while in Hungary the national and social movements were intertwined, is explained by the developmental characteristics of the two countries. When considering this aspect one has to bear in mind a factor peculiar to those countries which achieved their unity and national independence only late in their history.

It is here that the question of national unity arises. In every class society there are oppressed and oppressors, exploiters and exploited, whose situation is basically characterized by class differences. But economic, political and cultural links are formed between these classes, and these characterize the entire community. This does not in the least mean that one may suppose a total identity of interests between the classes in all historic situations, but this identity may play a role in certain critical periods and may serve as a basis for temporary collaboration.

As far as the relationship between the Hungarian nobility and the Hungarian peasantry is concerned, it is obvious that it is characterized by the feudal form of the class struggle. Nevertheless, at times of war against foreign invaders it was not rare to find an, always contradictory, co-operation, which corresponded to the interests of the two classes at one point: the defence of the country against the foreign conqueror.

The question is not therefore to paint an idyllic picture of "the lord and the peasant in the unity of Hungarian life", but to represent, in conformity with historic truth, the relationship—and its ideological reflection—between the ruling class and the oppressed. This common struggle could obviously contribute to the acceptance by the serfs of certain elements of the ruling ideology, and popular literature bears this out, but this does not mean that popular patriotism was purely and simply an emanation of this ideology.

Classes and Nations

How should one judge the relationship which existed between the class struggle and the fight for independence in the feudal era and in the era of capitalism?

Concerning the struggles for independence in the feudal era, it is necessary to ask whether an independent feudal state, liberated both from the Turks and from the Hapsburgs, was a postulate of progress in Hungary. Generally speaking one can say yes. This is valid especially about the wars against the Hapsburgs in the seventeenth and at the beginning of the eighteenth century, in which Hungarians and non-Hungarians alike participated, with the aim of re-establishing the fifteenth-century state of Matthias Corvinus. According to the political ideology of the times this state would have permitted an organic evolution without the intervention of the great powers. It is certain that in such a state the social and national conflicts would have appeared in a much clearer form and would have led to more rapid development from every possible point of view.[10]

The situation is more complex concerning the War of Independence of 1848–49 when—at a higher level of social and national development—the demands of the serfs and of the national minorities were only partially satisfied by the Hungarian ruling class, which on its part wanted to achieve national independence then demanded by historic evolution. This real contradiction does not mean that opposition to the Hapsburgs should be condemned, it proves only that the nationality policies of the Hungarian government were wrong and that the leaders of the national minorities were not aware that they had become the toys of the Viennese Court,[11] i.e. of reaction.

The national and social problem appeared in another light in 1919. The Hungarian Republic of Councils fought both for the cause of the nations and for the interests of the exploited classes. The intervention of the imperialists and reaction at home, but the bourgeois solution of the national question by the ruling classes of the non-Hungarian nationalities as well were responsible for its fall. Could it be said that the socialist revolution reached this part of Europe too soon?[12]

10 See Béla Köpeczi, op. cit.

11 E. Andics: *Das Bündnis Habsburg–Romanow*. Vorgeschichte der zaristischen Intervention in Ungarn im Jahre 1849. Budapest, 1963. Akadémiai Kiadó, 202 pp.

12 Béla Kun declared at the June 1919 Congress of the Party: "Incidentally, as partisans of a federal republic, we are striving to bring about the system of federated council republics, by assuring them the highest degree of national and cultural autonomy, self-government and independence." *Selected Documents of the History of the Hungarian Working Movement*. Vol. 6/b, Budapest, 1955. Szikra, p. 18. (In Hungarian). See: Béla Kirschner: "Société et nation au temps de la République Hongroise des Conseils." *Nouvelles Études Hongroises*, Vol. 4–5. 1969–1970. pp. 69–96.

The question of the role of the Hungarian ruling class—especially until the revolution of 1848-49—also arises here. In the struggles for independence, certain sections of the nobility were able to exercise a positive function and also—due to the particularities of development in Hungary and in other countries of Central and Eastern Europe—to achieve, even if in a very contradictory way, part of the objectives of the bourgeois revolution. The history of the struggles for independence and of the entire Hungarian past will be much easier to understand if we rid ourselves of a primitive Manicheism which opposes the evil nobleman to the good people.

All this does not mean that we should forget the fundamental antagonism of class societies or that we should idealize the role of the nobility, but a just appreciation of its position may lead to a better understanding of the complex links between the social and the national struggle.

Progress, Society, Nation

It is also necessary to give a concrete meaning to progress, which is often treated too abstractly. Progress serves, in the last resort, the bringing about of a classless society and the liberation of man, and every period does no more than offer its own contribution to the achievement of this final goal.

As far as Hungarian history is concerned, the abstract notion of progress implies that Hapsburg centralism was more progressive than the Estates system clamoured for by the Hungarian nobility. But in what guise did this centralism appear in the Hapsburg Empire until the end of the seventeenth century? It was rather weak even in the hereditary provinces and in 150 years it did not succeed in gathering forces sufficient to drive the Turks out of Hungary. And what did it produce later? It led, especially in the eighteenth century, to a certain economic and cultural development, but it maintained the framework of the ancient feudal society, including serfdom, and forced a semi-colonial system on Hungary. In the national question it applied the slogan *divide et impera* which was to contribute to the birth of embittered nationalist movements in Eastern and Central Europe.[13]

The greatest confusion rules historic consciousness as regards the relationship between independence and progress following the Austro-Hungarian Compromise *(Ausgleich)* of 1867. Some historians consider that this union between the Austrian and the Hungarian ruling classes completely satisfied the national demands of the Hungarian nation and that it assured

[13] J. Bérenger: *Les fondements théoriques de l'absolutisme dans la Hongrie du XVIIIᵉ siècle.* Mélanges offerts à Aurélien Sauvageot. Paris, 1971. pp. 23–28.

economic and social progress to the monarchy. The fact that a part of the Hungarian ruling class (the Party of Independence) supported an anti-Hapsburg policy which was wrong does not mean that demanding independence for Hungary was anti-progressive.[14]

The achievement of true national independence was the objective of democrats and socialists in Hungary in 1918–19.

When, on May 1, 1919, People's Commissar Jenő Landler appealed for the defence of proletarian Hungary, he was justified in proclaiming: "Today Europe watches us; today the cause of the European workers is in the hands of the proletariat of Budapest."[15] The emphasis on the international aspect of the struggle did not mean that, in 1919, Hungarian proletarians "did not defend the fatherland", at a time that is, when the representatives of the Hungarian ruling class conducted negotiations with the Entente Powers and their stooges, the Royal Rumanian Army.[16]

In the years following the defeat of the revolution, Admiral Horthy, in spite of his nationalistic propaganda, could not hide the evidence that he had linked the fate of the country to the policies of the fascist governments of Italy and Germany.[17]

In this period the only fighters for independence were the workers and the anti-fascist intellectuals who rose against the chauvinistic policies of the Hungarian ruling class and demanded social reforms, including the land reform.[18]

After 1945 those were right who—opposing the political forces which relied on the Western Powers—defended, with the support of the Soviet Union, the independence of the country and thus made socialist changes possible. Numerous examples proved that, in every country where the armed forces of the Western powers were present, the bourgeoisie prevented the satisfaction of even the most justified social demands.

There are some in the socialist countries as well who oppose proletarian

14 See The Austro-Hungarian Compromise of 1867. Material (reports and discussion) of the International Conference held in Bratislava, August 28–September 1, 1967. Bratislava, 1971. Slovak Academy of Sciences (Communications and interventions in French, Italian, Russian, etc.), particularly papers by P. Hanák and E. Kovács.

15 Jenő Landler: Selected Speeches and Writings. Budapest, 1960. p. 307. (In Hungarian)

16 See the documents published in "La Politique extérieure de la République Hongroise des Conseils." by Zs. L. Nagy, on the intention of People's Commissar Béla Kun to negotiate with the Four on territorial questions, extracts from the deliberations of the Council of the Four, etc. Nouvelles Études Hongroises, Vol. 4–5, 1969–1970. pp. 97–114.

17 See M. Ádám, Gy. Juhász, L. Kerekes: Allianz Hitler–Horthy–Mussolini. Dokumente zur ungarischen Aussenpolitik (1933–1944). Budapest, 1966. Akadémiai Kiadó, 409 pp. — The Confidential Papers of Admiral Horthy. (Prepared for publication and introduced by M. Szinai and L. Szűcs). Budapest, 1965. Corvina Press. XXII., 439 pp.

18 See Iván Boldizsár: "L'autre Hongrie". Histoire du mouvement de résistance hongroise. Budapest, 1946. Új Magyarország, 76 pp.

or socialist internationalism to national sovereignty, and independence to autonomy, and this attitude holds out the promise of some success to them since, in the past, the relations between socialist countries did not always develop on an equal footing. However, what was true in the past applies today as well: the question of national independence is inseparable from the cause of social progress. In the second half of the twentieth century only the direct co-operation between socialist countries and progressive forces can assure the independence of various countries.

The Nations in Central and Eastern Europe

A just appreciation of the relationship between Hungarians and other nations is, as far as nation, independence and progress are concerned, an essential problem of historiography and of historic consciousness. These relations take on particular importance in the case of the neighbouring nations, the history of which was deformed by the nationalist notions of past Hungarian historiography. In the course of these past twenty-five years efforts have been made to rid Hungarian historiography and public thinking of their nationalist character.

However, the elimination of this way of looking at things does not depend on Hungarians alone, since Hungarian nationalism is also fed by the nationalism of others. There are two themes in the writings of some historians of neighbouring countries which are wrong in my opinion: on the one hand that the Hungarians prevented the establishment of national states at the proper time, on the other that they exploited other nations. Marxist historiography cannot defend policies of exploitation and—starting with the end of the eighteenth century—the oppressive nationalist policies of the Hungarian ruling classes. One must recognize the right of other nations to independence and to autonomous statehood. But it would be unjust and contrary to the spirit of history to try to inspire a sort of "consciousness of collective guilt", seeing that in this multinational country it was the dominance of the Hungarian exploiting class and not that of Hungarians as such, that prevailed, a supremacy shared, incidentally, by the Austrian ruling class. Further, as far as the class struggle is concerned, it is not possible to argue that the Hungarian ruling class in any way differentiated between Hungarian and other serfs or workers.

It is true that in the past, that is from the beginning of the nineteenth century, when a bourgeois national consciousness was being formed, conflicts arose between Hungarians and the national minorities and that one of the causes of these conflicts was the nationalist and chauvinist attitude of the Hungarian ruling class. This, however, does not entitle anyone to disregard the class nature of the policies of all ruling classes in this part of Europe.

If one examines political developments that took place after the First World War, one has to bear in mind that nationalism manifested itself in Hungary as well as in the other countries of South-Eastern Europe, and that none deserves to be called more "progressive" than the others.[19] Marxist historiography has to fight firmly all manifestations of the nationalism of the Horthy regime, but it also has to adopt a firm position towards the nationalist tendencies which were then present in the other countries. This is indispensable if one desires to progress in scholarship and in the shaping of public opinion.

Co-operation between the historians of the socialist countries—which has already achieved appreciable results—will make possible the elaboration of a detailed history of the relations between the nations of the Danube basin, this being a necessary condition for the transformation of the national images which live in the everyday consciousness.

The modern—that is Marxist—view of history can reinforce the consciousness of a socialist patriotism which is, in the principles, internationalist, but which relies on the traditions and on the specific qualities of each nation.

[19] See some Hungarian works concerning the history of the neighbouring nations: I. Z. Tóth: *Hungarians and Rumanians*. Budapest, 1966.; D. Csatári: *Hungarian–Rumanian Relations*. Budapest, 1958.; E. Arató: *Fifty Years of Hungarian–Czechoslovak Relations*. Budapest, 1969. (In Hungarian)

RESTRATIFICATION OF A SOCIETY

by

SÁNDOR SZALAI

The fact that a social restratification on a vast scale has been going on in Hungary since the Second World War is so manifest that it hardly calls for a special study. We have in mind here not only the liquidation of the landowners' and capitalists' class but also the incomparably greater change caused, numerically, by the rapid growth of industry and the migration of the agricultural workers from the countryside to the towns to become industrial workers, or, in the village itself, by the employment, in factories or offices, of hundreds of thousands of women previously dependent or engaged only in household work. A major shift has taken place also in the ratio of physical and intellectual workers. Whereas in 1949 there were 13 employees per 100 workers, today there are 31, in fact in the state industry there are at present nearly as many employees —engineers, technicians, clerks, etc.—as there were workers in Hungary's entire manufacturing industry in 1938. In addition we have to mention the mass restratification caused by the changes in the state administration and economic management as a result of the complete transformation of the educational and vocational training systems. Just to quote an example: in 1937–38, 11,747 persons attended universities and other institutions of higher learning, 39.8 per cent of them the faculty of law and 9 per cent the Technical University. In 1964–65 the number of university and other students was 91,123, of which 4.7 per cent at the faculty of law and 33.1 per cent at the Technical University.

However, rough comparisons based only on general statistics, mainly census data, do not give a true idea of how this radical structural transformation of Hungarian society took place. They merely indicate the initial situation and the final result, but not what happened in the meantime—the career travelled by those individuals, families and social strata driven by the force of historic changes from their former status and induced to find their place in a new society, under new circumstances, either to their advantage or to their detriment.

What, in fact, were the dimensions of this landslide and how many of the ten million Hungarians did it directly affect? This question cannot be answered by merely adding up or subtracting census data. From the mere fact that in 1949 the state-owned industry employed 414,000 workers, and 1,006,000 in 1964, it does not follow that during the fifteen years in question 1,006,000 — 414,000 = 592,000 people looked for new jobs and became workers in state-owned industry. For out of the 414,000 workers in 1949, tens of thousands evidently became technicians, foremen, engineers, government officials (but how many?), while others, after all sorts of hardships, returned to the work-bench (but how many?) and tens of thousands reached retirement age or died (but again how many?). And of the 592,000 "new" industrial workers how many came directly from the school forms, or how many exchanged the life of an independent artisan, peasant or jobless functionary for that of an industrial worker?

To such questions general statistics—the census and labour data—cannot give a reply. The lives of tens of thousands, hundreds of thousands, even millions of people are tangled up here. Is there any means of tracing the individual threads, or at least the "typical" warps and woofs?

A few years ago, the Central Statistical Office, which is among those Hungarian scientific institutions that have the longest standing and enjoy an international reputation, began a large-scale and methodologically trail-blazing investigation to ascertain how such a vast restratification process in Hungarian society actually took place during the past several decades, what strata and groups of people it set into motion, where the careers of these people led to, and what kind of changes occurred in the composition of the population as a result of the rapid growth in social mobility.

The investigation required special methods. For where János Kovács, 38, section head in the Ministry of Heavy Industry, Mme József Nagy, 47, a cooperative livestock tender, or Péter Kis, 59, an unskilled worker at Csepel, were five, ten, fifteen, or twenty years ago, what they did for a living, or what qualifications they had, may generally be learned only from these persons themselves, because no central statistical data can furnish information about their individual lives. At the same time it is apparent that social restratification is realized through the ups and downs of individual life.

The problem, therefore, can be approached only through the methods of statistical sampling. The demographic research team of the Central Statistical Office selected a population "sample," that is, it picked out—on the basis of adequate census data—2 per mille of all families living in Budapest, 4 per mille of all families living in country towns, and 5 per mille of all families living in villages. In other respects, it was a random selection: every family, big or small, even a "one-man" or "one-woman" family had an equal chance of being included in the sampling. In this way the several thousand family units of the "sample" truly represented Hungary's 3.5 million families. These units were then individually visited by the representatives of the Central Statistical Office, who questioned each member of the family above the age of 14 about the facts of and changes in their lives, facts which—in line with the foregoing—the statisticians need to know in order to be able to trace the entire process of social restratification in Hungary.

This was a tremendous job of fact-finding and elaboration. The first volume, entitled "The Demographic Effects of Social Restratification in Budapest and Urban Centres" (1966), has recently been published, and a second volume will deal with the demographic changes in the population of the villages and hamlets, to be followed, no doubt, by many further studies dealing with other aspects.

Intellectual and physical work, town and country, office, factory and field, offer even today such divergent conditions of everyday existence, profoundly affecting ways of living in society, that it has become the established practice to divide the population roughly into three principal strata —brain workers, non-farm manual workers, and farm manual workers, together with their dependents (comprising those who are not and never have been engaged in a gainful occupation that would permit them to be classed as an independent stratum). Within this triple division into strata several groups may be distinguished. Among the brain workers there is a difference between the highly qualified and those of lower qualification (office clerks, administrative workers, employees in various professions, etc.). An important group among the non-farm manual workers is made up of skilled, semi-skilled and unskilled industrial workers, including manual workers of the artisans' cooperatives, independent artisans, and the like. Finally, the farm manual workers may be divided into members of cooperative farms, farm workers on wages and individual farmers.

This division into strata—and into groups within the strata—was used by the demographic research team of the Central Statistical Office in its analysis of Hungary's social restratification. It should be borne in mind that nowadays a similar three-stratum or three-sector division is used in all countries having a fairly developed industry and administrative or public utility apparatus. The main difference is that in the capitalist countries an important group consists of persons living independently on incomes derived from their property or their estate (house-owners, landowners, etc.); this group is mostly included in the stratum of brain workers, inasmuch as those capitalists that are actively running their enterprises and business executives in general are in any case classified there. In the socialist countries there are no such independent means of subsistence based on proprietor's income; here, on the other hand, the distinction between cooperative and individual farmers is of great importance.

On the whole, however, the tripartite classification into brain workers, non-farm manual workers and farm manual workers (not to mention at this juncture the marginal strata, the various subdivisions and subgroups) exists everywhere, and the decisive restratification process is denoted everywhere by the degree of mobility existing between manual and brain workers on the one hand, and between the farming and the non-farming population, on the other.

This movement can be traced along two main lines—namely, *intrageneration* and *intergeneration* mobility. Intrageneration mobility means, e.g., that a peasant leaves his village to become an industrial worker, or a factory worker takes an engineering course to become a qualified engineer or, *vice versa*, a former official or clerk becomes a factory worker. Intergeneration mobility, on the other hand, means that a peasant-father's son becomes a clerk, a worker-father's daughter a doctor or, conversely, the son of a factory manager becomes a bus driver, a civil servant's daughter a tram conductor.

Both the intrageneration and intergeneration mobility trends are manifestly an important gauge of social transformations. Naturally, both trends may be observed not only between the individual social strata but also between groups within the same stratum (e.g., when an individual farmer joins the group of cooperative farmers or when the son of a private artisan becomes an industrial worker). Nevertheless, the main changes in the structure of society are caused by the movements occurring between the three main strata.

A study of the data in the above-mentioned volume from this point of view reveals the truly extraordinary dimensions of the social restratification which has taken place in Hungary during the last few decades.

To begin with, it should be pointed out that according to this sampling more than one third of the gainfully employed—in Budapest 37 per cent, in the provincial towns 27 per cent—have changed their social stratum in the course of their lives. Taking into account intergeneration—rather than intrageneration—mobility, we find that the restratification ratios are even greater: compared with the father's social stratum in 1938, the proportion of restratified people both in Budapest and the country towns was 48 per cent, that is to say, nearly every second gainfully employed belongs to another social stratum than his or her father belonged to prior to the Second World War. Finally, if we also consider the social groups within the individual strata (e.g., independent artisans and tradespeople becoming industrial workers, individual farmers becoming cooperative farm members, clerks and specialists taking their degrees and switching over to higher level intellectual careers, etc.), a mobility that in Budapest involves 30 per cent of all gainfully employed and in the provincial towns 27 per cent, we come to the conclusion that only about one third of all gainfully employed have not changed either their social stratum or their social group in the course of their life. At present detailed data are available only concerning Budapest and the country towns, but the overall mobility ratio is unlikely to present a different picture. For though the *interstrata* movement in the villages and hamlets was smaller than in the towns—or, to be more precise, the overwhelming majority of farm manual workers transferring to another social stratum are now living in towns, whereas, compared with this migration, that from town to village has been insignificant—the largest *intergroup* movement in the villages and hamlets occurred when the bulk of the peasants joined the cooperative farms.

To sum up: among today's gainfully employed two out of three belong to a different social stratum or group from the one they belonged to earlier —whether the change took place during their own careers or in childhood (when their social status was determined by that of their fathers). This represents a historical transformation of staggering proportions, all within a single generation.

Of course, we must not "romanticize" the process that has taken place in Hungary. Restratification is not, in itself, identical with social advance— with urbanization, industrialization, the influx of peasants and workers into leading state and economic positions, or the increase in the number of brain workers. All this is an important factor but by no means the sole criterion of increasing mobility, because this movement is not always and in every case upwards.

Let us cast a glance at the table on the next page, relating to Budapest's present adult population.

What do these statistics tell us? Amongst other things this: of the present adult population of Budapest slightly more than one third have remained in the social stratum they were born into, while about 20 per cent changed their social stratum more than three times during their careers. Let us bear in mind that even a career in the course of which the

Restratification of Adult Population of Budapest According to Age Groups and Number of Changes
per Person (in percentages)

Stratum changed during life	Born before 1900	Born 1900–19	Born 1920–29	Born 1930–47	Combined adult age groups
Once	11.3	14.6	18.2	23.1	15.7
Twice	13.5	17.6	13.9	12.2	15.0
Three times	9.0	16.8	15.9	11.4	13.8
Four times	7.0	10.4	9.0	6.6	8.6
Five times	5.8	4.8	8.3	0.9	4.8
Six times	1.8	3.9	3.3	0.4	2.7
Seven times	2.0	1.8	2.0	0.4	1.7
Eight times	0.7	2.3	0.3	—	1.2
Nine times	1.2	1.0	0.3	—	0.8
Total	52.3	73.2	69.2	55.0	64.3
No change, or lived as dependent	47.7	26.8	30.8	45.0	35.7
Grand total	100.0	100.0	100.0	100.0	100.0

son of a landless cotter becomes a skilled industrial worker, then a qualified engineer or, if you like, a County party secretary, a Council president, even a Minister (a standard career on the screen), requires only two changes in social stratum. A triple change can only be imagined in a career which includes at least one set-back. And more than three changes in social stratum are conceivable only in the case of those who—scarcely of their own volition—had to cover a zigzag course in society, up and down, up and down... And when our chart shows that 1 per cent of Budapest's adults born between 1900 and 1919 had to pass through no less than nine changes in social stratum, then those terse and dry figures tell the tale of at least 15,000 human destinies full of vicissitudes, 15,000 "adventure stories," 15,000 Odysseys, each different from the other.

It is manifest that the life-stories of those born between 1900 and 1919 reflect half a century of Hungarian history, two world wars, with intervening revolution, counter-revolution, nazi occupation, Arrow Cross terror, followed by the transformation into a People's Democracy after the Second World War. A longer or shorter part of these series of stormy events was lived through also by the younger generations. It would be a mistake, however, to suppose that the decisive process of restratification occurred in those times or that since, say 1948–49, only minor "corrections" manifested themselves in Hungary's social structure. In fact, just the contrary is true. During the last fifteen years the process of social restratification has quickened and, strange as it may sound, 52 per cent of Budapest's gainfully employed and 57 per cent of those in the provinces joined their present social stratum since 1950. And this phenomenon cannot solely be ascribed to the younger generation which, availing itself of the incredibly increased possibilities of study and extension courses, strives to achieve more than its fathers did. Here is a striking example: 31 per cent of Budapest's gainfully employed over 60, and 41 per cent of those in the same age group living in provincial towns, entered their present social stratum since 1950.

As has already been said, mobility cannot simply be identified with rise in social status—for there are zigzag courses, even downward movements, as well. However, in the history of a people, the opportunity of rising to a higher status is decisive, in other words the preponderance of an unequivocally upward movement as compared with the embroilment and intermingling caused by mere change of place between "up" and "down."

There are some interesting data in this respect too.

The background of Hungary's present-day brain workers is as follows:

	In Budapest (per cent)	In provincial towns (per cent)
Brain workers from the outset	46.0	50.9
Non-farm manual workers turned brain workers	35.3	33.9
Farm workers turned brain workers	1.4	3.2
Farm manual workers turned non-farm manual workers, then brain workers	2.2	3.5
Brain workers turned non-farm manual workers, then again becoming brain workers	15.1	8.5
Total	100.0	100.0

As may be seen from the above, only about half of the present brain workers belonged to this category from the start, while about one third of them worked their way up from the masses of non-farm manual workers (mostly industrial workers). The ratio of those farm manual workers who went over from the peasantry directly to the stratum of brain workers is comparatively small. For them the path to the brain workers' stratum led through manual work of a non-farm character. These figures relate only to intrageneration mobility; but intergeneration mobility—from father to son or daughter—is even more pronounced among those moving from the stratum of farm manual workers towards that of brain workers. It is also worth noting that, according to the above chart, 15.1 per cent of the present brain workers in Budapest and 8.5 per cent of those of provincial towns started out as brain workers but in the meantime entered the stratum of non-farm manual workers from which they finally (mòstly from the status of an industrial worker) fought their way back among the brain workers. There was not one case—statistically demonstrable in the above survey of an exactitude of 0.1 per cent—of a brain worker turned farm manual worker again becoming a brain worker. Such cases consequently are very rare in our age. On the other hand, as we shall see presently, there are examples—though not many—of a man's abandoning his position as a brain worker, making his living as a farm manual worker and remaining in that stratum.

But let us examine the past of today's non-farm manual workers, represented, for the most part, by factory workers. Their background is illustrated by the following figures:

	In Budapest (per cent)	In provincial towns (per cent)
Non-farm manual workers from the start	71.4	70.6
Brain workers turned non-farm manual workers	5.6	2.1
Farm manual workers turned non-farm manual workers	15.8	23.2
Non-farm workers turned brain workers, then again becoming non-farm manual workers	7.2	4.1
Total	100.0	100.0

While, as we have seen, only about half of the brain workers have always been in this category throughout their lives, more than two thirds of the non-farm manual workers—nearly three-quarters—earned their living in their present stratum from the start. At any rate, this stratum has gained considerably from among the farm workers (in Budapest 15.8 per cent, in the provincial towns 23.2 per cent). Not very large, yet not to be neglected is the number of those who earlier earned their living steadily or transitorily as brain workers, but have now become manual workers in industry.

Finally, let us cast a glance at the stratum of farm manual workers, though their status cannot be adequately illustrated through data relating to the capital or to provincial towns, since in the former only 1.1 per cent and in the latter only 16.7 per cent of all gainfully employed come under this category.

The present farm manual workers have the following background:

	In Budapest (per cent)	In country towns (per cent)
Farm manual workers from the start	100.0	72.0
Brain workers turned farm manual workers	—	1.7
Non-farm manual workers turned farm manual workers	—	26.3
Total	100.0	100.0

In the provincial towns, "remigration" from industrial to agricultural work has been of considerable significance, a fact that can probably be ascribed to the new forms of cooperative farming as well as to the possibilities afforded by the mechanization of agriculture in general. Furthermore, in the provincial towns too, though to a very small extent, a return from brain work to farm manual work has occurred.

Taken as a whole, these comparative charts and tables bear witness to an imposing and definitely upward restratification of the population. There is an increasing mobility between the social strata, with the stratum of brain workers expanding most.

Let us quote here a few passages from the results of the survey of the demographic research team:

"The ratio of those having changed their social stratum (i.e., coming from other social strata) is highest in the stratum of brain workers—in Budapest still higher than in other towns. Even compared with the first gainful employment, the deepest-going change is to be found among those belonging to the present stratum of brain workers. The ratio of those that have gone back to manual work is about half that of those who found their way into the brain workers' stratum. . .

"From the point of view of the status of their fathers, the greatest change can be noticed among those pursuing an intellectual occupation, though in this respect there is no essential difference between Budapest and the other towns. Among the children of fathers with agricultural occupations more have shifted to the brain workers' stratum in the provincial towns than in Budapest. . .

"The greatest change from the social stratum of their fathers is to be found among those under 30 in Budapest and between 30 and 39 in the provincial towns. In this context, the proportion of males is higher than that of females."

Of the above quotations the last—referring to the great mobility of youth—is perhaps of greatest interest to us Hungarians. Here the detailed data too reveal an unequivocally upward tendency. Here the careers are no longer zigzagging, and it is no longer necessary for some to fall in order that others may rise. Urbanization, the growth of industry and the increasing modernization of agriculture open up wider vistas and give even more scope to our youth.

Let us conclude with another quotation from the survey:

"It is among farm manual workers' families that the social stratum of the young generation differs most from that of their fathers (71 per cent in Budapest and 59 per cent in provincial towns). In Budapest more than a third, in the country more than a fourth of the children of manual workers have become brain workers."

RESTRATIFICATION
OF THE WORKING CLASS

by

ISTVÁN KEMÉNY

I n Hungary, the first factory workers came from two places: abroad and the villages. Skilled workers came from abroad (primarily from Bohemia and Austria), and peasants became the unskilled labourers in the newly established factories. The workers were the non-bourgeois opposition within the capitalist economic system, but in society the feudal structure continued to exist side by side with the capitalist system. The industrialization of Hungary's economy proceeded fast in the second half of the nineteenth century, but progress in the democratization of the social system and in the urbanization of the way of life was slow and difficult. As far as the economy was concerned, workers lived in a capitalist system, but sociologically they did not live in a corresponding society; they formed an economically exploited and sociologically excluded class.

When Hungarian capitalism, and with it Hungarian workers, entered on the stage of history, Hungary did not have a unified social structure. Two societies lived facing each other, or to be more exact, gentry and aristocratic society imposed itself on peasant society in such a way that it completely closed off the latter, which could only be left rarely and by detours.

As the Hungarian bourgeoisie established itself, it did not endeavour to open up these closed worlds, but placed itself between the two as a third closed world. It became part of the Hungarian social order, but did not transform it. Its relationship to the workers was on the one hand that of the exploiter to the exploited, and on the other, that of a privileged stratum of the feudal society to an underprivileged one. Just as the gentry lived at an enormous distance above the peasantry as far as customs, culture and way of thinking were concerned, so the Hungarian bourgeoisie lived at an enormous distance above Hungarian workers. Hungarian workers, just as Hungarian peasants, had to develop for themselves, under pressure, a separate world to live in.

Factory workers lived in a system of strict subordination, as did Hungarian society as a whole.

At the start, the closed world of workers was itself divided into smaller closed worlds. Those who had come from abroad and those who had come from the country, the foremen, the skilled workers and the unskilled hands all formed separate groups which were sharply divided by income, education, prestige, culture and privileges. There was a workshop-system centred on the foreman, who had personal contact with apprentices and journeymen. A skilled worker learned his trade in the way craftsmen did, and he in fact knew it as well as any independent tradesman. He needed this skill, because the technology of the time demanded that he use it in coping with his work.

The first changes

The closed nature of this world was first broken by the organized workers' movement. Organized workers were more urbanized than their unorganized companions. They claimed all the achievements of the bourgeois way of life—while at the same time rejecting and even wanting to destroy capitalist society. The organized worker's scale of values had principles which agreed with the bourgeois scale of values and principles which were diametrically opposed to it. It agreed with the bourgeois scale of values in his respect for culture, in the high evaluation of achievement, and in the demand for increased production. It was opposed to the bourgeois scale of values in rejecting a social order based on inequality, in being based on faith in the possibility and necessity of the abolition of the system, the construction of a socialist one, and in the mission of the labour movement. The higher culture of the militant worker was inseparable from his being in political opposition. The ideology of the class struggle is rational and its acceptance requires a full understanding of the rational foundations of culture. A lack of culture, on the other hand, helps political adaptation; the worker living in a closed world sees the "sky" above him as something irrational, he is more prone to acquiesce, and to rebellions interrupting long periods of acquiescence.

Organized workers got farthest in the urbanization of their way of life, but there were other ways that led to urbanization. Some of the skilled factory workers became foremen or independent tradesmen. A tradesman's workshop on occasion grew and became a capitalist enterprise—although most tradesmen did not live any better than skilled factory workers—and the second or third generation sometimes already belonged to the bourgeoisie.

Other tradesmen sent their children to school, and with great difficulty and by hiding their origin, the latter sometimes wormed their way into the middle class, which led a petty-bourgeois life but had gentry pretensions. This road to urbanization meant leaving the working class, and also adaptation to a non-bourgeois social ambience, to the illusions and ideals which were then dominant.

In the 1920s the exclusion of the working class became even more pronounced. After the failure of the communist Council Republic, gentry society declared organized workers to be unpatriotic. This was only a sharper and more ideological wording of what was its more or less concealed conviction anyway. Gentry society identified itself with the nation, and excluded all other classes. This became an expressed view even when faith in it was profoundly shaken in those who apparently believed it.

In the thirties and forties the working class already presented an entirely different picture. A new technology had appeared, the autonomy of workers lost importance, semi-skilled workers became more important. The composition of the working class according to origin also changed. Those who had come from abroad, had become assimilated long ago, but the old skilled workers no longer formed any more than a nucleus. The numbers were provided by the masses that had come from the villages, who were less well trained, less versed in politics, and in culture, but who harboured very radical sentiments. The situation of the workers also changed within the social system of the factory. Industrial feudalism became tainted with rightist radicalism and social demagogy.

This rightist radicalism and social demagogy wanted to give a lot to the worker, or at least it promised to. The planning or development of the regulation of wages, labour safety, insurance, education, training in trades went hand in hand with emphasizing that workers should remain workers, obedient, ready to carry out orders. Industrial feudalism remained feudalistic, but became more paternal, more anti-intellectual, and more military.

The condition of dependence, of being shut out of political and public life, resulted in everything that happened in the superior world taking on a legendary, a mythical hue. People can only judge realistically what they participate in, what they know from their own experience. Correspondingly, the members of the "upper" classes also had a legendary, mythical idea of the world of workers and peasants.

During the Second World War industrialization received a new impetus. Production increased fast—by almost 40 per cent in the war years; new factories applying a new, modern technology were established and the technology of the old factories was also modernized. Quantity and quality of production achieved approximately the same level as in the second year of the post-liberation first five-year plan. This industrialization increased the number and weight of the workers—and of the bourgeoisie; it raised the standard of living. Industrialization offered an opportunity for the urbanization of the material framework of the way of life. But industrialization is in itself insufficient for the regeneration of the structure of social life. This requires the active co-operation of the forces that come from below, first of all of the workers. Without democratization there can be no regeneration. Industrialization without democratization only increased existing contradictions. Beside feudal elements, which were kept alive though obsolete and spurious, it created a fascist political superstructure, and it increased the forces that would have been interested in democratization, but prevented these forces from asserting themselves. By the end of the Second World War these forces were nevertheless in a position to create an up-to-date, democratic society.

Peasants turned workers

Today the closed culture of the working class is on the way to dissolution. Today's Hungarian workers are not a closed section of society with fixed customs, and an unequivocal system of interdependence, but much rather a huge camp of people on the way. One half of the working class were recently peasants, these lead a transitional way of life between village and town, between a peasant and a worker way of life. But those who were born workers are also on the way from being workers in the old sense to becoming a new type of worker. Some of them become foremen, technicians and engineers, others work in laboratories or a tertiary industry, others again seek supplementary work and live the more important part of their life outside the factory. In one way or another, the majority become divorced from their traditional way of life.

The transformation of the peasantry and of the working class are part of one and the same process, of the dissolution of the closed feudal culture and the urbanization of Hungarian society. This urbanization takes place step by step, in stages.

The *first* step is the turning of peasants into urban workers. In the preceding generation one half of Hungary's population were peasants, today one quarter are. This means every second son or daughter of a peasant has become an urban worker.

This is a process that is taking place almost everywhere in the world.

But in Hungary, in the past twenty years—especially in the fifties—this process was accelerated. This was made possible by the existence of a rural population surplus, larger in Hungary than in any other country of Europe. The exaggerated rate of industrialization at the beginning of the fifties provided jobs which drained off this surplus and—following the collectivization of agriculture—others who had not originally intended to do so, went to work in the towns. For the better-off peasants this change meant a lowering in rank, in prestige, in income, that is a downward mobility, but at the same time this also was part of the process of urbanization.

To become an urban worker when you were born a peasant is not a simple thing. It involves a change of culture. The first step is always unskilled or semi-skilled work, or the learning of certain trades that are particularly accessible to peasants, mostly those involving heavy physical work requiring great strength and stamina in bad conditions (great cold, great heat), or trades that are found and can be practised in villages. The sons of urban workers readily surrender those trades to the sons of peasants.

Two-thirds of Hungarian semi-skilled and unskilled workers are of

Trades	Percentage of those of		
	Peasant	Worker	Skilled worker
	origin		
1. Toolmaker	10.6	71.3	49.2
2. Turner	18.3	67.8	36.8
3. Fitter	19.1	65.8	38.1
4. Electrician	21.6	60.1	43.2
5. Welder	29.6	59.8	31.5
6. Adjuster	30.0	57.8	30.0
7. Grinder	32.2	50.4	25.0
8. Foundryman	33.6	46.2	28.6
9. Miller	35.2	53.9	37.4
10. Metal polisher	36.7	49.9	13.3
11. Furnaceman	40.0	49.4	18.7
12. Rollerman	40.2	52.2	18.4
13. Crane driver	42.6	50.6	14.9
14. Machine-moulder	42.9	46.5	17.9
15. Smelter	43.7	43.6	22.5
16. Joiner	44.4	44.4	33.3
17. First smelter	53.8	46.2	7.7
18. Solderer	55.0	35.0	12.5
19. Smith	62.2	35.5	20.0

peasant stock. The proportion of those of peasant origin is particularly high in mining, in metallurgy (foundrymen, smiths, rollermen, furnacemen, solderers), in the building and wood-working industries (bricklayers, carpenters, joiners), that is, in the "ancient" trades as well.

Thus, a survey of the 23,000 workers of the Csepel Iron and Metal Works gave the following picture of the breakdown according to origin of workers in 19 trades (see Table on p. 30).

In the same trades, the percentages of those who have come from a village are:

Toolmaker	28.6	Semi-skilled worker	50.4
Turner	29.4	Smelter	50.7
Electrician	24.7	Solderer	50.0
Fitter	37.0	Rollerman	51.7
Miller	39.5	Crane driver	49.1
Adjuster	38.3	Furnaceman	63.5
Joiner	42.3	Metal polisher	60.7
Welder	42.2	Machine-moulder	60.0
Grinder	40.2	Smith	72.3
Unskilled worker	47.8	First smelter	61.7
Foundryman	50.4		

Linking factory work and village life

A great part of workers who have come from the peasantry have taken only one step towards urbanization, they have gone to work in the manufacturing or building industries, but have not taken the second step, they have not moved to town. They commute from their villages by train or by bus. A great part of those who live in town try to get hold of some kind of small holding. Their majority has not even finished the eighth class of primary school. A large number went to work in a factory in the fifties, at the time of the first wave of agricultural collectivization, therefore many of them are men of forty to fifty who left their villages at the age of twenty to thirty.

This section of the workers as a rule can imagine their life only in a way that links factory work with agricultural work; they fatten pigs, breed chickens, produce vegetables and fruit. The bridge over the gap between a peasant life and that of the working class is that hard work remains the fundamental law of life. Rest almost counts as something immoral, reading as a superfluous luxury; permitted entertainments are drinking, the pictures, and lately television. Such a worker brings up his children in a patriarchal spirit, and this of course causes clashes between the generations. The children no longer accept this patriarchal treatment, but rebel against it. In their eating and clothing habits such workers maintain the thriftiness and simplicity of peasants. They are almost as distant from the world of bureaucracy as their parents were, or their predecessors, the traditional Hungarian working class was. They therefore find it difficult to protect their interests, either orally or in writing. They become entangled in a complicated description of superfluous details when presenting their case, and do not find the proper arguments. Abstractions are far from their way of thinking, the scientific, that is abstract, explanation of some fact or event is unacceptable to them. They have great difficulty in finding their way in public life, as a rule they do not know the organizational structure of the enterprise in which they work, and they do not clearly understand the rules that decisively influence their income.

This transitional condition is even more pronounced with those who stay in their village. Here commuting is added to factory work and agricultural work at home. Many of them build themselves a home with all city comforts, working from daybreak to late into the night, with boundless energy, and then they more often than not end up using the bathroom as a tool-shed, and they live in only one room of a house which they are not always able to fill with furniture, let alone with an urban kind of life.

There are others who cannot solve the problems of transition. The community of the factory does not accept them, because they are considered clumsy and slow-witted. But they do not wish and cannot be peasants any longer—so they are caught half-way.

There are others again who have not shown themselves able to stand up to the burden of transition weighing down on the soul, and have finally become incapable of leading an ordered life. These no longer commute between the factory and the village, but between the factory and some place where drinks are sold.

It is mostly the children of the latter—of those who have got stuck this way and whose life is unsettled—who stop on the level of their parents. They are a large proportion of the primary school drop-outs. Some pass all their annual exams but only through the benevolence of their teachers.

Acquiring skills

The majority of the sons of the others, of those who have taken the first step, do not carry on the occupation of their fathers. They learn another, more modern trade, where it is not physical strength but mental concentration and skill that count. This is the *second* step, if moving to town is not counted as a separate one. Two-thirds of Hungarian toolmakers, fitters, turners, millers, drillers, lathe-operators, grinders, metal polishers, precision engineers, electricians, printers are children of parents who themselves had taken the first step. The majority are young, they have almost all finished primary school, many of them have completed a technical secondary school or high-school course. To tell the truth, these trades are modern only in relation to the earlier mentioned ones, considering world-wide progress, they are also traditional trades. People operate machines as old as they are, and they are aware of this. They have ideas concerning modern technology which they think ought to be introduced. They clearly sense the transitional condition of their situation. The younger they are, the greater the distance between the way their family lives and the peasant world and the higher their schooling, not to mention that they are less satisfied with the work they are doing. They want to escape it through study or in some other way. Their clothing hardly differs from that of the young professional people and executives. If they save, it is no longer for a family cottage, but for a flat and a car.

The older generation of the section of the first step are skilled workers of the old type, with their roots in a period when the machine-operators were not yet the dominating figures in industry, and the skilled worker was really a "skilled" worker in the "craft" sense of the word. These live the old worker way of life, and do not wish to escape it. Hard work is the law of life for them also, they too have patriarchal ideas concerning family life, but even the thought of agricultural work is a long way from them. They grew up in a world where it was shameful for a skilled worker if his wife or daughter went to work in a factory, and where a man went and had a drink after work. They are perhaps the only ones who keep up the working-class culture discussed at the beginning of this article.

Moving further up the ladder

Half of their children are able to take the *third* step. This step leads away from being a worker in the old sense of the word. It can be taken in two ways. One is mobility within the career, rising to be foremen, technicians, engineers, or party functionaries. Most of the workers' sons proceed along this alternative. One-third, at the most, of skilled-worker parents send their children to secondary school, the others have them trained for a trade. (A larger proportion of girls attend secondary school. The explanation of this is that in the traditional female trades wages are lower. Therefore skilled-worker parents prefer to send their daughter to secondary school and let her obtain a leaving certificate, so that she may then become an office-worker or nurse, and marry.) If they encourage their children to go on studying, they start them off on a path which is expensive and risky and the results of which are doubtful. For nine years they do not earn anything and have to be kept. It is not at all certain that they will be able to finish secondary school, but if they succeed in this, the probability is still low that they can get a place in a university or college. Why should they learn a trade with a secondary leaving certificate, if they can do this with a primary school certificate? And finally, if they have succeeded in graduating from a university or college, they earn much less at the age of 23 or 24 than an 18-year-old skilled worker. If, on the other hand, they learn a trade, this is a sure livelihood, without being a dead end, the final stage of a career.

It is for these reasons that children of the section of society of the second step choose mobility within a career. They have a further reason—the difficulty they have at school in competing with children of white-collar workers and professional people.

Two surveys—one in the Csepel Iron and Metal Works, and one among workers in Pest County—have shown that every fifth skilled worker becomes a foreman or technician.

The role of environmental factors

Studying is an indispensable element in promotion; and with technical progress it is becoming more and more so. An important difference in the way of thinking of a physical worker and of professional people is the first's lack of an abstract rationality. The mode of thinking of which a mathematical formula is the extreme example is an accustomed and self-evident process for every intellectual. For a physical worker every relationship is a connection between real, concrete elements. The fundamental change occurs with the trained technicians and foremen. It is on this level that systematic thinking and definitions, conclusions following certain rules, verification, the use of laboratory methods and of experiments become common. The effect of this important change plays a major role in the decision whether or not children go on studying. Ten per cent of the sons of skilled workers, and already 25 per cent of the sons of foremen and technicians study at the day courses of universities and colleges. The explanation of this discrepancy is largely that the children of the latter are better able to compete. They are better able to compete because the change in the manner of thinking has already taken place with their parents.

At school, in competition among children, progress in culture as such is measured. In giving marks for individual subjects, not only knowledge of the prescribed curriculum is taken into consideration, but also the capacity to think systematically, discipline in learning, and general knowledge. The school teaches only one part of general knowledge, as much as is contained in textbooks; the other part, which cannot be found in the textbooks, is left to the family. The part of knowledge and culture which is left to the family includes the ability to think rationally and the application of a conceptual language, which in the families of professional people—but also in the families of foremen and technicians—are passed on to the children almost automatically.

A knowledge of mathematical formulae, definitions, logical verification, experimental processes and the ability to apply them do not yet add up to knowledge and culture. Culture of the kind not available at school has yet another, more concealed part, which is even less accessible to those who come from a worker family, which cannot be included in the curriculum, culture in the old humanistic sense of the term. The acquisition of this is perhaps the *fourth* step.

This can perhaps be expressed by saying that a man who grew up in a technical culture gets accustomed to the application of formulae, but is not on friendly terms with words, though this is an oversimplification. The meaning of words includes all the cultural content that can be associated with them. In their practical application they denote an object or an interconnection, but they are at the same time also symbols that may invoke an entire culture; they are elements of a secret language which is intelligible only to those who are in the know, and which excludes the uninitiated. Every communication refers to some interconnection. But beyond the first, most obvious interconnection it refers to a system of interconnections, to an entire culture. For elementary understanding communication on one elementary level, the straightforward interconnection has to be known to which it primarily refers, but the more remote interconnections someone is aware the more profoundly he grasps the communication. This is one of the reasons why the children of working men who have become professional people, so often remain—after having graduated from a university—at the level of white-collar workers doing routine work. Without the acquisition of culture in full sense there cannot be complete mobility.

*

Half the peasants are turning into unskilled and semi-skilled workers, half of the latter become skilled workers, half of the skilled workers technicians, engineers or others in professional employment. Every level is largely made up of those who come from below. Hungarian society as a whole is on the move and closed group-cultures are everywhere in a process of dissolution. An emphasis on the flowing and increasing process of mobility oversimplifies reality. Not everyone keeps to the rungs of the ladder, there are quite a few who progress by leaps. Others get stuck where they stand, and do not advance a single step. Others again, leave the path and find themselves outside society. Those who not only make no progress, but are also unable to maintain their large families, do not fit into this picture.

It would be a misunderstanding to believe that the continuous movement means social advancement for everyone and for every group. Becoming an urban worker meant going up in the world for agrarian proletarians and semi-proletarians, but not for well-to-do peasants. A semi-skilled or unskilled worker went up in the world when he turned into a skilled tradesman, but the owner of a small shop or workshop did not. Semi-skilled and unskilled workers went up even if they remained in their places, skilled tradesmen, clerks and professional people no longer did. The older generation of professional people and skilled tradesmen find that their income position has deteriorated. The consciousness of this is increased by the fact that their advantages over other sections have lessened—in some cases they have disappeared altogether. In the Csepel Iron and Metal Works, for instance, the income ratio between different sections was the following:

	Unskilled workers	Semi-skilled workers	Skilled workers	Foremen
In the thirties	100	125	150	190
The present position	100	110	128	160

The past as a basis for comparison is relevant mainly for those over fifty. For younger people the basis for comparison is either the neighbouring group, or the professional classes and skilled tradesmen of the more developed countries. They all consider that the difference between them and those immediately below them is not large enough, but that it is too large between them and their fellows in the West. Those who rose from below share this opinion. Their thoughts are not on the distance they have covered but on how far they wish to go.

The same paradox may be observed in the appreciation of the degree of mobility. Ten per cent of the sons of urban workers get to attend the day course of a college or university. (The figures are much lower for the children of the semi-skilled and unskilled.) This ratio is doubled if those who study at night are included. Seen from below, this does not appear too high a figure. Some of those who come from professional families, on the other hand, find that too many of their colleagues have risen from below.

The road upwards is a tiring one and it is full of trials and tribulations. Getting stuck on the way is even more painful. Exchanging cultures is often associated with a feeling of suffocation. One leaves the world into which one was born, loses one's inherited human contacts, and one is no longer understood by those from whom one descends. But it is equally difficult to find human contacts in the world into which one has arrived, to achieve mutual understanding with those who grew up in a different culture. Rising socially is often accompanied by loneliness, by a feeling of inferiority, by mistaken compensation, a flight into sickness and into an asocial attitude.

It should be pointed out once again that the process of dissolution of group-cultures is far from complete. The urban middle class, the gentleman-ly, the peasant, and the working-class ways of life still differ today, and the ways of life of their heirs also differ noticeably in the upper and middle layers. The value judgements they form of each—which are not always favourable—also differ and there are also differences in their image of the nature of society as well as in the ideal society which is postulated.

Some are saddened by the fact that the two-fisted working man, the man using his hammer, is gradually being replaced by a new type of worker in whose activities intellectual effort predominates, and who in his appearance and in his way of life differs hardly, or not at all, from clerks or professional people. But this process cannot be stopped, and delaying it would cause distortions in the economy, in society, and in the human soul. Sadness is out of place. Genuine democracy is unimaginable without the reception of the whole of culture, without the development of a common culture. Technological changes and the restructuring of the working class are creating the opportunities which will allow this to happen.

QUESTIONS OF SOCIAL EQUALITY

by

SÁNDOR LAKOS

S ocial equality is undoubtedly one of our most important objectives, but its achievement is one of the most complex and involved tasks in the building of socialism.

What is meant by socialist equality?

To be concise, we may say socialist equality is *equality according to work*. Not only in the distribution of income but in all domains of social life work is increasingly the factor that defines the position and situation of people. With us—at present—*work* is the centre of life. Yet we know that the ideal, equality according to work, will only be the outcome of a long historic process. Equality according to work necessarily involves, even in its fully developed form, temporary inequalities too, which, on the given level of development in the forces of production are inevitable. Therefore we take a stand, on the one hand, against mistaken "leftist", "new leftist", anarchistic views—emphasizing one-sidedly the ethical and moral aspects of equality—and their illusions and proclamations concerning some sort of complete social equality, and on the other hand, against the bourgeois interpretation of equality which wishes to exalt the inequalities temporarily existing in our system into a supreme social goal and project them into our future.

Property Relations

The starting point of the complex question of social equality may be the Marxian statement according to which the abolition of property relations which ensure exploitation makes possible the abolition of social and

Slightly abridged text of a lecture held at the Political Academy of the Central Committee of the Hungarian Socialist Workers' Party, on July 17, 1974.

political inequalities caused by these property relations. Social equality is expressed above all by the fact that the people are in power. Citizens of a socialist society enjoy equal rights to intervene in the affairs of society and to formulate policy.

By socialist equality we mean primarily the equality of social position and the increasing equalization of the relationship among the classes. The social structure of our country is characterized by the process of convergence. The different classes and strata are closer to each other in respect to living and working conditions as income relations of large groups in our society have become more equalized.

In spite of a more unified society, differences remain according to place of employment, scope of work and working conditions and life styles; differences between industry and agriculture, between white-collar and blue-collar work have not ceased. Inequalities may again appear in our society due to the shortcomings of our work but also due to objective causes. We must seek ways of gradually strengthening social equality while evaluating these circumstances. From this point of view we think mainly of the broadening of democracy.

People spend much of their time at their places of employment; it is there that they sense the equality or inequality of their social position most directly. Working people are, on the one hand, owners (as part owners of public property), and on the other, employees. In their capacity of employee they are structured into leaders, medium-level leaders, subordinates, etc., and thus they have opportunities for intervention and action of varying degrees. The dilemma of democracy in the work is to make possible and even encourage the increasing participation of workers in such a way that there is no obstruction to but rather strengthening of modern specialized management, discipline and organization. Decisions on production and technological processes cannot, of course, be transferred to collectives because expert personal leadership is required in modern production.

Within the plant, according to the position occupied in the decision-making hierarchy, there exist the right to issue instructions and the duty of implementation, and a dependence relation follows from this. This necessarily existing dependence may be counterbalanced by the collective and democratic judgement of the total work of the managers (not of partial measures). We think it only right to further develop democracy in the work in a direction which guarantees the right of a worker to express his opinions on the leadership and its work without detrimental repercussions; this implies a certain dependence of managers on the collective. Democratic control must also be improved in offices, a control which is fundamentally directed not at the evaluation of a single official or a single case, but of the entire work of an institution or office. The citizen who is in an unequal, often defenceless position in day-to-day matters should have access to a control mechanism which can rectify shortcomings that occur on a day-to-day basis.

In order to achieve a higher level of social equality, it is necessary to consciously reduce the differences caused by social division of labour, which are still being re-produced. We must strive to provide as many people as possible with convertible knowledge, knowledge that may be utilized elsewhere thus making greater social mobility possible. The establishment of greater social equality is especially important with the up-coming generation. We certainly must not accept—not even for a transitional period— that the division of labour or income be inherited, that decisive differences in starting one's career should be allowed to be recreated. This process must be restrained through effective regulators, mainly through the differentiated, long-range preference by state means for those who are in a relatively more disadvantageous starting position. We must make certain that the starting position of the up-coming generation becomes more and more equalized.

Last but not least, we must strive to prevent the transfer of inequalities in distribution, which necessarily live on in socialism, to other domains of social life. We must take a definite stand against income and property situations which create income and property prestige and resultant differences in social and community life. In socialism every man engaged in useful activity is equal from the viewpoint of social position, and this attitude must continue concomitant with our progress.

Differentiation

We may declare unequivocally that in our country opportunities for wide-ranging social equality are being created and that the main task today is only to complete and extend them; but we must emphasize just as unequivocally that in the economy—although unjustified inequalities persist—the main task today is not some sort of general equalization but a more consistent distribution according to work performance.

We may say without exaggeration that the establishment of equality according to work performance, which is based on socialist ownership of the means of production, is an achievement of historic, that is of epochal importance. The best of men have fought for centuries for the ideal that not

3*

privilege, nor property but work performed should be the measure of a man's worth. Today work performance—even if not fully and not consistently enough—is the decisive factor in our society.

In order to make the determining role of work unequivocal, we must endeavour, on the one hand, to achieve greater equalization commensurate to work and, on the other, to achieve greater differentiation. All situations must be equalized where income is not sufficiently adjusted to work accomplishment, therefore recently a uniform table of wages was elaborated the purpose of which was to ensure that identical wages are received for identical work no matter which branch, sector or enterprise of the economy is involved. For this reason economic regulators were altered in such a way as to make workers wages dependent to a larger extent on an individual's work and to a smaller extent on the company's profits, and great efforts are being made to see that the principle of equal wages for equal work should be fully applied to women too.

The above attitudes are also called upon to ensure that the differentiating role of our wage system become more consistent and that higher wages be received for economically more valuable and more responsible work. It is the ensemble of requirements of differentiation corresponding to work performance that we must be governed by. In this connection the regulation of the outflow of income deserves special attention.

The income ratio between the ten percent of those in the lowest income brackets and the top ten percent of wage earners is at present 1 : 4.5. In itself this does not seem exaggerated, but as far as the bulk of employees is concerned the spread of income differences is much smaller. Excluding for the time being the two extreme values, a greater differentiation of income is necessary for the bulk of workers. On this point we cannot stand for equality; it rather seems that we have not yet sufficiently recognized the magnitude of the forces that can be freed through additional income and wages rewarding more valuable and better work. We cannot leave out of consideration the fact that the bulk of differences in income is caused by individual differences in aptitude and knowledge. In addition to the multifaceted development of the personality, social and economic interests are also served by the stimulation of the development of aptitudes; here is where our largest economic reserves lay hidden. More effective stimulation for the better execution of basic activities is especially important. At the same time, we must demand to an even greater extent than before, equality in respect to discipline and work and the liquidation of laxity that has spread in many places. Distribution to everybody in accordance with his work can only be assured if everybody works according to his or her ability.

Income Ratios

Wage and income ratios between directors and subordinates are on the whole not exaggerated; in certain instances they are even insufficient. But a narrow circle of economic managers enjoyed huge incomes over a long period of time. This was due mainly to unjustifiably advantageous conditions for bonuses, which have since been altered by the government. In general, workers have a well-developed sense of justice and reality. Several surveys have shown that the overwhelming majority of workers do not take exception to the higher income level of the directors of the production process. Their criticism is rather directed at outstandingly high incomes which are disproportionate to work performance. Recent experience has led to the recognition that income acquired through work also has an economically justifiable and socially bearable upper limit which must be taken into consideration with the outflow and possibly with the regulation of income.

All sources which allow the acquisition of income disproportionate to work must be reexamined and a means of regulation worked out. In this respect the unusually high income of some groups of employees—especially in the tertiary sector—deserves attention. In many occupations, neither accomplishment of work nor training or social utility justifies the high income levels which are attainable. This also exercises a harmful effect on the consciousness of young people who are stimulated to look for opportunities of earning easy money instead of the more valuable activity that may be attained through knowledge.

The extraordinarily complicated and involved questions of the secondary, or more accurately the umpteenth, redistribution of the national income belong here. In the course of this process the ratios established on the basis of primary distribution are modified quite significantly. This redistribution involves a large number of different kinds of incomes, which fall under very different criteria, from overtime work in certain trades through various service activities to the renting and operation of certain means of production. Private allotments in addition to wages must not be underestimated either. We do not have primarily in mind classical "tipping" trades (hairdresser, waiter), where tips are mostly compensation for low wages, but of many other areas. Most of these activities are socially necessary and work-related; they are service activities which fill in gaps. Consequently our aim cannot be the reduction of these activities but only to make incomes more proportionate. An adequate, correctly differentiating income tax system may be suitable for this purpose.

It is not easy either to deal with incomes which do not originate from work. In principle there can be no income without work in socialism, but in societies building socialism, including our own, such sources may be present. We are not thinking of the well-known extreme examples of the lottery, the football pool and other winnings, the extent and importance of which do not deserve any special analysis, but of unearned incomes from making a profit with plot- and home ownership and the utilization of private or even state property in such a way which obviously does not bring an income commensurate with work but makes profits from more favourable situations and unsatisfied demands. This could include the income acquired by owners of plots and houses in the most beautiful spots in the country through letting the premises or rooms. Several measures have already been introduced to restrict this activity (tax increases on highly-valued property such as summer homes with several rooms), and the correctness of these measures has been confirmed by lively social response.

Our stand on such activities must nevertheless be circumspect and considered since these possibilities arise also from the fact that we cannot yet meet all recreation needs without use of private premises; consequently this renting does meet a genuine social demand. We may therefore restrict only the extent of the income, leaving aside the justifiable level of monetary incentives.

Differences in wages

Differences in wages persevering over a longer period of time may not only turn into income differences but into property differences as they become embodied in movable goods and personal property of varying size. If we accept the differentiating principle of distribution according to work, we must logically accept the differences resultant in the amount of personal property. We are not and cannot be against the frugal savings from earned incomes, and we even encourage them, for instance through tax exemption of Savings Bank deposits. The man who spends his income is not ranked above the one who saves it; the man who is building a house is no less a socialist than the one who uses his money for other purposes.

We must therefore reject all demagogy, all views which summarily condemn that accumulated wages can be converted into various objets in socialism and therefore condemn the objects themselves. On the other hand, neither can we disregard that in our country property may exist not only out of income, but—due to the relative proximity of the past—also as left-overs of property acquired in earlier periods. Similarly—to a limited extent—the possibility of employing outside labour has also survived.

Here we must make our position clear. From a long-range point of view it may be declared that the differences which derive from earlier property must gradually be reduced, and must eventually cease entirely. The reduction of other differences existing in property can be set as an objective only within reasonable limits. A great percentage of people save part of their income for themselves or for their heirs, and invest it in movable and landed property. The intention to care for one's descendants in this way is considered humanly justified, consequently laws ensure the right of inheritance. On the other hand, it is also just that the children of all working people should start life with equal chances, and viewed from this angle inheritance must not have a determining role. Only inheritance of a certain size can be accepted—in accordance with a recent governmental decree—and the unjustified portion is siphoned off by a progressive tax. At the same time, a great portion of society has already passed this stage and has entered, or is entering, the period of choice among possible life styles. It is here that a choice in the right direction becomes especially important.

It is clear for Marxists that existence determines consciousness. Obtaining better material circumstances may have a negative effect on ways of thinking and life styles in the case of those who ideologically are of socialist convictions, and of course even to a greater extent in the broader circle of citizens. It is also due to this trend that recently the so-called distortions of consciousness, exaggerated materialism and egotism had to be dealt with. We must fight these phenomena through our total policy, through a clear definition of our social objectives, through restrictive measures and through measures which increase esteem.

In summary we may state that in spite of considerable and truly significant achievements, differentiation according to work is inadequate and esteem for work is insufficient; on the other hand, there is too much differentiation which is not based on work or on factors commensurate to the work performed. While we must fight against incomes which are not earned through work or are not commensurate to it, we must continue to increase, by all possible means, esteem for authentic, socially useful, more valuable and better work.

Through a consistent and interdependent system of measures, the socialist state must reduce and counterbalance undesirable effects of income and property differences in living conditions, in public life, in the thinking of people. In order to counterbalance disproportions and to equalize disadvantageous situations it is thus necessary—and we have already taken important measures in this direction—for the state to offer graduated assistance. It is therefore entirely right that preference be given in matters of scholarship and placement in boarding schools and colleges to individuals with lower incomes or to their children on the basis of per capita income.

The enhancement of well-being is the objective and achievement of our system. Fundamentally it works towards the strengthening of socialist equality since it makes it possible for masses to rise from earlier backwardness. At the same time it is also clear that increasing well-being may not only strengthen socialist features, but may also work against socialist equality. In a society which has set out from relative backwardness and is becoming wealthier, it is impossible to prevent the quantity of material goods from also playing a role on the prestige scale of society. When an entire people rises at such a rapid rate out of such backwardness, even the satisfaction of fundamental needs becomes elevated into an important experience. There is no doubt that many people are still at this stage of evolution.

Social Policy

The principle of distribution according to work performed is necessarily supplemented in the period of socialism by social policy measures which correct or balance inequalities in all sectors.

How can the existence of social policy be theoretically justified under socialism, and what is its approximate content? By no means can it be identified with philanthropy, with charitable activity. In our circumstances this may not be a determining feature; it is not the giving of alms but the abolition of conditions which make charity become necessary which we consider fundamental. The important task of social policy is the equalization, to a certain extent, of inequalities of distribution according to work performance through, among other things, social allowances designed to this end. Care for those who are in disadvantageous situations through no fault of their own remains a permanent task of social policy, and the buds of Communism also appear in a certain sense in allowances which are in fact independent of the former principle.

Our Party has devoted much attention to social policy and can look back on significant achievements. Suffice it to mention universal social insurance, or the establishment of the pensioning age-limit—at a very favourable age by international standards too—and the relatively high level of pensions (in the most advanced capitalist countries men in general receive pensions five years later, and women often ten years later), the extension of recreation facilities at preferred rates, repeated raising of family allowances, the introduction of child care allowances, and many more.

We must nevertheless also recognize that our measures—although always designed to meet genuine demands—were not organically fitted into a concept of social policy which was carefully worked out, considered and justified in terms of long-range principles. There was, therefore, not sufficient assurance that partial measures always coincided with universal objectives.

Within the framework of a concept of social policy, the principal social-political areas for securing greater social equality may be formulated. The elimination of exaggerated differences between individual incomes or family incomes are of first importance. A situation opposed to the essence of socialism has developed in the fact that raising children has remained a financial detriment; it seems that this problem can only be remedied through increasing social support.

The improvement of the situation of those in the lowest income bracket and especially of pensioners is a fundamental problem. Social allowances play an important role in the development of social equality. Allowances may also be linked to employment, such as subsidized lunch in the plant, nurseries, day-care centres, etc., or may not be linked to employment, as for instance education, health and cultural care. According to another break-down, they may be free or given at preferred rates, in kind or money. In general, monetary allowances are more effective than free benefits given in kind because it may more effectively be guaranteed that they are used as intended. Consequently, it seems advisable in the future to increase allowances given in the form of money.

Social Allowances

In distribution policy economic and political factors are both present. While we consider it correct as a general objective that prices should approach input costs as much as possible, this does not appear achievable, even in the long run, in the domain of basic consumption (basic foods, mass transportation, housing, etc.). Consequently, subsidized (preferential) pricing which takes into consideration certain social groups and strata, and non-preferential pricing in respect to what are still considered today luxury items, is necessary. In this domain a peculiarly combined relationship of wages and allowances develops. In the prices of products bought with cash workers also receive enormous sums of state subsidies (amounting to several ten thousand million forints every year); therefore most people share in social goods in a greater proportion than simply in accordance with their work.

It is precisely this situation that we must rethink. Taking the various areas of subsidies and allowances together, it turns out that at the present socialist stage of evolution a not insignificant amount of social products goes to workers, not on the basis of work performed, but as an allowance based on social and other reasons. Thus means are tied down which could be used to stimulate better work. Consequently, in the next phase, the range of social allowances should be widened only to a justifiable extent.

But we must also take into consideration that we are entering a higher stage of socialist evolution, and at this stage within our long-range perspective of socialism, we must gradually develop the already existing "not-according-to-work" elements of our distribution system—which were introduced at an earlier stage perhaps prematurely or to an exaggerated extent—into communistic elements. Therefore, within our long-range economic-social developmental concepts, an increase in social allowances is planned to proceed at a faster rate than wages. A well-paced realization of this task is possible only if economic possibilities are taken into account, and its accomplishment will, at the same time, be an important factor in the completion and strengthening of socialist equality.

Only the Beginning

How can our position on the question of socialist equality be summed up? First of all, although equality of a nature and extent unimaginable in earlier societies has already been achieved or is gradually being achieved in decisive areas, socialist society is only the beginning of a society of equality. At the present evolutionary stage of society, our guiding principle in the most important tasks which affect all areas of social life is distribution according to work performance and the central role of work. Any view which questions this principle will only lead to utopias and mistakes. If we strive today for an equality which is not well-founded economically and if, in order to please, we overemphasize certain aims that are correct in the long run, we would not only fail to achieve greater equality but would jeopardize the equality that has already been achieved.

Socialist society is a society which is structured in many ways and under the given circumstances all differences caused by structuring cannot yet be equalized. Equality commensurate to work performance is the greatest equality which we are able to afford at this time, even if we recognize this is far from being a full or total equality. But a scale of values based on work performance, the universality of material and moral esteem—and the trimming off of every extreme which diverges from this principle—would constitute in itself en enormous achievement towards the realization of socialist equality. In the meantime, in many areas—since we shall never lose sight of our long-range aims—we may also proceed, as we have already, along the path of the gradual strengthening of communistic elements of equality.

THE HUNGARIAN ECONOMY

1945–1969

by

EGON KEMENES

An economic survey can only give an incomplete picture of the changes that took place in the life of Hungarians during the past quarter century. It would be just as futile to measure the development of a nation merely by economic indexes, as if we were to measure a child's development by its height only—however welcome development in either case might be.

Economic analyses can give answers to questions such as the extent to which the country has utilized its economic resources during the last quarter of a century, or how society has made use of the work done, or how much more is used to satisfy individual needs. But economic analyses can only give indirect information about many other changes or their effect on the life of society or individuals such as the extent to which individual choice in respect to social status, employment, mode of life and alternatives regarding the satisfaction of needs has increased as a result of a higher standard of living and the end of a class society, as well as to what extent security and human dignity are more general and worry and humilation rarer. Yet, these are, when all is said and done, the final ends and aims of every kind of economic development.

Besides, even the most exhaustive and detailed data about the present economic situation would only allow the drawing of indirect inferences as regards pressing question that arise in every country with a developed economy, including Hungary. How will people—freed from the restrictions of poverty—avail themselves of their increasing leisure, what will they do with more money and more time on their hands.

Yet, within its own limited field economic analysis can give answers to some questions of decisive importance from the aspect of the nation as such and the life of individuals forming the nation. A reader interested in problems of world-wide importance might wish to obtain information about Hungary's present economic situation as such as well as compare it with countries of a similar character. Economists might also be interested in the details of the process of growth that produced the present situation as well as in the internal factors and interconnections of Hungary's economy.

Both aspects raise a number of further questions. If the economic situation is to be regarded as the outcome of growth, the level from which development started is of considerable importance. One might also ask how the economy would have developed without errors, and without being misdirected. What sacrifices had to be made in order to obtain the actual progress made.

LEVEL AND GROWTH OF NATIONAL INCOME

The most frequently applied fundamental index of economic development is per capita national income or gross national product (GNP). In Hungary —and in other socialist countries—economic growth is measured by national income, whereas Western countries as a rule use gross national product* as the standard of measurement.

In Hungary in 1969, per capita national income was some $720. This sum is—if the difference between the two concepts, i.e. national income and gross national product is taken into account—by and large in conformity with data supplied by the World Bank.** Thus, as regards per capita national income Hungary's place is at the lower limit of that group of European countries to which Austria, Czechoslovakia, Italy and so on belong at a somewhat higher level. Therefore, Hungary belongs to the group of medium-developed European countries.

The development of the country's per capita national income in the immediate past permits the assumption that Hungary's position will improve in this respect, in other words, it is to be expected that the difference in level between Hungary and the more developed West European countries will decrease. In 1969, the national income per head was about two-and-a-half times higher than that in 1950 (1950 is the basis year used by the Hungarian Central Statistical Office for long-range comparison of indexes). This corresponds to an annual average growth rate of about 5 per cent, slightly surpassing that of most European countries. Between 1950 and 1966 the growth rate of the per capita GNP was 4.5 per cent per annum

* The gross national product surpasses national income by the value of services and amortization.
** See *Finance and Development*, a monthly of the World Bank, 1969, No. 1, p. 40. According to it Hungary's per capita GNP was $800 in 1966. If besides the difference between the two concepts, the difference in time is also taken into account, approximately the above value is obtained.

in the Common Market countries, 2 per cent in the EFTA countries, 3.8 per cent in France, 4.9 per cent in Italy and 2.2 per cent in Britain.* In view of Hungary's progress, particularly after 1958, it is hoped that its position will further improve. Between 1958 and 1969, the annual increase per head was 5.7 per cent on an average, whereas that of sixteen West European countries was 4.4 per cent per annum during an approximately identical period (1960–1967).

In order to appreciate the position Hungary takes in respect to per capita national income the level from whence the country's development started 25 years ago must be known.

During the Second World War 40 per cent of Hungary's improved assets were destroyed, and a considerable proportion of skilled people of working age were war victims. War damage in Hungary amounted to about $4,000–5,000 million. Due to losses in productive capacity, stores and manpower, the national income in 1945–46 amounted to only 45 per cent of that in 1938–39. Ten per cent of the national income was spent on reparations and another 6 per cent on the most urgent reconstruction works. After the war Hungary went through a severe inflation.

Due to enormous efforts economic reconstruction was successful so that the pre-war level was reached by 1949. At that time, per capita national income amounted to about $240.

From the end of the reconstruction period Hungary's national income developed as follows:

National Income Index Numbers
(at comparable prices)
1949 = 100

1949	100	1959	204
1950	121	1960	225
1951	141	1961	239
1952	139	1962	250
1953	157	1963	263
1954	150	1964	276
1955	164	1965	279
1956	146	1966	301
1957	180	1967	322
1958	191	1968	338
		1969	359

* In this study, Hungarian data are taken from publications of the Hungarian Central Statistical Office; data concerning other countries are taken from UN and OECD publications. Please note: the Hungarian Statistical Yearbook is issued in English as well.

The following diagram shows the development of national income:

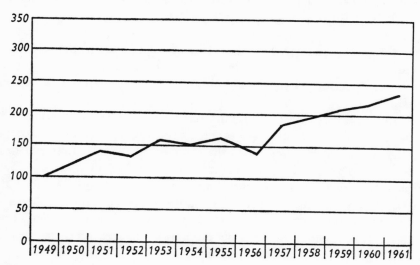

The diagram clearly shows the process as a result of which Hungary's national income grew from $2,100 million in 1949 to $7,400 million in 1969. According to the calculation below, the latter sum corresponds to a gross national product of $8,700 million:

national income	$7,400 million
national income + services =	
net national product	$8,100 million
net national product + amortization =	
gross national product	$8,700 million

Taking the period as a whole, the annual average increase was 5.7 per cent, that is, it was far higher than the average growth rate of 2 per cent per annum in the inter-war period.

It appears from the diagram that the development process of the national economy can be divided into two phases. After the spectacular upswing in some of the years between 1949 and 1958, growth slowed down, and a certain recession set in. Accordingly, in this period the overall increase was slower than in the second phase, from 1958 to 1969, during which fluctuation decreased and development became more steady. The difference is not due, or not only due to economic causes, but also and mainly to political ones. The steady development after 1958 indicates not only a realistic national economic policy but also that this policy rested on consistent basic principles.

In line with economic growth, the *structure* of the economy also underwent a transformation. Industrial production grew by leaps and bounds, while agriculture developed only moderately. The third sector (transport, trade and services) developed by and large in line with the growth of the economy as such.

Whereas industry and the building trade only produced 45 per cent of the national income in 1950, the proportion of these sectors rose to 67 per cent, in 1969. At the same time, the share of agriculture decreased from 37 per cent to 20 per cent. A breakdown by numbers of those employed between individual economic sectors also shows the transformation of the pattern of production. In 1950, the total number of those employed in agriculture amounted to 52 per cent and only 19 per cent were employed in industry; by 1969, however, this proportion changed to 30 per cent in agriculture, and 35 per cent in industry.

The decrease in the share of agriculture was only partly due to the fast growth of industrial production. Another cause was that agriculture only slightly developed during the past twenty-five years. This also manifests itself by the fact that in spite of the relatively fast decrease in the number of those employed in agriculture, a relatively large proportion of all those in employment is still working in agriculture as compared to other countries. The table below shows the percentage of agricultural workers in some European countries on the basis of 1965 data:

United Kingdom	3.5	France	18.2
Belgium	5.7	Austria	20.3
Netherlands	8.0	Czechoslovakia	21.1
German Federal Republic	11.1	Italy	26.1
Denmark	17.0	Hungary	34.0

It should, however, be noted that in the past few years agricultural production rose faster. While the annual increase was 1.8 per cent in 1961–1965, it amounted to an average 2.7 per cent int 1966–1968.

There is no doubt that the developed modern character of the structure of the entire Hungarian economy is due to the speedy increase of the share of industry. It was precisely industrial development (more machines and artificial fertilizer) that produced the conditions for a quicker increase of agricultural production the results of which started to show in the last few years.

The changing proportion between investments and consumption also pertains to the question of structure. The relationship between accumulation, the source of investments and national income indicates the kind of growth on the one hand, and shows, on the other, at the price of what sacrifices society has achieved the actual economic development.

In the light of the aforesaid it appears that a high rate of accumulation was characteristic of the allocation of national income in Hungary over the past 25 years. In 1938, the rate of accumulation amounted to around 7 per cent, in 1949 it already reached 21.3 per cent and, at the beginning of the fifties 25 per cent. The rate of accumulation fluctuated between 1954 and 1959; it was about 20 per cent in 1959, and rose—not steadily, though— to the present 25 per cent. In the past 7 to 8 years, it amounted to an average 25–26 per cent. Recently only some of the developed capitalist countries (the Federal German Republic and Japan) have reached a similarly high investment ratio. In Hungary the accumulation ratio is higher than in most of the developed capitalist countries. Detailed international comparative data are only available concerning the years 1961–1965. In this period gross accumulation as a percentage of the gross national product was the following:

Hungary	32
German Federal Republic	27
Austria	26
Sweden	24
Italy	23
France	22
United Kingdom	18

However, the efficiency of this considerable accumulation activity was not always high if it is measured by the effect it exerted on the growth of national income. In Hungary, the incremental capital output ratio (that shows the per cent increase of investments needed for one per cent increase of the national income) developed as follows:

1950–55	3.14
1955–60	2.18
1960–65	4.43
1965–69	2.10

Striving after spectacular successes, the economic policy in the years 1950–1955 neglected important investments, indispensable for a well-founded economy. These omissions were remedied and the high incremental capital output from 1960 to 1965 is due to a number of investments effectuated in the field of infrastructure and agriculture. Owing to their character, the effect of these investments did not manifest itself till a later point in time. The more favourable average index in 1965–1969 is due, among others, to the investments made in from 1960 to 65.

If the origin of national income is viewed through a breakdown by sectors it appears that almost the entire economic activity takes place within the state and co-operative sectors, in accordance with the socialist character of the Hungarian economy.

Origin of National Income by Social Sectors in 1969

State sector	77 per cent
Co-operative sector	20 per cent
Private sector	3 per cent
Total	100 per cent

SOME IMPORTANT FIELDS OF ECONOMIC ACTIVITY

During the past 25 years, industry was the fastest developing sector of the Hungarian economy. In 1969, net industrial production amounted to more than four times that in 1950 (index = 425). In the first half of this period the average increase was an annual 10 per cent whereas it was about 7 per cent after 1958. The rate of growth of industrial production surpassed that of most developed capitalist countries. A comparison of international data available up to 1965 shows the following:

Average Rate of Growth of Industrial Production per annum (per cent)

	1950–55	1955–60	1960–65
Hungary	13.8	7.6	7.3
Common Market countries	9.4	6.7	5.6
EFTA countries	4.0	3.3	2.2

In line with the fast increase of industrial production, the pattern of production also changed. The production of some sectors of industry that were particularly important for the development of the Hungarian economy increased to their eighteen to twentyfold in the course of 25 years.

The following table shows this process on the basis of gross production indexes:

Industrial sector	Index of gross production in 1969 (1950 = 100)
Heavy industry total	620
within it:	
chemical industry	1,210
telecommunication and vacuum technical industry	1,810
precision engineering	2,120
Light industry total	492
within it:	
textile clothing industry	765
wood-working industry	782

The production of some materials and products of basic importance developed as follows:

Name of basic materials	Unit	Production in		
		1938	1949	1968
Electric power	million kWh	1,399	2,520	13,155
Coal	thousand tons	9,360	11,838	27,213
Crude oil	thousand tons	43	506	1,807
Natural gas	million cu.metres	8	372	2,691
Steel	thousand tons	647	860	2,903

With respect to coal production it should be noted that the maximum output—31,548 tons—was reached in 1964. In view of the fact that the economic efficiency of Hungarian coal mining is declining since some mines are unfavourably sited, while other fuels—oil and natural gas—are used in increasing quantities, it did not seem advisable to develop coal mining, moreover the production by some mines working under adverse conditions was discontinued.

The economically unsatisfactory nature of coal mining was one of the factors due to which the productivity of industral labour did not increase as rapidly as industrial production itself. Up to and including 1968, the average rate of growth of productivity was about 4 per cent per annum.

Although this surpasses the corresponding data of some countries with old-established industries (e.g. Britain 2.7 per cent and Belgium 3.8 per cent), yet it is lower than that of Austria (5.2 per cent), and France (5.3 per cent), or of some recently industrialized countries such as Italy (6.5 per cent) and Rumania (8.7 per cent).

The breakdown by sector of industrial production shows that the socialist (state and co-operative) sector produced 98 per cent of the industrial output in 1969 and that 96 per cent of all persons employed in industry worked in the socialist sector (4 per cent were employed in the private sector). In the state sector, that produced 93 per cent of the gross in the sixties, considerable industrial concentration took place. As a result of merging smaller firms into large industrial units, the number of state industrial enterprises decreased from 1,368 in 1960 to 811 by the end of 1968. At the same time the number of employees and workers working in state industrial enterprises increased from 1,144,000 in 1960 to 1,470,000 by the end of 1968.

The new economic reform, that came into force on January 1, 1968, brought about considerable changes in the functioning of state industrial enterprises. The scope of entrepreneurial decisions—including a large proportion of investment decisions—was considerably extended; in the future, enterprises will have to draw on their own resources and bank loans to finance investments to a far greater extent than hitherto.

For various socio-political, economic and within the latter, investment policy reasons, agriculture developed at an only moderate rate during the same period. Ideas concerning the development of agriculture that rested on sound socio-political foundations on the one hand, and took into consideration the importance of agriculture in Hungarian economic life on the other, only became current after 1958.

Net agricultural production increased by only 28 per cent between 1949 and 1969 and grew steadily at the new, higher level since the beginning of the sixties only. It considerably fluctuated in the earlier years. Animal husbandry grew at a faster rate than agriculture in the strict sense.

The question of the ownership of land and the structure of enterprises was finally settled by the beginning of the sixties; the sectoral division of cultivated land developed at that time; in 1969 it was the following:

Arable Land Area by Social Sectors

State farms	14
Co-operative sector	81
Private farms	5
Total	100

After the sectoral division had finally established itself, a concentration process took place in both the state and the co-operative sector of agriculture, as a result of which larger production units were formed. However, the larger dimensions of the new co-operative units still permit supervision by the membership and do not hinder co-operative democracy. The data below indicate the extent of the concentration process:

Agricultural Units of Management
(mid-year data)

	1960	1968
State farm	333	208
Agricultural producers' co-operatives	4,265	2,846

Hungarian agricultural production only started to grow at a faster rate in the mid-sixties. The average yield of wheat, the country's most important cereal, reached 27 quintals per hectar (= 2,471 acres) in 1969 as against 13.7 quintals per hectare in 1931–1940 and 14.6 quintals per hectare in 1951–1955. This speeded-up growth—the result of which will manifest itself in the seventies only—is due, among others, to the fact that agricultural investments (and industrial ones related to agriculture) considerably increased since the beginning of the sixties. The higher level of mechanization made it possible to machine-harvest 93 per cent of the corn crops. The increase in the stock of tractors expresses best the development of the level of mechanization:

Number and Density of Tractors

Year	Number of tractors	Arable land per tractors, hectare
1935	7,014	799
1950	13,377	413
1960	41,015	129
1965	64,231	79
1969	70,000*	72*

* = preliminary data

Land under irrigation—in 1939 only 14,000 hectares, and even in 1950 not more than 33,000 hectares—reached 205,000 hectares in 1967. Due to progress in the chemical industry, artificial fertilizer production reached a high level by the end of the sixties leading to increased average yields.

Fertilizer Consumption (phosphorous, nitrogenous, potassic) by Hungarian Agriculture

Year	Total fertilizer consumption (1,000 tons)	Fertilizer consumption in quantities of active substance	
		Total (1,000 tons)	Per hectare of arable land (kg)
1938	73	13	2.3
1950	185	34	6.4
1960	748	141	31.4
1967	1,876	370	96.6
1968	2,277	450	124.0

FOREIGN TRADE

Apart from its considerable bauxite resources, Hungary is poor in raw materials. Hence, the growth of industrial production inevitably goes together with an increase of imports. In addition, Hungary is a small country with only ten million inhabitants. The restricted nature of the home market does not allow the mass production of many articles, this is only possible if export markets are available. Thus, it was obvious from the very first that the growth of the national economy is inconceivable without a simultaneous increase in foreign trade. At present, Hungary's foreign trade amounts to 40 per cent of national income.

Higher import needs—due to post-1949 industrialization and the necessity to pay for them by exports—gave the impulse to the development of foreign trade. In the years 1950–1955, an increase of the national income by 1 per cent went together with an 1.25 per cent increase in foreign trade. In the period of growth after 1958—referred to by Prof. József Bognár as the "intensive phase" of Hungary's economic growth*—foreign trade was of similar importance. Between 1960 and 1965, a 1 per cent growth in national income was accompanied by an 1.84 per cent increase in foreign trade.

* See the chapter "Economy" in the book: *Information Hungary*. Budapest, 1968, published jointly by Akadémiai Kiadó, Budapest, and Pergamon Press, Oxford. (Published as Volume 2 of the Information Series "Countries of the World".)

Hence, it was a matter of course that foreign trade increased at a faster rate than national income. The foreign trade index (1950 = 100) increased to 635 by 1969.

According to preliminary data obtained from official Hungarian sources, Hungarian imports amounted to $1,960 million and exports to $2,120 million in 1969. This means that foreign trade amounted to approximately $400 per capita as against only twenty dollars per capita in 1938. As regards the magnitude of per capita foreign trade Hungary is roughly on the level of Czechoslovakia, the German Democratic Republic and Italy. However, Hungary's per capita foreign trade falls short of that of Austria which is about $600, not to mention Switzerland and Holland with a per capita foreign trade of some $1,300.

Of course, this rapid increase in foreign trade led to considerable changes in the assortment of goods within foreign trade. Before the war, the overwhelming part of Hungarian imports consisted of raw materials and semi-finished goods, and that of exports of agricultural products. By the end of the sixties, the share of machines and equipment increased in Hungary's imports. Agricultural production fell behind and machines and consumer goods took the first place in exports. The table below shows the changes:

Pattern of Foreign Trade by Commodity Groups
(percentage)

Commodity groups	1938	1950	1960	1968
Imports:				
Machines and equipment	10.6	22.0	27.8	29.6
Industrial consumer goods	8.8	1.5	5.0	7.6
Raw materials and semi-finished goods	73.1	72.7	58.9	54.0
Foodstuffs and raw materials for the food processing industry	7.5	3.8	8.3	8.8
Exports:				
Machines and equipment	9.3	23.0	38.0	27.4
Industrial consumer goods	10.2	20.3	17.8	24.4
Raw materials and semi-finished goods	23.5	17.5	23.6	27.0
Foodstuffs and raw materials for the food processing industry	57.0	39.2	20.6	21.2

It should be noted that the socialist countries are Hungary's main commercial partners, providing a large and stable market. By and large 75 per cent of Hungary's total foreign trade is transacted with socialist countries. However, trade with other countries is also increasing; the auspicious growth of East–West trade is appropriately represented by the territorial structure of Hungary's foreign trade:

Development of the Hungarian Foreign Trade Broken Down by Groups of Countries
(in percentages)

Groups of countries	1960	1967	1968
Socialist countries	74	71	70
Developed capitalist countries	22	24	25
Developing countries	4	5	5
Foreign trade total	100	100	100

This short survey of the development of the Hungarian foreign trade would be incomplete if we were to disregard two new features which emerged since the economic reform was introduced in 1968. First, Hungary's exports to developed capitalist countries considerably increased in the first half of 1969 and surpassed by 25 per cent the exports of the same period in the previous year. This is due to two factors: in the first place, as a result of the reform, a number of industrial enterprises were authorized to establish direct contacts with customers abroad. In the past, foreign trade enterprises held a monopolistic position in this field, now, however, large industrial enterprises are increasingly active on foreign markets. In the second place, together with the economic reform, new and more realistic foreign exchange rates were established as a result of which production for export—that, as is well known, requires higher standards and more careful execution—became more profitable, so that enterprises are now more interested in exploring new markets.

Another new feature is that in addition to merely commercial deals, production co-operation agreements are being concluded more and more frequently, providing the opportunity for further commodity exports to third countries.

THE ECONOMY AND SOCIETY

In the last analysis, the yardstick of every kind of economic development is the degree society's standard of living—and within the latter that of the individual—improved.

Hungarian society became more urbanized as compared to the past. In line with this industrialization process, a considerable part of the rural population migrated into towns. In 1949, only 36 per cent of the population lived in towns, in 1969, however, the proportion of town-dwellers amounted to 45 per cent. The number of working women increased too: in 1969, 40 out of every 100 in employment were women. These two factors, to mention no others, considerably influence consumer behaviour and the pattern of consumption.

Hungarian society grows younger and older simultaneously. It grows younger because the proportion of young people as compared to able-bodied adults is large. In addition, infant mortality has decreased considerably: deaths under one year of age per 1,000 live births decreased from 1.31 in 1938 to 0.37 in 1967. On the other hand, live births which was at its lowest (1.2 per thousand) in 1962, is on the increase and has reached 1.5 per thousand in 1968. At the same time, improved public health conditions have lengthened the average life span and the proportion of the aged is continually increasing. 12 per cent were 60 and above in 1949, by 1967 they were 16 per cent. The proportion of pensioners amounted to 13 per cent of the total population at the beginning of 1968, although it was only 6 per cent in 1952 (in Hungary, peasants are also entitled to pension). Only 2 per cent in 1952 of the national income was spent on pensions whereas by 1967 it was 5 per cent.

The character of employment also influences consumption and the allocation of incomes. The breakdown of those in employment by occupations was the following on January 1, 1968:

workers and employees	72.3 per cent
co-operative members and helping family members	27.7 per cent
self-employed and helping family members	3.0 per cent
Total	100.0 per cent

By the middle of 1969—when the total population amounted to 10,250,000—the number of those in employment was 5,000,000. At present, there are only 106 dependents per 100 earners, a remarkable proportion by international standards. There are more than 2,000,000 women at work.

Real income has increased almost two-and-a-half-fold since 1950:

Per Capita Personal Real Income

1950	100
1967	219
1968	230
1969	240

One of the main factors in the favourable growth of real wages was the stability of consumer prices. Since 1951, the latter have not changed substantially, from 1965 to 1969 the price index shows a slight upward tendency amounting to an annual 1 per cent. Between 1960 and 1967, consumer prices rose by 29 per cent in Austria, by 27 per cent in Britain, by 35 per cent in Italy, and by 29 per cent in the Netherlands. The stable price level was convenient and secure for the consumer, but acted, to a certain degree, as a brake in the development of industrial production, i.e. from the point of view of the efficiency of enterprises. In view of this the economic reform did away with some of the price restrictions in 1968. This decision did not bring about considerable changes in the price index while it favourably affected the assortment and prices of the industrial production and stimulated enterprises to compete with each other.

In the retail trade in 1968, 67 per cent of which was in state ownership, 32 per cent were co-operative shops and 1 per cent were privately owned; the turnover in industrial products increased at a faster rate than that of foodstuffs; within industrial products durable consumer goods were in great demand. However, the fastest increase took place in the field of services. While the commodity consumption of the population grew by an annual average of 4.3 per cent between 1950 and 1966, the population's demand for services increased by 5.2 per cent p.a. during the same period. However, the service industries are limited for the time being and are at present the bottleneck in the Hungarian standard of life. 17 out of a hundred of those in employment worked in one or another section of the service industry in 1967, while 27 per cent did in Britain, in Belgium 24 per cent and in Norway 19 per cent.

The demand for services is partly due to the increase in the stock of consumer goods. For example, there were only 13,000 motor-cars in 1950 whereas their number amounted to 145,000 by the end of 1967. By 1969 their number had grown to 200,000. Today, practically every family has one or more radios and there were 114 television sets per 1,000 inhabitants by the end of 1967 (117 in Austria, 181 in Czechoslovakia, 151 in France, 132 in Italy, 125 in Switzerland and 254 in Britain).

On the whole, consumption developed favourably in Hungary. The annual average increase was 4.2 per cent between 1957 and 1967; this is higher than in Britain (3.3 per cent) between 1955 and 1964, but less than in France (5.0 per cent) or Italy (5.4 per cent) during the same period.

The growth in incomes enables the population to save considerable sums of money over and above the sums spent on consumption. The table below shows the growth of the National Savings Bank's stock of deposits during the past ten years:

Savings Deposits by the Population
(at the end of the year)

1958	2,300 million forints
1960	5,500 million forints
1966	23,000 million forints
1968	29,000 million forints
1969	35,000* million forints

* preliminary data

The supply and wider assortment of durable consumer goods as well as the building of privately owned apartment and one-family houses, and the possibility of making trips abroad, etc. has led to the spread of the habit of saving.

Since Hungary joined more intensively in international travel at the beginning of the sixties, travelling abroad has become a favourite way of spending money.

Year	Foreigners visiting Hungary	Hungarians travelling abroad
	(thousands)	
1937	383	220
1960	247	299
1968	2,403	929

In 1968, 2,030,000 visited Hungary from socialist countries and 373,000 from non-socialist ones. In the same year 778,000 Hungarians visited socialist countries while 151,000 travelled to non-socialist countries. The extent of the social security and public health system in Hungary covers the entire population. The number of medical practitioners gives some indication of the standard of the service provided.

Number of Medical Practitioners
(at the end of the year)

Year	Number of medical practitioners, total	Medical practitioners per 10,000 inhabitants
1938	10,590	11.6
1950	10,229	11.0
1960	15,698	15.7
1968	21,865	21.3

These figures are good by European standards if it is taken into account that the number of physicians per 10,000 inhabitants was 18.3 in the German Federal Republic (in 1966), 18.0 in Austria (in 1966), 14.9 in France (in 1965), 14.1 in Holland (in 1965) and 10.9 in Britain (in 1965).

The above data give some indication of the increased standard of living of the man in the street as compared to the situation in Hungary a quarter of a century ago. Well-being is not spectacular and does not reach the heights of some developed West European countries, but it is sound, well-founded and reaches the broad masses of the people. Hungary is not an "affluent society" but it is already a modern industrial society, a "consumer society"—together with the comfort and advantages of the present and the many problems the future holds in store.

The coming into being of a consumer society is not some kind of tolerated by-product of socialism, but the consciously realized result of Hungary's socialist economic policy. The Hungarian way of thinking is alien to the idyllic conditions described in Huxley's illusory *Island*, Hungarians are aware of the fact that in a modern world economy every "island" that takes no notice of technical and economic progress is doomed. At the same time, Hungarians are also aware of the danger of a consumer society as described in Huxley's other Utopia, *Brave New World*. This means that Hungarians neither reject the consumer society nor do they consider it an end in itself. In the Hungarian view, it is a means (although an indispensable one) by dint of which the life of man—freed from the worries of keeping body and soul together—obtains broader and fairer prospects and, thus, is able to show his better self. To search for the means and ways to reach this and to familiarize the members of society with these aims is a pressing need in view of the increasing abudance of material goods.

ECONOMIC GROWTH
AND THE QUALITY OF LIFE

by

JÓZSEF BOGNÁR

P roblems in connection with the quality of life are now timely and derive from the well-known fact that there are measurable and not measurable, at least given current instruments, phenomena and indices affecting the life of both societies and individuals. Things and phenomena may perhaps become measurable tomorrow though they are not measurable today, and the social sciences must endeavour to make measurable as many factors as possible. I consider it even more important that the broad interpretation of problems connected with the quality of life leads us back to those important questions which attracted the attention of the classics of economics, including the physiocrats, and of Marx, though his class position differed. These questions emerged once again in discussions connected with the welfare state and its rejection by a section of revolutionary youth, with various efforts and experiments in European socialist countries, as well as the concept of growth of those developing countries which are based on a strong traditional system, societies which endeavour to create an equilibrium between past and future.

These great questions can be formulated, briefly and summarily, in the following way: what is the function and aim of the economy, how far does its freedom of movement range within society and the state, what is the relationship between the economic and the non-economic objectives and functions of society? Which political, social and cultural preconditions (background) favour economic development, what kind of effect do mechanisms governing economic life exert on other (internal and external) objectives and power relations as well as on its scales of value? Whence derive the aims of economic development: are they to be considered independent aims, unrelated or superior to other factors, or do these aims derive from a given philosophical system, being an important instrument themselves in the achievement of more complex aims? Finally, what is the direct or indirect effect of economic development or the attainment of outlined or planned aims on the general disposition, behaviour and satisfaction of society as a whole, of particular groups and individuals?

One is justified in raising these major questions particularly these days since everyday life is becoming more and more complex. A given society or state (nation) has to achieve not just one great aim but an entire system of interdependent objectives. To give an example, in spite of scarce resources (economic questions) a certain equilibrium of forces (political and social questions) has to be established. Amidst divergent or even conflicting class and group interests societies and states have to provide for some sort of dissemination of knowledge, moreover, to improving it (education and science), and all this has to be carried out under given international political conditions the dynamism of which promotes or hinders governments in reaching their objectives.

The fact that the subject has been raised makes it obvious in itself that the quality of life is a problem of common concern; the question, however, does not emerge in the same manner in the major capitalist countries which, through the generations and as a result of industrial development, have accumulated a wealth of material, technological and intellectual resources; in the European socialist countries which—after consolidation and the development of a firm system of values—now strive for faster economic and technological growth and, finally, in developing countries which—after having attained political independence—have only recently started to build a new society and economy in the midst of enormous internal and international difficulties.

These societies, being apperceptive (adopting) media, are in very different situations; hence, they react to the same impulses, that is to the philosophy of the quality of life, in a different manner. I therefore propose to analyse the question from three different points of view and to draw separate conclusions and discuss problems separately in connection with developed capitalist, socialist and developing countries.

It is known that the classics, Adam Smith and Ricardo, established economic theory as a logically coherent system of causal relations. In this respect allow me to insist on the great merits of the physiocrats and to point to a few remarks by Aristotle who considered economics as a subclass of politics and attributed the same importance to the concept of value in the field of economics as to that of rights and duties in the sphere of law. The classics determined the concept of value, that of general value and not that of exchange value, discovered the existence of social economics, acknowledged the existence of interests, although they believed in the "harmony of interests" within the laws of economics, and they declared the possible happiness of man to be the aim of economic activity. In addition to the idea of welfare, the postulate of human (social) equality came to the fore right at the beginning, for Ricardo primarily aimed at discovering laws which regulate the proper distribution of goods.

The first views and theories on economics developed under the influence of natural law on the one hand, and under that of English empirical-utilitarian social philosophy, on the other.

This philosophy considered the interests of the community to be decisive, conceiving them as the sum total of the satisfaction achieved by individuals. This is what made the belief in harmony essential. It did not merely follow on the influence of Kepler or Newton.

Economic rationalism, called a system of rational aims by Max Weber, came into being against this philosophical background; it means, in the main, the relation between highest effect and smallest effort, that is, it looks for an optimum relationship between aims and means in the interest of public welfare.

It logically follows from the aforesaid that the postulate of "rational economics" in the practical sense is also a derived principle (an *a posteriori* principle, according to Gunnar Myrdal), i.e. it is a component or derivative of a system composed on a philosophical basis. Thus it is obvious that this postulate—however important it might be *per se* and/or in promoting economic development and in determining the priorities of development—cannot subject the system of values of society as a whole in a philosophical or logical sense. The individual is, as a matter of fact, not only a "homo oeconomicus" but a human being who has some kind of concrete relation to the system of values and aims of his age and society; accordingly, he maintains certain views about the equality of men, the right to learn and to work and about his own value-creating abilities. Society (the state), however, has to provide for the unfolding of every kind of faculty for the public good and must keep up a certain equilibrium between rational economic aims and the postulates of the adopted system of value.

Real problems emerged in theory when—at a later date—requirements of rational thinking adapted—not to social economics—but to capitalist enterprises were considered the peak of the system of values, while economics was treated as "neutral" in questions related to interests, and to the situation

3*

and conditions of life of the great majority of the population. Economics must be free of values *(wertfrei)*, economics has nothing to do with justice or injustice (Clark), it must consider what actually is and not what ought to be (Pigou), economics should only be concerned with subjective values for only such exist (Jevons). These views on the one hand imply that the interest of the capitalist in making profits takes priority over all other values; scholars abstracted from property relations and distribution based on them; real economic processes, however, developed on the basis of and through property relations. On the other hand, these views put bourgeois economics in a difficult position, it was not able to explain certain phenomena which caused increasing tension, what is more, it simply refused to admit the existence of these phenomena altogether. On the basis of the law of Say, for example, they taught—before J. M. Keynes—that supply creates its own demand, thus, unemployment cannot occur. It is true that John Stuart Mill and Alfred Marshall also said something similar, this, however, is no excuse for scholars to deny, under normal conditions, contradictions which have developed in reality and assumed considerable proportions. J. M. Keynes rightly argued that professional economists did not bother much about the fact that their theories and observable facts were inconsistent: this inconsistency, however, did not escape the attention of common people who did not respect economics as they respected other sciences, the theories of which were in accordance with facts observed in practice.

The disastrous economic crisis and unprecedented unemployment between the two world wars produced a new situation. J. M. Keynes showed that capitalism relying on earlier premises was not able to ensure full employment and that the distribution of wealth and incomes was unjust. At that time, an increase in wealth did not depend on the "self-restraint of the rich" any longer and one of the arguments usually adduced to justify property inequalities of wealth became pointless. Consequently processes which had hitherto been determined by individual initiative should—according to Keynes—be centrally guided. State guidance must influence consumer habits, and interest rates and a considerable part of investments must be socially controlled in order to achieve full employment.

J. M. Keynes's ideas more or less influenced all macroeconomic schools of bourgeois economics. Keynes considered himself and the consequences of his theory "moderately conservative", he was right, of course, in saying that, for he wanted to determine the volume of production only by means of forces outside the classical system of thought, but acknowledged the classical analysis according to which it is the privilege of private interest to determine what is to be produced, the proportion of the needed factors of production and how the value of the end-product is to be distributed amongst then.. It follows that Keynes, like most economists thinking along traditional lines, was only concerned with questions of production but was not interested in distribution or property relations. Economists have, however, drawn different conclusions from Keynes's theory: Joan Robinson, for example, emphasized that full employment cannot be achieved without a far-reaching socialization of investments. She therefore suggested firmer state intervention and central planning; Hansen, on the other hand, has stressed the importance of financial instruments and credit policy in the sphere of investments and has proposed to reduce the degree of state intervention.

"Welfare economics", too, has been rehabilitated along two lines: Kaldor and Hicks are relying on the principle of compensation and have refused to confront efficiency and justice. Other economists, Samuelson and Reder for example, consider "social welfare" a normative (moral) discipline and think —unlike other distinguished economists—that it is precisely economists who are qualified to deal with this complex of problems. Most continental economists, however—from Schumpeter to Gunnar Myrdal—reject the idea of harmony (common interests) which derives from the classical school and influences the Anglo–American way of thinking up to our days; they rivet attention on conflicts and on the solution of conflicts by transitional political compromises.

As a result of the ideas and activities of J. M. Keynes and of rehabilitated "welfare state" notions and of trade unions and the working class exercising greater control functions, the standard of living (per capita income) rose at a fast rate after the Second World War.

Technological progress was accelerated, ways of life changed and cyclic fluctuations have decreased in intensity, however, the institutions of capitalist countries continue to survive in spite of higher death duties, the taxation of profits and other factors, moreover, state interference relying on the power of arbitration, as well as state guidance and the direct economic activity of the state protect the established—though improved—order. The traditional institutions of the established order are bolstered by the political rotation system which—in our days—has spread outside the English-speaking world (e.g. to the Scandinavian states, the Federal Republic of Germany and Austria). That is, a kind of balance of powers has come into being in some countries between conservatives and progressives, and the outcome of elections is decided by what is called the "floating vote". In order to achieve power, progressives underwrite programmes palatable to the broad masses of the lower middle-class, which are not particularly interested in politics.

The order, which seemed to be relatively stable and to function satisfactorily at the beginning of the sixties, was fiercely attacked in the second half of the same decade. The concept of "welfare state" and economic life in the framework of the existing institutional order was exposed to hard blows from youth, a part of the intelligentsia and various strata subject to discrimination such as Negroes and foreign workers in addition to the usual attacks by trade unions and leftist parties. Trade unions advocated—true to tradition—a fairer distribution while leftists aimed to widen their basis, young people and the intelligentsia challenged the meaning and justification of the aim rational system, demanded and pressed for a more effective system of values and attacked the "manipulative" system produced by the slogan of free elections. Claims for a more effective system of values—which were sometimes confused from an ideological point of view and chaotic in respect to organizational forms (i.e. their import was emotional, not rational) —included equality, freedom to study, participation, better social services, the improvement of the infrastructure and the protection of the environment. At the same time, great masses of young people—and this is the more important process—reject the old institutions of society which had until now been accepted by everybody as the ground on which competition with the older generation took place. Nor do they in economics accept that mechanism which in the final analysis—in spite of many experiments and the best of intentions—is the economic derivative of an empirical-utilitarian philosophy (rational economy). It is true that these manifestations and ideas are still somewhat amorphous and contain more negative than positive elements: however, it is food for thought that the rebels reject traditional institutions the functioning mechanism of which relies on "rules of the game" as esatblished by traditional forces, and that the rebellion has spread to the children of the ruling class.

These new kinds of pressure coincide with the instability of capitalist society which derives from the overstrained state of the economy (inflation gathering momentum, crisis of the international monetary system: neither gold, nor dollar), radical changes in the system of international relations, growing tensions of the Third World, increasing armament expenditure in a number of countries, protracted unjust wars and so on.

As regards the economic aspects of J. M. Keynes's theory—which was the accepted economic policy for two decades—let me briefly mention that Keynes started from two assumptions:

(a) that there are fixed prices and wages; this, however, is not the case anywhere today, and

(b) that governments reduce budgetary expenditure when private investments reach an unduly high level; such a government, however, does not exist either.

The devaluation of the dollar means that there is no international reserve currency, that gold, too, can only play a very restricted role when it comes to establishing an international financial system. The devaluation of the dollar disposes of the question *ad interim* only, for the European market is overstocked with dollars; on the other hand, American capitalists are not ready to sell American-owned European enterprises, whereas European capitalists are not willing to buy US government bonds for their dollars.

Thinking over the many tensions, conflicts and absences of equilibrium, one arrives at the conclusion that ever increasing tensions have to be eased somehow. Tensions should be reduced in the field of external relations, on the one hand (restricted strategy of the foreign policy of the US, East-West co-operation, limitation of armaments, etc.), and internally, on the other. Bearing in mind the characteristics of the forces exerting pressure it becomes obvious that the value rational elements of the system must be reinforced; this means that the concept of quality of life will by far surpass the importance it plays at present in the life of the Western world. Increased emphasis must be laid, in addition to efficiency, on requirements of equality and justice, further, on the democratic supervision of economic processes, putting an end to discrimination, the right to study (not in a legal but in a real and material sense) and on the protection of the human environment.

Besides, everyday life has to be gradually reshaped in such a way that it should not merely be acceptable but found attractive by young people, failing which communication between the older and the younger generation will break down. Far greater attention must be devoted to problems of the Third World.

It is certain that the thus reshaped Western world will not be exempt from problems; we, of course, do not know what the new world in making will be like; one thing, however, is certain that the old one cannot go on any longer. It is undoubtedly distressing to part from the old world (this particularly refers to the older generation), and, perhaps, not only illusions but *real* values will also irretrievably get lost besides, uncertainty is always an unpleasant sensation; however, in harmony with the eternal laws of nature and society every rising generation tries to adapt the existing physical world to its own expectations.

This is why I think that the idea of quality of life will also obtain increasing importance in the Western half of our changing world.

II

In the case of socialist countries, the relationship between the value rational and the aim rational systems—which also includes the field of the quality of life—radically differs, for ideological and historical reasons, from what I have said about developed capitalist countries. The system of value of society is—as a result of firm ideological commitments—very complex and wide, and significant political and social forces back it. Consequently, the norms of rational economic thinking can only penetrate gradually—not, of course, to the peaks of the system of values but to their appropriate place.

This situation is partly attributable to ideological and partly to historical reasons.

1. The creators of scientific socialism, and particularly their disciples, had a vague notion as early as the nineteenth century that commodity production and the market will cease to exist and that society will directly control the production and distribution (without having recourse to the market) of the means of production according to needs. (It should, however, be noted in parentheses that Marx and Engels did not provide a concrete programme for the building of socialism and that their indications regarding the conditions of socialist society to be expected were expounded as a negation of capitalist production relations.)

2. Distribution is based on class and social principles and takes place without money, that is, the centrally guided economy expresses itself in physical terms. The same principles are expressed in the "Erfurt Programme" (1891) which was inspired by Karl Kautsky; moreover, Kautsky described socialist production in his early works as a closed autarchic economy. (Analysing what had to be done after the revolution, Kautsky wrote in 1922 that money will remain indispensable for a long time as a medium of circulation, but will lose its function as measure of value.)

Seen from a historical point of view it appears that—after power is taken over—such kinds of "ideological prognoses" can only materialize if a particular historical development leads to "compulsory actions" which give the impression that the prescribed principles were realized of necessity.

Such a peculiar historical development was the introduction of the war economy in the post-revolutionary Soviet Union; in the case of European people's democracies, it was social transformation in times of cold war aggravated by trade war. During a war economy the main task is to distribute commodities in scarce supply; legal buying and selling was discontinued, the economy was of a completely subsistence character and the obligation to work was introduced.

The term "trade war" in the case of people's democracies refers to the embargo initiated by the Americans, which was backed by the threat of sanctions. The embargo list included 50 per cent of commodities regularly handled in international trade.

At a time of revolutionary change, irrespective of the fact whether an armed revolt or political, that is, relatively peaceful means are involved, members of society are judged on the basis of loyalty to revolutionary ideas and institutions and sacrifices they are prepared to make for the sake of the cause; that is, every revolution is in itself a value-centric system. It logically follows that the aim rational system (a rational economy based on calculation, taking into account business risks, not to mention profits) can only play a very limited role.

Views and demands opposed to the above situation are frequently expressed by revolutionary leaders, but they generally cannot make a breakthrough in the middle of the battle. Lenin, for example, emphatically declared that socialism demands higher work productivity than capitalism and on the basis of results achieved by capitalism. It was also Lenin who said at a relatively early date that it is inevitably necessary to employ bourgeois experts and that this cannot be done in any other way than by continuing to pay them the high salaries they were used to.

One could point out that those formerly in charge of the European people's democracies frequently made similar demands and urged like measures. Thus economic questions increasingly come to the fore, however, under the conditions of intensified class struggle and in a strained international situation, the receptivity of masses backing the revolution is very limited in this respect. It also should be taken into account that under complicated circumstances (when progress is not impeded by resistance but our own foresight and circumspection as well as a careful weighing of the consequences of every of our steps) differences of opinion might also arise between those leading the revolution, for there are people who do not respect the limits of power and, taking maximum advantage of the situation they want to advance at the fastest possible rate. Others, however, think that moving at full speed, by aggressive or administrative means, endangers or wrecks future economic potentials of the revolution.

In this way such systems of direction developed which—in accordance with earlier ideological expectations and concrete historic circumstances—ordered enterprises to fulfil plan targets by means of and relying on the plan. Certain economic categories though, remained, but could not fulfil their function, therefore becoming reduced to a framework without meaning. Money continued to exist but mechanically followed the movement of commodities as determined by plan directives. The role of prices in influencing production was not acknowledged and calculations became inconclusive because of previously decided structural decisions, the embargo and because of chronic shortages of foreign exchange. Investments goods and means of production also were distributed on the basis of central directives.

The economic leadership regarded the national economy as a single large-scale enterprise (or trust) and the methods applied were in conformity with this view. Under such conditions economic interests (material interestedness) could not become the chief instrument of guidance and the regime had recourse to administrative coercion, that is, to force, in order to achieve economic targets and for the sake of adequate action and behaviour.

It must be pointed out in all fairness that economic development became complicated not only because of social change and the unfavourable international background but also because of the well-known fact that socialism first came into power in countries which were less developed, in which the role and influence of agriculture were large, where the overwhelming majority of the population in fact earned its living in agriculture, and large-scale industry was relatively underdeveloped.

The new system realized a number of social reforms in spite of economic difficulties. Of the reforms let me primarily stress the ones which are in close connection with the idea of "quality of life" and with the scale of values of the new society. The right to work, that is, full employment, became effective right at the start. (Naturally without making work obligatory for everybody.) Equal rights for women, in respect to work, wages and salaries, in social and political life, made considerable headway. The right to study was made effective on all educational levels, irrespective of the financial situation of parents. The children of sections of society which had been at a disadvantage in the past enjoyed preferences. (A new school system of eight classes with subject teachers was established, complete with hostels at places situated far from cultural centres. Social control was tightened in secondary schools and matriculation was made easier for young people of worker and peasant origin.) It is known that inequalities deriving from the past can only be done away with by providing temporary preferences to the formerly oppressed classes. The structure of the student population, and of the intelligentsia, has radically changed adjusting itself to the needs of an industrialized society. (Higher number of engineers, economists and extended education in the natural sciences.) The right to medical care became fully effective, for a first-class network of public health service covering the entire country was established providing medical treatment free of charge to every citizen with particular attention to prevention.

Cultural values were held in high respect and were popularized at a fast rate; at a farther stage of development, the production of cultural values thrived. This was due, at the beginning, to the fact that the state shouldered great responsibilities in this field. Entertainment affording cultural experiences such as theatres, concerts, opera and books, became available at low cost. Thus, the "purchase of cultural goods" also became possible for people in lower income brackets. As a result a wide section of a new public has grown up in the course of two decades which, in addition to classics, has also shown great interest in modern works provided that the new culture interpreted social problems of our times in a realistic way—ironically or humorously—but not in set formulae. Returning to the sphere of the quality of life one might say that a public keenly interested in cultural values has grown up which—thanks to state subsidies—was able to disregard the "traditional hierarchy" of goods although many at the same time badly felt the lack of a car and even of a flat. (If the traditional hierarchy had continued all this would have taken place 20–25 years later.)

It logically follows from what has been said that the value rational system considerably strengthened in the first period and became attractive in many respects (in the field of culture, science, dissemination of knowledge and education) and was highly instrumental in keeping up equilibrium, because it compensated hundreds of thousands, nay, millions for the scarcity of material goods.

In the second period of development, however, the relationship between the aim rational and the value rational system, and together with it, the structure of the developed system, considerably changed. (Let me remark in parentheses that I use Max Weber's terminology for lack of a more appropriate term. Although these two systems in fact develop and function in every society, it is not right to rigidly contrast the two since, on the one hand, every theory of economics contains the concept of absolute value while, on the other, there is a great interdependence between the two systems except in the case of traditional societies. I shall have more to say about this interdependence at a later stage.)

1. The new system consolidates and strikes roots, and its fundamental norms are accepted, so to speak, unnoticed and by mutual understanding. As a result the methods of leadership and guidance, which developed at the phase of struggle and in times of uncertainty, become disputable.

2. The development of a value rational system on so broad a basis—which by the way is one of the finest features of the system—entails relatively high costs and requires increasing material means. However, only a prosperous and efficiently functioning economy can afford these means.

3. Since full employment has absorbed the overflow of labour, intensive methods (i.e. technical progress) have to be adopted in order to increase production, improve the structure of the economy, develop services and so on. The systems of guidance applied earlier have proved suitable (in spite of deficiencies) to boost extensive industrialization, to absorb the excess of agricultural manpower and to develop new industrial sectors but are unable to step up technical progress, develop a new economic structure, increase paying exports and so on.

4. In line with conditions becoming more consolidated, people (particularly the rising generation) confidently expect democratic ways to become more general and increasingly take a dislike to administrative methods. Hence, what is called "revolutionary violence" can rarely be applied, that is only in case of emergency.

5. As a result of the cultural revolution and of the new educational system, citizens become more and more exacting in every respect. They refuse to attend cultural performances they would have readily gone to formerly nor do they read books which they would have liked earlier.

6. The population's demands for durable consumer goods increases, people are getting pretentious and furnish their homes in a more refined taste, an increasing number of people own cars and so on. Hence, the pattern of industrial production must be adjusted to the more and more intricate consumer demand structure.

Such and similar problems emerge in every European socialist country— to a different degree though and assuming different forms. Therefore, every country needs or will need reforms allowing a freer scope to economic rationality. Although the nature of these reforms may differ dependent upon the size of a country, composition of the population, standard and problems of the economy as well as upon the greater or lesser weight of foreign trade, certain fundamental elements will—in my opinion—be indentical.

(a) These reforms must provide greater freedom of action for enterprises, on the basis of harmony and interrelatedness of plan and market (commodity and money relations).

(b) One must allow the rational behaviour of enterprises to be influenced by the economic ambience, that is, administrative methods must be reduced to a minimum.

(c) Economic rewards for both economic units and individuals leading to a direct interest in production, technological progress and in the marketing of products must be increased.

Forms and methods of a more differentiated distribution must be introduced in order to speed technological growth.

(d) A method must be worked out allowing for comparative calculations of various development alternatives, including economic criteria, on the basis of which one can choose between mechanization and manpower.

(e) The position of consumers and user firms as against producers must be strengthened.

(f) Rational economic categories such as money, prices, credit, interests, profit, etc. must be employed to an increasing extent in order to step up technological growth and structural change.

(g) More attention must be given to problems of equilibrium and/or questions related to investments, stockpiling, etc. which generally jeopardize equilibrium.

There is no doubt that the coming into being, working out and functioning of reforms in many respects clashes with the value rational system and with certain groups backing it, their considerations ranging from the political to the arts. These conflicts, which involve considerable social tension, are probably unavoidable. Governments must, therefore, try to overcome differences which arise between the two kinds of systems and additionally maintain social equilibrium. The postponement of reforms could produce problems more serious than the tensions caused by the reform.

One can choose between alternatives but implement only one in social life, and this refers to both politics and economics. Consequently, if one argued that the alternative which was not chosen or keeping the earlier situation, would have been preferable, one can only deny this in argument but cannot concretely point to the defects or failure of established practice. It should be kept in mind that in spite of conflicts which necessarily soon arise interests show themselves to be common in the long run, for, on the one hand, the economy requires an intelligent, well-trained, broad-minded labour force leading a wholesome life, and the value rational system on the other presupposes a well-functioning and efficient economy.

Of course, the functioning of the aim rational system as such also raises problems which—failing governmental measures—could conflict with the system of value of a socialist society. Incomes, for example, must be differentiated—as pointed out earlier; these differences, however, cannot overstep the limits considered permissible by socialist society. Therefore, in addition to creating new income sources, the state must skim off excess incomes, that is, taxes must be imposed: this is a new kind of task in a socialist society and economy. It is not enough to provide new sources of income for those who adapt themselves more efficiently and flexibly to the requirements of consumers or to the dynamically changing requirements of external markets. Proper provision must also be made for those who spend many years of service with one and the same factory (loyalty bonus) or for those who by rallying their fellow workers further the growth of the team spirit in the community (socialist brigades).

European socialist countries therefore now face the task of strengthening the aim rational system for the sake of stepped up technological growth and higher efficiency in addition to maintaining and further developing the achievements of the value rational system.

Since Hungary has deliberately taken the road towards an intensification of the aim rational system, it introduced the new economic mechanism (system of guidance) on January 1, 1968; this caused a certain disquietude among supporters of the value rational system (including party and state executives, trade union officials, writers and artists) and became a subject of extensive debate.

Those concerned with political and social questions had scruples about the new way of life which, since it derived from the aim rational system, might undermine the public spirit, by "individualizing", that is making people selfish who may then become indifferent to their fellow-men. Writers and artists feared that cultural and artistic interests would decline in the age of the five-day week, week-end cottages, cars and pleasure trips abroad.

The answer to the first question is that forms of communal life have considerably changed—mainly under the influence of the young generation. These forms are looser, more informal and less regulated, in the view of older people at least, however, common experience, objectives, discussions, work and entertainment establish links today as well, through smaller collectives. Man today is attracted by intimacy and informality and looks for personal experience, he is more active, he is not a listener, as at meetings, he questions, argues and sometimes calls his debating partner to account; these forms of social living produce the kind of communal experience which satisfies man today.

My answer to the second question is that a truly attractive culture always finds new forms in its relationship with the masses. Young men of today possibly prefer clubs or the "underground theatre", however, the form should not be confused with the essence. In 1945–46 eminent Hungarian artists visited factories or went to the country in order to meet workers and peasants. Many people thought at that time that this was a forced gesture; it appeared, however, that actors established then and there human relations with their audience-to-be. It is certain that really valuable Hungarian and socialist culture will always find its way to people's hearts.

In further developing the notion of quality of life the increased competition (attractive consumption in pleasant surroundings) has to be taken into account. I for one firmly believe that economics and the system of value get on well together. Economics provides a life worthy of man, a life worth living for an increasing number of people. The system of values allows us to enjoy all the beauties of the world, not least that of our own inner life while the going is good, and to fight tooth and nail for our country and political convictions when this proves necessary. These are the two attitudes towards life which, as the century grows to a close, are indispensable for humanism and for the integrity of the human personality.

III

The nations of the Third World face the problems of the quality of life under peculiar conditions determined in many respects by their past. A system of value plays a very important role in taking a stand on issues such as national independence or the lack of it, forming an opinion on enclaves and enterprises within the domestic economy, the character of social reforms which makes economic development possible, the role of traditional institutions, culture and the vernacular and judgements passed on the quality of the way of life.

I do not want to overtax the patience of the reader by entering into particulars and, besides, the above subject would require a separate study.

Let me, however, point out some important interconnections:

1. Seen from a historical point of view, it appears that although national independence is not an ultimate object or an exclusive aim, peoples and nations consider it a value in itself and it is therefore well worth while making great sacrifices in order to achieve it. In this respect nations are inclined to fall into two kinds of error: (a) they continue with nineteenth-century ways of thought while living in an interdependent world where truly fantastic means of communication are available, and (b) they tend to interpret international co-operation in such a way that the stronger party—stronger from both a military and an economic point of view—dictates to the weaker party; if this takes place the real content of independence is reduced to nil.

2. Independence is not only a political concept but also an economic one. In addition to a country's right to dispose freely of its natural resources and to determine trends of internal economic development in a sovereign way, it is entitled to obtain the material advantages in international trade as the countries with which it bargains do. The latter requirement cannot be realized to the full while there are considerable differences between tech-

nological standards but can be gradually approximated if the more developed partner sees reason; otherwise colonialism, which is politically drawing to an end, will come to life again in the economic field.

3. In addition to achieving and consolidating national independence, the main aim is to step up economic growth. Hence social reforms are needed which liberate new energies in the interest of economic development and fairly equally distribute the burdens and advantages of economic growth between various classes, sections, nationalities and tribes.

4. In working out the notion of development expedient methods must be found which provide employment for a growing proportion of those of working age in spite of increases in population. Work-intensive industries must be developed the products of which are of the same quality as or preferably of a better quality than those of large-scale industry, allowing workmen to acquire special know-how which they can subsequently turn to account in large-scale industry. In those countries the right to work has to be interpreted in this sense for the time being since means, investment possibilities and technological-organizational experience are not available for the total mobilization of the labour force.

5. Comprehensive educational reforms are needed ranging from lower grade teaching to university education.

6. Most of these countries have inherited great cultural traditions. As a result of awakening consciousness, which increases with the progress of time, the peoples of Latin America will be able to preserve their culture of European—mainly Spanish–Portuguese—origin mixed with Indian elements and even to add new values.

In Asia inherited culture is particularly deep and varied and radically differs from the European one; the nations of Asia will certainly be able to achieve what Japan once aimed at: acquiring technology from the Barbarians (i.e. from the Europeans), while preserving their higher moral standards ("Samurai in spirit but businessmen in talent"). The Arab nations, having created a culture of their own (philosophy and religion included) are able to enrich it owing to increased national consciousness.

In Black Africa culture has not yet become separated from the way of life and those producing culture are not only and particularly not in the first place "professional" artists, writers or poets. This way of life imbued with culture—to which more and more conscious works of art are added—is sufficiently attractive to be able to influence others and to continue to develop.

7. It should, however, be stressed that certain attractive elements of the inherited cultures and ways of life derive from a traditional society or feudal-

agrarian conditions. Certain refinements of social intercourse, for example, can be attributed to the fact that time is not of value in traditional and feudal society. In an industrializing society, however, time will gain importance and, consequently, certain beautiful aspects of the ancient style of living will in fact disappear. This, however, happens whenever an agricultural society becomes transformed into an industrial one. The mode of life of an American plantation owner of the South was—judging by literary evidences —more enjoyable than that of an entrepreneur in the North, however, slavery was the condition of this kind of delightful and brilliant way of life.

Traditional society has kept certain fine features capitalism has completely wiped out in Europe. In this traditional society, however, people live in destitution and hundreds of thousands die of starvation.

The primary aim is to bring about material conditions worthy of man; accordingly, only those elements of beauty in traditional society can survive which are able to adapt themselves to the requirements of economic growth.

Most people cannot make a distinction between national (continental) traditions, on the one hand, and ways of thinking and behaviour patterns as produced by the conditions of a given society, on the other.

8. Thus, when rational economic thinking is introduced in developing countries, great care must be given to factors of the value system such as equality, the right to work and to study and social justice, and all values deriving from their culture as well as the beauty and attraction of their way of life must be preserved and further developed—provided they are reconcilable with the requirements of social and economic growth.

The situation of developing countries is particularly complex since they have to go through several historical periods concurrently. It is, one might say, the rule in late development that, thanks to knowledge and information acquired in an interdependent world by perfected means of communication, the masses require the realization and achievement of all that took generations in other countries. One has, therefore, to face the fact that developing countries want to enjoy elements of the system of value such as equality, the right to work and to study, a satisfactory health service and so on at once without first waiting for suitable economic conditions, that is, at a time when national income is still very low, and possibilities for accumulation are limited, the balance of payments shows a deficit and inflation is rampant. It can, therefore, be assumed that conflicts will arise between the above elements of the value system and the requirements of economic rationality. Achievements of a major social reform are generally followed by an absence of equilibrium and at this juncture governments take over which—in order to re-establish equilibrium—prevent reforms for a time and check a further growth in consumption. Experience shows that military regimes are better suited to perform such unpopular tasks which can be carried out by force only.

Other elements of the quality of life—related to culture, way of life, dissemination of knowledge and so on—can, of course, proceed in both periods and make their effect felt not only in the countries concerned but also in the outside world. These factors will be present in the life of every country and each continent as factors shaping knowledge, habits, mentality and fashion.

Conclusion

The idea of a quality of life, mentioned earlier, is not a fundamentally new idea or philosophy. Many scholars were concerned with it from classics to Max Weber and to the supporters of "welfare economies"—although the question comes up in a different form in our days. Marx and Engels and, subsequently, Kautsky also dealt with this question going into it from another class viewpoint and, in the course of concrete development, socialist societies made various attempts to reconcile the requirements of a value rational and an aim rational system.

It is probable that developing countries will have to continue these attempts—approaching them from another historical point of view, based on another social structure, and in a more interdependent world.

Although the philosophical notion is not a recent one, its present forms essentially differ from those in the past. The novelty of its present form manifests itself in that the pressure the masses exert in the interests of the value system has considerably intensified and that there are new power factors, such as the rising generation and the Third World, supporting it. On the other hand, this philosophical notion comes to the fore in an interdependent world (earlier world history consisted of parallel rather than interdependent processes) in which three worlds exercise mutual influence on each other while the technological and scientific revolution, advancing at an unprecedented rate, influences all three worlds.

The aim of the present study was to point out that one and the same impulse has very different effects on each of the three worlds. Since identical impulses exert very dissimilar effects in different media, I for my part do not believe in the convergence theory. This theory furthermore contains a highly obsolete element, the supposition that only systems approximating each other can coexist and cooperate. It follows, explicitly or implicitly, that non-converging systems are not able to co-operate. This idea, however, is absolutely untenable in the world of today in which the number of contradictions and differences one can perceive and notice has increased, because for one thing, many more nations and states have become involved in the current of world politics. It is probable that formerly there were just as many differences and contradictions these, however, were only reputed or understood in part only, since we considered our world "natural" and "normal" while that of others seemed to be a sort of peculiarity. However, in the eyes of an African, Europe is no less an oddity than Africa is in the eyes of a European! Both Europeans and Africans are, therefore, compelled to come into contact with so many strange practices that, when all is said and done, peculiarities outnumber "natural matters". Peculiarities, however, also depend on frequency of occurrence; peculiarities which turn up continually are no longer peculiarities but alternatives or simply a system of ideas and actions different from ours.

If we want to coexist and cooperate with others in the interest of peace and development we must learn to respect differences inherent in heterogeneous nations.

On this shrinking planet of ours, cooperation is imaginable in this way only since the technological revolution making headway at an increasingly fast rate and interdependent world politics as well raise identical questions addressed to all of us and our answers and the decisions we make also influence the other partner compelling him also to make his decisions.

This is the only international and human attitude which enables us to coexist and cooperate.

Only by adopting this attitude can we develop a system of conduct and action providing a solution to problems related to the quality of life. If we realize that there are three worlds but one planet only and that fundamental differences cannot be settled independently of each other, then we shall be able not only to meet the challenge of the quality of life, but also to surmount the obstacles put in our way by the complexities of our age and by development progressing at an unheard-of speed.

HUNGARIAN FOREIGN TRADE
IN THE SEVENTIES

The Transformation of the Commodity Pattern

by

JÓZSEF BÍRÓ

Hungarian foreign trade is determined in the main by production, world market demand and home consumption. The key question of the further progress in Hungary's international economic relations is the transformation of the production structure. The structure to be must be in accordance with the demands of international markets. It is obvious that in spite of measures so far taken in this field a number of major problems have still to be solved in the near future. This question has to be dealt with for the sake of the future showing how production and foreign trade have shaped in mutual interdependence, further, how and to what extent it meets the demands of international markets and what kind of tensions have to be overcome in the course of coordinating the market and production. Laying down the trend of the structural transformation means determining economic development—and also influencing the growth of productive forces—for a long time ahead.

The production pattern decisively influences the composition of exports and imports of every country while the repercussions of foreign trade are limited only, though it could well be that it is just foreign trade which conveys the impulses of international markets. Thus, the situation and the more or less stable position of a country in international trade are determined by the structure and market potential of home production that backs foreign trade. Speeded up industrialization in Hungary was not able to keep up with changes in the production pattern in conformity with the requirements of international trade; the structure of foreign trade has improved in spite of the fact that trade with capitalist countries demands conditions that differ from those required by commerce with socialist countries.

It is self-evident that Hungary aims to expand international economic relations with socialist countries, it is this that ensured industrial growth and economic growth as such as well as making it possible for a structure to come into being which permitted a link-up with the international division of labour. By the time this took place, Hungary was already among the "late-starters", a newer process was under way in the more developed socialist countries and in capitalist countries, and Hungary could not keep up. As a result contradictions came to the surface in the production pattern and in the foreign trade commodity pattern as well which threw the country's foreign trade out of balance. In the present case the first steps in easing inconsistencies aim at a narrowing of the pattern of production and at the concentration of productive forces; these measures are characteristic of small countries which undertook speedy industrialization. A further peculiar feature of these countries is a repeated or chronic deficit in the foreign trade balance. The causes of the latter vary from country to country. There is a clear marked relationship however between the trend of concentration and the foreign trade deficit. The core of the problem is that imports, particularly the imports of raw materials and energy bearers, are the basis of speedy industrial growth in these countries which have to pay for materials and energy by exports of increasing quantity and value. This obligation which goes together with a phase delay, that is with characteristic differences between imports and exports, is at the same time an important stimulus prompting the economy to adapt development to given conditions, for example, in the supply of raw materials and energy bearers, and to concentrate on the stepped up production of a few marketable articles which can be turned out profitably in large series, and are readily saleable. Important factors in the intricate web of efforts towards concentration are the high degree of capital intensity and research sensitivity of the modernization of production. When all is said and done it is clear that it is more remunerative to concentrate limited resources, such as labour and capital, on products which can be manufactured most profitably.

This process is the transformation and modernization of the structure of the economy, a calculation of the relationship of costs as against returns in order to achieve maximum results by a continuing regrouping of the factors of production.

Before looking at the commodity pattern of Hungarian foreign trade it is advisable to survey, in brief outline at least, the commodity pattern of world trade.

The Commodity Pattern of World Trade

Given modern large-scale production the commodity structure of individual countries has become differentiated owing to variations in the standard of productive forces. Technical progress has changed the commodity pattern of the world economy in recent decades and this transformation has not come to a stop yet.

Changes speeded up after 1955. The ratio of products of a raw material character and of processed goods was fifty-fifty in 1955, the former decreased to 35.5 per cent while the latter increased to 64.5 per cent by 1970. The equality of fifteen years ago thus changed to a $^1/_3$–$^2/_3$ ratio by 1970. This is attributable to the fact that the proportion of products of a raw material character decreased in world trade by 1 per cent a year while that of processed goods increased by the same ratio. Supposing that this shift in proportions continues—and all indications point to this—the proportion of products of a raw material character in world trade will shrink to about 25 per cent whereas that of processed goods will increase to 75 per cent by 1980. These figures indicate that the development of the forces of production changes the commodity pattern of world trade at a fast rate.

Trade in machines grew at the fastest rate: it amounted to 17.9 per cent of world trade as a whole in 1955, to 27.8 per cent in 1970 and will probably reach the double of the 1955 percentage (i.e. 35 per cent) by 1980. The sale and purchase of chemicals and other industrial products stands second as regards dynamism of world trade. The proportion of raw materials in the strict sense in world trade decreases steadily, they amounted to about one-fifth (19.5 per cent) of world trade in 1955 and to one-tenth (11.2 per cent) in 1970 but will decline in all probability to one-thirteenth by 1980. The proportion of agricultural produce also shows a decreasing tendency.

The shift in the commodity pattern of world trade reflects the fact that science and the power of the intellect increasingly determine the structure of production and trade indicating the main trends of technical development; in this respect automation, the use of atomic-energy, missile techniques, modern transport and telecommunications and chemization (new kinds of fertilizer) are the principal areas of growth.

It is now possible to keep track of the technological application of scientific research and its ultimate realization in production. Technical aspects become outdated within a far shorter time and the commodity structure quickly changes and is differentiated as a result of new products.

New basic materials are used by certain industries, more and more part units can be applied in a number of fields aiding both mass and individual production. Intellectual factors are given an increasingly important role, the concentration of research being a phenomenon observable throughout the world. Small countries—amongst them Hungary—can only develop along a narrow sector of one or another industry; for such countries the production and export of specialities is far more rewarding.

Development in the Commodity Pattern of Hungarian Foreign Trade

Considerable changes took place in the development of the forces of production in the past quarter of a century. This is demonstrated by the commodity pattern of imports and exports; the years 1938–1970 are particularly illuminative in this respect (see Table 1).

It was characteristic of the semi-feudal agrarian conditions prevailing in Hungary before the Second World War that the percentage of the machine and equipment imports amounted to about 10 per cent whereas the import of raw materials and semi-finished goods amounted to 70 per cent. The percentage of the raw and basic material import was unchanged, in the main, in 1950. The country, however, embarked on the building of socialism and it therefore became obvious that the import of machines and equipment had to be increased. The proportion of the latter reached double the pre-war figure, on the other hand, the proportion in imports of consumer goods, foods and materials for the food processing industry

Table 1

Development of the commodity structure of imports

	1938	1950	1960	1970
Machines and equipment	10.6	22.0	27.8	29.7
Industrial consumer goods	8.8	1.5	5.0	8.4
Raw materials and semi-finished goods	73.1	72.7	58.9	52.2
Foodstuffs and materials of the food processing industry	7.5	3.8	8.3	9.7
Total	100.0	100.0	100.0	100.0

Source: Statistical Yearbook of Foreign Trade of 1960 and 1970, published by the Central Statistical Office.

decreased—the latter to a slighter degree. This structural change was inevitable since conditions were not present yet for a decrease in the proportion of raw and basic materials imported; on the other hand, the changes in the commodity structure reflected the way of thinking of the times which concentrated on quantitative industrial development. In the years 1950–1960 the proportion of machines and equipment rose by 5.8 per cent. The fact that the share of foodstuffs grew by 4.5 per cent and that of industrial consumer goods by 3.5 per cent shows that economic policy to a greater extent took into account what the state of the economy made possible. The considerable decrease of the proportion of industrial raw materials of plant and animal origin in 1960 made it possible to increase the import ratio of raw materials of the chemical industry. In 1950 raw materials of plant and animal origin amounted to 52 per cent of Hungarian raw and basic material imports, however, this ratio decreased to 36 per cent in 1960. The relative decline of imported basic materials for the light industry—a phenomenon observable throughout the world—is also due to the fact that synthetics are used to a higher degree. Besides, light industry grew at a slower rate anyway, one reason being that Hungarian economic policy in the first half of the fifties relegated light industry to the background.

Figures show that the period of intensive development started in 1970. In conformity with the increased requirements of technical and technological development, the proportion of machines and equipment continued to increase within imports. In accordance with the living standards policy, the import of industrial consumer goods increased while the proportion of raw and basic materials further decreased.

Although the proportion of the raw materials of the light industry continued to decrease in 1970, but only by 3 per cent as against the 16 per cent of the prior decade. This also indicates that growth in the light industry received greater emphasis in recent years. The considerable increase in the import of raw materials and semi-finished goods of the chemical industry was the result of the stepped up development of the chemical industry and of the heavy demand for chemicals; this increase was partly set off by the decreased proportion of fuels and metallurgical products.

In the last resort it appears that the formation of the commodity structure of imports—at least as regards the main tendencies—furthered the continuous building of the Hungarian socialist economy.

As regards the commodity pattern of exports: a comparison of imports and exports figures for 1938 and 1970 shows that changes were far greater in the latter (see Table 2).

Table 2

Development of the commodity structure of exports

	1938	1950	1960	1970
Machines and equipment	9.3	23.0	38.0	31.5
Industrial consumer goods	10.2	20.3	17.8	19.5
Raw materials and semi-finished goods	23.5	17.5	23.6	26.1
Foodstuffs and materials of the food processing industry	57.0	39.2	20.6	22.9
Total	100.0	100.0	100.0	100.0

Source: Statistical Yearbook of Foreign Trade of 1960 and 1970, published by the Hungarian Central Statistical Office.

This is due to the fact that the shortage of raw materials—which determines the commodity pattern of Hungarian imports to a great degree—influences the commodity composition of export to a far slighter extent and indirectly only. Since reconstruction after the liberation of the country did not simply mean the restoration of the earlier economy, considerable changes took place in the structure of both production and exports as early as 1950. The proportion of machines and equipment in exports increased from 9 to 23 per cent and that of industrial consumer goods from 10 to 20 per cent. At the same time the proportion of foodstuffs and raw materials of the food processing industry as well as of raw materials and semi-finished goods considerably decreased as compared to pre-war exports. An overall picture shows that the improved commodity pattern of exports furthered the transformation of the internal economic structure. This became possible owing to improved trade links with socialist countries, primarily with the Soviet Union.

The proportion of processed industrial articles in exports further increased to 1960 mainly as a result of the large-scale development of the exports of the engineering industry. The porportion of machines and equipment in exports amounted to 38 per cent in 1960 and surpassed that of a number of developed industrial countries. This could be achieved thanks to the joint economic policy of the socialist countries in addition to particular stress being laid on the growth of the engineering industy. The same factors influenced the relative decreased in the exports of industrial consumer goods. The exports of raw materials and semi-finished goods reached the pre-war level. Between 1950 and 1960, as a result of the changing production pattern the proportion of agricultural products and those of the food processing industry decreased from 39.2 per cent to 20.6 per cent in exports as a whole. This decline was partially due to mistakes committed in the socialist transformation of agriculture.

The period 1960–1970, the decade when the necessary transition to intensive economic development took place, brought about decisive changes in the commodity structure of Hungarian exports. On the one hand, the proportion of products of the engineering industry declined for various reasons, on the other the proportion of industrial consumer goods, materials and semi-finished goods as well as of agricultural produce and products of the food processing industry increased more or less to the same extent. Some fundamental causes of the decline in the exports of the engineering industry deserve attention: (a) in line with the step by step transition to intensive economic development, the requirements of socialist countries regarding technical and technological standards rose; (b) because of parallel industrial development in the fifties, Hungarian foreign trade with socialist countries in products of the engineering industry could only grow to a relatively slighter extent.

The proportion of raw materials and semi-finished goods in Hungarian exports surpassed the pre-war percentage in 1970. This, however, took place against a background of changed home commodity consumption. The proportion of fuel, metals and mineral substances increased within exports of materials from 35 per cent to 60 per cent in 1970. The export of materials and semi-finished goods of the chemical and rubber industry increased at a fast rate as did that of ferrous and aluminium metallurgy. The considerable growth in the proportion of these two commodity groups took place at the expense of industrial raw materials of plant and animal origin. These changes are ascribable to both the fast growth of Hungarian industrial production and to changed demands on world market Thus, the same situation has arisen once again: demand for raw and basic materials of the light industry has been slight all over the world; besides the share of these products has diminished due to declining prices as well.

The Commodity Pattern of Hungarian Imports

Sixty-seven per cent of direct Hungarian imports in 1970 originated in the socialist countries, 29 per cent in developed capitalist countries and 4 per cent in developing countries. There are considerable differences in the commodity structure of imports deriving from different groups of countries. This is partly due to the economic conditions of various relational groups and partly to special reationships influencing the economic links which have developed between Hungary and the given relational groups. To take one example: it has become usual practice—and a very favourable one from the point of view of Hungary—for imports needs of energy bearers and electric energy to be covered almost entirely from socialist sources. In this respect the Soviet Union is qualified to meet Hungary's needs in the first place, in view of her natural endowments, and immense productive background.

The proportion of materials and semi-finished goods in Hungarian imports from socialist countries was lower than in imports as a whole, though this is the most important group of commodities imported from socialist countries and the basis of the raw material supply of Hungarian industrial production. The proportion of materials and semi-finished goods in Hungarian imports from socialist countries has gone down somewhat and shows an even greater downward trend in respect to agricultural produce and products of the food processing industry. It is characteristic of the latter that their share of imports from socialist countries is far below the average. This is so because the Hungarian economy needs to import agricultural produce and products of the food industry of a kind which are produced by socialist countries to a limited extent only or not at all, since the necessary geographic conditions are absent (protein fodder, citrus fruits, spices and so on).

In 1960 machines and component parts accounted for 31.3 per cent of imports from socialist countries.

This ratio showed a slightly increasing tendency in the sixties and reached 33.5 per cent in 1970. The share of socialist countries in Hungarian machine imports is high since these countries have already reached a high standard in this field and produce many kinds of modern machines and different types of equipment.

The proportion of industrial consumer goods was rather low in both 1960 and 1965 for all possibilities had not been taken advantage of. The fact that the improvement of living standards is considered something of the very first importance made it necessary to expand foreign trade in consumer goods, and with the socialist countries as such; as a result the proportion of consumer goods in imports increased to 13 per cent in 1970.

The commodity structure of imports from developed capitalist countries underwent a favourable change over recent years. In 1960, 70 per cent of imports from developed countries consisted of materials and semi-finished goods. This high percentage decreased to 55 per cent in 1970 although this ratio shows that Hungary is still dependent on the markets of developed capitalist countries in satisfying needs for raw and basic materials instead of being able to further expand imports of indispensable machines and other equipment needed for intensive economic development.

Between 1960 and 1965 the proportion of machines and other equipment imported from developed capitalist countries increased at a moderate rate but remained unchanged in the main in the past five years—apart from the unusual ratio in 1967. (An essential change in this field—a sweeping increase—took place in 1971.)

The share of industrial consumer goods increased from 3 to 6.4 per cent in the course of ten years. In order to improve supplies to the population at a fast rate almost seven times as great a quantity of consumer goods were purchased in 1970 than ten years earlier. Imports shot ahead in 1970. Imports of agricultural produce and products of the food processing industry from developed capitalist countries grew at a particularly vigorous rate in the first half of the sixties. This was connected with changes in the composition of import requirements: in the first half of the sixties it became necessary to import bread cereals, fodder grain and meat and these purchases, repeated from time to time, increased imports from developed capitalist countries.

The commodity structure of imports from developing countries is more uniform for it mainly consists of raw materials and agricultural produce; however, the proportion of these two significant product groups was reversed in the course of the past ten years: the import of materials amounted to 80 per cent and of agricultural produce to 20 per cent in 1960 whereas the former decreased to 40 per cent while the latter increased to 60 per cent in 1970. This is connected with changes in the composition of Hungarian raw material and agricultural imports as such which were discussed above.

The Commodity Pattern of Hungarian Exports

Sixty-eight per cent of exports are directed to socialist countries, 27 per cent to developed capitalist countries and scarcely more than 5 per cent to developing countries. The proportion in exports of the main commodity groups also differs. It is well-known that the main buyers of Hungarian-made machines are socialist countries while agricultural produce and foodstuffs are highly important export items to the capitalist world. It can be said that the commodity pattern of Hungarian exports is by and large in conformity with the structure of the most developed industrial countries, on the other hand, the picture is by no means unambiguous if the question is analysed from the point of view of main groups in terms on the type of country involved.

The composition of exports is particularly favourable in the socialist relation as shown by the fact that—in 1970—68.2 per cent of Hungarian exports to socialist countries were made up of processed industrial goods (that is, of products of the engineering and the light industry). The ratio was 67.6 per cent in 1960 and 65.8 per cent in 1965. The very high proportion of 1960 machine exports considerably declined by 1965; this could not even be offset by the dynamically increasing exports of the products of light industry. By 1970, however, the export ratio of machines increased again and the exports of the products of the light industry to socialist countries continued to grow to a slighter degree—in spite of stagnation in 1970.

The share in exports of agricultural produce and products of the food processing industry to socialist countries also shows an upward trend. The export of fruit and vegetables considerably increased in recent years. Although the Soviet Union continues to be the main buyer, the assortment of products of the food processing industry has considerably increased in relation to a number of socialist countries (Yugoslavia and Czechoslovakia) in recent years.

The commodity structure of Hungarian exports to developed capitalist countries points to a far lower degree of economic development as shown by the fact that the share of products of the processing industry in the narrow sense was a mere 23 per cent in 1960. This ratio slightly decreased in 1965 and receded to 21 per cent in 1970. In the first half of the sixties the decline was due to the relative decreased of exports of the engineering industry, recently slackening export activity on the part of light industry was responsible. The slow increase in the export of machines to developed capitalist countries between 1960 and 1966 was mainly due to the unsatisfactory improvement of the export capacity of the engineering industry. In recent years a turn for the better took place in this respect, partly as a result of expanding cooperation; the marketability of machines of Hungarian make has improved, this trend however, has not yet become general along the line.

In 1970 the increased satisfaction of home demand produced a considerable decrease in the proportion of industrial consumer goods in Hungarian exports to developed capitalist countries. This is a disadvantageous development for the country can loose its external markets if this tendency continues for some time.

The solution of this problem lies in the creation of commodity stocks by increasing imports, primarily however in the adequate increase of home production. Successful steps were already taken in this direction in 1971 and the share of consumer goods particularly increased in exports to capitalist countries.

In the last decade it became an important aim of both trade and production policy to decrease the share in exports of less processed and prosperity and depression sensitive products to non-socialist countries as well. This endeavour proved successful. The ratio of agricultural produce and of products of the food industry which still amounted to 50 per cent in 1960 decreased to 41 per cent by 1970 in spite of the fact that considerable quantities of bread cereals were exported as a result of the previous year's bumper harvest. The commodity pattern improved in general within this commodity group since—in addition to the wheat exports mentioned above—the proportion of products processed to a higher degree increased within agricultural and food exports to developed capitalist countries. In the ten years from 1960 to 1970 the boom and slump sensitivity of Hungarian exports to developed Western countries has increased more and more.

Finally the Hungarian exports to developing countries should also be mentioned. The large share of industrial consumer goods—mainly products of the light industry—was characteristic of Hungarian exports to developing countries in the first years of the sixties. Products of the processing industry in a narrower sense, including machines and equipment, amounted to 76 per cent of Hungarian exports to developing countries in 1960. This ratio decreased to 69 per cent in 1965 and to 58 per cent in 1970. These changes were mainly ascribable to the decrease in the exports of consumer goods from 41 per cent in 1960 to 22 per cent in 1970.

Demand for industrial consumer goods considerably increased in recent years. This was true of exports to socialist countries as well as of home demand. The proportion exported to both Western countries and developing countries decreased since industrial production could not keep up with the increased demand mentioned above. These changes made it obvious that light industry has to be reorganized; in fact, the reconstruction of this sector was decided on in 1970 in order to meet demand from all three markets (home, socialist countries and non-socialist countries) to a maximum degree.

The decline in Hungarian exports of products of the processing industry was offset—also in respect to developing countries—by exports of raw materials and semi-finished goods, that is, by highly prosperity and depression sensitive products. This was partly due to the boom of the late sixties. In addition developing countries became greatly interested in semi-finished goods, mainly of ferrous origin and in those produced by the chemical industry. In recent years Hungarian industry has achieved a fairly high productive capacity as regards goods of this kind.

In summing up it can be said that, in the commodity structure of Hungarian exports, deviations between the countries involved are too high. Important problems have yet to be solved in improving the price structure and lessening the sensitivity of exports to prosperity and depression effects.

International Aspects

In investigating the commodity pattern of Hungarian foreign trade the question of the extent to which the composition of commodities is in conformity with what is generally the rule and/or whether the trends of structural changes are in harmony with the main tendencies of world trade also has to be considered. It is obvious that this question touches on problems of the economic structure of the particular country the commodity pattern of the foreign trade of which is under discussion, and is also connected with the economic efficiency of production, and with the situation of big and small countries in world trade. The latter problem refers to the foreign trade structure to be developed in accordance with the given state of the productive forces, taking into account regional, natural, etc. conditions. In Europe there are a number of small countries like Hungary, with more or less identical raw material resources; although a parallel cannot be drawn between them, a comparison can be made, *mutatis mutandis*, bearing in mind that every comparison distorts to a certain extent. If the 1969 figures are scrutinized it appears that there is a marked difference as regards the import commodity structure of Hungary, the socialist countries and Western Europe, that is, the proportion of foods and consumer goods is smaller in Hungarian imports than in that of socialist countries as a whole, and far smaller than in West European imports. This is only natural considering that Hungarian agriculture can meet home demand for agricultural produce and products of the food processing industry besides exporting considerable quantities. The extremely high proportion of Hungarian raw material imports is the consequence of the country's natural endowments. The proportion of products of the chemical industry is relatively high in Hungarian imports indicating that the demand for chemicals is—due to the forceful development of the chemical industry—very high as compared with economic development as such.

The proportion of the extremely comprehensive group of products which includes semi-finished and finished goods of the light and other industries, black and non-ferrous metals, etc. is relatively slight in Hungarian imports. International cooperation is not satisfactory as yet, and relatively large reserves are available of these products, allowing for considerable future expansion.

The greatest difference in the export structure appears to be in the share of the food processing industry and food as such. It is obvious that, with regard to Hungarian conditions, the share of exports of this group of products is considerably larger than that of the socialist countries as a whole, or in the combined exports of Western Europe.

The proportion of raw materials and energy bearers in Hungarian exports is slight; it is somewhat higher in West European exports and highest in the combined exports of socialist countries. These figures truly reflect natural conditions. On the other hand, the relatively high percentage of products of the engineering industry in Hungarian exports is striking (in spite of a drop back since 1960).

Below average foreign trade in food and consumer goods on the one hand, and the large-scale increase of products of the chemical and the engineering industry in international trade, on the other, is a general tendency that has manifested itself throughout the world in the past 15 to 20 years. Thus, the structure of world trade changes to the advantage of machines and chemicals. This tendency is also observable in Hungarian foreign trade if a longer period is under review.

Yet, if a comparison is made between countries of about equal size and with more or less identical raw material resources, the question of the commodity structure—a perpetually timely question—merges, on a narrower range though, in respect to both imports and exports. As a result of their situation small countries have to overcome more difficulties, for many of them—Hungary included—have embarked on the path to industrialization rather late, their possibilities of development are limited, intellectual reserves are more restricted and the funds they can allocate for scientific research are far smaller, than is the case with, say, the Soviet Union or the United States. These smaller countries must to a large extent rely on the international division of labour, the commodity structure of their foreign trade must continuously be adapted to the permanently changing inter-

Table 3

Composition of exports and imports in 1968 (in percentages)

Main commodity groups Breakdown by SITC sections	Austria		Belgium and Luxemburg		Denmark		Netherlands		Switzerland		Sweden		Hungary	
	Exp.	Imp.	Exp.	Imp.	Exp.	Imp.	Exp.	Imp.	Exp.	Imp.	Exp.	Imp.	Exp.	Imp.
Foodstuff and livestock	4.5	9.1	7.1	10.7	38.5	8.3	22.7	12.2	4.0	11.1	2.3	9.6	17.6	7.6
Beverages and tobacco	0.2	1.2	0.7	1.5	1.7	1.8	1.3	1.3	1.6	2.2	0.0	1.4	2.8	1.2
Inedible raw materials (excepting mineral fuels)	10.9	8.9	5.1	13.6	7.2	7.7	7.5	9.8	2.4	5.9	21.7	5.9	16.1	
Mineral fuels, lubricants and related materials	3.0	7.5	3.1	9.5	1.5	11.6	8.0	10.1	0.2	6.7	1.3	12.3	1.7	9.7
Animal and vegetable oils and fats	0.0	0.9	0.3	0.5	0.9	0.3	1.0	1.0	1.0	0.4	0.3	0.4	0.4	0.6
Chemicals	6.3	10.4	7.8	7.3	7.3	9.3	13.3	8.1	20.5	10.1	4.0	9.2	6.9	9.7
Industrial products classified by basic material	39.3	22.2	47.0	26.8	9.6	24.1	18.8	21.9	16.5	22.9	28.2	21.7	14.9	19.7
Machinery and transport equipment	21.6	29.8	19.3	22.6	23.4	27.8	20.0	24.2	30.7	26.1	36.8	28.0	35.7	30.3
Miscellaneous manufactured articles	14.2	10.0	7.9	7.2	9.6	8.8	6.5	10.1	23.3	14.1	4.9	11.4	16.0	4.8
Non-classifiable commodities and transactions	0.0	0.0	1.7	0.3	0.3	0.9	0.9	1.3	0.7	0.5	0.5	0.1	0.3	0.3

Source: *International Statistical Yearbook*, Central Statistical Office, 1970. Data on Hungary were specially compiled from SITC as well.

national commodity pattern, flexible production must be carried on which is able to adapt itself to changes, moreover, their resources must be employed in a way that ensures that new products are competitive.

Developed small countries apparently try to meet the exigencies of the times particularly in those industries in which conditions prevailing in the country prove as well as in industries which have developed at about the same time at home and on a world scale. (The breakdown of exports and imports of small West European countries is shown on Table 3.)

It is striking that industries have developed in small countries in which they are competitive on a world scale. Their natural conditions indicate that they ought to concentrate on certain industries or groups of products and their deliberate industrial development policy also centres on the exploitation of given advantages. A case in point is the telecommunications industry of the Netherlands. From January to October 1971 the export of the electronic and instrument industry amounted to 942 million Dutch florins as against exports worth 692 millions during the same period of the previous year. Many more examples could be cited, for example, the Swedish engineering industry, typically of a "pace-making" character, as well as Switzerland's precision engineering industry. The foreign trade structure of Denmark deserves special mention: the country's agriculture and food processing industry continue to play a considerable role in the national income and the balance of payments; the proportion of the above amounts to 32–34 per cent in exports as a whole. Within the latter the export of products of animal origin is of primary importance, pork and bacon exports amounted to 48–50 per cent of exports deriving from animal husbandry. The main import items of Denmark are bread cereals, fodder, fertilizers and tractors. Its industry, tending to specialization, develops at a fast rate. The growth of the engineering industry as well as technical development concentrate on a few industries only e.g. on the production of agricultural, food processing and refrigerating equipment.

The development of the production of "pace-making" industries and commodity groups is a characteristic feature of small countries. This affects both the exports and the imports structure of the country. In the case of small countries efficient production can only be achieved in this way. These "pace-making" groups of commodities are, of course, export orientated and have to develop specialized productive methods, this, however, generally goes together with the marked increase in the imports of the products. In the case of small countries—Hungary included—restricted but specialized production with preference given to "pace-making" industries produces a foreign trade sensitivity which some countries, e.g.

3

Greece, Austria and Switzerland, try to balance by services. Joining in the international division of labour to a greater extent may help small countries to overcome production problems; this is perhaps the most efficient means to bring about a viable and rational commodity pattern at present.

Hungary's present economic structure is inseparable from the country's economic development. Joining the currents of the world economy only became possible as a result of the growth of the socialist world economy; the opportunity is now present for the sort of specialization other small countries have embarked on earlier. Traditional ways of production, that evolved through history, could be further developed to a limited extent only; the conditions of technical progress as required by the international market must be fought for now. Competition in foreign trade requires an export structure which is fully in conformity with Hungarian expectations. Twenty years ago the Netherlands, Ireland and the South European states concentrated on the food processing industry and on agriculture. The chemical industry of Austria was insignificant, Finland's timber and paper exports and Sweden's steel exports owe their existence to natural resources. In twenty years the production of these countries became specialized and continues to adapt itself to the trends governed by international trade since then.

External economic relations have expanded Hungary's economic borders and—like it or not—they compel the economy to become part of the international division of labour. This must be done, but in such a way that exports pay for imports, since international services cannot make up for gaps in the trade balance due to commodity imports. The Complex Programme provides favourable conditions for this country in establishing specialization in accordance with the requirements of the socialist market— the major factor in Hungarian foreign trade. Machine exports to the Soviet Union are particularly important for Hungary: the influence it exerted on the transformation of the country's economic structure manifested itself in the first year of the third Five Year Plan. Hungarian motor-coach exports, for example, increased eight-fold in the third Five Year Plan period and further increased by 7 per cent in 1971. As a result the export of motor-coaches which made up 3 per cent of machine exports as a whole in 1965, amounted to 19.5 per cent in 1970. Important changes took place in the production of equipment for the chemical industry which increased by 104 per cent and in the production of equipment for the food processing industries which grew by 63 per cent in the third Five Year Plan. The computer programme also influences the transformation of the commodity structure. The export of component parts of computers increased four-fold from 1970 to 1971 and further considerable changes are expected in this field in the period of the fourth Five Year Plan. Although economic agreements concluded with socialist states have an impact on the commodity structure, the main point is to develop those groups of commodities which can be sold without difficulty and whose production is economically efficient. This is required by today's internal development and the international market.

To sum up, it can be said that the most important task ahead is to catch up with the up-to-date requirements of markets in both socialist and developed capitalist countries. The development and production of the Hungarian economy must be directed and influenced in such a way that the products turned out should be in demand, permanently and to an increasing extent. Production should be able to adapt itself to the requirements of markets as regards technical indices, quantity as well as quality and finish and marketing should be more efficient. Although all this is elicited by the need to adapt to the requirements of the international market these aims also are in conformity with the government's economic policy regarding home consumption, since the requirements of such consumption are growing in a measure which surpasses the productive capacity of production. They are developing in accordance with world market tendencies and no difference can be made between the satisfaction of domestic and export demands.

Efficient and Marketable Commodity Structure

A basic condition of the economic efficiency of foreign trade is the economical scale of production; hence, we must advance towards specialization and concentrate the available resources on certain branches within one or another main sector.

It is therefore advisable to meet needs by imports in those fields in which the insufficient scale of production makes efficient production impossible; in other words: the labour input of the exported products must be less than the domestic production costs of the exchanged import commodities would amount to.

Comparative advantages can be made most of through foreign trade; hence, it partly depends upon the standard of foreign trade practices how and to what extent foreign trade enterprises take advantage of the terms of trade of international exchange and to what degree they are able to increase efficiency not only from the point of view of the enterprises but also that of the economy as such. However, exploiting changes in export and import prices demands flexible production. The adequate co-ordination of production and the commodity pattern of foreign trade allows one to reach almost optimum economic advantages by means of the international division of labour.

The main problem of the Hungarian export structure derives from the fact that the product patterns of various special provinces of the economy are rather broad as compared to the country's resources. This refers to the engineering industry in the first place. The aim therefore is to increase the efficiency of production in these fields not only by increasing output but also by improving the efficiency of manufacturing technology.

The Hungarian economy must concentrate on those fields of production in which international technical standards can be achieved, ensuring diversification within a narrower scope, so that every variant and size within certain type of commodity can be offered to meet any sort of demand.

In a more distant future it will become necessary to select between fields of production. Every one where development comes up against absolute barriers either for lack of research or sufficient experience, in view of the market situation or because basic materials and semi-finished goods are in short supply must be reduced and resources must be directed to areas where absolute limitng factors do not exist except for investment problems.

At present, however, production has grown to considerable proportions so that a small country cannot embark unaided on the development of a certain branch and on large-scale production. Co-operation in production can greatly further both specialization in the commodity structure and concentration. Specialization agreements reached with socialist states and co-operation agreements concluded between Hungarian enterprises and capitalist firms are only the first steps along this road. To mention but a few of the well-known advantages of joint undertakings: prime costs decrease as a result of optimum plant size and advanced technology investment costs are divided between the partners and the time needed for putting the new plant into operation shortens as a result of common efforts. Relying on common development one can, to a greater extent, take advantage of our intellectual resources and experiences. Instead of extensive industrial development, Hungary must increasingly have recourse to intensive development.

The finish and workmanship of Hungarian products has to be improved not only because, in the engineering industry, demand tends towards

automated machines—single-purpose machines to use a technical term—
and complex equipment, but also because the price of these kinds of
machines shows a tendency to increase while the price of basic materials
and simple products remains unchanged or rises at a slower rate. This
refers not only to the engineering industry but, also to agricultural produce,
articles of the food processing industry and to other products as well.
Only in this way can Hungarian export products become marketable
not only on certain traditional markets but on more exacting ones as well.
The marketability of articles of Hungarian make is an increasingly urgent
requirement depending upon the technical standard and improved quality
of our products. As a preliminary condition export-mindedness has to
become general in both production and foreign trade instead of the import-
mindedness prevailing today.

With regard to the aforesaid it seems expedient to change production
trends and methods in the following way:

— A basic requirement is to develop long-term economic policy on the
basis of given conditions and resources as well as taking into account
economic efficiency in such a way that it should serve as a yardstick not
only when it comes to deciding plans and problems of the economy but
that it also be instrumental when enterprises want to settle their own
problems, particularly in evaluating their long-term objectives.

— Instead of an economic policy based on group interests of single
industries a uniform economic conception has to be worked out in respect
to development trends aiming at the transformation of the commodity
structure of both production and foreign trade, so that plants of major
industries (mainly of the engineering industry) should turn out larger
series, or a greater volume of fewer commodity groups, and do so on a
higher technical standard than at present. In this way the Hungarian
economy will be able to increase exports of a higher technical standard
to CMEA and developing countries, and supply capitalist markets with
marketable industrial goods.

— Small and medium-sized plants should produce articles of sound
craftmanship, though not only labour exacting articles but mainly products
which call for intellectual work, for exacting markets.

— The present period—a transitional one from the point of view of
technical development—must be made the most of in order to catch up
with world standards in certain industries and types of agriculture given
priority; resources must therefore be concentrated on those fields of production where differences in technical standards are not unmanageable;
however, those fields have to be deliberately reduced in which technical

differences are very great and the required standards cannot be reached even through co-operation or the acquisition of licences.

— The long-term development of Hungarian raw material production (with the exception of bauxite and oil) seems inexpedient because of limited natural resources on the one hand, and high transport costs of voluminous goods as well as high investment needs, on the other.

The following guiding principles should be taken into account in respect to the transformation of the commodity structure of single industries.

Within selective industrial development particular stress should be laid upon the industries enumerated below, which should develop at a rate far above the average:

— tool engineering,
— professional telecommunication techniques (e.g. the production of acoustic equipment, special sound and video-recorders),
— agricultural machines and machines for the food processing industry,
— certain fields in computers and management techniques,
— the manufacture of medical, telecommunication, geodetical and geophysical instruments,
— health appliances and equipment as well as equipment for hospitals and surgeries,
— illuminants (Tungsram type lamps, etc.),
— the pharmaceutical industry (including veterinary medicaments),
— special sections of the chemical industry,
— wearing apparel (after considerable qualitative improvement),
— shoe and leather industry (after considerable qualitative improvement and in a selective way),
— certain special products of the food processing industry, meat products in the first place.

Soil and temperature conditions, the number of hours of sunlight as well as the rainfall in Hungary allow the country to produce:

— protein fodder (instead of basic materials of the food processing industry rich in carbohydrates),
— fruit and vegetables, further
— seed grains of high germinative value.

Those branches of production which can satisfy home needs efficiently and turn out large quantities of exportable products at the same time, must be chosen by a selective industrial and agricultural policy. The country's resources in respect to means of production, labour and money are scarce and can be increased to a limited extent only even in the long term. For this reason Hungary has to select possibilities for development on the basis of criteria which approximate economically efficient foreign trade in various ways. The criteria forming the basis of selection change according to the size of countries, further, from country to country according to the standard of economic development. Economic efficiency is the main criterion of the selection as regards both production development and trade development policy. The decrees of the 10th Congress of the Hungarian Socialist Workers' Party, the guide-lines of the fourth Five Year Plan and decisions of the government have placed selective industrial development at the centre of industrial policy. However, selective industrial development is the equivalent of an export orientated trend of development. Requirements can only be met out of own resources where sound conditions prevail. In other cases the smooth supply of the home market is provided for by relying on the international division of labour. Imports can be offset by a modern product structure which comes into being as a result of selective export orientated development. Just because of scarce resources Hungary will, in the future even more than hitherto, have to aim for economic and political objectives by the smallest possible expenditure. This aim includes the need to develop and modify both the production pattern and the commodity structure of foreign trade with a view to economic efficiency. This will be accompained by the purposeful regrouping of the country's resources.

HUNGARIAN CULTURAL POLICY
AND THE HEGEMONY OF MARXISM

by

GYÖRGY ACZÉL

The position and practice of the Hungarian Socialist Workers' Party in the struggle for the hegemony of Marxism–Leninism is based on the general principles of Marxism, the experience of the international working class movement and the lessons drawn from post-Liberation history. It therefore makes sense to review this period, naturally, without attempting a complete analysis. I would like to add that historians of this period, more specifically, specialists in party and cultural history, still owe us a detailed, scholarly study of the cultural policies of the past twenty years. One has to deal more thoroughly with this question in order to bring out better the continuities in the building of socialism in ideological work and in the party's cultural efforts, and also in order to acquire a better understanding of those errors which led to an impasse as well as the ways in which ideological work renewed itself.

In the year of change (1948) power was acquired by the working class in alliance with the peasantry. The reorganization of the institutional system of culture and ideology took place on the basis of, and in harmony with, the successful acquisition of political power. (The nationalization of schools and educational reform; the establishment of bodies coordinating and directing scientific activity; the nationalization of theatres, the establishment of national artists' associations; the founding of new literary and art periodicals, the reorganization of the publication and distribution of books; as well as the discontinuance of forums of discussion and periodicals belonging to non-Marxist and bourgeois cultural and artistic groups, etc.)

The meaning of this transformation was unambigous insofar as it created the necessary organizational and personal conditions for making the decisive influence of the party and state in the sphere of culture and ideology effective. This was one of the most important criteria of a socialist cultural policy and a guarantee that a cultural revolution in the Leninist sense of the term would be carried out. Looked at from the point of view of the subject under discussion party cultural policy was contradictory at that time, and virtually from the very beginning.

Direction did not proclaim a monopoly of Marxist ideology, neither in general nor specifically for culture, taking into account the division and contradictory nature of ideological and intellectual life. József Révai, basing himself on Soviet experience, unambiguously fought for the hegemony of Marxism at the time of what came to be known as the Lukács debate. He stressed that "...we cannot leap over the struggle for the hegemony of proletarian literature and socialist-realist party* literature, nor the objective and phase of intellectual competition between literary trends and writers." He further established: "The fight for the party-committed character of literature and the success of party literary principles does not prevent us from having companions and allies on the literary front." Accordingly, he gave priority to intellectual guidance: "The party desires to provide guidance for literature primarily with its ideas, by creating a literary public opinion which is not independent of, but an organic part of the people's, the working class's and the party's opinion, one which rests on an institutional basis."

At the same time, in spite of these expressed views, the battle for hegemony in practice, and consequently its interpretation also to a certain degree, became distorted. The doctrine of the constant sharpening of the class struggle, the principle that the enemy must first of all be sought within the party; the view that there can be hardly any talk of errors since it was primarily undermining by the enemy that had to be taken into account; the lack of confidence in the masses, which at the same time, was connected with the "prescribed" slogan that the masses were rapidly "becoming filled" with socialist consciousness; in addition to, and at the same time as a basis for all these, the strained pace of economic construction, beginning with the increased targets of the Five Year Plan, all these factors taken as a whole could only lead to the formal strengthening of positions of power in many cases and thus to an actual weakening. The principle of the leading role of Marxism became distorted on this political basis, partly in theory, and chiefly in practice. The leadership evaluated the situation and the possibilities in an unrealistic way not only in economic and social life but in culture as well, and though it did not consider the process to be completed it proclaimed as an immediate aim that Marxism–Leninism be generally accepted and virtually exclusive in the field of culture.

---

* In Russian partiynaya literatura. At one time this was generally translated into Hungarian as party literature, nowadays it is usually rendered as party-committed literature. The Russian permits both interpretations.

The demand that ideology should promptly accomodate itself to changes in power and the political situation grew to be characteristic. The leadership did not take reality into account, nor the Marxist principle that the rapid and relatively unambiguous transformation of power and property relations cannot be expressed immediately and with similar clarity by social consciousness which, by its very nature, lags behind it. They also neglected the factor of unequal development. In practice, the principle of hegemony, still maintained formally, that is the principle of the need for a leading role, was interpreted as if the all-embracing influence of Marxism–Leninism had already been implemented in culture, thus in this respect also mistaking abstract possibility for reality. József Révai, in the same article in which, basing himself on Soviet experience, he proclaimed and defended hegemony as a principle to be fought out through "competition", also argued in favour of an unjustified exclusion, a "placing *hors de combat*". "But the writers became silent, say the opponents," he wrote. "But does anyone think that the most important reason for this is that they are not allowed to write? Is it not rather that they cannot write because they have nothing to write about and no-one to write for? At the time of great revolutionary upheavals it is unavoidable that a whole line of older writers have to gasp for air, the ground slips from under their feet, because they do not know what to do with the new way of life and a new public."

We know that there were those who had nothing to say in the new situation. Actually, however, this evaluation was also applied to creative artists who objectively could have been considered as allies, and with whose views and for whom a struggle ought to have been waged, out in the open, in the interest of the hegemony of Marxism. József Révai was speaking about literature, although his declarations also applied to the whole field of cultural policy. We shall therefore also cite literary examples in the first place. At that time, László Németh's *Égető Eszter* and Zsigmond Remenyik's *Por és hamu* (Dust and Ashes) could not be published, nor could Áron Tamási's autobiographical *Bölcső és bagoly* (Cradle and Owl), though all three books looked on the past under the influence of the new socio-historical situation brought about after the victory of the proletarian dictatorship. In painting and sculpture also they at times excluded the most progressive artists of the period between the two world wars, some of them members of the Socialist Artists' Group.

This narrowing limitation also extended to the great progressive, and indeed, socialist creative artists of the past; Attila József, Bartók and Gyula Derkovits the painter were neglected and the main line to be followed was indicated in the work of Petőfi, Erkel and Munkácsy. This precipitate confrontation not only had the result that cultural policy only partly accepted the works of Bartók, Attila József and Derkovits, but also that it forced contemporary socialist writers and artists into an unnecessary choice and into a self-impoverishing limitation of style. Other examples could also support the fact that the principle of fighting for the realization of the leading role of Marxism became distorted in practice, and that the circle of possible allies was narrowly, and in a certain sense, arbitrarily determined.

The declaration of the exclusive domination of Marxism was given ever greater emphasis. That this was not contrary to the intentions of those in charge of cultural policy was illustrated by József Révai when he said in 1954, when an analysis of the preceding years was initiated also within the party: "It is certain that there were exaggerations in this sphere (that is as far as administrative measures used to an inadmissible degree were concerned —Ed.) but these were necessary and unavoidable in the period that has just passed... After the year of change (1948—Ed.) it was absolutely correct to use administrative means also to sweep out the bourgeois dirt of the ideological front, and to assist the success of Marxism–Leninism and socialist realism as well as to force the ideology of the enemy underground... In the new phase (after June 1953—Ed.) a greater role must, naturally, be given to methods of ideological education... But that we are able to contemplate doing this, that we can safely ease the too many forced measures, that we can allow literature much more freedom, is also due to the fact that after the take-over, in contrast to the anarchy of the coalition period, we furthered the monopoly of our ideas in ideology with a firm hand." (Contribution to "The Situation and Tasks of Our Literature" a submission drafted by the Agitation-Propaganda Department, 1954.)

This hasty voluntaristic "adjustment" of ideology to political monopoly resulted first of all in the exclusion of a valuable part of Hungarian and foreign culture from intellectual life, while another portion, also progressive but not Marxist, at times in good faith but erroneously, was "converted" in name and called socialist. Thirdly it also became possible for hostile views and trends to deliberately and consciously appear in the guise of Marxism.

The cultural policy of those years bears out that while aiming at the realization of the Leninist principle of party-committedness, it was precisely Lenin's directions that sank into oblivion. The policy of a "firm hand" was proclaimed even where it was not necessary, although Lenin himself called attention to the fact that "Nothing will be achieved in this by doing things in a rush, by assault, by vim or vigour..." and they were of the opinion that they had already reached the point of Marxist "exclusivity" not taking into account the warning "We must show sound scepticism for too rapid progress, for boastfulness. . . (Lenin Selected Works, Vol. 3. Moscow 1967. p. 775.).

Another usual accompanying feature of the voluntarism of "adjustment" was that cultural policy did not adequately take into consideration the special nature of the social role of various forms of consciousness. It brought science, the arts and their dissemination, education and culture into a direct relationship with politics and its most immediate demands. Occasional declarations to the contrary notwithstanding, they were expected to serve everyday political tasks in practice, to illustrate and agitate for the demands of the day.

The mechanical extension of political victory to ideological and cultural fields resulted in actual political unity itself becoming more restricted than warranted by the circumstances, in time a mere pseudo-unity, supported mainly by formal means. The unity which was established at the time of the political change, was naturally neither complete nor absolute, the contradictions of different ideologies straining within a political platform whose essential features were held in common. This unity should have developed further through a struggle of ideas and debates that cleared the air. Without these, however, it became rigid and could not become a dynamic unity mobilizing the public, expanding its own basis, that is a unity really strengthening the hegemony of Marxism.

The situation was further complicated by the fact that there was a conflict not only between political needs and ideological practice, but policy itself was replete with contradictions. The practice of making theoretical work and the arts subservient to everyday political demands, for instance, contributed to the additional tensions which rose out of errors in politics and economic policies. The underestimation of the peculiar characteristics of ideology resulted in the curious circumstance that the contradictions appearing in politics and economic policy frequently precipitated in culture and broke to the surface as cultural issues. For this reason the direct political significance of the fields of culture and ideology became distorted and exaggerated in an unhealthy way.

The realisation of political contents and needs by direct and overwhelmingly administrative measures in culture and ideology brought with it an excessive centralisation of direction. Predominant practice in cultural policy implanted the view that the only proper representative of Marxism–Leninism, who could develop it further, was the leader of the party, in a given situation, the person responsible for cultural matters within the party leadership. Thus, the role of every functionary, every ideological, cultural institution and its communists was essentially one of verifying that which was said "at the top", be that correct or incorrect.

An inevitable concomitant of a centralism burdened with bureaucratic features was that those in charge of cultural policy did not merely deal with matters of general interest in this field, and on the level of principle only. Ideological questions were connected with aesthetic observations, analyses of novels, short stories and poems in a manner that diverged completely from the role of politics and politicians, an injudicious practice even if these concrete analyses incidentally proved to be correct. This confusion of art criticism and the judgement of given works of art with a cultural policy designed to evaluate significant trends and with a real ideological position was harmful to art criticism but even more so to cultural policy. The criteria of political evaluation applied in those times could justifiably be criticized as reflecting individual taste, they consequently cannot be generally valid.

This declared monopoly also had the effect of producing complacency in many. In this position mainly ensured by power, an answer to current questions was apparently not urgent or indispensable, initiatives could wait, since these answers were essentially pre-determined and handed down by politics anyhow. In scholarly and intellectual public life the method of relying on politics and political prestige, substituting quotations for real argument, became widespread. Instead of discussing, that is analysing and therefore correctly judging, non-Marxist, bourgeois views, there arose a predominant practice of simply branding them with words. The weight of administrative measures could not replace the effect and authority of reasoning. Bourgeois views, in order to find a way to the public, were concealed under a "Marxist" cover, camouflaging themselves with Marxist terminology and quotations. In the ideological and cultural discussions of those times, the leadership at the same time acted quite narrowly and most sharply against artists who were either Marxists or close to Marxism, and only rarely, and in a much more objective tone, criticized the errors of "fellow traveller" intellectuals. This also derived from the fact that the dogmatism of the beginning of the 1950's just, as every other dogmatic-sectarian trend, saw the greatest danger in instability, either real or fancied, in its own camp, and indeed, spent much more energy in fighting against it than in convincing allies, or in the opposing and eliminating of the ideology of the class-enemy. In the meantime, a significant section of bourgeois and petty bourgeois views which were excluded but not defeated by argument, persisted and were influential since, in view of the lack of worthy Marxist criticism and argument, a large part of the public was defenseless against them.

Nevertheless, the politics and cultural policy of the early 1950's by no means consisted wholly of errors and misconceptions. One must not forget for a moment that these years opened the gates wide for a revolution in culture and the arts, that millions took advantage of the new possibilities offered by teaching, education and adult education, mass-oriented book publishing and arts, taking possession of culture, one of the most jealously guarded monopolies of the ruling classes of earlier times.

We can find people nowadays who, generally unintentionally but also superfluously, remember their former selves as if they had seen clearly but did not dare to act. The truth is that it was precisely these positive, and indeed, inspiring tendencies which in their eyes, and in the eyes of many people, clouded or diminished, or justified something that later proved to be erroneous, and actually criminal. Many of those personally attacked also accepted criticism even when the criticism was unjustified, they refused to be branded, that was all. This cannot be explained by a lack of character, only by the chaos of the situation, with which, lacking suitable experience, only a very few could grapple. The negation of the past in this sphere too, is wrong and meaningless since past errors cannot be rendered undone. They must be reckoned with in order to learn how to orientate ourselves much better than in the past. The one who does not recognize past errors, faces the danger of committing them again.

This cannot of course serve as an excuse for earlier ideological and cultural policy errors, or for the leadership of those times. On the contrary, this also proves the danger and harmful nature of concepts based on illusion, presenting as they did that which was actually contradictory as monolithic, and suppressing not only criticism but self-criticism as well, in this way making the situation invisible and concealing the contradictions.

The dangerous character of the dogmatic methods in the ideological struggle is not only reflected in the fact that in the final analysis they proved to be unsuccessful, but also because for a while they did produce results, and consequently hid unsolved problems or presented them as solved. The more "successful" administrative repression with which the intellectual struggle against bourgeois and petty-bourgeois ideology was replaced proved to be, the more vehement the reaction. Afterwards, revealing the actual situation in more than one case had the effect on creative artists and noteworthy intellectuals, that they began to doubt even those truths which proved to be true beyond doubt. This reaction was made all the more grave because there were those, and of course, not the very best who, ashamed of their failure, tried to compensate for their past by overbidding. They proclaimed themselves seers to make people forget how blind they had been before.

One ought to speak about this to help demonstrate to everyone that it was the party itself which revealed the systematic character, context and dangers of the dogmatic and sectarian mistakes of the period before 1953, that were so sharply brought to the surface by life and practice. This clarification is a matter of principle since without it all analyses of that period would be false. The fact that this criticism and elimination of mistakes started within the party and within the working class movement, and that this was not forced on the party by any kind of outside pressure, is at the same time the most striking proof that these phenomena were profoundly alien to socialism and Marxism–Leninism. Bourgeois opposition in Hungary just like the foreign bourgeoisie, did not, and could not have had anything to do with this exposure of errors, their fight was not aimed against the personality cult or the distortions, since they identified the mistakes with socialism and through this "identification" wanted to eliminate socialism itself. They had a lion's share in confusing misled people at the beginning with their slogans of fighting against errors, thus drawing these people under their influence and turning them against working class power.

The declaration of the exclusive domination of Marxism without any real foundation was also harmful because it resulted in the establishment of the "local" monopoly of various kinds of scientific and artistic groups. Under the given circumstances it was a simple matter for the representatives of certain cultural or scientific trends to silence others which were equally justified, by stamping them as "non-Marxist". All these "branch" monopoly situations damaged primarily those scientific and cultural endeavours in whose interest they had been formed in the first place, impeding their healthy development, and in many cases causing considerable harm.

To repeat: criticizing the distortion of ideology and its consequences by no means involves condemning all the cultural activity and its direction of the years after the take-over of power in 1948. Just as politics and economic policies, despite their burdens, achieved considerable and lasting results during this period, clearly in spite of all mistakes, so cultural policy also, despite the voluntaristic forcing of a "monopoly", attained considerable success in deepening the links between culture and the masses, in the development of socialist education etc. One must not forget that it was at this time that Marxism–Leninism really took root in Hungarian cultural life, in significant sections of the professional classes even if it was a period laden with dogmatism, and that this led to important socialist creative activity of lasting value, establishing the foundation for the further development of socialist culture.

Certain positive features of Hungarian cultural policy such as the attempt to battle against schematism, played a role in this process. Taking examples from literature, it was at this time that the generation of István Simon, Ferenc Juhász, László Nagy made its appearance, László Benjámin's verse, Péter Veres' prose, Gyula Illyés' dramatic writing etc. flourished then. Works like Déry's *Felelet* (Answer) and Németh's *Égető Eszter* were born on the basis of social and historical positions created by socialism, though in spite of the cultural policy of the times.

In the fine arts, it was this era that helped the painters István Szőnyi, Aurél Bernáth and Endre Domanovszky to create their monumental works, that gave further support to the sculptors József Somogyi and Jenő Kerényi in their careers, and gave many young and talented people the first push starting them on their careers. Several of them are active and significant artists today.

The party resolution of June 1953 created more favourable conditions both for the building of socialistm and the realisation of the hegemony of Marxism, by strengthening the worker-peasant alliance and by emphasizing socialist democracy. The theory of the constant sharpening of class struggle was not yet openly rejected but practical steps were taken essentially reflecting this recognition. Unfortunately, further development was first hampered and then distorted by two factors, which mutually reinforced each other in their consequences: a party leadership which was incapable of consistently eliminating sectarian dogmatic mistakes, and the revisionist group behind which the trends hostile to socialism, and later the forces of bourgeois counter-revolution, gradually drew together.

By and large, this was the atmosphere, one which also had a harmful effect on party unity, which prevailed at the beginning of 1956, when news of the 20th Congress of the Communist Party of the Soviet Union reached Hungary. Since the then party leadership did not draw the proper conclusions from the Congress or did so only inconsistently, it could not offer convincing perspectives for the future in the spirit of that congress, the revisionists on the other hand made the 20th Congress appear as the justification of their views. The party resolution of July 1956, the removal of Rákosi, theoretically provided a constructive basis for relaxation and further development. However, revisionism then assumed an organized form and the counter-revolutionary forces lined up behind it, increasing their attacks. The bourgeois forces of domestic reaction, with the help of revisionists and considerable support from abroad, took advantage of the situation to spark off the counter-revolution. Socialist power was shaken.

From an ideological point of view, we can describe the years before 1956, as the critical years of Marxism, when together with the collapse of "monopolistic" illusions, the positions of socialist ideology were also greatly weakened, and the Rákosi type of leadership, instead of sincerely and critically facing their errors merely undertook awkward and ambiguous adjustments in questions of detail only, while retaining their original notions and acting on this basis. It was not possible on this inconsistent basis to clarify the tasks involved in establishing the hegemony of Marxism–Leninism correctly. This was also true of other important questions. Lacking a re-evaluation of the notion of hegemony, and without a self-critical condemnation on principle of past errors, corrections inevitably appeared as "concessions" rather than steps towards the active realization of consciously constructed political principles.

Under these circumstances, the correct principle of "greater freedom—greater responsibility" (*Szabad Nép**, March 15, 1954) could not be realized. Communists working in the cultural field had no platform based on principles. Reviving bourgeois and petty-bourgeois views which openly appeared at that time could therefore take almost unlimited advantage of the declaration of "greater freedom", where there are only "concessions", there is no limit to demands. In such a situation, Marxists were incapable of argument, lacking a clear political basis, their battle against the right was necessarily linked to a defence of still virulent dogmatic errors end illusions. Those who correctly opposed revisionism and rightist reaction, could be branded as sectarian dogmatists while the revisionists could present themselves as the champions of "true socialism". The right wing, taking advantage of the left's lack of a firm principled position, could spread doubt to an ever greater sphere, compromising Marxism, it could always point to the inconsistency of the position of the leadership as far as the judgement of the past and current practice were concerned. It became possible, and revisionism, together with emergent bourgeois views used this opportunity, to identify the party with errors, socialism with the cult of personality, and Marxism with dogmatism and this without the counter-revolutionary, anti-Marxist character of such identifications being made openly evident in discussion.

In culture, primarily in literature, the attacks of the right were aimed at the main guarantee of the leading role of Marxism, that is the party guidance of culture. The criticism of errors was extended to the principle of party direction, something which was made all the easier, since as a rule the forces of sectarian opportunism predominated in the party leadership

* "Free People," the Hungarian Working People's Party's Budapest daily at the time.

and impeded a consistent elimination of the personality cult. The right-wing attacked socialist realism and socialist art at the same time, and with its criticism of the dogmatic practice of quotation it cast doubt on party committed Marxist scholarship. It began to undermine the institutions designed to guarantee the leading role of Marxism, transforming them into its own organizational bases, using open forums of debate, the Writers' Association, the Petőfi Circle, etc. for this purpose. The reasons for the loss of positions formerly held by Marxism were not, as some contended then, and still do today, endeavours to expose and correct past mistakes. On the contrary, it became evident that this struggle against reaction and revisionism could not be conducted on a sectarian basis, just as sectarian mistakes could not be overcome on a right-wing, petty-bourgeois or bourgeois, platform.

*

Following the defeat of the counter-revolution, the Hungarian Socialist Workers' Party began the ideological and organisational consolidation of cultural life as one of its most important tasks, parallel with political and economic stabilization. This complicated and complex process will be referred to here only in connection with the interpretation of the demands involved in the fight for the hegemony of Marxism, and the road chosen in that battle.

In this respect a more differenciated determination of relations between politics and culture and ideology, by the party was characteristic of 1959–60, priority being given to politics. The party considered their relation, but also consistently kept in mind the differentiated character of their roles in a socialist society. What followed from this primarily was that after the counter-revolution, that is in a period of extraordinary political tension when the re-establishment of proletarian power and a people's democracy was the order of the day, it categorically, and using the power at its disposal, secured the vital political interests of socialism. State power dispersed and dissolved all politically hostile forces, organizations and initiatives. From the very first moment, the party made it unambiguously clear that when it came to questions of power it was not willing to make any compromise with groups of hostile intention. This political principle was as a matter of fact the starting point of consolidation in the cultural field which first took place on the political plane. The Writers' Association had to be dissolved not as a cultural institution but as an organizational focus serving hostile political activities. It also became necessary to suspend other artistic associations which had become hotbeds of hostile activity, and to take legal action against politically guilty writers and artists, who were citizens who had broken the law.

But the party did not take over methods meant to secure political power into the fields of ideology and culture. From the very first moment, its objective was to restore, strengthen and develop the hegemony of Marxism through a fight for principles and ideas, and it chose the method of convincing by argument as its chief instrument. The party, besides giving far-reaching support to all forces which offered their help in restoring the people's power, dealt patiently with those who had been misled, giving them time to allow them to be convinced of the error of their views, attitudes and behaviour by life itself. It helped them to recognize their mistakes and to put a distance between themselves and foreign and domestic reaction. The party did not demand public self-criticism and did not urge declarations of loyalty, it did not force anyone, even indirectly, to express views contrary to his convictions. Those who proved through their works that they did not oppose the system were given conditions that allowed them to take part in cultural life once again. The method applied in the period that followed straight on the counter-revolution already reflected an attitude which persisted effectively later also. Granted agreement on basic political issues, a certain scope was allowed to non-Marxist, but not hostile, works of bourgeois or petty-bourgeois character; at the same time thorough criticism of these works from a Marxist point of view was encouraged.

The renewed practice of an intellectual struggle for hegemony meant initiating and undertaking open discussion on matters of principle. The free expression of non-Marxist but not hostile views, was, from the outset, coupled with theoretical and political orientation as the most important instrument of cultural direction, and with ideological discussion, as the most general method of developing further the leading role of Marxism. This was expressed in a whole series of party documents which, on the one hand, formulated the correct methods of Marxist ideological struggle, on the other themselves set an example, of principled intellectual guidance, and for polemical practice. (See the relevant section in the party resolution of December 1956, cultural policy directives of the Hungarian Socialist Workers' Party (1958), the first comprehensive summary of cultural policy, the position adopted by the Cultural Theoretical Working Collective affiliated with the Central Committee of the Hungarian Socialist Workers' Party on populist writers (1958), on certain questions of post-Liberation literature (1959); theses on bourgeois nationalism and socialist patriotism (1959), the Political Committee's 1958 resolution on the consistent but patient and differentiated intellectual discussion with religious views, etc.). All this was of course, a natural consequence of the Marxist-Leninist nature of the party's policy as a whole, and was an organic and inseparable part of the two-front struggle, of the policy of making alliances, that notion of socialist construction whose implementation is still carried on today.

As against right-wing revisionist views, the party emphatically established the absolute necessity of party and state guidance of culture. Against dogmatism, the party stressed and witnessed from the outset that direct (such as appointment, replacement, decoration, prohibition) and indirect (such as the distribution of material means) administrative restrictions were not, in the true sense of the term, a way to convince people but merely created a general political framework. Ideas can only be overcome by ideas. Principled ideological orientation is the chief instrument of party and state guidance of culture. The party critically analysed the essence and nature of counter-revolution and revisionism in a way that amounted to taking up an ideological position; the reasons for their existence and their various forms, and the relation between revisionism and nationalism in 1956, the role of a "populist" ideology in present conditions was described, as was the effect of mistaken revisionist ideals on literature, etc. At the same time, the party consistently rejected sectarian and dogmatic distortion. The mere fact of open discussion with hostile ideological views was a criticism of sectarian practices and at the same time made up for the omissions committed by an ideologically timid dogmatism which substituted administrative measures for argument. The party also carried out a retrospective analysis of revisionist tendencies in literature and art, and firmly excluded all politically hostile works. In contrast with the narrow methods employed by dogmatic cultural policy, the 1957 party meeting established that, besides giving special support to socialist realism, "a place must be ensured for other progressive efforts, naturally, always reserving the right of criticism."

The party opposed revisionist efforts to falsify, and "re-evaluate" the Hungarian cultural and artistic tradition, forcing socialist and revolutionary features into the background. To this day, the party, even in the face of a strong and stubborn opposition, has resisted every attempt to overvalue 20th century bourgeois decadence, or underestimate the achievements of Soviet culture, science, art and scholarship. At the same time it rejected the dogmatic view which even narrowed down literary and cultural traditions close to the working class, or indeed socialist ones. It rejected the isolationist cultural policies of sectarianism, and allowed 20th century bourgeois values their proper place. It rejected all merely formal glorification of Soviet culture and art, in this way ensuring and increasing the prestige and influence of their real values.

The two-front struggle does not mean, and never meant a search for some kind of "third way", nor is it a defensive attitude. On the contrary, it formed the guarantee and foundation for widening the communist basis and making it firmer. It made a convincing cultural policy that was consistent in its content and patient in form both possible and creditable, it made a far-reaching contribution to the shaping of the leading role of Marxism, to its popularity, increased attraction and last but not least, to a sharper delineation of the socialist features of intellectual and professional life.

As a result of the party's new cultural policies, the socialist basis of cultural life was strengthened, and supplemented by a generation of talented young people who were committed to Marxism–Leninism and socialist realism. Those who had been excluded by the lack of trust inherent in the earlier cultural policy became active and recognized participants in cultural activities. The writers' strike (1957) proclaimed by propaganda from abroad failed, and the intellectual groupings which had been formed in the name of hostile ideals were realigned or dispersed.

The period of consolidation was essentially over by the beginning of the 1960's. The greatest achievement of the ten years that have passed since then has been that the ideological situation of cultural life has been developing in proportion, and largely in harmony, with the construction of a socialist society. The cultural level of the working class and the peasantry is rising. Though the ideological range of cultural life is wide and not exactly free of contradictions, the positions held by Marxism–Leninism have become stronger. The situation is complex but conditions which promise a further strengthening of this position are taking shape, intelligent, open discussion is one of the contributing factors. In various fields of science, art and culture, it is becoming obvious that creative workers who started out from alien ideological climes are coming closer and the taking shape of attitudes approaching Marxism is quite evident not only in their statements but in their works as well. One could name more than one Hungarian writer, artist, scholar or scientist belonging to the older generation, many of whose works now enrich the values of socialist culture. It is true on the other hand, that some of the young, in the early stage of their career show the confusions of incomprehensibility produced by alien ideological climes.

Ideological work conducted on a Marxist–Leninist basis is not a simple task even today, it is certainly more complex than the earlier exclusiveness which was necessarily ensured mainly by administrative means. For that very reason, this work demands definite principles, their consistent practical application as well as the necessary forms and organizational structures. In the decade following the consolidation, and as its unchanged continuation on principle, the party worked out the principles and methods of ideological activity with particular care in the knowledge that, always taking into consideration concrete conditions, it is they that most effectively further and ensure the extension of Marxism–Leninism in society and the gradual realization of an integrated socialist ideology.

What are the most essential basic principles of the realization of this leading role? It not only presumes the party and state guidance of culture, but also demands that it become stronger and more differentiated. A permanent condition of the fight for, and the growth of hegemony was and is a categorical rejection of the bourgeois interpretation of the "freedom of culture". A few in Hungary and many more abroad, reject party guidance of culture on principle and see a threat to cultural "freedom" in the notion of hegemony.

The same unconditioned rejection is the lot of another view chiefly characteristic of revisionism, which champions what is called the principle of "indirect" direction and places it in opposition to party and state direction of culture.

Being Marxists we are fully aware that an ideological superstructure is finally determined by social reality. Marxists nevertheless also know how relatively independent and significant the role of ideology, the whole of social consciousness can be, reacting on and influencing the basis, the development of social existence.

The objective process of the growth of a socialist society naturally creates the possibility for the formation of a consistent socialist consciousness. This possibility, however, is not realized automatically, but as a result of the creation and widespread implantation of ideological "regulators" securing the growth of socialism. This also presumes a conscious, organized struggle against bourgeois and petty-bourgeois influences. For this reason the party can never, and will never abdicate its right to direct ideology and culture in an immediate way. The past history and the present of the international working class movement prove this. It is evident that the attempt to eliminate party direction from this extraordinarily important sphere is hostile and aimed against Marxism–Leninism, socialism and Hungarian culture. The party's direction of culture has the closest possible relationship with the implementation of Marxism, it is the most important pledge ensuring the leading role of Marxism–Leninism in the formulation of new issues as they arise and in the initiative and dominance of Marxism–Leninism in the argument with hostile views. It also makes sure that the cultural freedom granted to non-Marxist views does not become deformed into a cultural "freedom" in the bourgeois or revisionist sense, that is licence, but leads to the strengthening of the positions of Marxism–Leninism and socialist culture.

Looked at in this way party cultural guidance is certainly not restricted to a mere definition of the scope of the ideological struggle or to prescribing "the rules of the game". In the fight for a strengthened hegemony, party guidance is not some kind of passive refereeing role. On the contrary thanks to party direction, the principle of the party-committedness of culture is dynamically realized. In the first place by the help given to socialist tendencies in every field of culture with all ideological, moral, propaganda and material resources. Not only for simply political considerations but because Hungarian communists echo Lenin in professing that the revolutionary working class movement, party-committed culture standing at the side of, and openly accepting socialism, at one and the same time requires a more profound reflection of objectivity and a fuller grasp of the context and trends of reality, resulting in a deeper knowledge of, and increasing commitment to the working class, and the great objectives of historical progress.

The most important intellectual safeguard of the leading role of Marxism is Marxism itself. More accurately, the support of socialist aims primarily means the defence of Marxist–Leninist theory, ensuring its further creative growth. The pushing back of anti-Marxist, bourgeois revisionist views is one "side" of the ideological struggle. It can only become comprehensive and persuasive if questions raised by social development, by a creative use of Marxism are fully explained including questions that arise in connection with hostile views. Successful competition with non-Marxist ideas can only be carried on with the help of an attractive scientifically well-founded and constantly growing theory.

The further extension of Marxism can only be achieved in constant debate with bourgeois and petty-bourgeois views. For this reason, the party encourages discussion which serves to strengthen the positions of socialism and Marxism in scientific and creative workshops, and in periodicals which frequently have a nationwide circulation, and also endeavours to create a suitable atmosphere and framework for such discussion. Above all there is a conscious and organized effort to aid Marxists to raise the vital questions of the age, to take up a scientific and scholarly position on issues arising out of these questions, and finally to help shape public opinion in the right direction in opposition to views deriving from an alien ideology.

The party initiates and encourages such creative discussion in order to make sure that it really serves the enrichment of Marxism–Leninism. For this very reason, aimless argumentation and discussion that casts doubt on the basic principles of Marxism–Leninism is discouraged. Discussion is not supported for its own sake and the principle of discussing issues and not personalities is observed and efforts are made to ensure that others observe it also. We believe in the strength of our arguments just as we believe that human beings can be changed for the better.

It is very important to keep the theory unadulterated. It is clear that, even granted a Marxist basis, an issue can be approached in different ways and can be the object of a fruitful exchange of ideas. In any given concrete question therefore the road to establishing a position often leads through long and difficult discussion among Marxists. The necessary conditions are ensured. A pluralism of Marxism is, however, most firmly opposed, that is the theory of "several roads to Marxism". Pluralism is politically used as an ideological basis by splitters, it undermines the leading role of the party. In international affairs it destroys the unity of Marxist–Leninist parties. Looking on various tendencies within Marxism as independent and equally justifiable Marxist systems opens the gates to relativism in philosophy, leading finally to the denial of objective reality, and of Marxism–Leninism as a scientific world view. Although Marxism is a living and growing system of ideas, there is no such thing as 19th century or 20th century Marxism, proletarian and intellectual Marxism, party and non-party Marxism, conservative and modern Marxism, there is only one kind of Marxism which is constantly developing by studying a changing world and a changing reality and the processes involved, and generalizing the lessons to be drawn from them. The integrity of Marxism is, however, maintained in spite of the variety of analytical methods and starting points if these are put forward by people who are conscious of their limitations and inevitable onesidedness, if they do not claim a monopoly position for themselves but strive for a newer and newer synthesis by making use of the conclusions that can be drawn from the manysided debate.

Though criticizing revisionist notions of the pluralisation of Marxism and the relativisation of scientific ideology, one must not, however, forget the constant danger of dogmatism, which is also expressed in efforts to limit, or even eliminate discussions that serve to further the progress of theory. If truths which were valid in a given period of social development are allowed to rigidify, if they are not confronted with changes in reality, if Marxists do not differentiate between their wishes and reality, if they do not take into account the real direction and conditions of development, then their decisions become dogmas and barriers to progress. The counter-part of a revisionism which turns everything relative and doubtful, are notions which do not take into account the fact that Marxism must be enriched by every momentous scientific discovery, as it were taking on "new forms" in changing social conditions. This way of looking at things replaces careful and thorough Marxist analysis and the clarification of a new situation in the course of prolonged discussion by a single demand on ideological work: apologetics for statements once they have been made. This applies not only to the past. If we are not vigilant dogmatism may revive again and again.

There is one basic principle which cannot be neglected in the course of implementing the leading role of the party, that is that Marxism and bourgeois and petty-bourgeois ideologies are opposed to each other. This has to be particularly emphasized in connection with the policy of peaceful coexistence, since some equate this policy with "ideological reconciliation". The party, unambiguously and repeatedly declared that peaceful co-existence is a political and not an ideological category. There cannot, and will never be peaceful co-existence between proletarian and bourgeois ideologies, only intellectual discussion and struggle in its various aspects. Peaceful coexistence between Marxism and anti-Marxism cannot be imagined.

The ideological struggle is also going on on an international level. It is a commonplace that imperialism uses every means at its disposal ranging from economic, trade and scientific contacts, the significant growth in tourism, some Hungarian emigrants in the West, and the radio, right to open diversionary acts, to further its attempts to create disintegration. Its most general aim is to produce a confrontation between the socialist countries and the Soviet Union and between the various socialist countries, primarily nationalist incitement and the propagation of a number of variations of the "third way." It endeavours to cast doubt on the construction of socialism in Hungary and on party policy in order to conserve and revive bourgeois views. The glorification of the western way of life is an integral part of its propaganda, including western science and culture. Part of this is the advertising of its superiority.

The successful construction of a socialist society is the most telling argument against this loosening up strategy; the establishment and constant growth of a structure of economic, political, moral and cultural conditions which justifies the historical validity of a socialist form of society to the broadest masses. A direct struggle against loosening up must be, and is, conducted on this basis. Even the most indirect appearance of liberalism and nationalism is consistently opposed. At the same time, socialist patriotism is strengthened, national consciousness with a socialist content is deepened among the people, as is the sort of patriotism which includes proletarian internationalism as an organic part, the sort of consciousness which acts and thinks in the awareness of the necessity for unity and harmony between national and international interests. At the same time, in every sphere of education and culture, and with an intensive use of mass communication media, the true face of modern capitalism is exposed in argument; its political aggression, economic exploitation and its inhuman morality and culture, and contrasted with the true values of socialism.

The implementation of hegemony also demands a differentiation among the various bourgeois ideals. We live in a transitional society, therefore, in the fields of culture and the arts, we often encounter transitory ideological formulae, which although they are non-Marxist, and thus bourgeois, are not expressedly anti-Marxist. One must also remember that various ideological elements merge eclectically in the consciousness of a significant portion of Hungarians. Awareness of this factor which crops up every day, does not in any way mean the theoretical recognition of an ideological "third way". It is the task of Marxist critical thinking to separate such formulae into elements which agree with Marxism and those that are alien to it, and this separation means ideological struggle and argument. We cannot, and will never accept bourgeois views which are foreign to Marxism as our own, and under no circumstances can we abdicate our right to criticise them. One must be aware however that there is an anti-imperialist, anti-capitalist culture in the capitalist countries also, science and art with a progressive function, which though not Marxist, tells the truth in a most authentic and outspoken way about the bankruptcy of today's highly developed capitalism, this dead-end of human development. Such relative values, given the right critical attitude, have an important place in Hungarian cultural life. Marxist criticism is a necessary ideological condition for the understanding of the values inherent in these creative works. I consider it obvious, although it is not superfluous to note this here, since a great many see bourgeois and petty-bourgeois anti-capitalism in the cultural activity of the capitalist countries at most; there is a most significant, Marxist-inspired, communist-committed science and art, in the West also.

In Hungary bourgeois ideology makes its appearance as a rule with a characteristic content and in a characteristic fashion. In Hungarian artistic life, for example, a number of creative people, not only in words but in important works, commit themselves to such basic moral categories as the people, work, peace, reason and so on. It is also characteristic of them, however, that in many cases they do not closely relate these great human values to the working class movement, to socialism, often leaving questions connected with this relation open, or avoiding them. Certain features of this, for lack of a better word let us call it "abstract humanism", are acceptable if critically apprehended even if their theoretical basis does not have a Marxist content. Their presence and effect are strong forces against that bourgeois decadence which does not even believe in the humanist values mentioned above, and therefore they are valuable. It is not "liberalism", that "permits" such progressive, but non-socialist art, but the policy of alliances of the working class and the working class movement in both the home and the international sense of the word, which necessitates contact with other anti-imperialist, humanistic forces in the field of culture as well, precisely in the interest of socialism and the working class. What is emphasized is that this Janus-faced humanism is considered a value, not in itself, but as something to be apprehended in a critical spirit.

*

The principles and practice of Hungarian cultural policies further the strengthening of the hegemony of Marxism–Leninism, ensuring that it should fill a leading role in the ideological life of Hungarian society, permitting a further development and re-enforcement of the positions that have already been conquered. Progressing further along this road, we shall eventually achieve the full implementation of the complete, all-embracing influence of scientific socialism when the ideas of Marxism and Leninism will determine the consciousness of the whole of society. But this era will be a world of silence and uniform views even less than the present one. Reality always poses further questions and man is always forced to answer. The distant future can only be characterized by a lively intellectual atmosphere, rich in discussion and argument, when the rapid and wide comprehension of objective truth will not be impeded by unscientific illusions and various kinds of prejudice. The fact that this is our goal, and only this, cannot be a matter of doubt for Marxists. To find the road that leads to this goal, to discover the most useful methods and means to approach this goal: this is our task.

ACCESS TO AND PARTICIPATION IN CULTURE IN A SOCIALIST COMMUNITY

by

GYÖRGY ACZÉL

I

Institutionalized and organized action designed to ensure easier access to and greater participation in culture has recently been much discussed in Hungary. It was an important subject at the March 1974 session of the Central Committee of the Hungarian Socialist Workers' Party which passed an appropriate resolution.

It is part of the "prehistory" of this resolution that, soon after the defeat of the counter-revolution, to assist consolidation, in the course of formulating fundamental ideas in 1958, the Central Committee adopted directives for the cultural policy of the Hungarian Socialist Workers' Party, laying down the long-term principles of party and state guidance of the whole of Hungarian cultural life. In 1969 the Central Committee elaborated and adopted directives for science policy, and in 1972 it determined the duties of educational development. It was these preliminaries that made an analysis of the present subject possible.

However, these ideological and cultural statements and directives are not the only, or the most important, antecedents of this proposal. Indispensable preconditions were above all the progress of socialist reality, the modernization of economic guidance, the further development of socialist democracy in state administration, an examination of the situation of the working class, the resolutions on the position of women and young people, and the work done to implement them; all that was done, allowing one to maintain that Hungary has reached a higher stage in the construction of socialism, when the importance of the further development of socialist consciousness, mode and way of life impresses itself with even more imperative necessity than before.

Carrying out objectives demands a higher general level of culture, the situation does not only allow but demands that social change should —through the mediation of larger and smaller communities—produce a socialist outlook and socialist ways of living at the family and personal level. This is, of course, not primarily or exclusively the task of institutionalized activity within cultural policy, though this has an important role, since with its own special means, which cannot be replaced, it helps to shape socialist consciousness.

It is therefore unnecessary to stress that reexamining this question was prompted neither by a bottleneck, nor a crisis. Results of far-reaching importance were achieved in the implementation and fulfilment of the Leninist cultural revolution. It is this that prompts the question: what must be done now

—with the difficulties which are the left-over of the "legacy" history bequeathed on the country;

—with the tensions, contradictions and duties which are the side-effects of what has already been achieved;

—with the demands of the future;

—and with the problems caused by shortcomings in our own work.

What Lenin had to say about the two cultures naturally applies to the present subject as well. The socialist point of view on the education and culture of the masses has always been in sharp conflict with the bourgeois one. The fundamental question is—besides the ideological content of culture—the relationship of politics and power to the education of the masses.

To give an example, in 1919–20, at the height of the White Terror, the ideologists of those in power argued: "It has become clear that the slogan 'science belongs to everybody' may lead to extraordinarily dangerous demagogy, and we have reached a stage where it may become necessary to put a brake on the popularization of the sciences for the sake of the morals of the masses."[1]

Kunó Klebelsberg, for many years Minister of Education and Church Affairs in the Horthy regime, wrote: "The foundation of my cultural policy is the thought that in small and large nations three or four thousand people stand for culture."[2] The advocate of "cultural superiority", Gyula Kornis, wrote: "The intensity of culture is in almost inverse proportion to its extensiveness, the wider and more quickly it is spread the shallower it becomes, like a flood that is reduced in power as the waters cover a larger

---

[1] *Új Idők*, No. 13, 1920, p. 264.
[2] Kunó Klebelsberg: "On the Development of Hungarian Culture." *Dunántúl*, May 28, 1925. (In Hungarian)

area."[3] This was the way in which this cultural policy expressed the aims of the Hungarian ruling class as it was progressing towards open fascism. Progressive forces, on the other hand, considered the positive link between people and culture to be a fundamental issue. As the late nineteenth-century poet János Vajda put it: "A more educated people is more sensitive to the material and moral suffering engendered by its oppression; it feels it as more unbearable and it finds the ways to express its dissatisfaction."[4] What the progressive intelligentsia, the Social Science Society, the periodical *Huszadik Század* (Twentieth Century) and the Galileo Circle did for culture and education early this century can only be briefly mentioned here. This applies also to the educational plans by the movement of populist writers which, in addition to some utopian features, contained much that was inspiring and valuable but—as the 1958 declaration on populist writers rightly pointed out—these good intentions and beautiful ideas and reform plans, which wanted to change the cultural situation of the people not through the class struggle but by avoiding it, proved to be mere illusions.

The cultural history of the communist, that is the left wing working-class movement, stands for the most valuable traditions of cultural work. The first workers' clubs already were founded for the "intellectual training of members, as well as the defence and promotion of their moral and material interests."[5] Ervin Szabó explained in 1907 that libraries were needed in which "an industrial worker, who seeks the fermenting elements and justification of his struggle for economic and political progress in the new results of technology and the natural sciences, but mainly of the social sciences and social policy finds the books he wants".[6] The Constitution of the Hungarian Republic of Councils stated that "an end is put to the cultural privileges of the bourgeoisie opening up to the opportunity for actually acquiring culture to those who work".[7] The underground Hungarian Communist Party, together with the Social Democratic Left, and organized workers, continued, even in circumstances of inhuman persecution, and during the war, with its work of cultural enlightenment; this was an important instrument in its political fight, particularly in maintaining contact with the masses. It endeavoured to make sure that the best members of the proletariat acquired, at worker-seminars, which entailed great risks,

3 Gyula Kornis: *Culture and Politics.* Franklin Publishing House, 1928, p. 69. (In Hungarian)
4 János Vajda: "On the Situation of the Working Class." In: *Politikai Újdonságok,* May 16, 1883. (in Hungarian)
5 Selected Documents of the History of the Hungarian Labour Movement. Vol. 1, Szikra Publishing House, 1951, p. 256. (in Hungarian)
6 *Fővárosi Könyvtár Értesítője,* 1907. p. 1.
7 Selected Documents of the History of the Hungarian Labour Movement. Vol. 6/B, Kossuth Publishing House, 1960, p. 215. (in Hungarian)

fundamental ideological and cultural knowledge, that choirs be formed, including such as recited prose and verse, since the communists well knew that cultural work was a community-creating force, such communities being indispensable in helping the political struggle, preparing the intellectual advancement of the people about to be liberated.

Liberation produced a fundamental change in the relationship between the working masses and education too. Between 1945 and 1948 the Hungarian Communist Party—while fighting for political power and the reconstruction of the economy—consistently represented the cause of the democratization of education as well; it intensified educational activity within the movement, and opened breaches in the walls of the educational system through which tens and hundreds of thousands of gifted young workers and peasants passed. One was able to witness the accumulation of communal experience covering hundreds of thousands; new, socialist community movements were formed with a newly liberated vigour. Under the leadership of the Party and party organizations, the youth movement, and in another sense, the colleges of young workers and peasants and the hostels for apprentices were turned into communities not merely by the educational intention of those in charge but first of all through their actively taking part in the shaping of history.

The socialist cultural revolution got under way after 1948—in the wake of the conquest of political and economic power by the working class. An end was put to the cultural monopolies of the erstwhile ruling classes, an integrated state system of general schools was created, and cultural institutions, such as publishers, theatres, cinemas and film studios, came under state ownership, but it was a revolutionary feat of no lesser significance that large numbers of adults—workers and peasants, the veterans of underground work, war and privations—covered the syllabus of secondary schools in abridged courses, entered universities and studied economics, the social sciences and history, law, administration and politics. Within a very short time a new socialist intelligentsia, that is a new leadership, was born.

The "leftist" and rightist political distortions of the first half of the fifties were present, or reflected, in the cultural life of that period as well. Nevertheless, important results were achieved at that time, the number of educational institutions was considerably increased, the basis of culture widened, hitherto unimaginable opportunities were opened up for the working class, for the masses.

After the defeat of the Counter-Revolution and the stabilization of socialist power and in harmony with socio-economic evolution, the process that had begun in 1945 was accelerated.

The entire structure of cultural activity was transformed largely due to the effect of the rapid spread of television, radio and the press.

Radio and television already play a leading role in educational work as a whole, that is the spreading of culture. They not only spread and mediate culture, but organize as well. Various nationwide competitions and quizzes ought to be mentioned there, particularly Fly Peacock, the folk-song competition that grew into a movement. The work of television and radio is especially important in those villages and settlements whose size does not permit a sufficiency of locally based cultural institutions.

In recent years dailies and weeklies, county newspapers and periodicals have done more than ever before to spread culture and knowledge, and shape public taste. This is shown by a large and growing circulation, and by the greater space taken up by art and literature. Hungary's cultural map is still far from uniform, there are blank spots, but the meaning of the latter term has changed and is changing. The term blank spots is used to refer to homestead-clusters and villages far from urban areas where the number of newspaper and book readers, cinema-goers, library subscribers, of people interested in and receptive to culture is below the national average. Today it means that television has not reached every home yet and that there are still people about who do not make a habit of reading; thirty to forty years ago it meant massive illiteracy. "Not reading" is also relative. We are well aware that there are still quite a number of people in Hungary—and unfortunately not only the elderly—who, for subjective or objective reasons, have so far been left out of cultural advancement. This is a warning that ways of coping with this must be found—and in a good many places these have already been discovered—which do not lay primary emphasis on the school, that put the stress not on some certificate or diploma but on fundamental education and the awakening of interest in culture. The primary aim must now be to make sure that as few as possible of the younger and future generations be left out, that they not only be given the opportunity but a basic education as well. As regards the majority of the people, attention has to be concentrated on the extension of culture, the raising of standards, the intensification of cultural educational work and first of all on the spreading of the socialist consciousness, of education suffused by Marxist ideology.

Taking into account all the anxieties and difficulties it can still be said that in the past thirty years the Hungarian nation has become more educated, more enlightened, more broad-minded and incomparably richer in knowledge and better informed than at any time in the past. And what is no less important, men and women have become educated and conscious in their actions in the socialist sense of the term, they know that they have a right to live in a human way, a right to justice, that they have a part to play in public affairs; they make their calculations and plan ahead, they live in awareness of their future.

The culture of every class and section of society has increased, to a differing degree, and in various forms.

The largest increase has occurred in the case of workers, both as regards their acquired skills and general level of education. The most highly skilled workers show themselves most receptive to culture. The relationship of the socialist brigades to culture is especially noteworthy. The socialist brigades were originally formed to increase production, improve quality, or reduce costs, but the workers soon discovered that they could meet these requirements only if they read, became informed in the world of culture, went to the theatre and watched good films. An interesting aspect in the cultural activity of socialist brigades is that they often discuss what they have read or seen, and so lead to a new, spontaneous form of community life. The number of skilled workers who are in possession of the secondary school leaving certificate is also increasing. The rise in cultural standards has a beneficial influence on the development of living conditions. In socialist brigades the demand "work, live and study in a socialist way" is ever present and to a growing extent. The trend is basically sound but there are many shortcomings. Approximately one and a half million of those in employment have not completed the general school course; only one-fifth of manual workers use libraries, and much of what is read is of the best-seller type and much that is done by the socialist brigades in a cultural way has a merely formal character.

The socialist reorganization of agriculture and the technological progress that accompanied it radically changed the nature of agricultural work, transforming working conditions, village customs and traditional culture. Socialist large-scale farming does not only make the acquisition of higher skills and a higher general level of education possible, but even demands them. Nevertheless, the cultural standards of the peasantry, and of villagers in general, and their educational opportunities, lag behind those of other sections of society and the urban population for historic and objective reasons.

The majority of professional people can be said to be highly trained and well-educated. Their role and responsibility in the spreading of culture —especially at their places of employment—is most important; but they do not do as much as is desirable.

Reciprocal contact between the classes and sections of society is much livelier, the earlier rigid barriers are disappearing; this too has an influence on culture, on changes in ways of living. Most families number manual workers, peasants as well as professional people among their members. The marks of earlier class culture are disappearing, and in the way of life, in culture (home, language, reading matter) the strengthening of socialist national unity has helped a new socialist culture to come into being and grow which includes not only national and internationalist values but the progressive traditions of mankind as well.

Young people ask for an active community culture. Two-thirds of those making use of the facilities of houses of culture and libraries are young people. This is promising for the future, since those under twenty-four make up 38 per cent of the total population, and those under twenty-nine 45 per cent.

II

There must be mutual trust between the masses and the party. All citizens who honestly do their daily work, serve the cause of the people and of the working class, even if they hold views regarding one or the other aspect of socialism, the past, the present or the future, that differ from those of communists. What did and what does this mean for ideology? Patience must be exercised but there must be no acceptance of erroneous views, continuous efforts using education and explanation as its main tools must be made to shape the thinking of the backward. It has to be taken into account that in Hungary there are still a fair few who keep up customary habits and folkways, still believing in unscientific superstitions. Although they will have no part of the old socio-economic system, they still enjoy its cultural left-overs. In this respect, communal education, and the understanding and patient transformation of public opinion, are of great importance.

Requirements are increasing all the time. As progress is made, society needs people who consciously accept the struggle for socialism. As a result, not only socialist relations of ownership but socialist thinking on public questions and socialist culture and morality are becoming more general.

Influencing the minds of men and deliberate action has always been important to progressives, socialists and communists, to all those who desired and did continue to shape the future together with the millions. To those —to us—the cause of educational action in culture is important for this very reason. Communists have always opposed rightist and "leftist" views which mechanically differentiate between or confront economic and cultural construction, Leninist principles do not allow one to forget that these two are inseparable and dialectically related. The firmer the material base of socialist society is, the higher the standard of living rises, the more necessary it becomes and the less possible it is to postpone the answer to the question "how shall we live?"; in the Marxist sense of the term this does not come about by itself but must be built up in a planned and systematic way.

Socialism is being realized consciously, and this is the only effective antidote to "consumer-mindedness". What people attend to all over the world when observing socialist cultural progress is whether we are able to develop—and in what way—the socialist alternative of human and cultural progress. Take literature and art, they do not only exist in a socialist society. The essential difference between the two systems consists exactly in that the other social system may exist without literature and art, but these are organic attributes of socialism, and parts of its essence. Socialism cannot exist without art and literature of a high and continuously progressing standard, it cannot be constructed without this, just as many-sided, advanced socialist man cannot be imagined without literature and art, without socialist culture.

It is an achievement of cultural policy that 20 to 25 per cent of the listeners and viewers of valuable, high-standard art may be considered a more or less permanent public. The audience which is receptive to high-standard works as well, e.g. the ratio of those listening to serious music (5 to 10 per cent), is increasing slowly but all the time. Light music is favoured by a larger camp, though it must be said that what different age-groups are interested in is not identical.

The cinema still satisfies the requirements of the masses for culture and entertainment. Films are not only an important instrument of education in art, but also a guide to ideology and politics; the policy of distributors does not always however satisfy requirements that derive from this.

Theatre attendance dropped somewhat as television became more widespread, but numbers have picked up since.

Interest in and demand for the contemporary fine arts as well as for industrial art is on the increase. The progress of visual culture has been furthered and speeded up by the increasing number and improved standard of art works erected in public places, the progress of artistic life in the country, developments in the provinces and greater liveliness in the field of exhibitions.

Valuable work today already reaches a major part of the population; television and radio help a great deal. There is however a large section who have remained impermeable to the masterpieces of culture. It is they who are most exposed to shallow works, to the second-rate and trash, all of which can have a damaging effect. It has to be taken into consideration here that society in Hungary is in constant transition, and this often involves mobility in the literal sense. A large number of people are, so to speak, permanently on the move, those who work in the construction industry or who, while working in cities, maintain their homes in distant villages. This way of life places a heavy burden on those concerned and they have less time left for cultural interests. The interest in literature and the arts of the older generations who grew up at the time of the previous social system, is more difficult to rouse.

These days when the international class struggle is continued under the conditions of détente, that is the peaceful coexistence of the two systems, the capitalist powers keep on intensifying their ideological manoeuvres directed against the socialist world.

Culture is not a commodity: that is one of the basic tenets of Hungarian policy. This means that the state supports, not sparing the cash, every valuable cultural work, book, play, film, exhibition hall, concert, the radio and television. In Hungary the state subsidizes every theatre ticket by approximately the same amount as the client pays at the box-office. This principle also results in higher prices for products that are light entertainment, such as thrillers, or musical comedies, than those of good books or serious drama. The former are barely subsidized or not at all. A sense of responsibility towards need to increase culture and to bear in mind the sound needs of society is still insufficiently in evidence in artistic and scientific activity, in those who transmit the achievements, and some of the leaders as well.

In spite of these manoeuvres, Hungarian cultural policy does not reduce but increases and intensifies the cultural contacts with nations living in a different economic and social order, since it looks on cultural coexistence as part and parcel of political and economic coexistence.

The consistent policy of the Soviet Union and of the Soviet Communist Party, and the growing strength and authority of the community of the socialist countries have produced new conditions in the international class struggle, in the domains of ideology and culture as well, including access to and participation in the latter. At the Moscow Conference, last December, of the Central Committee Secretaries of the fraternal parties responsible for ideology and foreign relations great attention was necessarily devoted to the realization, development and active propagation of the socialist way of life as an important part of the struggle against capitalism. If we put our own ideas and ideals into practice we shall be able to stand up most effectively to the old and new weapons of subversion. Here as well the best form of "defence" is a sound example, that is persuasive achievements. Bourgeois society is unable to create—though the material welfare of part of society may be ensured—what we call the good life; it is not able to solve fundamental human problems, nor to offer men and women a real purpose in life. The everyday practice of socialist society as well proves what has been undeniable in theory from the very beginning, that it is socialist society alone that can satisfy these needs. The more obvious this becomes the smaller the chances of enemy propaganda are at home, and the more attractive we make socialism—not only in principle, but as realized practice as well—to the workers living in capitalist countries.

Quantitative indices without qualitative co-ordinates have less and less to say in cultural life. The comparison is invalid that, for instance, both there and here six and a half "publications of a book nature" per capita are produced, if one does not add that in Hungary the decisive majority derive from the humanist, noble and valuable part of world and Hungarian culture. This goes for music as well, and the production of films, and is even —to a very important extent!—also valid for television programmes.

Bourgeois ideologists and politicians still frequently talk about the irreconcilable contradiction between "élite" and "mass culture". This shows they sense danger, a fear weighs heavily on the politicians of the oppressing classes, the leaders and spokesmen of monopoly capital, when the genuine desire for knowledge and demand for culture of the masses surfaces. It is then that they pour forth a spurious culture, cultural trash designed to disarm under the heading of "mass culture". This manipulative differentiation which is sometimes expressed in a hidden way in this part of the world as well, is rejected outright by us. It has been demonstrated, day after day, that the people, acting in a deliberate manner, are not only able to make use of cultural products of a high standard, they in fact demand them.

Making cultural products of great worth available is, of course, not a way of providing "alms", or "gifts" to the people, but a duty—it is a mandatory part of socialist evolution. At the time of the scientific and technological revolution, both up to the minute production techniques and the modes of civilization require to be met by permanent study and autodidactic activity. This is a clear condition of progress, but even more is involved. Socialist society needs skilled workers and cooperative farmers who are able to see their work in a wider context, who know where their place of employment and their industry are located within the economic system; who then can voice their views with self-assurance in the arena of socialist democracy— democracy at the bench and at the plough. It must become part of the normal situation that the majority of workers should be men and women who are lent courage to participate in political life by their familiarity with the questions at issue, men and women who are liberate and articulate in the common idiom, able to express the wealth of their ideas with precision. It largely depends on active education that more advanced production techniques and a higher standard of living should also result in a rational, free and harmonious life and a way of living in which the community is involved.

What must the socialist alternative rely on in practice? What is the new "prescription for life"? Let it be said right at the start that this pharmacopoea does not include any panacea. The major elements are well enough known: work, the community, culture—and the organic, socialist unity of these three. As Marx and Engels put it in the German Ideology: "Only in community with others has each individual the means of cultivating his gifts in all directions; only in the community, therefore, is personal freedom possible."[7] Socialist educational communities of a new substance and with a new meaning which permit a full unfolding of the personality and of individual abilities, can only be organized autonomously and not autocratically. Life brings forth numerous community forms, but we are already well aware that the place of employment, the production organization, offers the primary opportunities. Integration with the community, with the other people is realized primarily in productive work, and that not only and not even always as concerns place, but internally and in its content. Identical goals and problems, the common tasks that have to be solved, to which a genuine community is dedicated, are present here to the highest degree.

Brigades in plants and cooperatives, as examples of the socialist communities, are at the same time indispensable bases for cultural and educational activity. Much that is worth emulating in the cultural activity of the socialist brigades bears out the Leninist truth: "The workers will not forget for a moment that they need the power of knowledge."[8] The time approaches when there is little justification for a brigade calling itself socialist if it does nothing or hardly anything for the development of socialist culture and thought.

Communal forms of education must at the same time be given an impetus where people have their homes. It is necessary to fight the spirit of isolation that tries to introduce, even to modern housing estates, the obsolete view: "my home is my castle". It is true that the housing question still causes great anxieties, but it is becoming increasingly important that those who

7 Karl Marx and Frederick Engels: The German Ideology. I. Feuerbach. In: Selected Works in three volumes. Progress Publishers, Moscow, 1969. Vol. 1, pp. 65–66.

8 V. I. Lenin: How to organise Competition? In: Selected Works in three volumes. Progress Publishers, Moscow, 1970. Vol. 2, p. 519.

have already moved into new homes should learn how one must live there in a socialist way.

The proper and worthwhile use of a rising standard of living, in other words, of a socialist way of life, cannot be passed on as instructions for use when housing and other goods and commodities are handed over to those who will utilize them.

Socialism is a movement which today feels responsibility for the tomorrow, a movement which faces the future. This makes the education of youth particularly important. One of the characteristics of youth is activity, the desire for action which, if it is not provided with the right goals or given the proper help, will in the case of some, and not always the least valuable, find itself in a blind alley, even seeking satisfaction in a destructive community. Let it never be forgotten, closer acquaintance with members of beat clubs or with the most enthusiastic groupies often leads to the discovery that they were assembled by an elementary but insufficiently guided need for communal ways. Many of the young leave the parental family but, not yet having founded a family of their own, seek communal forms elsewhere. Community creating forces must therefore be promoted in a professionally and politically sound manner, the desire for communal forms that is alive in the young must be given socialist forms and substance, and attractive and bright opportunities must be provided. More clubs, groups giving free play to initiative, literary stages, choirs, amateur theatrical societies and similar opportunities must be created and the good example of the existing ones must be publicized in full awareness of this.

III

One of the most important present objectives is to develop and continue to develop an integrated attitude to educational activity of a cultural sort, improving its social status. An integral dialectic view must be in evidence all along the line from productive work to a proper use of time off, from science and art to the operation of voluntary bodies. Such an integral attitude is built on the foundations of Marxism–Leninism, and its principal political objective is the full realization of that Leninist cultural revolution whose requirements keep on growing all the time. In Lenin's words: "Far from extinguishing competition, socialism, on the contrary, for the first time creates the opportunity for employing it on a really *wide* and on a really *mass* scale, for actually drawing the majority of working people into a field of labour in which they can display their abilities, develop the capacities, and reveal those talents, so abundant among the people whom capitalism crushed, suppressed and strangled in thousands and millions."9 It is this political and social aim and creative intent that establishes the high status of education for culture in a socialist society; it is the integrity of ideology, morality, culture, the arts, ways of life which must be brought to cognitive awareness in all its aspects. To this end, intellectual and material energies must be rationally developed, concentrated and made use of.

The connecting link is the requirement that all questions should be dealt with from the angle of the recipient millions. More intensive attention must be paid to ensure that the values of art really reach the masses, that works that show understanding for the future of socialism, that shape socialist ideology and morality should become part of the general awareness. Never in the course of Hungarian history has there been an opportunity for the meeting on such a massive scale of art and the public, of creative work and those for whom it is meant that equals what socialism provides today. The people's power creates the conditions which inspire genuine and rational creative work, but it also imposes great responsibilities on creative artists: a responsibility towards truth, that is the historic truth of socialist reality, aims and ideas. Making works of art available to millions—and only socialism produces the right conditions for this—does not mean a mere quantitative change, but a qualitative one in the first place, a new era in the history of culture. The achievements of education for and in culture react productively on creative artistic activity, the improvements in the taste and the growing demands of millions offer encouragement to artists, in whose interests it is that the public should receive their work with understanding. Society therefore has every right to demand in return that artists do all they can to help an understanding reception of their works.

Hungarian culture has room not only for art but also for entertainment, as long as it is in good taste and does not make use of cultural refuse. Let me add to this that though no regulations are made on questions of taste, the taste of millions is a matter of public concern in a socialist society. Works called "entertaining" may, of course, also offer and do offer artistic experience of a high order and lasting effect. The opposite of "entertaining" is not "valuable" but "boring"; and if a piece of work is complicated, abstract and difficult to follow, it is by no means certain to be "valuable". There is, of course, room not only for the spreading of meaningful and practical knowledge, but also for collective and individual pastimes that are rich in content and are agreeable.

9 V. I. Lenin: How to organise Competition? In: Selected Works in three volumes. Progress Publishers, Moscow, 1970. Vol. 2., p. 517.

The rapidly rising mass demand for literature and art is also borne out by the figures. More than 60 million books were sold in Hungary in 1973, the turnover in books is rising, and the fear of those who predicted that the spreading of television would atrophy reading, has been shown to be baseless. On the contrary, instead of "competition" between the various forms of education in and for culture the number of examples that are evidence of good cooperation and a wholesome reciprocal influence is on the increase; successful television programmes recruit readers, and the readers take a different view of the television programmes. Things have to be done in the further development of reading as well; the results so far achieved in the "For a Reading People" movement must be developed further in such a way that the selection of the quality of the reading matter should increasingly be decisive. What might be called basic books must be placed into the hands of the hundreds of thousands who still do not read. These "basic books" are the classics of Hungarian literature and that in other languages, poems, novels, plays, some important modern works, not only Hungarian, which on the one hand reflect and on the other develop thinking in this age of transition. It should be obvious that these basic books include the classics of socialism, since it is exactly through these that one can size up and properly appreciate the most valuable creations of the human mind. One must also make sure that school-leavers who are critical readers indeed remain readers for life. Not only new beautiful library palaces satisfy the needs of the present although one will, of course, wish for as many as possible of them! It must be understood that until we are able to build such libraries everywhere, it is possible and necessary to serve the cause of culture and of reading also by modest, small libraries.

Television is in our time the most important way in which culture is brought to the people. But its effect goes beyond this: it may play an important role directly and indirectly in the formation of the socialist way of life, doing so if it shows a positive example. Television is not only an instrument for the satisfaction of demands but also for the rousing of new sound ones. It has a complex educational purpose, to an increasing extent it is turning into an artistic workshop and institution seeking its own ways. It has been shown that the "age of television" does not lead to a withering of traditional educational institutions and forms, but on the contrary helps them to flourish while modernizing. It may well accelerate the process which transforms the public into a community.

In the development and rejuvenation of adult education—lectures, series, free universities, language courses—professional men and women may find a major opportunity for selfless social work. It does not reduce the authority and importance of museums and their staff either, but on the contrary increases them if the latter undertake more consistently to fulfil their educational calling and do more in the spreading and popularization of scientific knowledge.

Encyclopaedic knowledge is not the equivalent of education, an educated man is one in whom an interest in culture and knowledge lives permanently and recurringly, someone who asserts acquired knowledge in everyday life, enriching through it community contacts with friends and at the place of work.

It is part of an integrated approach to the subject that we argue against views and attitudes which, even if they are not general, are nevertheless frequent enough to cause trouble.

It happens even within social and political organizations that culture and education are "handled separately". It is lost from sight that this work, from central directives to local practical implementation requiring great independence and responsibility, must be in harmony with the general party programme.

In some factories and agricultural cooperatives economic interests, are used as an excuse, and there is a failure to recognize that it is not only in the interests of socialism in general but in a narrower sense also of the enterprise in question that there should be money and energy left for the library, for the further training of workers and for the club of the socialist brigades. The time has come where it is possible to call to account a manager who neglects the mental "development" of people just as if he left the valuable machines of his firm to "rust". It is a part of the personal example that the chairman or manager, the Party secretary, and Communist leaders in general are required to give that they attend theatrical performances, that they read and buy books. Luckily there is hardly anybody today who is proud of being uneducated, but there still are some who say: "A proletarian does not need culture or the arts." They affirm this without really knowing that, by this, they come close in their thinking to the bourgeois who says that the worker does not require culture.

In the age of socialism it is also a manifestation of lack of belief in the people and in the cause of socialism if some who work in this field declare that there are places and sections of society where and among whom it is impossible to create and spread culture. This view hides complacency and laziness.

An attitude is, of course, also unacceptable which refuses to undertake mental effort in order to receive culture. Medical practitioners warn against inactivity, mental sloth should be included in this warning.

Progressive bourgeois ideas of adult education generally projected the teacher-pupil relationship within the schools to extra-curricular education. The role of schools in Hungary is of increasing importance. But the methods of the schools—which incidentally are also being developed in the direction of initiative and activity—cannot be copied mechanically outside the school, in adult education. The submitted resolution must be implemented in practice: "active, voluntary, independent and organized education outside the schools must become more efficient, it must be raised to a higher level and become more widespread through the cooperation and assistance of various institutions, voluntary organizations and movements, serving a useful and valuable way of spending one's time off."

Although this is an important question, I can only briefly touch on the frequent misunderstandings concerning the interpretation of folk traditions in culture. Two false extremes must be rejected. One considers folk culture in the narrow sense of peasant culture, wishing to conserve the old peasant culture creating a myth around it. The other wishes to differentiate between working-class culture, that is socialist culture, and traditional folk culture, and does not take into account that a healthy socialist culture can only grow in the soil of the earlier worker and peasant traditions, by further developing their most valuable features.

In Hungary the number of members of national minorities is not large, their percentage of the population is not very significant. It is nevertheless necessary to speak of them in connection with this subject since in a socialist country the equality of the national minorities, the care and esteem of their culture, native idiom and traditions cannot be determined by numbers. However small the community may be, we consider it a moral duty to satisfy and support their national and language need in all the details of everyday life and of culture and education, be it street names in their own language, right to a thorough knowledge of their own literature and the cherishing of their ancient, traditional culture. It is our firm resolution to give the cultural needs of the national minorities who live in Hungary the same care and attention as that accorded to those whose native language is Hungarian. It is therefore not only the business of the associations of the minorities themselves but a public matter, a social and political question, in which we follow the principles of socialist internationalism and of Leninist national minority policy.

*

The document submitted to the Central Committee does not only formulate immediate practical aims but has the character and importance of principles. It speaks both to the leaders and to the people who long for education. But it determines only the directions of what has to be done so that, in its wake, the elaboration of the measures, plans and long-term programmes should be possible in accordance with local conditions, and the concrete areas of activity. This demands protracted, tenacious and persevering work. It is necessary to bear in mind Lenin's idea that, in this domain, it is not possible to win battles by cavalry charges. But this does not mean either that immediate great efforts and perseverance are not necessary. Lenin was not lenient in this question affecting revolution either, but keeping the particularities of this area in mind, he declared war on spurious and apparent solutions, which always chose the easier way.

The essence of the question is the appreciation of the content of socialist culture, the interpretation of what is meant by culture. If somebody means by culture that the people should get by heart numerous quotations from the works of Chairman Mao, then he can carry out the cultural revolution in one go; but if he sets out with the demand that everybody should be literate, then much more time is needed. And how much more still if one counts with all that which must be demanded in the interests of the people!

We wish to make all human values of every age accessible to educated socialist men and women. The anarchists and those associated with the Proletcult movement as well as the contemporary ultra-left and Maoists argue that, with the proletarian revolution, the "old" culture loses its validity; it must not be learned, it must even be annihilated. This view, if it becomes a policy, endangers—as experience has shown—not only culture but socialism itself, that is why we reject it. Lenin's starting-point in his teaching on the cultural revolution was: "Marxism has won its historic significance as the ideology of the revolutionary proletariat because, far from rejecting the most valuable achievements of the bourgeois epoch, it has, on the contrary, assimilated and refashioned everything of value in thought and culture. Only further work on this basis and in this direction, inspired by the practical experience of the proletarian dictatorship as the final stage in the struggle against every form of exploitation, can be recognised as the development of a genuine proletarian culture."[10]

A substantial part of the difficulties with our school system and our educational activities derives from this broad interpretation—which we avow as our own. We must, for instance, face the overburdening of students in our school system, and we are trying to mitigate this, not in order to give up knowledge, but on the contrary: for the sake of the bringing up of

[10] V. I. Lenin: On Proletarian Culture. In: Selected Works in three volumes. Progress Publishers, Moscow, 1971. Vol. 3, p. 485.

more educated, more receptive and more intelligent young people we try to liberate tuition from the burdens of superfluous encyclopaedic knowledge.

We face similar, and still different, if possible even more complicated, difficulties in adult education. But if we ask ourselves whether we should continue to undertake this broad range or limit our efforts—the answer is obvious. We shall undertake it. It is true that the tension—as reflected also by the report—between the requirements and the financial resources is very great. Cultural demands grow, and hopefully ever faster, and possibilities, especially financial resources, are limited. It is therefore important to mark out a realistic path. If too little is undertaken, and no efforts are made, the negative consequences can be foreseen as clearly as those of the other extreme: if the plans are unrealistic and failure is discouraging.

Our Marxist order of values functions well, and I believe that in general we select more or less appropriately, we broadly know what forms part of our values and what does not. The question is what values shall reach—in respect of their substance and standard—increasing numbers of the people, and at what pace. What we have achieved so far is certainly not little. Let me mention one figure only: twenty years ago people bought books worth 70 million forints in Hungary. Now, in the last year, books worth 1,400 million forints were sold, at roughly comparative prices. I believe that reading was the first step of the cultural rise, and will continue to remain the most important. The first step was that as broad masses as possible should read. But today the qualitative requirement becomes more important. Of course there is no mechanical, rigid sequence. It was never unimportant for socialist cultural policy what people should read, and the Marxist order of values was not unimportant either. We have always tried to influence the internal structure of the demand for reading with the instruments at our disposal: the assertion of the principles of our cultural policy, e.g. size of editions, criticism, publicity, etc. Even though there were distortions, the total process is healthy and serves our goals well. It is a matter of course that the more we progress, the more the people rises culturally, the higher the ideological, aesthetic and taste standards must be.

We are sometimes inclined to underestimate our achievements, but life refutes our faint-heartedness. It may seem a trifle, but allow me to give an example. A weekly publishing nothing but serializations of novels of literary merit has been started. It has turned out that 100,000 copies, which everybody considered too much, were sold out within two hours, and at the railway stations, commuting workers who do not buy books for 40 forints, buy this periodical. In the second week no less than 160,000 copies were sold.

With the progress made by our society, the evolution of socialist public thinking and public morality, of socialist consciousness, the requirement becomes more and more emphatic that every person should have a socialist future recognized by himself. All that is decisive in the great transformation of society as a whole, must also be created in man as he is becoming a community being.

We have to reckon with progress in this domain not being spectacular, an extraordinary number of larger and smaller difficulties in the implementation of the educational work programme will be encountered with, but in the long run it will be proved that in the wake of the resolutions of the Central Committee, concrete new and important results will have been achieved, which will basically accelerate progress, and shape the cultural image of the entire working people. A people hungry for culture will turn into one living with culture. Both the demand and the opportunity are present. Our task is to realize them.

SOCIALIST TASTE
AND THE SOCIALIST MIND

by

MIKLÓS SZABOLCSI

T
he question of socialist public taste has been occupying Hungarian public opinion for several years, and a growing number of articles, studies and surveys related to this topic have appeared. This sudden interest is understandable. Indeed, this past period can rightly be called one of extensive development of Hungarian cultural policy. The increase in cultural media complicated the cultural structure. And questions, currents and stratifications which had been hidden came into the open. The question of which way to go became more acute.

On the other hand several factors have revealed the necessity of updating the question of social consciousness, thus giving it a new importance. Among these factors were events on the international scene and in the international working-class movement in recent years, as well as the turning-point that occurred in our own development. The latter was characterized mainly by new phenomena brought about by the economic reform, or, more broadly speaking, by the fact that Hungary is now ranked among the medium developed industrial countries, and is embarked on a scientific-technological revolution. This has fostered a growing interest in, and need for, the scientific examination of social realities and processes, and a desire to see our situation as it is, without illusions, in all its contradictions, and the tasks that stem from it.

Since 1965, therefore, many articles and discussions have appeared dealing with the development of Hungarian taste today.

I

The debate in fact was initiated by a special consultative body of the Hungarian Socialist Workers' Party, consisting of representatives of the professions and the intelligentsia. In 1965, under the title "The Role of

Literature and the Arts in our Society" it published, not a study, but rather a series of theses which discussed problems and stimulated debate.

In 1966, the journal *Alföld* (The Plain), appearing in Debrecen, began a longer series of discussions on popular education. Almost all the problems, difficulties and new experiments in the field of mass culture were discussed in this debate. A logical consequence of this was another debate (in 1967–68) which was mainly concerned with taste. In the first place it drew attention to the contradictions between public demand and the expectations of those supplying the goods, and to the fact that taste is often underdeveloped, showing how conservative habits impede the influx and reception of new cultural material. The participants in the *Alföld* discussion were mass educationalists, journalists, teachers and librarians (the excellent article by Mihály Bimbó[1] was an attempt to discuss the more theoretical questions in this field). A year later, in the Budapest journal *Valóság*, artists, critics and writers on aesthetics raised the same questions. The main topic on the agenda was modern art and the difficulties of its reception. Let me emphasize that in this debate an effort was also made to grapple with the problem of public taste, mainly in the article by Miklós Szántó.[2]

Thoroughgoing investigations can also be found in several other comprehensive sociological studies. Not only in empirical investigations, but also in many leading to general conclusions worthy of attention. I am referring to the valuable works of Zsuzsa Ferge,[3] Judit H. Sas,[4] and, in this particular field of interest, to the work of Ágnes Losonczi.[5] Let me add to these the interesting experiments of Ernő Gondos,[6] the studies of Pál Miklós,[7] and finally the material for the conference on popular education held in Hungary. Naturally the whole question of taste is the subject of a large international debate and there are many artistic and cultural-philosophical points of view. Since Levin L. Schücking and Arnold Hauser the problem of taste has been discussed in both bourgeois and Marxist criticism. But the literature on socialist public taste is less extensive. As far as the topic of this article is concerned, the most thought-provoking book was that excellent work of Richard Hoggart, *The Uses of Literacy*.

---

1 "Cultural Policy and Taste", Alföld, 1968, No. 6.
2 "Public Artistic Taste through the Eyes of a Sociologist." *Valóság*, 1967, No. 6.
3 Zsuzsa Ferge, *The Stratification of our Society*. Közgazdasági és Jogi Könyvkiadó, Budapest, 1969.
4 Judit H. Sas, *People and Books* (Social Studies). Akadémiai Kiadó, Budapest, 1968.
5 Ágnes Losonczi, "*The sociology of musical life*" (For whom, when and what kind of music?). Zeneműkiadó, 1970.
6 Ernő Gondos, *Jonah and the Whale in Óbuda*. Budapest, Magvető, 1968.
7 Pál Miklós, "*The Value and Meaning of Reading Today and Tomorrow*." *Új Írás*, November, 1970. (All in Hungarian).

2

I shall begin with questions. First, what is taste?

From the psychological point of view, it is an apparatus which evaluates and selects; it is an ability to filter, evaluate and in general relate to one another, reject or receive incoming experiences and impressions (originating in art, the environment, etc.). From the sociological point of view, it is an element of reception, a precondition for the reception of works. And if we want to describe it in aesthetic terms, then one can say that taste is one element of the ability to "assimilate" a work of art, a need to "assimilate" certain works and to reject others. In this sense, and using Lukács's terminology, it belongs to the "after" of the work of art. We are consequently dealing with a complicated notion which can be differently defined according to whether it is viewed from the psychological, sociological or aesthetic point of view. No matter which definition we consider, it designates not only a state of affairs, a static system, but an active, dynamic apparatus.

And what do we call "public taste"? This question was also the subject of several debates during which several different opinions were voiced. Public taste, one can say, is the average of many individual tastes, and we can therefore refer to the taste of a group, a stratum, a class, a nation or, more correctly, to the general direction of the taste of these groups. It is also clear that the larger this group is, the coarser the average taste is, and the less correctly its direction can be determined. The public taste of a nation or a society can only be regarded as a system of contradictions and a strongly stratified structure. Thus public taste is not mainly a psychological but a sociological notion, i.e. it can be examined by sociological means. And as a natural consequence, neither individual nor public taste is constant, but is ever changing, in constant formation, developing or regressing. It is historically, socially, geographically and nationally a determinate, mobile structure. So we cannot speak of taste or public taste in general, nor, as we shall see, can we really even speak of socialist public taste in general, but only of the public taste of the socialist Hungary of the 1970s, or rather of the types of taste which compose it.

3

What are the components of taste as a dynamic, selecting and filtering structure? How is it developed and formed? There has been very little research on this subject, so it is mainly by summarizing everyday experience that we can describe its components as follows:

(a) Certain psychological factors.

(b) Family upbringing and education.

(c) The artistic traditions, legacy, accumulated resources of the collective or people in question.

(d) This basic disposition is moulded by impressions acquired later, experiences acquired both spontaneously and apparently-spontaneously (e.g. the aesthetic quality of the environment as well as consciously acquired, learnt, artistic qualities; aesthetic ideals as well as impressions interpreted and systematized not by aesthetic but by ideological demands. In this field, mass communication media play a large and ever increasing role.

(e) Taste is formed and developed by the social environment, by the opinion of the power élite, by prestige factors, the micro-milieu transmitting the culture.

(f) A significant role is played in the formation of taste by prevailing fashion, which on one hand selects a few objects from the multitude of objects forming the artistic environment, puts them in the limelight and thus influences choice; on the other hand it makes its effect felt through "prestige" factors.

(g) Finally, the latest (including Hungarian) sociological investigations have convincingly shown that taste is strongly influenced by the position of the individual in the division of labour, by his material level, his living conditions, his housing situation.

It consequently also follows that, as Mihály Bimbó pointed out, taste belongs to the sphere of what is known as everyday consciousness rather than to the sphere of theoretical consciousness. To put it another way, consciousness, and within it the ideological factor, is only one of the components of the development of taste, effective, though mainly indirectly, through complicated transmission mechanism (and among these the life style and social environment are of great importance).

In its genesis—that is, looking at it diachronically—taste is very complicated, often consisting of contradictory elements; nor, looking at it synchronically, is it homogeneous either, i.e. the individual does not use the same system of values and norms to evaluate various fields of art and life. That is why people with excellent literary taste often have bad taste in the plastic arts, or connoisseurs of music, or excellent *literateurs* are hidebound in their attitude to interior decoration.

4

Complete relativism?

Does taste develop spontaneously? Is it formed under the influence of various and illusive factors which can themselves be neither influenced nor grasped? Paradoxically, taste can at the same time be strongly influenced, developed (and "regressed") by individuals as well as by groups. It can be modified with the help of "direct" conscious factors as well, i.e. through a direct ideological or aesthetic influence, and even in an indirect way by creating a variety of choices, by modifying the economic and living conditions, by the "prestige" factor, by various kinds of education. It can be changed, developed in a good direction, or regressed to a low level. It can also be orientated in a mediocre direction. The question is whether we can single out the direction in which it should be developed.

5

And here I reach one of the most difficult questions: what is "socialist taste" and what is "socialist public taste"? How can the adjective and the word it modifies be related? How can "socialist (individual taste)" be characterized? It is very difficult to define this, precisely because of the complicated components, the many instinctive or already mechanical elements comprising "taste".

We can only represent an ideal picture, a "model" to be realized, to be constructed. Socialist taste is more strongly influenced by ideology. In its choices and system of comparisons, socialist ideas contained in the works of art, or rather the place occupied by the single works of art in the whole of socialist culture, play a greater role. (Of course this statement has to be understood in all its complexity, taking into account the peculiarities of the artistic representation of ideology and ideas.)

Thus socialist taste embraces works which fulfil a demand for universality, large works representing the world in its complexity; it even prefers them. But it is also receptive to other, and different types of art, it accepts not only the harmonious, but the inharmonious and grotesque as well. And socialist taste is not some kind of rarefied ascetic taste, hence it receives, assimilates and claims as its own "lighter" or more entertaining works of art, evaluates and accepts more "restful" artistic qualities; it can experience relaxation and escape as well as catharsis.

Socialist taste is not settled, conservative. It is alert, open to receive new cultural material and actively participates in its development. It is not a completed structure, adapted to certain types of work. It is not a system of unchanging norms, not even in the sense that it adapts to "great works"; it represents rather an open, evaluating and selecting ability. It follows from all this that socialist taste relies on a minimum of educational requirements, both with regard to subjects and level, and presupposes certain abilities (e.g. to "decode" the works, understand the meaning of their symbols).

Thus socialist taste in general accords with socialist ideology and the general ideals based on it. That is how taste can become a part of one's conscious thinking, that is, more and more part of one's philosophical equipment. So we can speak of the close connection between socialist consciousness and socialist public taste, as well as of how socialist taste can help the conscious element, that is, the ideology. It can put more life into ideologically conscious elements, making them more complete, motivating and colouring conscious actions. Socialist taste contributes to the development of a rich and meaningful life. It plays a significant part in the formation of "man and his environment", in the development of relations between people, in regulating the operation of collectives, in shaping the forms and styles of social action and in increasing its effectiveness. Socialist taste can display its most effective activity precisely in the re-interpretetation and filtering of fashion, and even in the possibilities provided by technology and production.

In the session of the Academy of Sciences in which the question of taste was discussed, a number of questions were on the agenda: How can the new system of economic management in Hungary be further developed so as to serve the total development of the individual? How can short and long-term interests be reconciled? How can the worth and prestige of civilized and moral values be preserved when material standards are constantly increasing? In general the question is, how can the possession of material goods be reconciled with the interests of the collective society? And still further, how can a way of life for new collectives of another type, worthy of today and valid in the technological era, be created, i.e. how can we represent the model of today's developed socialist society? Here, developed socialist taste can be very helpful.

It is probable of course that taste will always include instinctive, half-conscious and occasional-casual elements, which belong to the sphere of everyday consciousness; but the distance between socialist theoretical consciousness and taste can be decreased.

6

Perhaps the above picture of "socialist taste" is too general, too abstract an ideal picture. But perhaps it is an ideal picture to which we can relate, which can be approximated, and whose formation we can help.

And socialist taste? According to what we have said so far, this is also a sociological notion, which can designate the average level of taste to be reached as well as its general direction. Of course, socialist taste also changes in time and space; since it is based on different traditions, in different national environments it takes on different nuances. The socialist public taste of different collectives, nations, countries sifts out different things from the multitude of artistic products, changes, adapts and uses fashion in different ways.

Thus a socialist public taste is not the same as the public taste of the socialist countries, since as we have said above, included in it are many different kinds and variations of taste co-existing with one another. Nor does socialist taste mean the taste of any particular class or stratum of society. This is worth emphasizing, since there are people here today who claim that socialist taste is exclusively the general taste of an imagined or genuine class or stratum.

(In Budapest in the 1930s, for example, the taste of a certain intellectual group was based on an appreciation of the highest values of the progressive, humanist culture of the time, almost inevitably, however, marked by an acceptance of certain types of art which have proved ephemeral, and by a certain confused snobisme. On the other hand, just after the War the strong and vigorous People's College movement (Nékosz) threw up a young intellectual group with a taste and standard of beauty largely determined by their peasant origins which they professed with a certain fervour. United with cultural elements of the worker's "movement" it threw up a peculiar, individual mixture of both, badly dated today.)

Socialist taste is not bound to any single class. It is based on socialist relations of ownership, and on the socialist social structure which influences it. It is stratified, but fundamentally homogeneous, that is, it has no "low" and "high" levels. One of the characteristic peculiarities of socialist taste moreover is precisely its width of range and democratic, as opposed to aristocratic, leanings. Socialist taste is consequently also a collective term: it embraces on a large scale many different types of taste. It includes "lower" types of taste as well, constantly evolving towards the "higher" types of taste. Like individual socialist taste, which embraces the objects of everyday use, light entertainment as well as the great works of art, s ɔ socialist public taste must also be imagined as wide ranging and varied.

Looking at the problem from another angle, a socialist taste could also be defined as characterized by a rational adaptation to the social system and to conditions of life created by the social order, with a demand for the creation of a suitable artistic environment.

But why call this type of individual and public taste "socialist"? Isn't it simply the same as the highest order of taste created by earlier developments? Certainly the work, traditions, ideals and norms of human and individual national culture are built into the system of ideals and regulators of socialist taste, and socialist taste starts from the highest level of the pre-socialist culture and is nourished by it. But it adds to this foundation the values of socialist culture, and is at the same time wider and greater than its predecessor. The ideological factor plays a bigger role; in certain fields it even plays a regulating role, not only in connection with past works of art, but also with those of the present and future.

Contemporary Hungarian socialist taste is not as yet fashioned, not even in a rudimentary form. It is still only a possibility. A possibility, and an obligation. Hungarian socialist taste has yet to be developed, created on the basis of a conscious programme. We might go so far as to say that the model has to be created as well, and plans and actions adjusted to it. In the first place, of course, the future of Hungarian socialist education has to be planned, and taste adjusted accordingly. This ideal picture, or model, has to be designed on a basis of the facts as they are, building on both obviously known and latent demands, and taking into consideration all the changes in taste which may be affected, for good and bad, by modern technology.

7

To add a few further remarks about contemporary Hungarian public taste and a possible model for it:

A. What are the traditions which nourish contemporary Hungarian taste and the nature of its various elements?

(1) The genuine "folk element" (taking for its ideal in behaviour, music and customs the peasant way of life, folklore, and a taste developed around 1890) both in its original form and a more sophisticated version of those tastes which can be called a "popular trend". József Erdélyi and István Sinka, the eminent adherents of this movement, developed in opposition to a certain overripe, overrefined luxuriance in the poetry of the early

twentieth century, turned back to the folk arts and ways, which they believed were simpler and more deeply-rooted, while discovering, like similar movements in other European countries, elements of a certain mystique in them. This "secondary" "popular trend" is also divided into several strata, separated in time. The most recent is perhaps the taste integrating within it the traditions of the Nékosz movement.

(2) The type of taste represented by "Jókai", a liking for romanticism and dramatic situations, conservative in its choice of cultural values, a less developed kind of taste. Mór Jókai is one of the great classics of Hungarian literature, a representative of the nationalist, patriotic, romantic, dramatic trend of writing, and the most widely read Hungarian novelist of all times. But what most of his followers, mainly those only now just beginning to have a taste for reading, like in his works, are first of all the dramatic situations, the heightened romanticism and the angel-devil, black and white of his characters. That is why we consider that the type of taste represented by his name is only the first step or first phase in developing a literary taste.

(3) Almost as wide is the Catholic type of taste of "gentry-bourgeois" origin. It is a kind of old-fashioned taste, stubbornly preserving the traditions of a particular stratum of society at the end of the last century. Typical of this type of taste is the dark, massive furniture which preserves the atmosphere of homes of the upper bourgeoisie at the end of the last century, the antiquated suite of the big family cupboard and the double bed, crammed into small country houses or modern flats, the complete bedroom suite, the Hungarian songs, hackneyed by the superficial interpretations of commercialized gypsy orchestras, far from the real folk songs and folk music of Hungary and which recall the atmosphere of the Hungarian lesser nobility of the end of the last century; the operetta exuding the air of late nineteenth century Vienna, and the pseudo-moral, stereotyped literature which catered to the taste of the "patriotic Hungarian middle class".

There is also a more urban, petty bourgeois variation of taste. Some of the works preferred by this type of taste are now beginning to loose their original class characters, the Hungarian song, for example, which has nowadays become generally popular.

(4) Another variation of present taste can be characterized as "the culture of the Worker's Clubs." In a peculiar way, Péter Veres, the writer of peasant origin, was representative of this cultural form, so characteristic of the working class. He was an agro-proletarian writer, who came from the remotest Hungarian countryside, the Puszta, but who was educated to political consciousness, literacy and the higher articulate values by the culture

of the Social Democratic workers' movement. In literature, this culture is characterized by a preference for the naturalists such as Zola and Gorki, uniting of worker and peasant life, for realistic and naturalist works in general, with a liking for more scholarly and committed works, and also group poetry recitals and in music for folk and movement songs, rejecting at the same time more apparently sophisticated works.

(5) And finally, the taste of certain intellectuals and a smaller group of workers. It is oversimplifying to describe this type of taste as homogeneous, because it too has many variations and forms, but fundamentally it can be defined by a spectrum ranging from Attila József and Bartók to Thomas Mann, modern films and modern furniture.

B. To these different types of taste representing roughly the trends dominating round about 1945–48, new elements have been added in the past 20 years. We cannot speak of completely developed new types of taste, but rather of the influences, factors and educational media and material, which form and modify public taste, such as non-Hungarian—European and world—culture. In the first half of this twenty-year period, the products of Soviet culture exercised a great influence; for the past fifteen, influences from other directions have been penetrating the country. Certain aspects of world literature, of jazz and the different variations of beat music have certainly penetrated the Hungarian world of taste and become part of it.

Thus in its "high" variation, a type of taste is being formed which is increasingly susceptible to the more twisted, loud and fragmented impressions of world culture, and which in general feverishly searches for the new, the surprising, the shocking. Although only barely perceptible, a kind of taste is growing which rejects the old, the traditional past or "semi-past", and always chooses and adopts as its own whatever represents the living present.

On the whole we are not fully aware that the various efforts aimed at the conscious development of tastes have had considerable success in various cultural fields: the quantitative increase in educational or cultural media and material and its delivery to the "consumers" has provided a wider basis for the development of taste; in literature, music and, for instance, in interior decoration and fashion we can see the result of much enthusiastic initiative, and devoted activity in developing taste, increasing cultural standards and disseminating knowledge, over the past twenty-five years. One must add to this the influence exercised quite spontaneously by technological achievement on the taste of the public and, first of all, through the development of the townscape, architecture, interior decoration and clothes. These influences almost imperceptibly but continuously form and modify public taste, by awakening the demand for different shapes, colours, harmonies and lines.

The mass communication media of course also exert a very strong influence on the formation and modification of taste. Above all television, which in a very short time has changed and formed Hungarian taste. Perhaps it is still too early to say that a new type of taste has been created under its influence but it has certainly begun to reshape both in mixing and unifying the earlier types of taste—and this is not necessarily a bad thing— but also by equalizing, assimilating and levelling them. It is also clear that certain inherent features of television, its visual quality, its tendency to simplification, quizzes, games are already creating a definite type of taste. Today we are living in a changing world of taste, and although it is too early to speak of completely developed new types of taste, we can observe certain processes, certain consequences and certain dangers. We are witnessing a relaxation, an interplay of existing forms of taste, an assimilation of frontiers. Social mobility, the possibility of breaking out of the framework of a class or stratum, and the accelerating flow of the agrarian population into industry, as well as the changes in professional structures, have all had an important effect on the formation of taste. Perhaps the rapprochement and interplay of town and country, agrarian and urban types of taste is its most characteristic feature. There is a certain receptiveness of taste; in spite of its strongly conservative character, many signs point to its increasing receptiveness. There are, of course, certain dangers of bias, or mediocrity or simplification, but there is no need to consider them fatal. They are the consequences not only of the effect of the mass communication media, but also of the technological factors in contemporary life.

8

Considering the future model of Hungarian socialist taste, one wonders whether Hungarian socialist taste will have a national character which is different from a general socialist taste. The fact that in addition to the universal stock of cultural material it depends on specific cultural materialism as well effete and traditional, gives a different character to the taste of a particular society. And this cultural and traditional material also forms peoples, assists in encouraging certain tendencies while suppressing others or restraining others. No doubt this is part of the reason why we can speak of "Italian" or "Russian" or "German" taste, and as a broad, first generalization these terms are valid.

A peculiarly Hungarian type of taste can therefore indeed exist; and today it is more clearly visible in the field of literature in general than in the plastic arts. Of course, with the increase of the cultural media and wider choice, even characteristics which appeared to be "traditional" or even "eternal" can be changed and shaped. In the future therefore old and stereotyped forms of taste will not be so identified with the national character as in the past. The difference between "town" and "country" will very probably decrease still further and with it the type of folk and popular art developed in the 1890s. Taste of a "national" character will in general not show itself in a predilection for certain pseudo-national traditions but in the constant interaction of an indigenous art based on the conditions existing in any given country and influences from abroad. When the two influences come together, enriching each other, they will give rise to a specific form, and further enrich the structural pattern of taste.

It is probable that socialist taste will have a greater impact in the future. That is, it will exert a more effective influence, comparing, evaluating and selecting, in more fields of the arts and in daily life. The representatives of future Hungarian socialist taste will, we hope, be well versed in literature, music, the plastic arts, architecture and the cultural world of everyday life.

9

Following this brief sketch, I would like to consider what is to be done, in terms of research and the practical orientation of culture, to form a good socialist taste.

One of the aims of scholarly research could certainly be a further thorough scientific investigation of the level of taste by using and developing what has so far been done. An especially urgent task appears to be an investigation into the psychological character of the mechanism of taste and precise investigations into the field of experimental aesthetics and the determination of certain psychological characteristics of taste and perception.

Literary people and historians are in general reluctant to accept cultural prognostics, that is to commit themselves to any exact outline of the future of culture and to any artistical measurement of the paths leading to the future. I believe however that we shall have to familiarize ourselves with certain forms of investigation into the cultural future, by at least accepting that a model has to be set up, and regarded as the goal to be attained, and that the specific steps to be taken should be adjusted to this model.

It is a platitude but socialist public taste, the power to select, can only be formed if there are things from among which to select, if there is something to be preferred, and something on which we can rely. In other words, it has to have a firm foundation. To realize this model and carry it out as soon as possible certain economic and organizational measures are also necessary, similar to those which have been most successful in the Scandinavian countries. In those countries, the production of industrial products of a certain type and level of taste is not permitted, nor indeed are they in demand. We should also make sure that the formation of taste should be increasingly taken into consideration in the course of economic development, on one hand by effective propaganda, and on the other by preventing the circulation of bad and tasteless products.

Nor should we ignore the different social and moral means we can use to influence and form taste. Here we are referring to the function of critics, the role of the mass communication media, the leading role of political, intellectual and economic attitudes, and the "prestige" factor. We have to take into consideration the role of those directly involved in cultural life (the so-called micro-milieu) as well as cultural fashions, which admittedly can degenerate into forms of *snobisme* but can also prove to be a most stimulating force in the development of taste.

And finally, in the development of taste and the formation of a socialist taste, education and teaching both have fundamental roles to play, both in school and in extra-curricular activities. Today, questions of school and what is generally known as public education are increasingly becoming important, and the question of the development of socialist taste is closely connected with them.

WHO READS AND WHAT?

THE GUTENBERG GALAXY IS STILL SHINING

by

BÉLA KÖPECZI

The goal of the socialist cultural revolution is to put an end to cultural monopolies, in other words to the privileged position which certain strata and the ruling class in general enjoyed in respect of culture as well, and to accord everybody—irrespective of the social class to which he belongs—the opportunity of becoming educated, and thereby to create not only his general and professional culture but to assist his human evolution as well.

What this means for socialist publishing and book-distribution is that they must serve primarily the interests of the fundamental classes of society, awakening and satisfying their demand. In the course of the last quarter of a century this view has led to a large-scale quantitative increase in the volume of publishing. Capitalist publishing issued in Hungary 2,438 titles in 1938 with a total number of 9.1 million copies: in 1971, on the other hand, 5,536 titles were published with a total number of 53.5 million copies. As regards the number of publications the increase has been more than two-fold; but what is even more important, the number of copies printed has grown more than five-fold. These data refer only to books, i.e. to publications of more than 64 pages. The number of all publications (including booklets, textbook notes, scores, pictures and maps) was 28,942 in 1971, in altogether 88.8 million copies, as against 8,156 publications in 1938, in 17.2 million copies.

The quantitative increase has been general, but there has been a certain differentiation according to the branches of publishing. Scientific literature, which was very neglected by Hungarian publishing before 1945, issued 300 to 400 works at the beginning of the fifties and this number grew to more than 600 by the end of the sixties. The number of copies in this bracket was 6–700,000 at the beginning, and exceeded one million at the end of the sixties.

There has been an especially noteworthy development since the beginning of the sixties in the publishing of educational works and popular science. This branch of publishing was in fact established at the end of the forties and the beginning of the fifties, and it is characteristic of the growth of recent years that not only the number of works rose (to 6–700 by the end of the sixties), but especially the number of copies, which reached—counting only books—11–12 million. It should be noted that in this branch booklets also have their importance, and although the number of copies dropped after the exaggerations of the early fifties, the number is still considerable, reaching 6 million annually.

Trade and professional publishing, which was also developed after the Liberation, has been on a rather steady level, since the number of books seldom surpasses the annual 1,500, and the number of copies is around 3–3.5 million.

There has been a rapid growth in fiction, where the number of titles exceeded 700 at the end of the sixties, as against 300 in the fifties; but it is even more interesting that as against 2–3 million copies two decades ago, the yearly number has already reached 15 million.

As against 100 works of juvenile and children's literature at the beginning of the fifties, the number of 200 was surpassed at the end of the sixties, and the number of copies has increased from one million to 5 million.

Finally, the gigantic scale of textbook publishing must be mentioned, where differentiation is indicated by the number of approximately 1,000 books annually in 15–16 million copies.

Growth has been most dynamic in fiction, in juvenile and children's literature and in educational works, and this seems natural since it is these three branches of publishing that speak to the widest public. Scientific and trade literature is characterized mainly by the extension of scope and the increase in the number of works accompanying it.

It is often said that socialist publishing does not consider books as a commodity. This is true, but a certain reservation is nevertheless necessary, since books have a price in Hungary too and this necessarily influences their distribution. But prices are set in socialist publishing not on the basis of cost but mainly in the spirit of the goals of cultural policy. The price of the book is determined by its character, i.e. the branch of publishing to which it belongs, by its genre and public. It is on the basis of these criteria that the so-called uniform price per sheet (16 printed pages equalling 40,000 letters) has been developed, from which the publishers may deviate only in certain cases. The socialist state generally shoulders the difference which exists between the retail price of books and their cost. The state makes an exception where value is not the determining aspect, and this applies mainly to entertainment literature, the revenue from which feeds the culture fund, i.e. the subsidy for valuable works.

The average price of books was Ft 20.30 in 1971, i.e. Ft 1.21 per sheet (40,000 "n"), with an average thickness of 16.7 sheets. The average price of books was Ft 18.60 for fiction, Ft 30.20 for trade, professional and scientific literature, Ft 24.80 for educational literature and popular science, and Ft 7.20 for textbooks. It is one of the characteristics of the preferences of the Hungarian reading public that they like the more expensive, bound books, and this is also taken into consideration in the calculation of the average price. The textbooks and juvenile and children's books are the cheapest. These are followed by educational works, fiction, and trade and scientific books, in this order. In certain branches of publishing and in certain genres there are cheap series as well, which are published as paperbacks.

It is part of the democratism of socialist culture that books should not only be published in as many titles and copies as possible and that their price should make them accessible, but also that they should reach the appropriate public. This necessitates a distribution network which can publicize the books not only through the bookshops (the number of these is under 400), but the potential buyer should meet with the books in the factory, on the co-operative farm, in the office, in the hospitals, and at places of entertainment as well. At present, three specialized enterprises distribute books in Hungary but the publishers and other organizations also participate in this activity.

The results are reflected by the fact that while 12.2 million volumes were sold in 1951 at a value of 143 million forints, in 1971 62.6 million volumes were sold at a value approaching 1,150 million forints. Book purchases by the population and by public bodies were approximately equal in 1951, while in 1971 purchases by the population exceeded 80 per cent. It follows that, on average, every inhabitant spent 88 forints on books, including children who cannot read or write. Examining the volume of book purchasing by branches of publishing, fiction is in the first place, followed by juvenile and children's literature, then by textbooks (which amount to approximately 10 per cent of book sales annually), and educational literature.

Another way of disseminating books is to gain attention for them through the libraries and to satisfy demand through them. The number of educational libraries and book-lending points operated by the councils and trade unions all over the country exceeds 9,000, with a stock of books of approximately 25 million volumes. The number of registered readers is on average 2.2 million each year, the number of volumes lent is around 50 million, i.e. every registered reader borrows on average 24 volumes per year.

According to surveys, 70–80 per cent of readers borrow fiction or juvenile books, and the rest mainly educational literature and popular science.

All these data prove that the traditional ways of disseminating books, i.e. selling and lending them, have not only survived but have been further developed, mainly in the sense that they reach people in their homes, at their places of work and entertainment, everywhere they go. This does not, of course, mean that books have reached everybody or that everybody makes use of the opportunities offered.

It may be stated that through the quantitative development of publishing, through its price policy and the means of distribution the socialist state has endeavoured to realize also by way of books the goals of cultural democracy, and has achieved considerable results in this field.

BOOKS AND VALUE

One of the principal goals of socialist cultural policy is to carry genuine values to the broad masses. The selection is especially difficult in respect of contemporary fiction, or juvenile and children's literature, although it is these that speak to the broadest public. In scientific, trade, professional and educational literature even the works representing a lower value are apt to communicate at least certain information and data, but in respect of fiction, children's and juvenile literature even this cannot be said in the case of trashy works. True, worthless scientific, trade and educational works may also spread false views, but the effect of fictional publications in this direction is deeper, because they are presented in a more attractive form. The great advantage socialist publishing possesses over capitalist publishing, which is built on business interests, is that it is not forced, even in the branches of publication mentioned earlier, to publish easily saleable trash. If it makes concessions in respect of value, this is done for two reasons. One is the experimenting taking place in contemporary literature, which cannot always create great values. In this respect any aristocratic view may restrict creative activity, hinder competition, and thereby impede the bringing about of a wholesome cultural atmosphere. The other concession may be made due to the consideration that entertainment literature is a natural need which must be satisfied on a certain level without giving free play to violence, sexuality, and to the cult of inhumanity in general. In both cases the debate is about the right proportions and about the limits. There is no doubt that in recent years adventure, crime and spy stories, as well as spurious historical novels have been published in large numbers of copies. This is certainly giving rise to some concern, but only as regards the level of entertainment and not from the aspect of the evolution of genuine literature.

In examining fiction publishing from the point of view of value, the "rebirth of the classics" must be mentioned first, the popularity of the classical works of world literature, including Hungarian literature. As far as contemporary literature is concerned, in addition to the products of entertainment literature those works have been published in the largest number of copies which draw attention to essential social and human questions. The same may be said of contemporary foreign literature, in the publishing of which Hungarian publishers have been truly generous, since they have published not only outstanding works but also those which represented only fashionable trends and proved to be of ephemeral success.

From the point of view of education, the publishing of encyclopaedias must be mentioned. Following the publication of the New Hungarian Encyclopaedia, the Hungarian Literary Encyclopaedia, the Hungarian Biographic Encyclopaedia, the Scientific Encyclopaedia, the Encyclopaedia of Art, of Music, and the Film Encyclopaedia, the publishing of the Encyclopaedia of World Literature has also begun. A whole number of small encyclopaedias have been or are being published. Specialized encyclopaedias and series are being published in the various branches of the natural and social sciences. These attract various strata of the public, and in addition to basic knowledge, also include the latest advances.

Books may attract not only through their content but through their outward presentation as well. It is one of the characteristics of Hungarian publishing that the collection of books has developed on a massive scale, which is shown by the fact that bibliophile books are not bought by a few experts only but may reach tens of thousands. In addition to the specialists in the publishing houses, outstanding typographers and graphic artists take part in the designing of books and their covers. This co-operation has given an impetus to the art of publishing such books, leading to recognition at home and internationally.

Window onto the World

Hungarian publishing does not only endeavour to make known the old and contemporary achievements of Hungarian literature but also mediates in an ever increasing sphere the achievements of foreign cultures. The progress in the publishing of fiction since the liberation is especially characteristic of this endeavour. Today approximately the same number of foreign authors have their works published in Hungary as Hungarian authors. The nationality break-down of the authors of books published between 1945 and 1971 is as follows: Russian and Soviet literature 25.7 per cent, French 14.6 per cent, British 9.5 per cent, German 8.3 per cent, American 6.9 per cent, Rumanian 6.4 per cent, Czech and Slovak 4.8 per cent. In addition to fiction, foreign scientific, trade and educational books are also being published, and their number has been increasing in recent years. If one considers the number of copies in which especially fiction and educational works are published, it may be said with justification that it is not only the selection that is wide, but many books reach an extraordinarily broad public. In 1971 for instance, more than 100,000 copies were printed each of Sholokhov's Human Fate, Dumas's Vicomte Bragelonne, Feuchtwanger's False Nero, Colette's Wandering Life, Sinclair Lewis's Dodsworth, H. G. Wells's Kipps, Walter Scott's Kenilworth, Aragon's Island on the Seine, Leonhard Frank's Disciples of Jesus and Chekhov's The Lady with the Dog.

Hungarian publishers also endeavour to make Hungarian works accessible in foreign languages. Although quite a number of Hungarian works of fiction and juvenile literature have been published abroad in recent years, there is a rather large backlog even in this field, let alone in the other branches of literature. According to the statistics published by UNESCO, the number of Hungarian works of fiction translated between 1954 and 1969 approached 3,000, most works having been published in Czechoslovakia, the Soviet Union, the Federal Republic of Germany, the German Democratic Republic and Rumania (to mention only those countries which published more than 200 Hungarian works). The Akadémia and Corvina publishing houses publish scientific, professional, educational, art and musical works and, to a smaller extent, fiction, by Hungarian authors in foreign languages and make them available abroad through joint publications with foreign publishers or through the sale of assortments. The achievements of Hungarian science and culture are also reported in foreign language periodicals, the number of which has already exceeded sixty.

This is interpreted by some people as the natural interest taken in the wide world by a small country. It is true that in small countries the need for information is often felt more acutely than elsewhere, but this systematic two-way activity is in Hungary the result of a conscious attitude of cultural policy, which opposes any kind of national isolation and takes internationalism seriously in culture too.

FAVOURITE AUTHORS AND THEIR READERS

According to the data issued by the Central Office of Statistics, 56 per cent of the population over the age of ten read books. There are no substantial differences between the sexes in this respect, but there are considerable differences between the age-groups. In the age-group of 15 to 24 years, 96 out of 100 young people read books, but among the older people one quarter of the population do no look at books at all. The most important relevant factor is education. Among those who have completed less than the 8 years of the general school, only 40 per cent read fiction, whereas the figure is 92–93 per cent among those who have completed secondary school or some form of higher education.

One of the yard-sticks of book-reading is the family library. According to a representative survey, not a single book is possessed in 48 per cent of those families where the education of the head of the household is less than 8 years of general school. Among those who have completed the general school, this proportion is 19 per cent, while for those who have completed secondary education it is 5 per cent.

The investigation of the situation of the different classes and strata of society from the aspect of literary culture requires special attention. According to a survey made among the workers of the Mávag factory, 70 per cent of skilled workers, 52 per cent of semi-skilled workers and approximately 44 per cent of unskilled workers read regularly or from time to time. The importance of education is shown by the fact that 76 per cent of those who have completed five forms or less, 50 per cent of workers who have completed 6 or 7 forms, and 27 per cent of those who have completed the eighth form are not in the habit of reading. According to another survey which covered a wider field in 1968, 75 per cent of workers read regularly or from time to time. 48 per cent of the non-readers have not completed the eighth form of the general school.

As far as the peasantry is concerned, according to the data of the Central Office of Statistics, 27 per cent of co-operative members read more or less regularly. A representative survey shows that 41 per cent of the peasants questioned read some kind of book in the four weeks prior to the survey. The transformation in the villages has changed a great deal in the cultural situation, including the reading of books, but there are still a large number of non-readers among the peasant population, especially among the older peasants.

While precise data are available from the quantitative aspect, i.e. as regards who reads how much, much less is known about what people read and with what result. It is concerning fiction that the largest number of surveys have been made and it is perhaps in this field that the most general conclusions can be drawn. Examining the various genres, classified mostly by topic, it has been established that the most popular genre is the historical novel, followed by adventure and love stories, travelogues, biographies, war novels, scientific fiction, and finally by the contemporary novel. Professional people are mostly interested in historical novels, travelogues and works with a contemporary topic. Agricultural physical workers are mostly interested in juvenile works. Young people like historical novels in addition to juvenile literature. Housewives prefer love stories. Poems interest mainly professional people and white-collar workers.

At the end of the sixties the order of the most favoured authors was as follows: Mór Jókai, Géza Gárdonyi, Zsigmond Móricz, Kálmán Mikszáth, Jules Verne, Leo Tolstoi, Victor Hugo, Alexandre Dumas père, László Passuth, and Ferenc Molnár. This order was, of course, not brought about by spontaneous interest alone, but was also determined by the works that were published in the largest number of copies at that time.

This question is worth investigating according to classes and strata as well. According to the already mentioned 1968 survey, the most read books among workers were: Gárdonyi's novel, The Stars of Eger, Jókai's novels and the works of Berkesi, Rejtő and Dallos. It says perhaps more that out of quality fiction 45.7 per cent was represented by the romantics, 35 per cent by the traditionally structured classics (Tolstoi, Móricz, Thomas Mann) and 19.3 per cent by modern authors (Hemingway, Semprun, Sánta). Out of all reading-matter the so-called quality fictional literature represents 45.2 per cent, and light-weight reading-matter 38 per cent.

As far as the peasantry is concerned, their favourite authors are Jókai, Mikszáth and Móricz, but they also like to read Sholokhov and Péter Veres.

Among university students (according to a survey taken at Szeged) the most favoured Hungarian authors are László Németh, Mór Jókai, Kálmán Mikszáth, Attila József and András Berkesi. The most read foreign authors are Thomas Mann, Hemingway, Leo Tolstoi, Steinbeck, and Dostoyevsky. According to an investigation outside Budapest, romantic works attract 10 per cent of the intelligentsia, traditional classical works 38 per cent, and modern authors 52 per cent. This survey shows, however, that the latter include a fair quantity of light-weight reading.

It would be risky to draw general conclusions from these surveys, which often cover a very narrow sample. It would be risky not only because the samples are small, but also because the reading habits of the various strata change, their cultural level rises and their taste is being developed. Nor should it be forgotten that considerable changes occur in publishing and these also influence reading.

It is also worth looking at what motives move the reader to choose this or that book, or why he likes the books he reads. According to Judit H. Sas's survey of three villages, the following proportions could be established concerning the various motivations: 28.7 per cent of respondents sought entertainment, 6 per cent factual knowledge, 11.4 per cent considered self-recognition as the experience they looked for, 17.8 per cent the so-called search for happiness, 12.2 per cent were mainly interested in social problems, 20.7 per cent in ethical problems, and a mere 3.7 per cent took an interest in artistic form.

A survey taken among workers in 1968 ranked the categories of demand in the following order of frequency: entertainment, interest in moral questions, activity, the acquisition of knowledge, self-recognition and search for happiness, need for prestige, and compulsory reading.

In comparing regular readers among the workers, peasant library members and intellectuals, one finds that there is no substantial difference between them as regards the satisfaction of the demand for entertainment. It is interesting that among intellectuals prestige, the search for happiness or self-recognition play a smaller role. These investigations prove, on the one hand, that entertainment is a natural requirement and, on the other, that those motives are also important which are somehow connected with the formation of the personality—whether the search for happiness, self-recognition, or moral questions are concerned.

It could be observed recently that some genres of fiction also spread knowledge, and some educational works take a literary form. In recent years educational literature of an essay type has gained ground. This appears to be not only a Hungarian but an international trend. The main factors in the spreading of educational literature are the degree of education, age to a certain extent and, of course, the need to learn of the great social transformations of the scientific achievements, and also the growth of consciousness.

DEBATES AND PLANS

The problems of the Hungarian culture of books are connected with the general cultural situation, therefore it is only possible and worthwhile to discuss them in this context. According to the data of the 1970 census, in Hungary 0.9 per cent of the active earning population of 5 million had not had any schooling at all, 10.2 per cent completed only 5 forms of the general school, a further 27.5 per cent seven forms and 42.3 per cent completed all eight forms of general school. What this adds up to is that 38.6 per cent of the active earning population had not completed even the eight forms of general school. It is true that these include many older people, but there is also a stratum of younger people who do not proceed to secondary education. 2 million people are involved, and it is a great task for our publishers and book distributors to arouse their interest.

As a consequence of the educational differentiation of the population, considerably more people have completed secondary school or have a diploma from an institution of higher education than was the case in the past. Their number together approaches one million. Our publishing trade has discontinued uniformization for some while and has endeavoured to take the requirements of the various strata into consideration. The substantial increase in the number of active earners with higher education presents, however, a warning that further differentiation is necessary with respect to this stratum.

One of the most important topics for debate in recent years has been how publishing should be further developed as far as content is concerned, and especially how it should satisfy the demands of the masses and stimulate new demand. It is obvious that entertainment is a natural requirement, consequently the problem is not to treat it as some kind of socially prohibited and harmful passion, but to find ways to satisfy it, bearing in mind higher standards. Incidentally, entertainment never appears on its own, but always entails a certain fund of knowledge and naturally education for a certain way of life and as regards taste. Consequently, there are many genres of entertainment and the value concerned is not necessarily an aesthetic value. The attitude which wishes to measure the various historical and biographical novels, adventure stories and travelogues against the greatest literary works, is mistaken. On the other hand, it must be seen that the greatest classics can also be entertaining, depending on how the reader approaches them and on his erudition and pretentions. The extent to which light-weight reading on the one hand and quality literature on the other spread in the different strata is worth thinking about. When light reading is the exclusive reading-matter, the question arises whether it is possible to proceed from here to genuine literature.

An interesting problem arises concerning interest in new and old literature, and in respect of up-to-dateness in general. Surveys prove that those with lower schooling are more attracted to old literature, while the younger age groups are more interested in the new. But new literature must not be generalized either, because according to experience the most popular new works are often those which present easy reading-matter. In recent years there has nevertheless been a welcome change in interest, which has occurred in the attitude of at least some strata. This is not only welcome because it assists the progress of contemporary Hungarian fiction, but also because it shows that the world-view of the readers, and perhaps their taste too, are becoming more modern.

It is part of the question of up-to-dateness, that the Hungarian reading public should avail themselves to a greater extent of the opportunities offered by educational and professional literature. In recent years considerable progress has been made in this respect, but both the scientific-technological revolution and the transformation of society demand the intensification of this interest and especially its extension to new strata.

All this is connected with the need for the Hungarian publishing and book trade to become more modern too. In this respect great importance must be given to cheap and satisfactorily printed mass series, not only in fiction but in educational and professional publishing as well. As long as our publishing trade is unable to overcome the shortage of printing capacity, it is unable to fulfil fully those tasks which are connected with the modernization of the structure of reading and with the stimulation of the demand of the broad masses. This also entails the utilization of new means for promoting the distribution of books, and primarily taking advantage of the new communication media, especially television, in the publicizing of books. The Gutenberg galaxy continues to "twinkle" above our heads, but there is no doubt that the new technological instruments may strengthen its brightness.

*

Socialist publishing in Hungary has compensated in two decades for the omissions of centuries: it has established the essential conditions for cultural democracy, it has made value and its dissemination the centre of its activity and has served the education of the masses and the satisfaction of their needs. We may remember the 500th anniversary of publishing and printing in this country in the knowledge that everything that was valuable in the past has been continued, and goals have been realized which for centuries appeared humanistic dreams.

Bibliography

1 *János Bak:* Magyarország könyvkiadása 1945–1969 (Publishing in Hungary 1945–1969) MKKE, Budapest, 1970.

2 A magyar könyvkiadás adatai (Data on Hungarian book-publishing) 1921, MKKE, Budapest, 1972.

3 Mit olvasunk? (What do we read?) Budapest, Central Office of Statistics, 1965. 104 p.

4 *Piroska Dobos:* A munkásolvasók irodalmi ízlése a Fővárosi Szabó Ervin könyvtárban (The Literary taste of worker readers in the Municipal Ervin Szabó Library) Budapest, FSzKK. p. 65 (Investigations into the sociology of reading 1.)

5 *Ferenc Gereben:* A középiskolás fiatalok és a könyv (Secondary school pupils and books) Budapest, KTTK. 1968. 78. p.

6 *Ernő Gondos:* Kutatások az olvasói ízlés világában (Research into readers' taste) – Társadalmi Szemle, No. 4. 1969, pp. 56–67.

7 *Ernő Gondos–Péter Polonyi:* Írók és olvasóik (Writers and their readers) – Valóság, No. 5, 1967. pp. 55–59.

8 *István Kamarás:* A munkások és az olvasás (Workers and reading) Publicity Bureau for Popular Education, Budapest, 1969, 202 p.

9 *István Kamarás–Péter Polonyi:* Értelmiség, olvasás, könyvtár (Intellectuals, reading, libraries) Budapest, 1970.

10 *Máté Kovács:* A magyar könyv és könyvkultúra a szocializmus kezdeti szakaszában (The Hungarian book and bibliophilism in the initial period of socialism) Budapest, 1961.

11 *Péter Mándi:* A könyv és közönsége (Books and their public) Budapest, Publishing House for Economics and Law, 1968, 295 p.

12 *Péter Mándi:* Könyvolvasás és könyvvásárlás Magyarországon (Book-reading and book-purchasing in Hungary) Budapest, KTTK. 1965. 78 p.

13 *Péter Mándi:* A munkások és a könyv (Workers and books) Budapest, KTTK, 1968, 62 p.

14 *Judit Sas:* Emberek és könyvek (People and books) Budapest, Akadémia Publishing House, 1968, 214 p.

15 *Miklós Szántó:* Életmód, művelődés, szabadidő (Way of living, education, leisure) Budapest, Akadémia Publishing House, 1967, 169 p.

16 *László Szentirmai:* Olvasás, elemzés és néhány következtetés (Reading, analysis, and a few conclusions) Szeged, 1966, Acta Bibliothecaria, Tom. V., Fasc. 2.

17 *Jenő Ughy:* 1000 falusi lakos és a könyv (1,000 villagers and books) Budapest. KMK. 1965. 119 p.

MIKLÓS SZÁNTÓ

LEVELLING AND INEQUALITIES
IN CULTURAL DEVELOPMENT

An imaginary map of culture would show peaks, plateaus and deep valleys. An indispensable aid in orientation, perhaps, but such a map would present, of course, a static picture, while culture is a process. The majority of those who write on mass culture today, going back to Ortega, picture this as a levelling process which takes place as a result of the wide dissemination of mass-culture media. They claim that, with the disappearance of the peaks, culture has become the province of mediocrity, a view which has adherents in Hungary, too. Erroneous judgements have occasionally gained ground in the working-class movement as well, mostly in the form of utopian illusions based on a sort of "obligatory optimism". The process of culture has been viewed as a single phenomenal, straight-lined rise, problem-free, where plains and valleys disappear, where all differences are levelled out and a vast "plateau" spreads out at the level of the peaks. In reality, however, the situation is different. Some of the old inequalities have disappeared while others persist but have taken on new forms. In the course of cultural development new inequalities spring up, new contradictions arise and are resolved.

Certain levelling trends are noticeable in developed capitalist countries as well. But equalization caused by technological development takes a different direction. There are some who would equate the two kinds

of equalization on the ground that the levelling process is a world phenomenon; what they forget is that equalization in Hungary is taking place in socialist soil, within a national framework and with a changed content. What is the same is also different, and every general phenomenon occurs in the specific, particular context of "here and now".

In referring to levelling and inequality, the terms themselves imply a comparison of certain reference points; differences or similarities of the chosen points of elevation, a decrease or increase of differences, the convergence or divergence of values are all determined within a given system of measurement. Thirty years after the liberation of Hungary we are attempting to survey as Marxists the way we have come and the historical antecedents of the present situation, and in so doing to clear up the real factors and contradictions of the concrete situation. For this reason the special features of the present cultural conditions in Hungary, the relations of the different classes and strata of Hungarian society to one another and the observable trends of levelling and inequality need to be examined.

Every cultural historian is confronted with the very complicated question of the standards by which to measure social progress. The classics of Marxism have illustrated the development of successive social structures by the developmental levels of forces and relations of production. The evolutionary curve from the stone-axe to the laser beam is evident and tremendous, but technological progress in itself cannot be the sole index of the genuine affluence of a society. In their investigation of the main trends of social evolution Marx and Engels came to the conclusion that the epochal stages of the continuous process of equalization must be sought in an analysis of the basic forms of the division of labour. On this basis it can be said that socialist society is characterized by the obliteration of sharp social differences between classes, and that, by relying on social ownership of the means of production, the thousand years old differences between town and village and between manual and mental work will gradually disappear.

Characteristic of our time is the production and large-scale dissemination of ideas to broad masses on the part of a large number of specialists. The efficiency of dissemination has increased enormously and knowledge is spread with fantastic speed. "Consumers of ideas" have multiplied along with a host of highly trained skilled workers, technicians, university graduates and, in another dimension, politicians. Mass information requires a lot of material, a need which is also expressed by the fast-growing demands of the consumer "market".

We live in an atmosphere of competition between the socialist and the capitalist systems, of international exchanges and discussion. Publicity throws light on vast areas, extending the frontiers of public opinion. We live in a time when ideas and knowledge rapidly become obsolete, and life calls for new ideas daily.

Research, however, indicates that "cultural demands" have not grown uniformly in all the different strata of consumers. It is very difficult to transmit new knowledge to the older generation of workers and peasants who did not go beyond the sixth grade of elementary school. It is only with great difficulty that they are able to accept works of art differing from their accustomed taste, which is based upon traditional ways of narrating stories, the traditional gamut of melodies and colours, and works with plenty of action.

Mobility therefore is of two kinds. In relation to the starting-point of 1945 marking the liberation of the country, the whole of Hungarian society has moved forward and upward. This process is sometimes faster, sometimes slower in rhythm, but it is steady. At the same time the cultural development of certain sections of society progresses unevenly and relative shortcomings do exist. The total structure has changed vertically, but horizontally there are differing levels and rhythms. While society as a whole is in continuous motion forward and upward, there is a vertical levelling of large social groups within which there exists a horizontal inequality of strata.

In Hungary the juridico-social foundations of "vertical" equality are built upon the working class having achieved political power and having passed social ownership into law. "Horizontal" inequalities, however, could not be eliminated, for the inequality of income distribution and the inequality of culture and life-style between different classes and strata of society have remained. Life-style differences are due not only to a difference of available supplies but also to a difference of demands. We carry many things with ourselves: a peasant turned worker, for example, who brings an established system of customs and a given body of knowledge from the village, is able to absorb the new for a certain period of time, but there is a limit to his flexibility beyond which he is unable to adjust. It is a process of assimilation which does not take place uniformly, for example, in respect to the satisfaction of so-called "civilized demands" or artistic tastes. For the most part it takes place much sooner in spheres closest to innovation in technology, ranging from the operation of the washing machine to the mechanical techniques of factory work, because daily practice aids the development of new reflexes. It is accomplished with most difficulty in conceptual and symbolic systems of knowledge which are less frequently used and which frequently lack a basis on which one can build.

The Democratization of Culture

How did we get where we are today? What characterized the cultural conditions of the country in the decades before 1945? What was the significance of the cultural monopoly of the old ruling classes?

1 Inequality was institutionally secured. The exploiting classes restricted admission to secondary and higher education. For all practical purposes, education was not available to children of working-class and poor-peasant origin because of the system of tuition fees, the hardships of subsistence during study years, the scarcity of job opportunities afforded by college and secondary schools, the threat of future unemployment, etc. All these factors perpetuated and deepened the cultural gap between manual and mental work on the one hand and between town and village on the other.

2 The body of cultural knowledge, works of art, the instruments of civilized recreation were monopolized in such a way that, on the one hand, the working class was largely deprived of the culture afforded by schools and thus had no incentives and, on the other, poor people could not—even if they wanted to—buy goods such as radios, books, theatre tickets and musical instruments.

3 The culture of the ruling classes was dominant, and in its role as defender of capitalist society it paralysed the thinking of people by espousing religiousness, sentimentalism, shoddiness and by preaching submissiveness.

4 Intellectuals—who are of decisive importance as steadfast innovators, developers, guardians and transmitters of culture—were

made to serve the purposes of the ruling class which was also the exclusive provider of its reserve forces. The little industry there was did not require a great number of technicians. Vacancies requiring secondary or higher education—mainly legal posts—could easily be filled by members of the ruling classes, which also controlled distribution. The way of life of intellectuals was shaped by forces which were under the influence of the ruling classes.

Therefore interpreting the democratization of culture which has followed in the wake of the liberation as a countercurrent to the cultural monopoly, one must say in the first place that the educational standards of large social groups are becoming equalized. The meaning of equalization can be summed up as follows:

1 Control of the institutions of secondary and higher education with equal opportunities for working-class and peasant youth.

2 Legally equal conditions which tend to become equal in practice; utilization of extra-curricular forms of cultural development; acquisition of cultural tools with a view to shaping cultural discrimination.

3 Conscious propagation of a dominant Marxist culture with the help of institutions which pursue a socialist cultural policy and which consider it their main duty to draw into cultural life the heretofore culturally isolated masses.

4 Increasing the proportions in accordance with the tasks of the building of socialism, creating a new generation of professional people from the ranks of the working classes; winning over the old professions and enlisting the active participation of all in the realization of the aims of socialism; structuring the professionals in conformity with the requirements of a developed industry and large-scale farming; considerably increasing the number of those with technical qualifications.

The new structure can come about only if the various large social groups are able to make use of the available means. Improved conditions guarantee that anyone can obtain the qualifications which best suit their abilities, and that on the basis of an appropriate work assignment, and its accompanying income, they can fashion their own demanding or unambitious way of life. The position occupied in the division of labour, income, educational levels and lifestyles underlie the shaping of the cultural structure of a society building socialism.

The Indices of Development

Today's situation is the result, the summation as it were, of thirty years' changes. If we fail to take this into account it is impossible to measure either the distance from the starting point to the present position or to determine diverging velocities or setbacks of partial processes in some areas and the cultural trends of different social groups. Nor would it be possible to evaluate the significance of phenomena and map out a course of action to be taken. However, it is not easy to find the "milestone"; in historically different circumstances it is difficult to use identical categories to measure progress. The varying standards used by researchers and the absence of a clear periodization of post-liberation cultural history are a source of many errors. There are no indices of different periods which would make comparison possible at specific points and this causes further difficulties. In this necessarily brief survey such an attempt appears to be one of the possible, and hopefully controversial, solutions which will stimulate further effort.

The present system of cultural institutions came into being step by step; scientific and technological achievements, literary and artistic works characteristic of given stages emerged at every point and the masses "consumed" the different cultural productions, re-creating them in their own image in accordance with their specific capacity.

A network of schools, scientific institutes, theatres, cinemas, the press, radio and television, publishing houses, libraries and other institutions not specified here have been established. Mass media came into being which are capable of satisfying the needs of millions of people, transmitting indispensable knowledge, information and cultural products to Hungarian homes day after day. There are a large number of talented specialists in this field and the indices of the supply of cultural facilities testify to considerable development. The question is whether the growth rate is fast enough and whether development complies with both needs and what can be done. According to the cultural policy resolution of the Central Committee of the Hungarian Socialist Workers' Party there are alarming signs of serious shortcomings which make it imperative to examine thoroughly the present situation.

Some discussions of the present situation are far too "aesthetic"; they fail to make allowances for the conditions which determine choices of action, their hierarchy of values and hence the place and role of culture in their lives. Cultural contradictions cannot be understood, nor can they be resolved, within the limits of cultural conditions; they can only be inferred from the whole of social practice, keeping in mind, of course, the relatively autonomous development of a particular field.

In accordance with the basic Marxian position, let us begin with differences in production and the social division of labour and its cultural consequences. Within the total number of wage and salary earners in agriculture, industry and the service sector alike, manual and intellectual workers are differentiated according to training, the degree of responsibility in concrete productive labour and the amount of physical effort required by the work.

There are further subdivisions, the stratum of manual workers itself its heterogeneous and is subdivided according to qualifications into skilled workers, semi-skilled workers and unskilled workers. There are also degrees of inequality in distribution, for example in wages. (Another basis for classification is the aggregate income, on which calculations of per capita income are based.) The income level determines the scope and composition of the family "assets", and also influences the pattern of household expenses.

One of the most profound cultural contradictions of our time, at a period of transition to intensive production, is found in production.

Production and Culture

People live and work in conditions that are getting better but the improvement is not in a straight line. Productive labour is the basis of existence and, as a result, contradictions and tensions is this sphere are carried over into private lives, influencing the way we feel in particular about culture. A substantial part of tasks stems from the fact that the level of training and education of the labour force is not in keeping with the technological level of production. While industries complain of a labour shortage, in some areas overqualification is a problem. Modernization of production is a way out, but the mechanization of hard manual work is made difficult by the prohibitive cost of machines. What is more, a considerable number of skilled workers do jobs that could be performed by the semi-skilled and—as we read in one study—"they rightly ask themselves if it was worth their while to undergo special training. For, while there is a growing number of skilled workers with a secondary education, there will be an ever increasing need for mechanics or semi-skilled workers as automation advances."[1] Today

[1] György Pogány: "Társadalmi-gazdasági követelmények a fizikai dolgozók képzési-oktatási struktúrájával szemben" (Socio-economic Requirements in the Training and Education Structure of Manual Workers). *Közgazdasági Szemle*, 1974/12, p. 1342.

the general education of manual workers is lower and their average qualification is somewhat higher than socially needed. Not much has been done to stimulate interest in the enterprise, so the workers' personal interest abates; thus it is only natural that the prestige of culture does not rise. The demand for extension training does not express a need within the enterprise, but arises as a result of outside prompting on the part of the state, and this encouragement occasionally even conflicts with the every-day interests of enterprises.

What can thus be expected? Qualification levels will generally continue to rise, while technical work will, for some time, require the monotonous semi-skilled tasks of assembly-line production or, at best, work with semi-automated machines. How much monotony can be tolerated depends largely on a person's educational and training level. "The more abilities and skills you feel to be unused in any given job, the more you suffer from the monotony," a prominent Hungarian economist writes in this connection. She also formulates the consequences as follows: "Parallel with the ever more widespread satisfaction of material needs, the kind of work done, together with related cultural differences, is fast becoming the most important kind of social difference."[2]

Many professional people are "semi-skilled" intellectual workers who do not perform work of a creative nature. The end-result is unpleasant feelings they try to escape from, and culture becomes a kind of "protective device" instead of a source of human wealth.

Let's make no mistake, however; this process is not a mysterious stroke of fate: technology is not an enemy to culture. First, advanced technology is a welcome development which brings with it qualitative changes in production, a widening choice of products, improved supplies and a higher standard of

[2] Katalin Falus-Szikra: "Képzettség és munkaszervezés" (Qualifications and Work Organization). *Közgazdasági Szemle*, 1974/12, p. 1424.

living. Furthermore, the working conditions of an up-to-date, modern factory, skill in a new trade, productive collective activities, the wholesome, democratic atmosphere of factories in, and even in spite of, mass production can, and necessarily will, prove to be constant stimuli for the cultural improvement of youth, those of rural origin, and women. We also hope to be able to discover modern forms of work organization which will provide a remedy against monotony, render work more varied and eventful and increase labour productivity at the same time.

In speaking of the dialectics of work and leisure and the different aspects of contradictory relations, what Marx said of the true significance of leisure activities should be kept in mind.

"The saving of labour time (is) equal to an increase of free time, i.e. time for the full development of the individual, which in turn reacts back upon the productive power of labour as itself the greatest productive power. From the standpoint of the direct production process it can be regarded as the production of *fixed capital*, this fixed capital being man himself."

"Free time—which is both idle time and time for higher activity—has naturally transformed its possessor into a different subject, and he then enters into the direct production process as this different subject."[3]

Hungarian society cannot afford to let this fixed capital of the human force of production, knowledge and experience remain unutilized by wasting creative energies. The question is frequently asked why people cultivate gardens, investing their ideas and energy in them to such an extent that they withdraw from community life. In my opinion, the most instrumental factor is that the choice of profession is often accidental; positions often turn out to be uncuitable to the real or imagined abilities of

people; but the negative atmosphere of a factory or the weakness of a collective can also contribute to a lack of involvement in public life. Often work does not grow into a vocation and a good many people do not feel the joy of accomplishment in their productive activities. All these factors are also related to the weaknesses of unsatisfactory workshop-democracy. The garden, the week-end cottage or the car as a goal or as an occupation may offer only a "mini-perspective" but one which is at least tangible. And so many withdraw into their private worlds.

Of course, this is but one aspect. To the city-dweller the garden means recreation, a closeness to nature, fresh air, healthy surroundings, relaxations, frequently a change of company, meeting with people of similar interests, exchanges of opinion, companionship, "supplementary sports", and sometimes, encounters with new fields of knowledge.

The car is a vehicle which helps one to see and know hitherto unknown cities and people, countries and cultures; its operation sets in motion skills and abilities which might rarely be used, thus giving rest and pleasure. The above "values" do provide pleasant experiences if they serve as tools in personality development. The trouble begins when the garden, car or cottage becomes an end in itself and turns into a mere status symbol; when it serves as a refuge for the owner to hide in; when it is a cave of withdrawal from society and community life; when it is not a source of new strength for man to live more affectively in the community but dwindles into a fenced-in "property", raising an insurmountable wall between society and the proprietor.

The basic requirement of advanced socialist societies of equalization between manual and mental work is not only a matter of raising the levels of education and training. Productive culture is also a unity of knowledge and behaviour, which is manifest in man's morality as a whole, in his willing-

3 Karl Marx: *"Grundrisse"*. *Foundations of the Critique of Political Economy* (Rough Draft). Translated by Martin Nicolaus. Penguin Books, Harmondsworth, 1973. p. 711 and 712.

ness to make sacrifices. As György Aczél said: "By culture we do not only mean the level of technical knowledge (although this, too) but primarily the so-called 'inner culture', the culture of thought, of feeling, of the total human attitude. It refers to the individual's capacity for comprehending the entire working process, the social interconnections and significance of labour, and recognizing and sizing up the role it plays in society, in man, in the world."[4]

The leading class of a society building socialism is the working class, and the unity and progress of that society depends on their enthusiasm for productive labour and political consciousness. This is why we consider important the socialist brigade movement whose motto and practice so accurately express the requirements of socialist humanity: to live, work and learn in a socialist way. We are working to make the socialist brigades genuine communities and workshops of culture.

Much has been said about the scientific and technological revolution having renewed and restructured the cultural ideal; the rapid obsolescence of knowledge necessitates continuous training, even after formal education is over. It has been noted less frequently, however, that it takes great perseverance, diligence, self-abnegation and sacrifice over many years for a working person to make up gaps in formal education. The chances for success are greatly influenced by the participant's age. After 40 the success of school-type learning seems quite hopeless. In addition to age, family status and sex are decisive. A single woman is more likely to study, but the situation of a housewife with two children is difficult and she has less opportunity to do so.

Figures on the educational level of the gainfully employed indicate that nearly half

the population of Hungary has not completed eight years elementary education. If we examine the figures by ten-year periods, it appears that in the 20 to 30-year age-group there is a high ratio of secondary-school graduates, while among working people over 50 the number of those who have completed only six or seven years of elementary school is astonishingly high. In the coming decade there will still be hundreds of thousands in production who have a low level of education and general culture and who have very little chance of finishing their elementary-school studies. At the same time the rate of technological progress is extremely fast and enterprises introduce more and more new machines which people must learn to handle. The lower the level of general education and professional training, the more difficult the switch-over. Older workers naturally cling to what they have become accustomed to; their self-esteem is based on the routine of decades. The younger, more highly educated workers are also better qualified professionally and adapt themselves more quickly to new conditions, finding it easier to switch over to the new. Such situations imply contradictions and create tensions between different strata of workers.

The prestige of culture varies from stratum to stratum; its standing is not only a cultural but a social question. Béla Köpeczi writes: "Until general culture, professional training and income come into a closer and more reasonable relation with one another, the social prestige of culture cannot grow."[5]

Urbanization

During the past few decades vigorous urbanization in Hungary has considerably raised the cultural level of the labouring masses. New, incomparably broader pos-

---

4 György Aczél: "Szocializmus, életforma" (Socialism, Life-style). Based on short-hand notes taken at the meeting of the Central Council of Trade Unions on June 29, 1973. *Látóhatár*, No. 1973/9., p. 179.

5 Béla Köpeczi: "A kultúra társadalmi rangja" (The Social Status of Culture). Extract from a debate. *Látóhatár*, 1973/3., p. 168.

sibilities were provided than had been available in the traditional village. Urban life requires the acquisition of new knowledge necessary for a new way of life and the adoption of relevant norms and customs. Concurrent with rapid and extensive urbanization has been the diminution of differences between the capital city and the countryside, on the one hand, and between the towns and the villages, on the other.

Industrial plants were established in traditional towns, engendering new cities, but the development of the infrastructure did not keep abreast of this rapid industrialization. Hundreds of thousands of new industrial wage-earners solved this problem by retaining their rural residences and commuting between home and work. Characteristic of the position of commuters is that they spend too much time commuting. The fatigue of the daily rides resulted in a cultural disadvantage which was further aggravated by their working as auxiliary labourers in co-operatives, on state farms or on their own household farms, especially at the peak of the agricultural season. Thus they were left out of general cultural development.

City-dwellers acclimatize to urban life through an uncomfortable "crash course". In cities technological development is higher and the interrelation between the spread of electricity and the rise of the cultural level, for example, is self-evident. The appearance on a mass scale of audio-visual instruments has transformed life-styles. Some household appliances have an indirect cultural effect. The city, with its abundance of cultural facilities and regular schedules, provides cultural stimulants around the clock.

But there are also drawbacks. Every sociological or socio-psychological study on city living points out that amid urban conditions there are more impersonal relationships than elsewhere, that opportunities for new acquaintances are fewer and the circle of acquaintances smaller. There are indications also in this country that families become introverted, a trend which is promoted

by better housing conditions and increased television viewing. There are many lonely people. It is paradoxical in a society building socialism that the cohesive force of the community does not grow as it should.

The continuous one-way influx of people from village to town has slowed down; the resources of agricultural labour are dwindling. The village itself is no longer an entirely agricultural settlement. In most villages located in the vicinity of some city, the majority of the population are gainfully employed in industry, commerce, the service sector or in public administration. In many places villages grow into suburbs and are being supplied with public utilities in widening concentric circles. The car enables villagers to go to the theatre and concerts in the city and the radio offers the same culture to them as to city-dwellers. Collective work and uniform interests bring people together, and this factor, in addition to and in place of family relationships, is the basis of the reorganization of social life.

A reverse movement which could be seen a decade ago in developed industrial countries is now beginning here: families are swarming to settlements outside the city. The increasing use of cars, the development of mass transportation and more highways have made it possible for the strata with surplus income and higher living standards to have family homes built in villages which are growing into suburban zones around larger cities. At the same time the strata with more modest incomes take advantage of relatively less expensive plots of land in districts farther out and build their own family homes with gardens. This ties up all their money and energy over a period of several years; in the actual construction, especially on week-ends, they enlist the help of the whole family, relatives and friends, and colleagues; then after moving into the new home they repay in kind, working Sundays on the plot of another relation or colleague.

Nor is this process free of contradictions.

On the one hand, a relatively large number of villages, following the pattern of the unification of co-operatives, become so-called primary villages and develop more rapidly as emerging industrial centres; on the other hand, some communities remain backward and face the possibility of depopulation. The system of detached farmsteads, which came into being in some parts of the Great Hungarian Plain during the eighteenth and nineteenth centuries and whose scattered houses are still inhabited by a million people, demonstrates certain features which in some places are still viable under the new conditions. In other places, under different conditions, they survive for a time, only to become obsolete as their occupants lag hopelessly behind rising national living standards. In this respect there are great differences between more and less industrialized areas; communities linked to the transportation network develop more rapidly, while others are virtually abandoned. The total abandonment of villages such as Gyűrűfű and rapid urbanization occur simultaneously, are interpenetrating phenomena. All strata, of course, cannot equally utilize the possibilities of the changing situation. It depends first of all on income, education and age as to whether families benefit from the new conditions, or whether it all only adds up to inequality between those moving forward and those remaining behind.

Contradictions of Cultural Consumption

All researchers of cultural conditions are in agreement that there has been considerable improvement in the living standard of Hungarian families; their cultural "reserves" have been enriched, and within a few years' time it has become a matter of course to have a radio and a television set. Household culture has changed; electrical appliances help in housework and the demands for services have grown too. The process of equalization in respect to per capita family income has progressed.

At the same time there is a relatively broad stratum which still lives under bad conditions and must struggle with housing difficulties; there are retired people who receive low pensions and families with too many dependents for the family income. The past four to five years of accelerated improvement has not equally covered all strata of the population. Per capita income depends to a large extent on the number of children, and the ratio of earners to dependents is one of the determinants of discretionary income which, over and above the satisfaction of basic necessities (food, dwelling, clothing), makes such things as cultural demands impossible to satisfy.

Culture costs money. Therefore it is essential to know what use people make of available material resources and whether the ratio of cultural allocations is growing, absolutely and relatively, within family budgets. And here we encounter a serious contradiction, for the ratio of the sums expended on culture within the pattern of household expenses is stationary.

The prices of cultural facilities in Hungary are comparatively low. Considerable state subsidies make books and theatre tickets accessible to any person of modest means who wants cultural entertainment. But even inexpensive cultural products are only within the reach of one who has a developed taste for them and a "free" income. The moment you have to stop to consider how to spend your money and, we may add, your time and energy, the value factor intervenes. In the whole system of decision-making the position culture holds in the scale of values, the prestige of culture, the social esteem given the cultured man and the real or fictitious values which underlie social prestige all play a role. (In capitalist societies, social status is determined by success, money and career.) The question arises whether ability, culture, social usefulness and participation in decision-making constitute the value standards of socialist society. One of the causes of the harmful manifestations of petty-bourgeois mentality is that in our transitional society certain types of personal property lend "private proprietary features" to their owners, and an attitude of "consumption for consumption's sake" can also be observed.

Culture is a particular commodity the nature of which is restricted by the Hungarian state's policy of subsidization. But let us entertain no illusions in this respect either: the national income devoted to this purpose is produced by the entire people. The buyer has a definite need which presents itself as a buyer's demand. If we examine, for example, the social stratification of theatre-goers, we find that the number from each stratum grows according to the degree of education. The people who enjoy the subsidies granted to theatres come primarily from the higher income groups with secondary and higher education. This does not mean that state subsidies to theatres ought to be stopped, but it does give cause for greater sacrifices in order to create such demands and to seek means by which disadvantaged people can be effectively helped. It must be recognized that equal chances often augment inequality. Therefore efforts must be redoubled in order to achieve the cultural advancement of those living in difficult circumstances.

At this point, however, it should once again be noted that the "consumption" of culture does not automatically go hand in hand with the socialist way of life. Socialist life-style also demands a communal attitude and active participation in public life.

*

Many questions have to be answered, constructive debates have been going on for years; the recent Party resolution on cultural policy has complemented an entire series of previous resolutions. Socialist culture as a whole has been brought into the limelight. Interesting discussions have been held on the role of intellectuals, the structure of institutions and the prestige of culture. For example, in a meeting of the Cultural Research Committee of the Hungarian Academy of Sciences, the theoretical and practical problems of socialist culture were discussed by leading specialists.

These useful and interesting debates have been marred by an overemphasis on aesthetics while work and its culture have been pushed into the background; not enough stress has been placed on the fact that socialist culture encourages not only study and a search for artistic experience, but also a communal attitude that manifests itself in productive work, in public consciousness, in behaviour and in knowledge alike. In my opinion the solution should be approached from the side of the socialist way of life, taking into account conditions of personal circumstances. In production we have in part already discovered ways of switching over to the intensive stage, but in culture many vestiges of the extensive period still survive: the qualitative approach is strong, the worker is often regarded merely as manpower, not infrequently planning is one-sidedly investment-oriented and we have not yet found sensitive, accurate indices for a system of effective incentives to create interest in culture; long-range thinking which takes into account the chain-reaction effects of all our economic and social arrangements is sometimes lacking and these effects can promote or hinder cultural processes, too.

Most contradictions go hand in hand with progress. Marxism-Leninism is a good compass and on the basis of the Marxian scale of values we can work out necessary tasks, fight against unfavourable tendencies and strengthen everything that points to the future.

BÉLA BARTÓK

On the 25th anniversary of his death

by

GYÖRGY LUKÁCS

These lines were not written by a musician, their author cannot even claim to be a connoisseur in music. So the experts are free to ignore them if they wish.

And yet I believe, or at least hope, that these non-professional lines have a close connection with Bartók's true significance, even if they are no more than suggestive hints and far from fully exhaust the subject. In any case, it is this true significance that inspires them.

The mere fact of being his contemporary provides no adequate excuse for this article, even in spite of the fact that—being a few years younger than Bartók—I also am one of those whose early years of development were overshadowed by the patriotic traditions which hardened into the rigid and obtuse academism prevailing after 1867. At that time only the first faint indications of the ideological revolution were visible. So if I claim to be a slightly younger contemporary of Bartók, it is first and foremost in terms of the community which stifled all genuine protest common to both of us in our youth.

And when the ferment of protest began it was Bartók, alone with Ady, who raised his far-reaching voice; he was one of those whose personality and creative work made the period from 1900 to the revolutions the truly great epoch of Hungarian culture.

After the collapse of 1848, Hungarian society and Hungarian policy followed "the Prussian way." Following Lenin's definition this meant that Hungarian capitalism and the development of bourgeois Hungary produced no more than slight changes in the economic, social and political hegemony of the vestiges of the past still surviving. The unequal alliance between the feudal latifundia and developing capitalism for the joint exploitation of Hungarian workers and peasants was then called liberalism, on the grounds that within this alliance, where the leadership of the feudal partner was always unquestioned, large-scale capital was no longer relegated to a social ghetto; on the contrary, it was sometimes tolerated even in the corners of the exclusive National Casino; and under this system the great Jewish-capitalist landowners duly fulfilled their allotted roles side by side with the big bank presidents of ancient lineage.

Capitalist Hungary, consequently, except for the brief episode of the 1919 revolution, remained the country of the nobility, a "gentleman's" country. Of course such a gentleman, as one of István Tisza's supporters said about his leader, was "a gentleman who worked." This meant that any one of the minor gentry, if he chose to go into business, could even rise to prominence in economic affairs, or if he chose to remain a simple country gentleman, a ministry or county official. Everyone knows that all the estates of feudal origin were only finally broken up and divided among the peasants in 1945.

Hungary was not the only country to follow this line. It was equally the destiny of the German nation after the sad end of 1848, and of the Russians until the Great October Revolution in 1917. But this social and political similarity produced different intellectual attitudes in each country. 1848 put an end to the radical trend in German thinking and German art which, from Lessing to Heine, had dominated those attitudes there. A new phase began in the development of German literature which has been aptly characterized by Thomas Mann as "power-protected intimacy." In Russia a definite revolutionary contradiction developed in the field of ideology and political thinking which characterized the great epoch of Russian literature from Pushkin to Chekhov. And if we consider the main line of Russian literary development we would be mistaken if we assumed the trend represented by Bielinsky, Chernishevsky and Dobrolyubov as the antithesis of the ultimate aims of Tolstoy and Dostoyevsky. The real essence of Tolstoy's and Dostoyevsky's work was the same sharp, uncompromising protest against the social bases of Czarist Russia as the direct attack waged in the criticism of the revolutionary democrats.

Hungarian literature (because we cannot speak of independent Hungarian philosophical thinking at that stage) embraces the major extremes of world development in a specific way. "Power-protected intimacy" was the ruling trend in Hungary as well. This is no exaggeration, but it is as well to make clear at the outset that this did not invariably and inevitably mean always a conservative and hidebound satisfaction with the long-enduring vestiges of feudalism in Hungary, nor with the capitalism superimposed on them. This kind of ideological backwardness was equally to be found in the German "alldeutsch" trend and Russian reaction, extending to the "Black

Hundreds." But I am now speaking of something fundamentally different: the basic frame of mind here is an attitude which could perhaps be best described as a state of mind reluctant to grumble or show discontent.

*

Honest and sincere political thinkers, at least the best of them, despite the difference in the degree and clearness of their vision, perceived the great deformation of human beings through the alliance between the remnants of feudalism and the beginning of capitalist production. Feeling and thought protested against it, but they believed *a priori*, that even theoretically, any possibility of radical opposition leading to or encouraging action was hopeless. The abdication which sprang from this attitude was one of the essential features of "power-protected intimacy" and ranged widely, both subjectively and objectively from open desperation to cynical resignation, at which point the man and the political thinker comes to a full-stop, renounces all intermediate attitudes and becomes a cynical and active supporter of the regime he despises. A glance at German developments after 1848 will show us the evolution of Richard Wagner in the ranks of the "power-protected," he who was a revolutionary in 1848 and became a follower of Feuerbach and later of Schopenhauer; it will show us the fundamental and deep melancholy of Brahms which had its origins there, and the self-ironical humour of Raabe and Fontane.

In Hungary 1848 was also the point of departure for "power-protected intimacy" as a dominant trend. It is hardly necessary to mention Zsigmond Kemény and Mór Jókai in this context, men who in all other respects were so different from each other, although there is no doubt that not only their direct impact, but also these effects considered as a model, have influenced the development of Hungarian thinking up to our days.

János Arany, who ought be mentioned here as the first great representative of this very typical attitude, was never a born revolutionary by nature as Petőfi was. It is however remarkable, and worthwhile pointing out, that during the revolutionary years which brought so many personal disillusionments to Petőfi, Arany was the only one with whom his relation remained without conflict to the end. And of course the true image of Arany is only complete if we bear in mind that his relation with Petőfi was never shaken or even questioned. Arany's belief that 1848 could never be repeated was no mere passing mood, and he never even considered the effect of an eventual revolutionary protest on his personal life. But an understanding of the truth of 1848 and the fact that it could never be repeated became the basis of Arany's outlook and thinking in his last years. And there are some perceptions in "The Love of Toldi" which on occasion go farther than the more revolutionary parts of it written before 1848. The only disillusionment of the ageing hero in "The Evening of Toldi" was King Louis's personal conduct. But "The Love of Toldi," which basically rejected the former attitude of protest, called him "the king of knights"—a very exact class characterization.

This is not the place to analyse these very profound inconsistencies. After all, I am only attempting to sketch the background which shaped the significance of Bartók's œuvre through its very contradictions. There is only one more thing to add to the image of Arany: in his manhood and old age, which were considered by Hungarian liberalism as the eternal and classical manifestation of what a poet's attitude should be, he deeply despised life in Hungary as it was around 1867. It is perhaps enough to quote here the well-known stanza of the poem entitled "Epilogue":

> When a gentleman horsetrader passed me
> Who spattered me with mud
> I never argued.
> I stood aside and wiped it off.

And it is no accident that Arany's "Album", his farewell to poetry, ends with these lines:

> Comus did not stay with me,
> Nor the gentle Muses
> Only unsmiling
> Naked misery.

Many have been aware of this "power-protected intimacy" in the works of Kálmán Mikszáth but they do not generally conclude with this definition. With Mikszáth these contradictions are perhaps even sharper than with Arany. It was Mikszáth who painted the most realistic, the most cruel test and the most cynically damning picture of Hungary in the epoch of the Tiszas. That is why we respect him as the most significant master of Hungarian critical realism. And we should therefore make it our business to understand, in analysing his poetic attitude, what is perhaps the biggest paradox in the development of Hungary: how could it happen that Mikszáth, the writer of such criticism, became the best-known writer of an openly admitted reactionary epoch, and why did he not become an outcast like Ady in the eyes of the Tisza epoch? His criticisms were no less sharp than those of Ady.

The most complex representative of the Hungarian "power-protected intimacy" was, undoubtedly, Mihály Babits. It would be an oversimplification to remind the reader that Babits rejected the first real poems of Ady which attacked the whole feudal establishment. But even these emotional motivations have to be investigated. Babits wrote to the friend of his youth, Dezső Kosztolányi, who felt the same about them: "I wonder if Ady comes from an ancient Hungarian family?... Even if that is so, he should handle this subject with love... I am a Hungarian, from a Hungarian noble family (yes, I am proud of it!) on the side of both my mother and my father: and my grandfathers on both sides have been county officials for many years (is there a more Hungarian occupation?): my father was the first of the family to take service with the State, but he was still the true type of the Hungarian gentleman and man of law."

It would, of course, be quite wrong to trace a direct connection between the more mature declarations of the later, mature Babits on what he considered the true substance of Hungarian culture and the right lines of its future development, to his somewhat callow outburst, but it is also true that Babits's attitude of mind on the essential characteristics of the Hungarian people never quite rid itself of this basic premise. It would be very interesting to follow up and analyse this development factually from phase to phase. It would show that his early article in *Nyugat* contrasting the petty bourgeois parochialism of Petőfi, which according to him was closely connected with his revolutionary attitude, with the distinguished sensibility of Arany, was by no means fortuitous. He describes this quality in a very characteristic way: "In those who always carry their past within them, the basis of their conscientiousness is their attachment to the past and a moral consistency."

Here, again, is not the place to illustrate the development of Babits, and the ripening of his opinions. I must add, however, that when he no longer rejected Ady he consistently tried to fit him into the historical development which, in his opinion, formed the unchanging and unchangeable essence of the Hungarian nation. His later writings, his attempts at autobiography, his essays written for the anthology "What is it to be a Hungarian?" consistently followed the same line. And this attitude remained, even when he voiced a powerful protest in his "Book of Jonah" against the fascism that was preparing in Hungary.

*

For the sake of clarity in this important matter I must criticize myself as well. When (in 1941) I enthusiastically welcomed this very fine poem I also discussed in some detail Babits's contemporary statements on his attitude and his views on Hungary. I recognized in my explanation the contradictions in them, I based this powerful anti-fascist demonstration in the main on individual moral motives. I had not then fully understood that he rejected fascism chiefly on the grounds of its objective nature, because fascism—unlike the nineteenth-century reactionary trends which respected and developed historical continuity and historical traditions—was a special type of reaction which, as the still unconscious ideology of the new phase of capitalist evolution, was not simply a further development of the old conservative trends, but indeed was often in sharp opposition to them. I should have seen this all the more because I actually quoted the following excerpt from Babits's autobiography, which had been recently published: "I am part ot the old intellectual era in which the bond with the nation was a sacred and spiritual bond. This present epoch despises the spirit and spiritual bonds. Those who call it 'epoch of nationalism' do not really know this unhappy nineteenth century, which created modern national communities by simply giving the different elements equal rights and seeing that they shared in the common culture and tradition. Our century dissolves these spiritual bonds, it prefers the physical bond of race or the class community of interest." So the final philosophical viewpoint of Babits remained the same, he even enthusiastically idealized the transitory epoch which Arany despised, the Prussian road to capitalism.

All this by no means lessens the poetry and beauty of "The Book of Jonah" and its moral and social significance. But it demonstrates at the same time that the final philosophical foundation of Babits's anti-fascism was his attachment to the essentially conservative "power-protected intimacy." We know that the conservative Stefan George emigrated to Switzerland as a silent protest against Hitler. Babits did not keep silent, he spoke out and this, from every point of view, makes him considerably superior to his German contemporary. But this just and legitimate evaluation cannot and should not wish to conceal the final ideological foundation of his attitude which is very similar to the other's.

I have taken a devious route to reach Bartók himself. But this detour was necessary. If we wish to evaluate correctly how "power-protected intimacy" was overtaken by revolution we must not devalue these opposite philosophies and artistic trends by vulgar simplification.

It is only on the basis of these considerations that one can compare the "Russian" trend in Hungarian thinking, Csokonai, Petőfi, Ady, Attila József and chiefly Bartók, with the best and most progressive manifestations of the "Prussian way." Ady's famous article, "Petőfi does not compromise," was the first proclamation which was conscious of this contradiction.

Of course if we—quite rightly, I believe—draw a parallel between this trend in the Hungarian development and the great Russian revolutionary trend, we shall have to bear in mind another difference which is apparently only a difference of genre. The Russian form of development included all the important domains of poetry and thought: epoch-making creative work in the novel, drama and comedy appeared in the course of this development. The same trend in Hungary was almost exclusively confined to the best representatives of lyric poetry and the subjective type of literature, and then—in the works of Bartók—it reached its deepest expression and most exquisite manifestation in music.

*

The problems of genre, as everywhere in the development of world literature, are based mainly on philosophy of history. The medium in which any people in a given period wishes to give conscious expression to their self-knowledge, the criticism of their past and their present, and the way their future development lies, offers many types and very different possibilities of expression, and not only in purely artistic terms. The structures of and directions taken by the movements which create these differences are closely connected with the social foundations of these movements, and particularly with the extent to which a protest movement can penetrate the life of the masses. From this point of view the domination of lyric poetry in Hungary is *a priori* a reflection of the social weakness of its radical movements. It is not that the particular Hungarian development did not know the exquisite forms of expression provided by epics and drama: such forms of expression are very well known in Hungary. But the Hungarian writers who thought it their mission to describe the fate of their people purely objectively, could not, just because of their knowledge and experience, be resolute and combative opponents of the remnants of feudalism and emerging capitalism. The lonely lyric poet who, despite eventual fame, has to rely upon his own personality and the exclusive and direct manifestations of his ego, can draw the fundamental accent of his verse from this very situation. When Petőfi wrote his great ode about his desire to die for world revolution he opened with a meditation on his personal death, and the desire for revolutionary martyrdom grew out of this, and not inversely. And Ady, for example, reproachfully summoned the "lingering, languid red Sun," addressing it like a loved woman.

Only music is able to objectivize this deepest subjective attitude into a vision of the world without weakening the subjective verse of the lonely lyric poet. Music, indeed, can even augment and intensify it into a protest by the world against its own condition. So the unique place and significance of Bartók in Hungarian culture is built to a great extent on the fact that he was a musician. I wish to give an objective, generalized basis to this statement, and consequently would like to refer here to an important category of my aesthetics, viz. undetermined objectivization. This category has its source in the very substance of art. The extensive and intensive objectivity of the heterogeneous world can only be expressed by art through a process of homogenization which starts from man and returns to him. This process or homogenization, however, prohibits in advance the direct objectivization of certain decisive elements of reality. So literature cannot sensibly and directly represent people and facts, painting and sculpture cannot illustrate real movement and expressed thought, and music cannot exactly be perceived by thought, it is compelled to remain in the realm of pure feeling and experience, which cannot be articulated in a determined manner.

In the development of art, as everywhere, these insurmountable obstacles to the possibilities of expression do not constrict but, on the contrary, broaden and deepen the possibilities of artistic expression. The true basis of the creation of types on the scale of world history very often starts here. The dissolution of Renaissance culture can only be expressed in indirect phrases, but in the later works of Tintoretto, in the music of Monteverdi it finds a deep and unified expression in a unique artistic way: neither contemporary Italian literature nor philosophy were able to convey this picture. This undetermined objectivity makes this exquisite typicalness possible where many concrete and directly perceptible determined elements disappear or at least fade into the background; these are the elements which make the change of an epoch manifest even in daily life. These elements are then replaced by the deep and poignant human emotions through which the beginning of a new era can mean a memorable turning-point in the development of the human race, in the historical development of man as a human being.

This level of creation, which is rooted directly in the artistic limits of the forms of a genre, appears really as a problem of content. Merely to eliminate or obscure the direct forms of historical change only degrades art into dullness. Where undetermined objectivity ignores these symptomatic directly objective forms not for profound reasons concerned with content, but purely for directly formal reasons, nothing remains but dullness and indifference. Dutch painting is a great example of the positive aspect of this development. This painting sprang from the victories of the Dutch in their war of liberation against the feudal and autocratic Spanish kingdom, and from Van Goyen to Vermeer they laid the bases for the new painting of the new world. Rembrandt is the only painter who stands apart from this line of development. Why? Because Rembrandt turned to his own use, yet put aside, the great majority of the conquests achieved by this line of development, which directly created reality, and represented the most profound problem of the new man, the new vision of the world, on the basis of undetermined objectivity, this deepest problem being the manifestations of life of the new man which have developed into irreparable tragedy. Many artists and thinkers, then and later, felt and perceived the true insoluble problems of the new man, and of a world advancing towards capitalism and then establishing it. Neither Diderot, nor Rousseau, nor even Goethe can be properly understood without this knowledge. And yet: there is no other intellectual or artistic reflection of this epoch of great transition, which expresses it as it is expressed in the undetermined objectivity of Rembrandt's pictures, revealing as they do the fundamental and insoluble inner contradictions of the new man in a manner which also gives it contemporary validity. (There is one exception: the last part of *Gulliver*, with the opposition of wise horses and vile men.) If we wish to experience this problem in its true reality and depth, and if we are looking for a way to lead us out of these contradictions of humanity, we should look at Rembrandt's pictures today.

Without a comprehension of this situation we cannot fully understand the real greatness of Bartók. The Kossuth Symphony, even if it sprang from revolutionary sentiments, could still be welcomed by conservative Hungarian critics who saw in it the appearance of a new Hungarian musical genius. This appreciation was not without foundation; the specific substance of the Hungarian people, the essence of their life was already expressed in it, even if as yet in an immature form. It was still limited, it was only an inner generalization of the true Hungarian people, it was the first attempt of a people wanting to renew itself, the first attempt to express its intrinsic self, in music if in nothing else. If at the same time the young Bartók and his followers struggled against the pretension of gipsy music to represent essential Hungarian quality they fought for what Ady fought in his attacks on a fashionable minor poet of the period. They were perhaps more radical, and they generalized more on the basis of the maximal undetermined objectivity of music. So the enthusiastic welcome given by some conservative critics was already an error at the time.

*

The substance of Bartók's development can be expressed in a brief, and of course too generalized, form as follows. Although Hungarian folk music always remained the foundation of Bartók's compositions, he did not stop at this first and powerful impulse: he went further, towards a comprehension and artistic utilization of all folk music. Here the right wing ceased their praise; it is well known that he was even accused of high treason because he praised Rumanian folk music. Nor did he stop there; he included Czech, Slovak, Arab, Portuguese, indeed all folk music among the ever-broadening and deepening basic elements of the new music. For Bartók the central problem of renewing the world (i.e. music) was the true life of every people, and the insoluble contradiction of the distorting effects of capitalist pseudo-culture upon it; the irreconcilable contradiction between the natural life lived by the peasant and the distorted and alienated life of modern man provided him with the point of departure for solving the problem of human living today.

If the peasant is here mentioned as a central figure who is the authentic social basis for revolt, we must remember not to regard it only in a directly social or political context. Here too—with the help of the undetermined objectivity of music—the crux of the matter is the turning-point in world history, just as in the case of Rembrandt's bourgeois. Directly, in the literal sense of the term used here, we could say that neither of them "existed" in this artistically realized form, but at the same time both expressed a turning-point in world history in an artistically perfect way clear and understandable to all. If we wish to understand correctly the historical role of this peasant in its full significance, neither the real role played by the peasants in contemporary political and social life nor the personal political views of Bartók provide a clue. Bartók himself considered the peasants a natural force, and this is why he could, in both his criticism and by his positive influence, artistically transcend the artificial alienated human type created by contemporary capitalist development.

When Lenin said to Gorky of Tolstoy, "before this count there was no real peasant in our literature," he did not think, or at least he did not think exclusively, of the great political and social significance of peasant revolution which played a major role in his own activities; rather he thought (or at least, also thought) how the peasant created by Tolstoy became the criterion of the genuine popular substance of revolution. If this role of the peasant was not as immediately apparent in the works of Tolstoy with the same historical universality as later in the works of Bartók, the difference must not be ascribed to their different positions in the evolution of society nor even to the differences in their respective personalities but rather to the fact that the undetermined objectivity of music is capable of deeper and wider generalization, even in a universal historical sense, than the most exquisite literature.

The concrete methods which led to the domination of this plebeian type in the works of Bartók was also the result of inner development. The basis of the playful fairy-tale style of *The Wooden Prince* is undoubtedly the final victory of the people's forces over the distortions of alienation. Here the natural force which informs Bartók's oeuvre expresses itself in almost the literal sense of the term, because he appears to be saying that if we honestly take hold of ourselves, if we genuinely experience our own human self, then these threatening air-castles of alienation will fade into the nothingness they deserve. A few years later, in the music of the *Miraculous Mandarin*, the struggles of the contradictions of alienation are painted in quite another manner. In our average "civilized" world alienation has become a second nature to us, and must be borne as such. "Natural forces" like the Mandarin can only break in from "outside": against these "natural forces" the general alienation which is common to all men who have become estranged from their human selves is powerless. Bence Szabolcsi, in his excellent essay, has centred his analysis on Bartók's rage against alienation. But we must not forget that this rage is much more than a personal emotion: it is a passionate criticism of a whole world.

The Mandarin himself—in the sense of determined and determinable objectivity—is as far from being a peasant as the idyllic and unambigously victorious figures of *The Wooden Prince*. But I think that we are entitled to suppose that even on the level of the undetermined objectivity of music—in a contrasting manner, and with a constrasting outcome—both figures are the personifications of Bartók's peasant revolution against the "conquests" of capitalist civilization, which merely satisfy the wishes of the particular Ego through the market, but divest him of his original character, his human self.

This trend reached its peak in the *Cantata Profana*. Here the peasant of Bartók enters the scene—in the climate of musical undetermined objectivity of course—and, probably not accidentally, his original superiority and his later rage and passionate protest are replaced by a revolt against alienation, an open revolt full of horror and tension, when the youths who have turned into stags do not even wish to return to his pseudo-human and distorting environment. Bartók is here perhaps the only great and resolute representative of the social criticism which openly declares that what usually is called civilization and recognized, even if criticized, as a human mode of life, is in reality the negation of man's humanity. The peasant youths transformed into deer are not only right in not wishing to return but even—by maintaining a profound universal truth—they, as great revolutionaries, declare the human justification of this world invalid.

Some two hundred years after Swift's wise horses Bartók's deer were the first to raise their voice as radical revolutionaries against the dehumanizing effects of capitalist culture. And it was an odd accident of development (if it was only an accident) that the *Cantata Profana* was presented to the public at about the same time as Kafka's great novels which, similarly, also followed the hoofmarks of Swift's horses. It is impossible here to go into further detail on Kafka's significance and the connection of his negations with those of Bartók, but there is one aspect of them worth noting here: Kafka, like Swift, believed that the human situations they described and condemned were the unchangeable conditions of existence. And here two more points must be mentioned: it is one thing to prophesy some kind of development, as was done by Swift, and quite another to represent realistically an existing state of things, as was done by Kafka. A world-wide view of the general development of mankind is one thing, and the currents of our daily life which confront us and provoke our direct action are another. They are different because their relation to the everyday conduct of people is different. And secondly, it would be an error to believe that Kafka's world vision was consistently fatalist. He saw what the characters he created did not see: that from an objective point of view individual issues may exist, though those in the middle of them do not perceive them. But only individual issues. Bartók, on the contrary, condemned the whole world and system of this social reality, *a priori* to destruction.

But quite apart from the great difference between Bartók's and Kafka's vision of the world it needs only a slight comparison to show a decisive element in Bartók's work, if we consider it as it came into being in terms of the continuity of Hungarian development, that is in its division into basically different phases. The movement of the poor and dispossessed at the beginning of the last century represented by those prototypes of peasant heroes (*Ludas Matyi*—Mat the Goose-boy, *János Vitéz*—Gallant John and *Toldi*) was the ideological preparation for the Hungarian 1793 which never occurred. The literary movement of the time had consequently to try to renew popular forms in an appropriate style, bring them to life on the national level at least. When Ady and Bartók began their career, the position from a social point of view was quite different. And no devices of art or form could reestablish, in terms of valid art, the connection which had its roots in reality. So Ady, Bartók and Attila József had no choice, but to be modern artists in both the form and the content of their works.

Ady's development and influence is a clear demonstration of this. Everyone knows how Bartók, whose beginnings were influenced by Richard Strauss, broke with the continuation of the Wagner–Brahms tradition dominating Hungary at the time and became the great representative of the new music, in its formal aspect as well. But today, at a distance of several decades, we have a better view of the real image of the new epoch. Hanns Eisler, the disciple of Schönberg, a man who always remembered his master with gratitude, once characterized Schönberg's basic attitude towards life, which included of course the essential content of his art, in saying: "A long time before the discovery of bombers he expressed the feelings of people crowded in the shelters." If we translate this into a social language we find that Schönberg fundamentally condemned the new world that grew up with himself, but he believed it was the fate of mankind to be unable to change this situation; it was impossible to attempt any change. There was only one possibility: hide in the shelter and try to survive individually.

What else is this if not the new, modernized form of "power-protected intimacy"? It is new because society has a great deal changed. And it is new especially and above all because the ideology which grew out of the new situation expressed the belief that the ultimate forms of existence were the pseudo-lives attainable in manipulated capitalism: it thought that the final incarnation of man was that unlimited rule of particularism developed and supported by this manipulation. It therefore proclaimed the need to extinguish all ideologies together with the need to oppose every old art guided by and struggling with ideologies.

The right thing for every really up-to-date person was to despise ideals, especially those of the nineteenth century. Thomas Mann who by temperament never belonged to those who represented open revolutionary protest left this prejudice of his time far behind him in his last great novel. His hero was a musician who composed works very like those of Schönberg, and who accepted the ultimate consequences of this outlook (which, according to the author, was inspired in the last resort by the devil's hostility to man): he withdrew his Ninth Symphony. Here an honest-thinking great writer drew the consequences that followed from the dominating artistic trends of his epoch. Bartók's specific position in the evolution of his time could perhaps be most exactly determined by saying that he never withdrew a Ninth Symphony but sought a genuinely modern and musical form of expression which through contemporary music could fully and worthily be measured against the best of the music of the past. So here is no so-called historical continuity. On the contrary. He recognized that

Beethoven had exhausted all the possibilities of renewal for humanity following the great but unsuccessful revolution of his time, whose content remained a living actuality in the consciousness of the human race until its realization. This is the true continuity of human history, as against the attempts to describe today's manipulated and particular alienation as an achievement.

The way from folk music to Beethoven and Rembrandt: this is what distinguishes Bartók from his famous contemporaries, stuck fast in today's human degradation. It is not surprising, therefore, that many of the theoreticians of this specifically new music have criticized Bartók because of his compromise with the music of the past. It was also no accident that Adorno, whose musical theory postulated Schönberg's standpoint as the only one leading to salvation, saw something suspicious in Bartók's folklorist approach. The liberalist opponents of fascism who uncritically accepted the universal validity of this shelter-particularism, the "power-protected intimacy" of new capitalism, with any and every innovation of form, quite naturally shrank from the truly great innovator whose truly revolutionary attitude blew up the human foundation underlying the merely formal innovations.

This period of development which lasted over several decades, is now over. The open and patent crises of the ruling regimes have now to create new movements in all fields of political thinking. So it may well be argued that Bartók, as the great representative of the pre-1945 era, can now be viewed in historical perspective. But I think that this perspective reveals him as one of the truly great. He, like Rembrandt and Beethoven, joins the ranks of those whose works have expressed a major turning-point in the development of mankind in a perdurable form of art.

The Hungarian people, who have not yet resolved the great dilemma of "power-protected intimacy" and true human protest in their cultural life, have to reach a full understanding and carry further the works of Csokonai, Petőfi, Ady and Attila József, and base themselves, above all, on Bartók in order to find the truly progressive way to their national development. But Hungarian culture will only be able to appreciate Bartók at his true value when the answer is found to the question which history has repeatedly asked: What does it mean to be a Hungarian? This question must not be answered in the old way, tricking out the most odious historical compromises by representing them as qualities of the Hungarian people; Hungarian culture must have the courage and social and moral basis to say: Bartók has opened for us the historical way to true Hungarian culture.

AIMS OF EDUCATION
IN A SOCIALIST SOCIETY*

by

GYULA ORTUTAY

1) Socialist aims in education are essential principles in the building of a socialist society. The aims of our education policy follow from the objectives of a socialist society and the plans designed to bring it about. Therefore, in speaking about the values and aims of a socialist education policy, we are in fact speaking about the socialist society in process of construction, and about the phases in which this process is carried out. I propose to survey the main features and some important problems related to the development of the aims of a socialist education without attempting to cover the whole field, and to do so relying on Hungarian experience in the domain of public education.

2) If we wish to give a general definition of the main features of the aims of a socialist education the following should be kept in mind:

a) according to Marx, socialist education policy is "centred on man";

b) Our socialist aims in education are determined by the demands of social development in accordance with the various stages in the construction of socialism without however abandoning any of the principles of Marxist "man centredness";

c) Our third general determinant is concerned with the distant future, and sounds somewhat Utopian: in a society which has completed the building of socialism or rather communism, the true inner unity and harmony of the structure of society has to be expressed by a socialist education which on a high level and in a manner appropriate to the times integrates a scientific approach to the social and the natural sciences, to history and to technology.

Two comments though have to be made regarding the latter requirements which today may still appear to express a "maximalist" attitude. Laying

---

* Lecture delivered at the plenary session of the Hungarian Academy of Sciences, November 14th, 1967.

2*

the foundations of an education common to all and developing a common education across class barriers is already a requirement at the initial stages of realizing the aims of a socialist education though, of course, on a lower level. This was expressed in our plans before the liberation of the country and, after 1945 in the need to establish a general school* and the debates which followed regarding its character. On the other hand, an antinomy has to be pointed out which became clear to many of us (long before the debate on "the two cultures"), namely, that although in a modern industrial society—and this refers to capitalist society as well—a common cultural basis is needed, specialization divides quite early, and the requirements of the separate branches are soon apparent. The need for specialisation together with that for a common attitude creates increasingly contradictory situations. These contradictory situations accompany the development of socialist aims in education right from the start and it is easy to understand that the difficulties of the problem grow step by step as progress is made.

It is clear that these three determinants follow each other step by step, at the same time a socialist society which is resolved on developing its educational aims has to take into account all three determinants from the start and follow with attention the effects of the three fundamental determinants. There is no doubt, that socialist society as a whole will be "man centred." The distant objectives to be realized at a later stage have to be kept in view right from the beginning as soon as the building of a socialist society is started.

3) In the first place, I wish to deal with the teleological principles of socialist education policy which are a consequence of the Marxist concept of "man centredness." In his early writings already, for example, in his criticism of Hegel's Philosophy of Law in 1848, Marx emphasised this principle in the following way: "...for man, man is the supreme being." This principle informed all his work throughout his life, it is so to speak the draft of his humanism. There is no need to prove that *Marx's man centredness applies to men living an active life within and for society*—a working class and creative life in contrast with bourgeois aims in education which—from Herbart to our days—placed the isolated individual into the centre, socialist educational aims, considered the individual as a dialectical function of his/her social (class) relations and commitments. This dialectical relationship has to decide our educational methods, the tendencies and objectives of our educational policy in the most varied fields. It would be

---

* Attendance at general schools is compulsory from the ages of 6 to 14. The eight year course of studies of the general school must be completed before any form of secondary education either technical or academic can be started.

interesting to analyse the interrelationships which these social-moral principles produce in kindergarten education, the smallest communities, right up to what the notion of commitment means as far as writers and scientists are concerned. All this is the categorical imperative of the same continuing aim in education. Here it should be noted that our discussion is concerned with the aims and the desirable tendencies, the teleology of socialist education. However, reality, educational practice and the realization of educational policy show many contradictions, slips and errors. Although the two decades and more which have elapsed since the liberation of the country substantiate the aforesaid, we do not now wish to engage in a critical analysis of the past since we propose to set forth principles and tendencies for the future. In certain cases however, we shall have to point to certain concrete measures and organizational forms of our educational policy.

Thus, Marxist socialist aims of education should be considered from two aspects:

a) from the aspect of the individual. Our education aims to bring about the development of the human personality in a way that allows all potential qualities to flourish. It follows from the organizational form of our school system that in spite of the different rhythm at which individual qualities and faculties develop and tastes and interests become apparent, it is possible to develop *all* individual qualities and find a place for all personal aspirations as long as they are in harmony with the interests of society. (The requirements for an *open* school system and questions related to it will be discussed later.) It is in the interests of precisely a socialist society that true human (intellectual, moral, etc.) qualities should not get lost but help to raise standards instead. Earlier historic-social systems wasted human assets and it is visible even today to our own eyes how wasteful the capitalist and imperialist world is where human qualities are concerned. The loss of talents and qualities through neglect and non-recognition is a dominant theme of Hungarian literature, and this accords with observations I made almost daily when I collected ethnographic material. Socialist education tries to bring all assets to the surface and use them to the highest degree in the interests of society. Therefore it must endeavour to bring out all potentialities in order to ensure that harmonious development of the human personality which leads to effective social activity. In addition to other principles connected with the class struggle, Hungarian school policy was and is bound to help overcome the difficulties of the children of peasants and workmen. During the long transition period more had to be done for them than normal educational practice required so that their personal qualities may develop. Lately, we seem to have forgotten this more than once, though the transition period still continues, as was proved by the conditions prevailing in schools for children living in isolated homesteads. The essence of socialist education is to fuse inseparably the balanced personality and the talents of the individual with social activity and social commitments.

b) Our second objective is to bring up human beings who adapt themselves harmoniously to society, live for it and find within it the satisfaction of their personal interest. This is another aspect of the same educational principle. The salient feature of this dialectic unity is that the two viewpoints are stressed simultaneously, and one objective cannot prevail against the other, otherwise our educational work would be of no use. In modern philosophical and educational literature—or to put it more precisely in modern sociological literature—fear of the masses stands again in the centre of interest. Ortega y Gasset's fear of mob rule, and of a general decadence in culture and society re-emerges again, meaning, in this terminology, the debasement and degradation of human qualities. On the other hand, the debate on alienation—a concept analysed by Marx in a classical way—is going on with renewed zeal. Modern industrial societies seem to dread both the influx of masses which threaten to level down standards to the extent that they are afraid of crowds as such, and the solitary human being who becames alienated though he, too, is one of the crowd. It is just this fear which socialist education combats when it sets against anxiety the individual who is fully alive to his responsibilities and who works for a socialist society. Socialist society is opposed to both the amorphous mob and the isolated alienated individual. Neither is a socialist social category.

One might say that these are only ideals, since our socialist society, which we are now in the process of building, does not yet know this harmony of conscious individuals and the community. Every day one can see the symptoms of *Vermassung*—of disintegration into an amorphous mass in more than one field and in the view of many the problem of alienation also appears in socialist society, though the latter problem is based, in our view, on false preconceptions. This much is certain: the unity of the individual and the community, as well as that of a balanced personality and a harmonious socialist society have still to be put into practice. However, prior to this a socialist economy must be built and a society relying on it must come into being.

It ought to be said that it is our duty to work out rules of conduct valid in a socialist society, in other words socialist norms and to do so on the basis of our experience in the building of socialism and of a socialist system of values. In this respect we failed to do our duty. Starting with the laws of Hammurabi, continuing with the Ten Commandments, hitherto every social and economic system created its scales of value and settled the relations between society and its members. Every previous system of moral precepts and rules of conduct (to mention the two extreme points) originated from and was justified by metaphysics. The ethics of the socialist society, i.e. the standards and rules of conduct as well, must rely on the revolutionary experience and practice of the daily life of the working class. Socialist ethics must be rooted in sociology and its imperatives must result from the structure of the socialist society. It is not mere chance that the working out of moral problems has been neglected since sociological investigations as such were also neglected for a long time. Exhorting people to work more efficiently and regulations for safeguarding common property can hardly be looked on as socialist ethics. The harmonious cooperation of a creative, working class personality and socialist society cannot function without socialist ethics and a socialist system of norms. It is our firm belief that relying on actual social experiences and on certain ideological preconditions, the working out of socialist ethics is urgent, and possible and should not be delayed.

We know that this is not done in a day, nor as the result of the work of this or that philosopher or sociologist. But both society and educational policy have every right to expect at least a beginning from our institutions and our philosophers.

c) Having examined the relationship between the individual and the community, and the individual and society we shall return to a problem of historical character. In order to realize our aim i.e. the evolution of a balanced personality, living according to socialist ethics, ready to develop his talents, and to use his work capacity for the benefit of socialist society, we had to demolish a school system which was built on the perpetuation of educational monopolies. After 1945, we started to build up the new system at once. I would like to draw your attention to two principles established at that time, for they are even now essential aspects of our system of education. One of the requirements was that a general school of eight years be established with the aim of providing a common "language" in which education could be carried on. This was, of course, that type of school which demolished the walls which enclosed educational monopolies. The second requirement, a school system open in every direction had to be developed more slowly. Our school system was built up in such a way, perhaps with an excess of orders issued to secure reforms, that students could proceed from lower types of schools to higher ones in accordance with their abilities. Without going into particulars, it can be said that the efficiency of the educational system of a developing socialist society established on these principles proved itself by the quantitative and qualitative results achieved in twenty odd years.

Although the general school produced very good results, it cannot be denied that there are some disquieting features. For example, the principle that the upper forms of the eight-year general school should be taught by different subject teachers, was not established everywhere in the country. At several places the dropout of students after the sixth and even after the fourth form is not insignificant. Our educational administration is taking effective measures against this happening, such as abolishing the small schools catering to children living on isolated homesteads in favour of district schools.

This new arrangement has already produced results, in spite of difficulties (the great distance between school and home, etc.). Let me here mention a thought which may seem heretical to some. I have some right to do so I think, since I acted as midwife when the general school was born. * These days the question of breaking educational monopolies is no longer a problem. On the other hand the question whether we rightly distribute our resources amongst the various types of schools is.

Further problems connected with development are on the one hand raising the school leaving age, on the other the future structure of the secondary school system. In time, and within the range of possibilities we shall have to consider reorganizing the general schools on a broader basis which might include certain elements of the present secondary curriculum. The idea is that in the future the general school should consist of two sections: a lower one of four years and an upper one of six years. This arrangement would raise the number of years during which it is compulsory to attend a general school by two. Based on this second stage students could then at the age of sixteen start a two year course preparing them for entry to colleges, universities and higher technical schools, after a choice based on their wishes and their abilities as shown by the results they obtained. In this way guiding young people of 16 to a certain profession and stimulating them to continue their studies would rest on sounder foundations, and from an educational and a psychological point of view it would be sounder to decide on important questions e.g. the choice of an occupation and the question of continuing with one's studies, after the difficult years of puberty are over. It is even conceivable that in the next

* The author was Minister of Education from 1947 to 1950.

stage of the development of socialism this kind of general education might be compulsory, aided by a network of district education and supporting boarding schools which may come into existence by then. We must not touch the general school until this new organization can be fully realized. This will mean a rise in standards from the point of view of school organization, educational practice and methodology, and therefore political progress too. Compulsory education up to the age of 18 and the structure and content of it are not yet topical questions.

4) Another group of questions within the domain of how to shape the socialist aims in education can be defined in the following way: the aims, means and objectives of socialist education policy are always determined by the social demands (and possibilities) of the given period and phase in the building of socialism. I think that most of the errors committed in the practical execution of our education policy are due to the fact that the above rule was disregarded.

a) The comments I wish to make in this connection are primarily related to the XXIst Congress of the Communist Party of the USSR and the VIIIth and IXth Congress of the Hungarian Socialist Workers' Party. These congresses emphasized that science also became a productive force in socialist society and that this increases its importance. In our view a socialist view of education rightly demands that this statement should be completed by the following: *science, but also every stage of education which is a necessary preparation for scientific work* (i.e. from general schooling right to voluntarily undertaken adult education) *are forces of production.* It is clear that the entire system of school education up to voluntarily undertaken adult education is not only a productive force, but it might also be said that it is the essence of social development in the highest sense of the term, it enriches man and makes it possible for him to reach his objectives. Thus from the point of view of education the development of society and the education of the individual have to be considered together. Therefore it is obvious that every stage of socialist education is a productive force too. In every mode of production and every productive relationship the role of man, his work and creative faculty are of central importance, hence, not only science—which *is one* of the higher stages of education—education, too, is of central importance.

I am emphasizing this not only from the point of view of the state owned economy, though from that too. This is worth pointing out especially today in the initial stages of the new economic reforms—though it should have been emphasized long ago. Education always seems to be on the defensive. It is one of the so-called "non-productive" sections of the economy.

This view is mistaken. It represents a narrow "treasury" point of view, and not true state, social and economic interests. Education, training to perform work for which one is suitable in order to be able to take part in the social rhythm—all this is of primary importance to the state, and serves the central actor of production, man. This cannot be shown in the production figures of this or that section of the economy, but it is there behind all production, and its value is incalculable.

This seems a good place to point to one of the most sensitive and not sufficiently acknowledged spheres in our educational system, namely, to the importance of teacher training colleges and of chairs at universities dealing with the training of teachers. In our view, the quality of the entire educational system is determined there. The educational system which takes young people to their 18th year decides in the main the level of learning, the human qualities and the character of those who then enrol at universities and colleges. The better educated matriculants are, the better can universities or colleges achieve their objectives. They must endeavour to specialize as early as possible and it is a severe handicap indeed if they have to spend much time on rudiments and elementary moral and political questions. The responsibility for all this rests on teachers, that is on teacher training. There is no doubt, that in a modern socialist society, high-grade technical education and a knowledge of the natural sciences is most desirable—but this, too, cannot be achieved without the good work of those sections of universities and colleges which are engaged in training teachers. This is the first and a necessary link in the chain. Our doctors, engineers, technologists and all those engaged in research will bear the marks of the education they have obtained from their secondary school teachers. Their basic learning will be acquired from them before the age of eighteen. The danger at present is not only that teachers of mathematics and the sciences leave their job (though there are signs that this too is taking place) but that institutions training subject teachers are unable to meet the qualitative requirements of a socialist society.

The aforesaid have to be taken into account at every stage of building socialism if we want to maintain the efficiency of our educational work.

b) It has been mentioned earlier that after educational monopolies had been broken down it became a guiding principle to build up a non-exclusive school system open to all who want to get a higher education. Amidst the political struggles of the first year after the liberation it was sufficient to declare this only as the principle of a school system which was to be one of the means for realizing an integrated socialist society. Of course, today, in the final stages of building socialism this is no longer enough. The fact that even the highest grades of education are open to each talented young man or young woman and that it is out of the question that a socialist society should block the way to any available education for the children of the working or any other class is guaranteed by our policy. At the same time, it should be noted, that it would be most desirable to improve the education of children in villages and isolated homesteads. There the dropout even while attending general schools is the highest while the proportion of those who enrol at universities and colleges is the lowest. It is possible however to establish a fair balance and it is moreover our duty to do so, for even in the initial stage of building socialism, when we fought for a People's Democracy under far more difficult circumstances, we were able to do something even though sometimes they were only improvised solutions.

Now that we are over the hump the network of general schools seems to be increasingly suitable for the realization of our objectives. In addition to emphasizing that our school system is open to all for the betterment of their education, we must endeavour to think out systematically what our qualitative requirements are, and to introduce them. We have no intention of developing some sort of elite, the sham-democracy of the "school of the highly gifted," or to give prominence to a few hundred pupils. This was never a revolutionary socialist educational idea. Looked at from the point of view of socialist society as a whole we think it important that suitability and aptitude should be preconditions in all types of schools. The system of university admissions has proved sufficiently how very difficult it is to elaborate qualitative indices, aptitudinal and vocational selection procedures and admittance tests. Although it is a good thing that we are able to chose the best due to the fact that there are far more applicants than can be admitted, the entrance exams draw attention to the many deficiencies of our educational system. It became apparent that tuition in general, or that of some subjects, is on a high standard in certain secondary schools, while in other ones inferior teaching is compensated for by liberal marking. (Not to mention other unforeseeable difficulties at the entrance exams e.g. it may easily happen that a young person with a special talent might be eliminated from further studies, while a very good student of average ability and commonplace knowledge may continue his studies—a fact which is undoubtedly socially damaging.) It is our firm belief that the criteria for qualifying to a higher type of school must be re-examined. In this connection let us neither hesitate to think things through, nor let us delay the introduction of long overdue psychological tests.

Much has been said and written about the connection between school and life, and between school and work, and our school reform paid attention to the political views expressed in this connection. In my view, educating young people to work cannot be reduced to a few hours technical work—which usually means that some very simple work is done over and over again—particularly in view of the fact that this kind of work is of no importance in our plants and it will be of little use in modern automated industry. Industrial or agricultural technical work that forms an organic part of tuition and truly serves educational purposes as well as the demonstration of creative work throughout history and its significance in reshaping societies, means a genuine addition to the knowledge of the students and an influence on their political and ideological bearing.

The aforesaid had to be mentioned because the stages of our school system, the relation of these stages to each other and the qualitative selective criteria of getting on to the next stage—as they were briefly expounded above—must be established in conformity with the needs and demands of the construction of a socialist society. Much remains to be done yet! A socialist society has to sit up and act if conspicuous interest is shown in some lucrative but peripheral professions and certain fashionable subjects taught at universities, and at the same time, the standing of vocational training declines, and interest in a number of socially necessary middle level industrial, agricultural and white-collar trades decreases or ceases altogether. It is indeed a serious contradiction if, on the one hand, technical education is stressed so that work will be respected and, on the other, the respect for work and the worker decreases, as shown by fashions in the choice of training. I want to make it perfectly clear that the highest asset of the socialist society is the working man, the creative individual. For this reason, among others, the working class takes the lead in the building of socialism. Now if what we want is that respect for work should mean improved training for skilled workers, and this is now a requirement in agriculture too, then we ought to realize that these schools of vocational training do not get their standing and value from the fact that they issue a certificate of equivalent status to that issued by academic secondary schools, but from the fact that in addition to basic education they provide vocational training instead of teaching a lot of dry facts by rote. It is more important to teach young people to think, to form sound opinions and to act properly rather than to teach them to hoard an overabundance of dry as dust so-called facts. Here as everywhere else, a systematic demand for quality must form the basis.

In our view it seems necessary to establish a system which, on the basis of the student's talents, interests and character, is able to give the parents and society some indication regarding the choice of a profession, already in the upper forms of the general school. A system that relies on adequate aptitude tests and qualitative standards will help students and parents, school and society in guiding young people to choose a career while at secondary school. It is obvious that we need experts, teachers and psychologists, in order to elaborate the flexible yet effective principles of this kind of system, for in this case rigidity and petty severity are almost as harmful as immoral favouritism. For example, in the Soviet Union great care is devoted to the care of specially talented pupils already in the general schools whereas we have only been concerned with this in the case of admittance to universities, and even then only in the past one or two years. Thus, we have to consider simultaneously both the proper guiding of outstanding pupils and the putting into effect of a socially fair attitude to aptitude.

I would like to add by way of concluding this subject that in Hungary's economic pattern the proportion of foreign trade amounts to 35 per cent; this means that in international competition the country can only hold its own if its industrial and agricultural products are up to standard in every way. Similarly, our literary, art and scientific achievements will only arouse international interest if their standards are high enough. The means, content, methodology and organization of our public education must therefore adapt themselves to international standards. This means that we have to support the standing of educational institutions which train for industrial and agricultural work, we have to think about the right proportions, and establish aptitude tests and qualitative norms for obtaining admission to higher grade schools and what's more we have to work out the socially useful, fair and adequate educational forms of this system. Of course, this is easier said than done.

c) It has been mentioned earlier that the socialist ideal of education always adapts itself to and serves the requirements and tasks of building the socialist society. In this context I would like to touch upon another problem. Social needs, the development of the economy, and the structure of socialism determine not only the qualitative indexes of admission to higher education but also the relationship to each other of various types of schools. I referred to this relationship earlier, and let me say right now that in my opinion we did not think this question through thoroughly enough at the time of the last school reforms. The authorities concerned will have to reconsider carefully the organizational forms of secondary schooling. As far as the relationship of types of school to each other is concerned the situation of general schools is clear. It was already mentioned that it might become necessary to alter the time spent at general schools when secondary schooling becomes obligatory. This however remains to be seen. The actual question is whether the proportion of academic secondary schools, specialized ones and industrial and agricultural vocational schools to each other has been determined correctly. It is a basic principle that in a socialist society there are no "exclusive" school types, for all are equal in rank though each of them fulfils a different function in public education. There is no point in creating differences in value because students are admitted to universities and colleges not only from academic secondary schools. What is serious—and this refers to every healthy society—is if those who have secondary or higher qualifications cannot find employment according to their qualifications and therefore do not produce what is the most efficient work from a said point of view. Consequently, we have to develop more useful proportions between the different secondary educational forms in accordance with social needs, and it is necessary to analyse again and again the indexes which determine the number of university and college students. The proportions must be in conformity with the requirements of the national economy. It has been pointed out more than once that the proportions determined earlier were neither correct nor in conformity with the requirements of life, not even in the short run. The exaggerated differentiation of secondary vocational schools does damage and does not serve the actual requirements. Overdone specialization in vocational schools according to industrial and agricultural trades can lead to the unjustifiedly large number of qualified specialists in a narrow field and the retraining of a number of students for a new profession is often more difficult. In our view, exaggerated specialization at a too early stage of secondary education renders both planning and thorough professional training more difficult. At a university specialization does not start in the first year either. We believe that it is worth while to re-examine the problem of secondary education. Though we are opposed to school reforms every four or five years and think that the organizational forms of public education should assume a final shape we nevertheless had to draw attention to this question. The fact that academic secondary schools receive too much attention and questions connected with the Final Secondary School Leaving Examination have been discussed critically before, in the near future a reorganization of various branches of vocational schooling, and their unification in more comprehensive units will have to come about, that is the training of skilled industrial and agricultural workers will have to be improved in accordance with the requirements and needs of a socialist society.

5) Finally let us refer to that particular stage of development of socialist principles in education which is appropriate to the time when the construction of socialism will have been completed and following that the communist society will have come into being. In the introductory part of my lecture I mentioned that it certainly seems utopian to discuss the classless society and its economic, social and cultural harmony, amidst our present troubles. We should not however avoid this question.

a) It is obvious that in a socialist society the open character of the present school system will be continued, moreover, that the open system will adapt itself in an even more flexible way to the increasing demands made by economic and social development. In addition, both personal and collective adult education will also continue to develop. Although educational policy has to be planned well in advance the organizational forms the changing educational system will assume in the next 20 to 30 years cannot be known at present. Audio-visual education and teaching by means of television and scientific films, are at present only in their infancy. We should, however, keep an eye on them and study how these new methods could be turned to good account. It is impossible to prophesy in what way curriculum and teaching methods will determine the shape of education on a school, a family, or an individual level. This much is certain that due to more efficient means and teaching aids, individual pupils will learn faster. It is important to follow these experiments with attention. However, there can be no doubt that neither the intensive and continuous influence of home education nor the role of the guiding teacher is dispensible, however perfect audio-visual equipment may become.

b) The individual who develops his abilities in harmony with his social commitments—as described at the outset of my lecture—is able to do so in a fully developed socialist society without serious obstacles, and the more the contradictions and conflicts between the individual and the community will become eliminated at this stage of social and historical development, the closer we will be to the best possible society. It is obvious, that this subject can only be dealt with in the conditional, for we are living in a transitional period amidst the worries and anxieties due to the serious conflict between two hostile social orders, therefore thinking about the educational aims of a fully developed socialist society produces merely idyllic phantasies. (Not to mention Marx's ironic comments on Utopianism. His plans for the future were always built on a criticism of things as they were in the present.) We do not think that when socialist and later communist society becomes a reality idyllic harmony will prevail from the start. That what we are trying to bring about is the harmony of the individual, society and nations in the period of international and classless society, is something that ought to be said already today although our present anxieties make it clear how remote all this is. A further requirement of socialist education is, that through it other contradictions should be resolved in a harmonious way. For example, the difference between those whose culture is predominantly literary on the one hand, and those with a technical or scientific bend on the other, must be integrated in a common comprehensive world outlook. This problem exists in the western world, too. The foundations for a common conception are given in the philosophy of Marx and Lenin, since Marxism–Leninism contains within it the laws according to which nature, society and history develop. It therefore provides the basis for an integrated world view. The basis and final principles of our aims in education also rely on them.

ISTVÁN GÁBOR

THE FUTURE OF SECONDARY SCHOOLS

Unanswered Questions in Public Education

It has become a commonplace in our time that, throughout the world, secondary schools are that particular type which give plenty to think about and much trouble. This statement still holds good although worries have somewhat lessened recently and certain reforms have acted as a safety valve protecting secondary schools and many excitable young people against the danger of blowing up. According to UNESCO's *Statistical Yearbook* the number of young people educated in secondary schools grew by 139 per cent between 1950 and 1965, which indicates the size of the increase *(The Times Education Supplement*, 1969, No. 2,802, p. 309). *Education* (No. 10, 1969) reports that an increase amounting to 6.1 per cent in the number of secondary school students was expected to take place in Britain between 1968–9 and 1970–1. In Hungary the number of secondary pupils grew from 96,000 to 236,000 between 1950 and 1965. The increase amounts to 435.9 per cent as compared to 1937–8: 52,000 in 1937–8 and 228,000 in 1968–9.

The serious problems secondary education has to grapple with everywhere are connected in the last resort with the considerable increase in the number of students. Hungarian secondary schools are, obviously, not exempt from the same worries although the Education Act Parliament passed in 1961 has eliminated a number of hindrances to further development. However, quite a few handicaps

and obstacles have remained, and in line with the transformation taking place in industry and agriculture, as well as the changes in the average cultural level of the country, newer and newer problems are banking up in respect to Hungarian secondary schooling.

Before 1945 schoolboys and schoolgirls came to the cross-roads when they reached the age of ten. After the fourth form of the elementary school, three-fourths of the ten-year-old children enrolled in the fifth form of the elementary school, the remaining 25 per cent could choose between the *polgári iskola* (then an inferior form of secondary schooling) consisting of four classes which took them to the age of fourteen or the *Gimnázium* (some with a classics, others with a science bias) consisting of eight forms. Thus even that 25 per cent did not necessarily get to *Gimnázium*. The *polgári iskola* provided a not too high level of general education, with a practical bias mainly for town children. It was possible to get to a *Gimnázium* from this type of school—by passing a supplementary examination but it was extremely difficult. Clerks and manual workers could not afford the luxury of having their children educated until the latter reached their 18th year. Besides, after the final secondary school examination those who passed had to face new problems. Only few could enrol in a university course—mainly for financial and also for other reasons—and the classical grammar school did not help very much in securing suitable employment. Up to the end of the fifties, the *Gimnázium* stubbornly stuck to an outdated cultural ideal, and took no cognizance of the world we are living in and the growth of natural sciences and technology.

No wonder that under such conditions the 174 state and church *Gimnázia* provided education almost exclusively for the children of the aristocracy, landowners and the urban middle class.

General Schools and Gimnázium

Shortly after the end of the Second World War, in August 1945, a governmental decree called into existence a new type of general school and many people rightly said that this was the "land reform of public education." This decree established a school of eight forms compulsory for all, with a uniform curriculum; accordingly, the age when further decisions had to be taken was 14 and no longer 10. When general schools were established and church schools were nationalized (in 1948), *Gimnázia* were reduced to the top four forms. A 1947 plan provided for three sections: a Latin (classical) section, a modern languages section, and a natural sciences section. This plan was modified and—true to tradition—two sections: a science one and a humanistic one, continued to exist although the number of hours of Latin in the timetable was reduced and that of natural history subjects was increased after 1945.

After 1945, a not entirely new type of school, the technical secondary school, was given greater importance, due to the growing development of industry. The aim of this type of school was to educate technicians for industry and agriculture at a secondary level, which it did well at the beginning; it reached its zenith at the beginning and middle of the fifties when accelerated industrialization made newer and newer demands.

However, close observation of international developments in technology showed at the end of the fifties that the technical secondary school was less and less able to fulfil its assigned role. The 18–19-year-old young people with little practical experience and even less executive experience were not capable of holding their own in factories in junior managerial posts on the basis of the secondary education they had obtained. Later, the greater part of them only found employment after becoming skilled at a trade, a fact which diminished the popularity and appeal of technical secondary schools and produced tensions. The exaggerated specialization that later developed in technical secondary schools made it difficult for young people to switch from one trade or section of industry to another without trouble and loss of time. When all this became evident vocational secondary schools of four forms were set up providing students—who had first completed the general school—with a skilled tradesman qualification plus the secondary school-leaving certificate. Act III of 1961 which deals with the school system established two fundamental types of secondary schools in Hungary: *Gimnázium* and the vocational secondary schools. Some technical secondary schools have survived to the present. They are being gradually transformed into vocational secondary schools, and higher grade technical schools are being established for students who, to be admitted, must have finished a secondary school course and passed the final secondary school-leaving examination *(Érettségi)*.

Thus a vocational secondary school also leads to the *érettségi*, that is, students have to face a board of examiners and answer questions, both orally and in writing, covering four years' work. In Hungary the *érettségi* traditionally enjoys considerable prestige. In recent years the question whether the final examination should be abolished or continued has on several occasions been the subject of discussion, it was finally decided to continue it after all. And, in fact, there is a case for it: the summing up and revision of work done in four years demands an intense mental effort from young people which prepares them for other tests in life, particularly at universities and colleges. In addition, the final examination provides useful information for teachers of special subjects and the school on the one hand, and for those who direct public education on the other; it shows both the successes and the gaps in teaching which appear more clearly in a severe, one might say, overstrict examination.

The final examination is an important summing up of secondary education but it is not a precondition for finding employment although it is doubtless an advantage; it is a necessary qualification for study at a tertiary level and it should be noted that it underwent important reforms in recent years. In the first place, the number of compulsory subjects was reduced and its main point is no longer checking on book learning but investigating how a student, after having finished his secondary education, applies the knowledge acquired in school and combines knowledge with everyday life, whether he can think logically, and what he knows of his country's and the world's affairs.

At present subjects on which students are examined are the entire four years' syllabus in Hungarian language and literature, history and mathematics; a written examination has to be taken in Hungarian literature and mathematics plus a subject that had been taught for at least two years in the secondary school. The examination in the latter is compulsory too, but the subject of instruction can be freely chosen. In classes with a specialized curriculum—which will be discussed more fully later—the final examination also includes that special subject.

The Education Act of 1961 together with a decree of 1965 outlined the aims, tasks and prospects of Hungarian secondary schools. This, however, does not mean that all those problems no longer exist which beset secondary education in many countries throughout the world. Here I only want to mention a few problems without aiming at completeness but allowing for the fact that social and economic development continually produces new tasks in the field of public education, and alternative solutions as well.

The basic question is to determine the objectives of secondary schools. Clearly, the primary function of the *Gimnázium* is to provide an appropriate grounding for higher level studies; it is however questionable whether this objective and function should unambiguously determine the entire curriculum and cultural policy, and the teaching methods used. Only 25–26 per cent of *Gimnázium* pupils who have passed the *érettségi* are able to go on to a course of higher study, since the present capacity of universities and colleges as well as the demand for graduates and jobs available do not make it possible for more to be admitted. If the number of *Gimnázium* students goes down while that of vocational secondary school students increases, the proportion of *Gimnázium* pupils able to continue their studies at a university or college might rise to 40–50 per cent at the most. Even then the question: What will become of young people who have passed their *érettségi* but have no chance to continue their studies and are insufficiently prepared for practical life, remains unanswered. Those responsible for the school reform anticipated this and therefore decreed that the *Gimnázium* must adjust the education they provide to the needs of practical life. In addition to modernizing the curriculum in general, making it more relevant, practical training was introduced into the *Gimnázium*, at first for a whole day per week, training students in one or another skill. Known as "5+1"—i.e. five days of theoretical learning + one day of practical training—this system had many drawbacks: a shortage of appropriate workshops and equipment, difficulties in establishing continuous and systematic training in plants, lack of preliminary training, etc. Therefore, the 5+1 was transformed into two hours practical teaching per week in most *Gimnázium* with the more modest but far more realistic aim that the students should acquire a certain manual skill and obtain, at the same time, direct and personal experience of manual work.

Two well-known contradictions appear in all Hungarian secondary schools: first that the comparatively rigid unchanging curriculum, and secondly that between optimum modernization of the curriculum and old established teaching methods, outdated equipment, buildings, class-rooms, etc. In other words, secondary education has to make increasing efforts in order to prepare students for real life outside the school-walls while it is less and less able to keep students and the great cultural, technical and communications revolution of our times in contact. The curriculum is, admittedly, being gradually modernized under social pressure, the other inconsistency, between the modernization of the curriculum and outdated teaching methods and the increasingly narrow limits of education, still continues. P. G. Munday rightly emphasizes (*Visual Education*, April 1969, pp. 25–9) that modern education cannot be carried on within traditional institutions by old methods without making use of the new technology of education and new means of communication.

In Hungary, these inconsistencies are aggravated by certain peculiar circumstances. Such retarding factors are, for example, the many obsolete schools planned at the time for a smaller number of students, with a view to the requirements of a humanistic culture and disregarding practical demands; further, class-rooms which only permit traditional teaching, but are unfit for group-work in laboratories. There are considerable differences in the equipment of schools, for instance, in some there are audio-visual linguistic laboratories and closed-circuit TV systems while others cannot arrange even

the most simple demonstration lessons for lack of projectors. This lack of uniformity in equipment—which is also shown by an inequality of staffing—leads to students being taught under widely differing conditions. At present there are considerable differences in standards, a fact proved by comparisons between marks obtained at final examinations and at university entrance examinations. Students from *Gimnázia* in the country have less chance of being admitted to universities than students who were at school in the capital or in large industrial centres. Young people are allotted to secondary schools—and to general schools as well—according to their place of residence and admittance to a school elsewhere is subject to special permission. More ambitious parents sometimes take advantage of the latter loophole hoping to send their children to a school with a higher reputation, however, the basic principle of admission according to place of residence cannot be changed since it would lead to overcrowding in some schools, while others would remain half empty. It has also to be taken into account that schools can scarcely provide boarding places for students who don't live in the neighbourhood. It is obvious that the solution of the problem is not free choice of schools but the gradual abolition of the differences in standards.

Specialization within the Gimnázium

The desire to reform *Gimnázia* is expressed in the first place in a desire to accommodate to the needs posed by life. A significant aspect of it is practical training and education for work. The 5+1 system was mentioned above and although it did not stand the test, it indicated the changing and more up-to-date demands society made. In 1961, at the initial phase of the 5+1 system, 67 per cent and 1963–4, 89.7 per cent of all *Gimnázium* students took part in one day per week training. It is, of course, another matter—and this was the main reason why the experiment proved a failure—that preconditions were lacking for this often debated training system, there were neither adequate workshops nor adequate staff and tuition itself was often not organized purposefully. However, the quick spread of this movement clearly showed that the often expressed demand for a change in the traditional framework of secondary schools and for teaching to be based on more practical grounds was justified.

When it became obvious that the *Gimnázium* in its present structure—designed first of all to prepare young people for the university and to give them a good general education—was not able to give an adequate grounding in a skill, another more direct approach was suggested. This was connected with the fact that only 25–30 per cent, 40 per cent at most, of the students could gain direct admittance to universities or colleges. (There are, of course, evening and extension courses, not admittedly in every faculty, which allow a few thousand more young men and women to continue their studies.) Thus, different sections were established in *Gimnázia*, called classes with a specialized curriculum, in which more than the usual hours in the timetable are devoted to the teaching of one or another subject under more favourable conditions and, obviously, with a better effect. This covers languages such as English, Russian, French, German, Italian, Spanish, etc., also mathematics, and physics, biology and chemistry, chemistry and physics, art, music, and gymnastics. In 1968–9, of 126,000 *Gimnázium* students more than 28,000 attended classes with an emphasized language curriculum, more than 12,000 classes which specialized in the natural sciences and about 1,500 classes where art, music and gymnastics were given more time and emphasis. This means by and large that about one-third of all *Gimnázium* students received a more differentiated education and were prepared in certain subjects on a more thorough and

more practical basis. Although this system cannot fundamentally change the objective of *Gimnázia* it helps to orientate pupils towards certain careers.

Thus, specialization to a certain extent means the revival of the earlier *Gimnázium* and better opportunities for gifted young people. Unfortunately, in most cases the opportunity only is given, putting it into effect does not quite work out. This is due to certain difficulties in the system of specialized classes.

The latter became very fashionable at some places, it spread like wildfire, as such things are likely to do in Hungary. Earlier, the $5+1$ system also spread rapidly, though the foundations had not been laid carefully. The system of specialized classes requires far better conditions than average, competent trained teachers, linguistic and other kinds of laboratories, a smaller number of students per class and class-rooms other than the ones available at present. Without these preconditions a higher degree of knowledge can be acquired in certain subjects but it is not at all certain that the real aim, that is providing specialized training, can be achieved. In view of the fact that one-third of the students are already attending secondary school classes with specialized curricula and the number of these classes amounts to half of all secondary school classes, the results seem more than doubtful. After a quick initial upswing, it will certainly become necessary to content ourselves with more moderate results in this field and to reconsider the possibilities; there is no doubt that the highest directing authority of secondary schools, the Ministry of Culture and Education, will exercise careful supervision and only permit—though to a slighter extent than hitherto—the establishment of classes with a specialized curriculum where the preconditions thereto are suitable. The system of specialized classes as such gives excellent opportunities for those with special talents and for the transformation of a type of school—which has perhaps been too much reduced to a pattern—into a more attractive and diversified one. If fashion will however dominate, the relations between both teachers and pupils of the specialized and the general sections are likely to develop in an undesirable way.

The Training of Skilled Tradesmen

All over the world industry increasingly demands more and more skilled tradesmen and better trained workmen than formerly, with a comprehensive general education in addition to the technical knowledge required. One of the greatest problems of both economic life and secondary public education is the way in which training in certain skills can be harmonized with a general education. Linking the two is the only way to meet the increased demands of industry. P. Ducros justly argues in "Problems of Developing Vocational Training" in OECD (Organization of Economic Co-operation and Development): "How can vocational training be combined with general education? Up to now we have not yet succeeded in giving a satisfactory answer to this question. Each country can be considered a living laboratory, and the results achieved as well as the failures in vocational training stand in the full glare of publicity." He quotes R. Regaire according to whom "the solution is to be sought in comprehensive vocational training which lasts until the adult age and is closely correlated with general education. This mode of education will be many-sided in the initial stage and gradually tend towards specialization."

All this also applies to Hungary, Hungarian public education is also a "living laboratory." The structure of the Hungarian economy underwent radical changes in the course of the past twenty years. In 1949, 50 per cent of all gainfully employed persons worked in agriculture and scarcely 21 per cent in industry and the building trade, whereas today these figures are 30 per

cent as against 40 per cent. However, agricultural employment amounting to 30 per cent does not simply mean that fewer workers are needed in agriculture; the speedy development of the latter and changes in the agrarian pattern going hand in hand with mechanization, more chemical products, etc. require another kind and better trained labour force. The same applies in an increased degree to industry where techniques changed to an even greater extent during the past 10–20 years. These tendencies are making themselves felt just after the Hungarian economic reform. Thus unskilled workers tend to be used in services rather than in production. Considerable labour mobility is needed; in view of this, it is absolutely necessary that young people should be able to change easily over from one trade to another. Between 1949 and the present about a hundred trades ceased to exist in Hungary and 120 new ones came into existence.

In Hungary in the past industrial apprentice schools as a rule dealt with the vocational education of skilled tradesmen; children were generally admitted to this type of school when they were 14 years old and had previously completed primary school; this basic form of training of the rising generation of skilled tradesmen has been kept up. However, it was difficult to establish a suitable proportion between theoretical and practical subjects in view of the short period of attendance (only 2–3 years) (the proportion of general education plus theoretical instruction of a specialized kind to the practical training in the student's future craft was generally 75:25); hence, a justified demand arose for a modern type of school in which more time was given to the teaching of general culture on a broader basis. (In vocational schools for the training of skilled tradesmen higher standards of general education were also introduced. The ratio of lessons to practical training changed to 35:65 and young people who completed these schools had, in addition, the possibility of finishing secondary school within two years.)

Act III of 1961 established for the first time a type of school in which general education and vocational training are combined, taking pupils to the *érettségi* and training them in a trade as well. "The specialized secondary school extends and deepens knowledge acquired in the primary school; it leads to further growth in the educational level of students, and provides training in morals, aesthetics, physical education and socialist ideology, and qualifies them in a trade." Later, however, as a result of experiments and experiences and, last but not least, when the new methods of economic guidance were worked out, the objectives of the specialized secondary school also had to be diversified. The 1965 decree on secondary schools determines the objectives of teaching and education in vocational secondary schools as follows: "Vocational secondary schools provide an up-to-date general education and middle grade vocational training. The students are educated to be versatile men and women in a socialist spirit, provided with theoretical and practical knowledge, skill and ability in a trade, relying on which they are able to solve tasks assigned to them within the special field they were trained for, from productive work to directing partial processes as well as tasks in a particular line; moreover, it enables them to pursue higher grade studies."

This definition makes it clear that vocational secondary schools have to perform a multiplicity of tasks. The possibility for continued education has to be ensured, for about 12–15 per cent of those who took their final examinations at vocational secondary schools continue to study at higher grade institutions; therefore, the syllabus of the subjects providing a modern general education was determined in such a way that it should by and large meet the requirements of general education and allow for studies to be continued. As regards vocational training, vocational secondary schools have to deal

with a complex situation. In view of swift changes in trades, working processes, technology, etc. such a school cannot train students for one trade only. Today's vocational secondary schools correspond by and large to English secondary technical schools and teach students in five main sections and in about 30 occupational groups. The earlier overdone specialization of technical secondary schools which was not suitable to the needs of a relatively small country such as Hungary was discontinued. Ten to fifteen years ago technical secondary schools, the forerunners of vocational secondary schools, adjusted themselves too much to the almost daily changing demands of industry and agriculture: in 1953–4 there were 14 different sections in agricultural technical schools.

Taking into account changes in industry and agriculture on the one hand, and the fact that about 82–84 per cent of young people who have completed primary school continue to study, the proportion between *Gimnázia* and vocational secondary schools —which lead to immediate employment— had to be changed. In 1958–9 and the following years 67–68 per cent of secondary school students enrolled in *Gimnázia* and 28–30 per cent in technical secondary schools; this proportion, however, changed by 1968–9 and only 55 per cent enrolled in grammar schools, 30.4 per cent in vocational secondary schools and 14 per cent in surviving technical secondary schools. This process goes on even today, and as a result the above ratio continues to be shifted towards vocational secondary schools which provide occupational skills while technical secondary schools are gradually abolished.

The curricula of the first three years in vocational schools are relatively uniform, differentiation permitting not only specialization but also mobility between trades, intensified in the fourth year. A new and more modern syllabus for theoretical subjects and vocational training taking into account changes in industry and technology is being prepared now.

*The Shackles of Convention and the Spirit
of Irreverence*

The World Educational Crisis (Oxford University Press), by Philip H. Coombs, the former director of the UNESCO International Institute of Educational Planning, has aroused world-wide interest and caused a great stir. Mr. Coombs declared that educational systems adopt themselves far too slowly to the fast changes that take place in science and technology and in economic and social life. Education—according to Coombs—can only fall into line with this speedy development if the spirit of innovation and irreverence becomes prevalent everywhere.

His words contain a great deal of wisdom; without justified disrespect for hoary concepts and without a passion for reforming changes, the school—particularly with such problems as the secondary school—cannot meet the requirements of changed and continuously changing demands. This is the basic issue of public education and further development is impossible without dealing with it.

Obsolete conventions are most likely to assert themselves when it comes to defining culture. Discussions about what is part of it and what, sometimes important, subjects have to go, though relinquishing them may be distressing, still hang in the balance in Hungary and elsewhere too. This battle has to be fought out on a broad front by those who direct secondary schools, for the battle-line reaches from "higher" strata where distinguished scientists fight in defence of special subjects to the "lower" spheres of simple teachers and even laymen.

Conservatism, which together with many other popular views hinders at present the radical transformation of secondary schools, shows itself among others in a sort of resistance against the natural sciences. The defence of humanistic cultural ideals often bars the way to a more modern teaching of natural sciences and stops the development of the right relationship between humanistic

education and the teaching of sciences. One ought to listen—in Hungary and elsewhere too—to the views of Roger Gal, the eminent French educationist: "Teaching of the natural sciences must become an essential part of modern humanism for sciences provide the most reliable knowledge for the human spirit striving to understand itself and the world... There is no general culture without some kind of knowledge of the general laws of technology." (Roger Gal: *Où en est la pédagogie?* Edition Buchet–Chastel, Paris, 1961.)

Conservatism and the fight against it cannot be reduced to deciding, say, the hours given to history and physics in *Gimnázia*. Even if it succeeds in establishing an optimum proportion in this respect, old-fashioned ideas can create serious difficulties for many students. According to Coombs—who bravely broke away from petrified traditions—modern educational methods imbued with the spirit of irreverence are needed, the growth of which—as is known by experience—is by no means devoid of problems.

The Comprehensive High School, by James B. Conant, a former President of Harvard University, includes facts describing a thorough investigation he had carried out in secondary schools in the USA. From these data it appears that only 10.9 per cent of the headmasters interviewed attributed importance to television in the teaching of single subjects and only 16.2 per cent of the headmasters considered programmed teaching important and effective. These facts speak for themselves and throw a strong light upon the battle-line of secondary schools.

How long will this fight be going on? Perhaps as long as culture is not interpreted in all secondary schools as it was expounded by an eminent Hungarian teacher, György Kálmán, at present a Departmental Head in the Ministry of Culture and Education: "Education includes the development of talents as well as the demand to get to know new results and facts in the life of humanity... Thus, culture does not only mean completion but possibilities for further development... Hence, an educated man is actively cultured, in other words, he is active in the development of his mind. He is open to the new and ready to receive it for he has improved faculties for turning it to good account."

Throughout the world experts grapple with basic questions in education such as how to make room in the curriculum and in teaching for new and quickly changing facts. This is not only related to the amount studied, the number of hours and subjects or to the prolongation of the time of education for—as it has been mentioned earlier—it is mainly a question of methods. In order to improve the faculties of students, the educational methods in secondary schools must be perfected and modernized. It is not a question of a reform once and for all, for what is mainly needed is to endow the spirit of education with a new life. Without being exaggeratedly pessimistic it does not seem likely that this will ever succeed fully, if, however, it does happen even only in part one can entertain hopes for the future of secondary schools.

FERENC PATAKI

THE SOCIAL WORLD OF SECONDARY SCHOOL STUDENTS

The social and practical experience of age-groups following on each other and entering into the educational process, into educational institutions, differ from each other to an increasing extent, and differ especially from the content of the social experience of their parents. The world of experience, the mass media and the structure of the mode of life (pattern of consumption, demands, aspirations, etc.) of the younger age-groups "entering" one after the other demonstrate radical differences. Whereas earlier an identical or hardly changed mode of life, customs and traditions were bequeathed from generation to generation, today these change considerably even within the life of a single family or educational institution, and build up a peculiar tension. The effects of horizontal and vertical mobility add further hues to this picture.

The age structure of society is changing and undergoing substantial rearrangement. Although there are considerable differences from country to country, the increase of the proportion of the older age-groups, on the one hand, and that of the "young generation," on the other, are typical features, and these have become the source of interesting, novel developments. In Hungary, for instance, the proportion of those over sixty has increased from 5.5 per cent to 16 per cent since 1920. The middle-aged and older age-groups are active for a longer time. For the young this often means that older people "keep positions occupied" and hinder a faster progress in career and society. This creates a number of tensions and difficulties. The sort of situation has arisen in the most advanced industrial countries for the first time where the young (those under 29) form an increasing part, in some places the majority, of the total population. This circumstance has added to the social weight of the young, it has accelerated its stratification and the homogenization of its mode of life (increasingly uniform schooling, particular consumption patterns, fashions, etc.).

Continuous change is taking place in the method and organization of the transmission of information. Today the quantity of accumulated information (the stock of scientific, production and cultural achievements and knowledge which the young have to make their own) are increasingly becoming divorced from direct, personal experience, and are being passed on more and more as abstract knowledge. But thirty years ago, in the world of the Hungarian peasants or craftsmen-artisans the young grew into social work by learning know-how, traditions, customs, the spiritual values and the norms regulating behaviour within the framework of the family, primarily through personal participation and the imitation of living examples. Today (partly due to the extension of schooling, and partly to the rapid growth of the quantity of information) knowledge and experience become increasingly divorced from their personal carriers, from those who apply them, from collective forms (such as the village way of life so rich in patriarchal traits not so long ago), and are passed on more and more as rational information. Today we pass on also the behaviour patterns increasingly in the shape of rational material, and are therefore increasingly forced "to moralize," "to preach." Education has been shifted from a basis of experience to a basis of explication. One reason for this is that the family is becoming less the scene of common production, and increasingly only the scene of common consumption. In this situation, the behavioural patterns, evaluation mechanisms, customs and moods existing in the groups and communities of the young come more and more into their own.

In the wake of the growth of the scientific-technical and social demands made on man the preparation-and-learning period of the socialization process has definitely been extended, and as a consequence of this the period of the "pedagogic situation" has been lengthened radically in the life of the young. A growing part of youth for an increasing time live a "student way of life": in a basic situation oriented mostly towards the passive reception of information. This fact has numerous consequences which cannot be analysed here, including the lengthening of the "intermediate zone" between biological and social maturity, a more lengthy period of life regulated from outside, and greater complexities in the relationship of education and self-education. As a result of all this, numerous elements of traditional education in schools and other traditional forms of education have also become full of problems. The essentials may be summarized by the fact that the role of the "age-groups" (Riesman) becomes more and more important in the life and orientation of the young, as a consequence of which their world is becoming more complex and expanding wider all the time. It is well-known that the integration and intensity of family life are generally being reduced by the changes in the structure and mode of life of the family (the radical reduction in the number and often the complete absence of brothers and sisters; the employment structure of the parents; the definite reduction and often complete absence of the neighbourhood and other traditional institutions as example, control or sanction; the extension of free movement and uncontrollable activities outside the family, etc.). In numerous cases, the family can no longer be considered a coherent group. The "children's world" with its particular system of relationships can hardly develop in families with one or two children, and consequently the children must go outside the family whenever they wish to step into the activities of companions of more or less their own age. (This is so even if the scene of this organization and of their activities is the home provided and maintained by the family. In this case the home is but the scene of that particular social life and activity of the young.)

The extension of the characteristic social-communal "student way of life" is linked with the increase of the relative sectional differentiation of the young, the rapid spread of peculiarly juvenile consumption patterns and fashions, and with the growth of a spontaneous social life which is being organized "behind" the "official" communal organization of the school.

General Picture of the Social World

The influence of the urbanization processes on the forms of existence and the modes of association of youth are mostly examined apart, in the context of various phenomena (deviation, changes of the family, the conditions of "school society," the "street-corner societies," etc.). It may, however, be assumed that one can speak also of a social field structured in a particular way in the conduct of life of groups of young people, a field the inter-related elements of which may be investigated as parts of an integral system.

We have tried to test this assumption through research into the social world of secondary-school pupils in Budapest.* Hungarian secondary schools, in which boys and girls spend four years from 14 to 18, are of two basic types: academic secondary schools and vocational secondary schools.** (Vocational secondary schools also provide preliminary training in certain trades.) The first three forms (age 14 to 17) of both types of schools were covered. We did not include the fourth form since the pupils were about to take their school-leaving examination, which makes considerable demands on their time and energies.

The general picture took shape after the two fundamental questions had been answered. These two questions were: "In

whose company do you prefer to spend your free time?" "Who is the grown-up person, or who are the grown-ups with whom you can talk most frankly about your personal problems?" The criterion "with whom do you prefer to spend your free time" is not entirely unequivocal, since it can unite and express together at least two elements, i.e. subjective attraction, the wish to be together on a social occasion and in a common activity, and competence, skill, sometimes even prestige. Somebody may like to be together with a companion who is outstanding in some activity (e.g. sports), although he is not attached to him by attraction or affection as he may be to others. In spite of this limitation, we are inclined to argue that the information received may be interpreted in both the dimension of affection and attraction. The fundamental data appear in the table on p. 112.

Since we have not limited the choice to a single person, the totals exceed 100 per cent. But the relative proportions provide an accurate picture of the extent to which the individual persons are preferred.

Some facts are conspicuous at first glance. The ratio of pupils longing for solitude, preferring to spend their free time alone is very high (especially among the girls). This was expressed by every fifth pupil, among the girls by almost every fourth. It is enticing—but entirely without foundation—to put this category unequivocally under the heading "solitude." But this group includes also those who prefer a free time activity which does not require a social situation. In addition to this, the group includes those who are aloof "on principle," as well as those who have been forced to the outside

---

* This study to some extent used data of a representative survey in Budapest. This was planned and carried out by Ferenc Gazsó, Pál Sántha, György Várhelyi and the author.

** The Hungarian secondary-school system is described and discussed in "The Future of Secondary Schools" by István Gábor on page 101 of this issue.—The Ed.

Person with whom co-operation is desired	Total (N = 770) per cent	Boys (N = 311) per cent	Girls (N = 459) per cent
No one	21.4	17.7	24.0
Parent	31.0	29.6	32.0
Brother or sister	16.5	14.5	17.6
Classmate-friend	42.7	39.9	44.7
Schoolmate-friend	6.8	7.4	6.3
Friend from outside the school	46.5	54.3	41.2
Friend of the other sex	3.2	3.9	2.8
Unusable answer	0.3	0.6	0.0

by external compelling reasons, and those who are little or not at all integrated in the family and in school. But it is also demonstrated that a considerable group of secondary school students is not sufficiently integrated either in the family or at school, but live in a loose social medium of little efficiency. In this context we are justified in saying that in spite of their appearance in many kinds of social situations, numerous secondary-school students are in essence without companions and feel alone.

It is somewhat surprising how small the number of those is who prefer to form mixed couples. Hardly 3 per cent of the pupils admitted to preferring to spend their free time with members of the opposite sex. Looking at the choice of the students (in respect to both sexes) the existence of three main centres of attraction, three principal directions of social ambitions take shape: parents, brothers and sisters, i.e. the family; classmates; and friends outside school. The obvious preponderance of the two latter groups supports without doubt the prior assumption that the interest of secondary-school pupils is directed primarily towards those of their own age-group.

There is no essential difference between boys and girls in the direction and character of social orientation. The girls' bias towards parents, brothers and sisters, and classmates—i.e. more intimate, frequent and direct forms of contact in personal relationships—is somewhat more pronounced. On the other hand, boys make contact outside school over a much wider field; the majority endeavour to establish social co-operation outside school and the family (54.3 per cent as against 41.2 per cent). In this fact a traditional—although gradually fading—norm has also become manifest; the freedom of girls, their movement outside the family, is still more restricted than that of the boys. We cannot really be surprised that this is a natural phenomenon even in strongly urbanized conditions and under co-education. The family continues to control girls much more resolutely, and there are numerous traditional elements linked to the social role of the female.

Links within the school are localized almost exclusively in the form. Attraction to friends who are not classmates but go to the same school are in one but last place on the list of priorities, ahead only of members of the opposite sex. Within certain limits this has to be accepted as a natural fact; it is obvious that co-operation and existence together in the school form day after day, a social structure taking shape continually changing, influence the commencement and the consolidation of social links more forcefully than the looser field of the whole school which is more difficult to survey and to observe. Our school communities mostly still exist in secondary schools as isolated, self-contained form communities. The institutional surfaces of co-operation between the various age-groups (forms) are extraordinarily limited, and as a consequence of this we cannot speak of a community structure on a school scale. Since a certain frequency of contact and regular co-operation are preconditions of the commencement and the stabilization of personal links, in the absence of this, community relations within the school are formed only in a simple and rudimentary way. Makarenko already mentioned the disadvantages of this, and new educational analyses point again and again to the damage caused by it. Nevertheless, the characteristic situation is still present unchanged in Hungarian secondary schools where community links are organized with an unwholesome one-sidedness mostly only on the basis of forms and not of the whole school.

The co-operation of various age-groups and their interaction is accompanied by an "exchange" of behaviourial models, modes of activity, ambitions and motives (and not only for the benefit of the younger) without which social links which are adequate in content and manifold, and are effective in the formation of personality, cannot develop.

Stratification according to the social status of parents shows little variation in available data, whereas age, the type of school, marks obtained, and sex are factors that produce considerable differences. (See table below.)

In the group of the students attending a secondary school the wish for solitude and the attraction of the family are more pronounced. (The proportion of girls is higher in secondary schools!) The links limited to the form appear to be stronger among those attending secondary schools while orientation towards friends outside the school is somewhat more pronounced in the case of vocational secondary school students.

The fluctuations that occur according to age (school forms) are much more interesting; especially as they offer an insight into the

Person with whom co-operation is desired	1st Form (N = 292) per cent	2nd Form (N = 251) per cent	3rd Form (N = 224) per cent	Gramm. School (N = 478) per cent	Voc. Sec. School (N = 292) per cent
No one	26.0	17.1	20.5	24.7	16.1
Parent	32.5	29.9	29.5	31.8	29.8
Brother or sister	57.5	13.9	19.2	18.2	13.7
Classmate-friend	36.9	53.4	37.9	46.9	35.9
Schoolmate-friend	8.2	6.8	4.9	6.9	6.5
Friend from outside the school	41.8	42.6	57.1	45.2	48.6
Friend of the other sex	2.4	2.4	5.4	3.6	2.7
Unusable answer	0.0	0.8	0.0	0.0	0.7

dynamic qualities of the phenomenon which we are investigating. It is only surprising at first sight that the wish for solitude is strongest among those who attend first form. Difficulties involved in the change of school, the competitive situation (for a favourable social situation, for achieving a good position in the schools' pecking order) which occurs openly or concealed in the newly organized first forms and the already mentioned paucity of links on the school scale equally contribute to this.

In the second form the number of those who wish to be alone takes a dip. These forms are the most stable groups in secondary schools; the primary formation of social structures, relations of influence and authority have taken shape. The children generally "feel good." Adaptation to secondary school has been completed, everybody has been sized up. The zones of achievement have also been confirmed. This is characteristically reflected in the fact that the intention to co-operate with classmate-friends is strongest in those attending second form.

The third form is in many respects a critical period in secondary education. The first two years are the closing wave of puberty, while the second two years (17 to 18) are already the period of youth, turning more resolutely towards the future, of the reorganization of social links, of the appearance of new demands and tensions. Symptoms usually become stronger which indicate that students "outgrow" somewhat the school boundaries which hedge them in. The more definite interest taken in the opposite sex, the expansion of the field of free movement, familiarity with new forms of entertainment and activities, all indicate this. The figures show the symptoms of the changes and of the new tensions more or less accurately; the wish for solitude increases again, the social field outside school becomes more important, the attraction of the family is somewhat reduced, and the importance of the partner belonging to the opposite sex becomes more pronounced.

The gradual but clearly visible decay of school links beyond the form underlines the validity of what has been said of this subject before, now from the dynamic aspect as well. The outstanding students—as a group—tend to concentrate their interest more definitely on the family, to a lesser extent seeking contacts outside school or links with schoolmates, and desiring more solitude. They are also less orientated towards siblings. If we select the four most important directions of linkage and relate their order of importance to each other, we get the following picture:

Outstanding student: parent — friend outside school — classmate-friend — brother or sister

Average student: classmate-friend — friend outside school — parent — no one

Failed student: friend outside school — classmate-friend — parent — no one

The tendencies are very characteristic: with the deterioration of study results the domination of links outside school becomes more pronounced. We should add straightway that it would not be right to interpret these figures as if this were a linear determination. It is quite natural that the group of students who are not sufficiently appreciated in the "official" dimension of evaluation at school "leave" this hierarchy, which mostly holds only failure for them and which offers them very low social prestige. They seek and find instead informal-spontaneous structures the evaluation patterns of which—irrespective of their content—provide more favourable opportunities for their ambitions to assert themselves. But the phenomenon itself may occur also in the reverse order, although the former is probably the preponderant. It may happen that joining a group or circle of friends which is outside school and the family (sports club, beat orchestra, gang, etc.) become the reason and source for neglecting school work. Although it may be caused by several reasons, the fact itself undoubtedly exists.

The firmness and desirability of links to parents is in a direct ratio to the success achieved in studies, and this is completely understandable.

The other approach to the general picture of the social field was the attempt to find out the adult person in whom the student under investigation confided. In this dimension we were interested in the degree of intimacy and in the situation of the "persons of confidence." The data obtained are suitable partly for checking and partly for supplementing the extensive picture which the answers to the first question provided.

Person in whom confidence is placed	Frequency of occurrence, percentage of the sample
Father	40.4
Mother	67.8
Friend	5.6
Brother, sister—other relation	16.4
Member of the opposite sex	0.6
Teacher	5.5
Coach, band-leader	1.2
Nobody	8.1
Unusable answer	3.1

(Friends may come from two sources: the students have either mentioned adult friends, or it escaped their attention that the question was limited to "grown-ups." Therefore this figure cannot be interpreted here.)

The figures are startling on several counts. The absolute preponderance of the narrower family circle is already an unexpected result, especially the extent of the role of the mother in this. This shows first of all that—at least in the case of secondary-school students—the mother continues to be the confidant,

and is the main representative of care and of an emotionally strongly coloured relationship for the children. Two-thirds of the pupils mention their mother as the person with whom "they can most frankly discuss their personal problems." Although the father too has an important role in this respect, as against the mother he is only mentioned by two-fifths of the students.

We must feel reservations concerning the general belief in the disorganization of the family and the separation of the young from the family, at least as far as secondary-school pupils are concerned. The sociological literature discussing urbanization also points out that the first wave of the process of urbanization is indeed accompanied by the loosening of the primary organizations and social groups and by symptoms of disorganization, but the stabilization of the process and of the conditions for urbanization enhance again the role of the primary social groups, including the family.

The increase in numbers of certain symptoms of disorganization (e.g. divorce) does not at all exclude in principle that another (perhaps major) part of families might show greater consolidation. Certain traits in metropolitan conditions—such as the cessation of neighbourhood links, the strongly formal-bureaucratic and impersonal character of employment, the frequent situation of anonymity, etc.—may lead to an increase of the subjective evaluation and attraction of the intimate family sphere.

The two other facts which deserve attention are: the low frequency of teachers in the capacity of intimate confidant, the relatively large number (8.1 per cent) of those who have no confidant.

The low percentage of teachers is a rather disquieting and frightening development. It indicates that the school has taken on an exaggeratedly impersonal-institutional (not to say bureaucratic) character, and that the personal attraction of teachers, their contacts with students is insufficient. That only five students out of a hundred should mention their teacher as a person in whom they confide, shows the extent to which this unfavourable process has advanced. We are of course aware that this harmful situation is strongly connected with certain disadvantageous aspects in the working conditions of teachers, and in their recruitment. However, a school system which lacks effective educators who radiate confidence, can fulfil its educational functions only to a limited extent.

The generally unfavourable picture of the students' links to teachers is somewhat modified if we examine figures in terms of forms. It turns out that the number of teachers in whom students confide increases with the time spent in the school (first class: 3.4 per cent, second class: 5.6 per cent, third class: 8.1 per cent). The dynamics of the matter are obvious: time is needed for the development of confidence. But the length of time the process takes and the figures referring to the average must still give rise to anxiety.

The proportion of students who answered "member of the opposite sex" and "nobody" (i.e. student having no confidant) correlates in its tendencies with the figures obtained from the analysis of the answers given to the preceding question, and supports the conclusions drawn there. (The answer "nobody" may be related to the students who express a wish for solitude.)

Pupils in the Family

We can evaluate the substantial role played by the family as a social structure in the process of socialization only if we first get an answer to three questions: (a) What type of common activities dominate in the lives of families? (b) What is the scale of magnitude of the time spent together by children and parents? (c) How frequent are the occasions of intimate conversation with the person in whom confidence is placed?

Let us first see the types of common activities of parents and children, and the frequency of their occurrence:

Types of common activity	Frequency of occurrence, percentage of the sample		
	Total	Boys	Girls
No common activity	3.3	4.3	2.6
Family events (family holidays, visits, traditional occasions, etc.)	31.2	27.9	33.5
Meals	29.3	29.8	28.9
Conversation	16.5	15.4	17.3
Household work	8.9	7.7	9.7
Play	1.5	1.5	1.5
Excursions, walks, summer holidays	32.3	26.1	36.7
Public entertainments (theatre, concert, movie, etc.)	36.6	29.1	41.9
Watching television	30.9	32.8	29.6
Unusable answer	4.9	6.7	3.7

Within the total of the families in the sample there are:

both parents at home	82.7 per cent
parents separated	2.3 per cent
parents divorced	10.3 per cent
father deceased	3.6 per cent
mother deceased	1.1 per cent

Number of siblings:

None	29.8 per cent
One	45.0 per cent
Two	17.8 per cent
Three or more	7.4 per cent

The order of frequency of "being together" situations can be established easily from the table.

It is conspicuous that the "occasional" common activities are much more frequent than the continuous activities of everyday life (e.g. household work, conversation, meals, play), although TV viewing, this less frequent than the expected situation of "social solitude," must probably also be counted here. This life rhythm of organizing the family around "occasions" and events is characteristic of the rather harassed metropolitan families, which rely on employment "outside the home" of both parents. The disappearance of the family as a working community is indicated accurately by the relatively and absolutely small occurrence of household work performed in common.

The fact that public entertainments lead in order of frequency amongst common activities must certainly be appreciated as positive. The overwhelmingly professional-employee social background of secondary-school pupils, the combined effect of the opportunities presented by the capital and the student mode of life, are reflected in this favourable development.

The difference between boys and girls again supports an earlier—incidentally quite natural—conclusion: the girls are much more family-oriented. They take part in larger numbers of intra-family activities and do so more frequently.

An analysis of the types of common activities can only be complete if we include the time-dimension. We asked the children to estimate with the help of a detailed scale the average time that they spent weekly in a common activity with members of their family (whatever its form and mode). If we form larger typical groups in respect to the whole sample (little = 1–10 hours, average = 10–20 hours, much = 24 hours and over, and no time at all spent together), we get more tractable figures. The ratio of typical groups is the following: 4.3 per cent spend no time at all with their families, 36.5 per cent spend little time, 20.1 per cent spend an average amount of time, 39.1 per cent spend a considerable amount of time with their family.

It is disquieting that almost 40 per cent of pupils spend little time in activities that are organized and carried out in common within the family. Whatever our judgement about normative requirements and favourable educational situations may be, this position appears unfavourable from both an educational and a wider social point of view.

At the other extreme, the group that claim that they spend a considerable amount of time with their families, also number almost 40 per cent. This strong dispersion and these opposing tendencies again show that conditions and characteristic trends of metropolitan families cannot be described in unambiguous formulae.

The symptoms of disorganization and of loosened ties in a considerable number of families may exist simultaneously with an inclination of family members towards each other, and the increased intensity of family life in another group of families. Extreme and one-sided judgements appear to be out of place; the picture is more diverse and intricate than may be thought on the basis of superficial and hasty generalizations. The simultaneous co-existence and shift and movement of opposing trends is certainly a characteristic of today's Hungarian educational (and social) reality.

The frequency with which students discuss with their parents (or with one of them) their personal problems is an important yardstick of the intimacy between children and parents. The expression "personal problems" may have many meanings, and we did not investigate its content. We simply assumed that students would understand by it the situation of more intimate conversations of a personal interest, irrespective of their concrete content.

How often do they discuss their problems with their parents	Total	Boys	Girls
	Percentage of the sample and of the two groups respectively		
Daily	36.9	28.6	42.5
Several times a week	29.4	27.9	29.7
Once a week	6.6	7.3	5.8
Seldom	24.0	33.3	18.7
Never	2.7	2.6	2.8
Not usable	0.4	0.3	0.5

It is interesting that this question shows the same polarity—at least in tendencies—as in the investigation of the amount of time spent with parents. If we confront the daily, several times a week categories with the seldom and never categories, the former—and this is something definitely positive—add up to two-thirds, and the latter only to just over one-quarter of the sample. The extent of the polarity is not so accentuated and asserts itself only as a tendency.

The figures referring to the whole sample hide the essential differences between the sexes. While 72.2 per cent of the girls discuss their problems with their parents daily or several times per week, and only 21.5 per cent belong to the seldom and never category, as regards the boys the same figures are 56.5 per cent as against 35.9 per cent. This shows that the boys are in a less favourable position, more precisely that they turn their backs on their families to a much greater extent than the girls. Only every fifth girl (but every third boy) is in the situation where she can (or wants to) discuss her problems with her parents only seldom or never.

The peculiar "father-deficiency" which shows in family education, as we have already seen in another context, appears again here.

Friends and Groups of Friends

The introduction of three types of structure of friendship appeared practical on the basis of research into the social structures of the young. This survey also justifies speaking of an intimate-closed (one to two friends), a small group (three to six friends) and an extensive-loose circle of friends (seven friends or more). If we investigate the position of the individual, we also have to consider the condition of friendlessness in addition to the position occupied in the structures here mentioned. Those elements which are particularly interesting become clear in the table below.

Structure of the circle of friends	Sex	
	Boys per cent	Girls per cent
Intimate-closed	19.6	27.5
Small group	51.8	46.6
Extensive-loose	21.9	17.9
No friends	6.1	5.2

(The total of the percentages is here—as well as in the tables below—somewhat under 100 per cent, unusable answers not being included.)

Girls definitely prefer the intimate-closed structure, while boys are linked somewhat more forcefully to wider and at the same time looser groups. The relatively low occurrence of intimate-closed links indicates that the role of looser and more superficial but extensive links is on the increase among metropolitan youth. It appears that some of the groups of two or three friends can also be considered only functional and partial, and not a formation that involves the whole of the personality.

It appears to be beyond doubt that the increase of the extensiveness of social links, social co-operation taking place in many ways and in many situations, is not necessarily accompanied by an increase in the intensity of these links. This appears to be one of the aspects of urbanization. The young are mostly involved with groups, with loose or tighter social formations, but within these, pairing off, and ties of friendship remain rudimentary and superficial.

Certain fashions contribute to the development of the "background atmosphere" of the situation. Generally, emotionalism is not fashionable among the young; they often have reservations about "showing their true selves in front of others." Sometimes a relationship to a member of the other sex also fulfils the function of friendship, and does not leave room for intensive and extensive, unconditionally frank links with a companion of the same sex. The fact itself, the extension of the dimensions of personal links, and simultaneously a reduction in their emotional intensity and completeness, seems to be beyond doubt. The educational conclusions to be derived are amongst the most important of our investigation. The social condition characteristic of the majority of secondary-school boys and girls is a superficial life beside one another, co-existing together and co-operating in occasional situations, rather than ties of friendship involving the full personality. In this the effects of one of the possible consequences of metropolitan conditions are reflected: the loosening of ties into something impersonal, empty and formal. It may be assumed that the already mentioned lack of sophistication and the amorphous nature of school communities, and the diminutive role played in education by co-operative and active forms of work, also help to give rise to this peculiar phenomenon.

The encouragingly small proportion of those who have no friends at all, explains one of the figures given earlier; the wish for solitude in various activities is not necessarily accompanied by social isolation, by a complete lack of friends. The number of pupils who are in fact lonely is more truly reflected by this latter figure than by the number of those who like to do things alone.

If we look at the figures in terms of age-groups (forms), we are again able to establish certain dynamic processes.

Friendship structure	Form		
	First	Second	Third
Intimate-closed	28.4	21.9	21.0
Small group	48.2	52.2	45.5
Extensive-loose	15.5	18.3	26.3
No friends	6.9	6.4	3.1

In keeping with the earlier figures, the proportion of those without friends is highest in the first form here too. The role of the intimate-closed groups is most important here, and as the other side of the coin, the proportion of extensive-loose structures is smallest. In consequence of the particular situation already mentioned, students in the first form "latch on to each other" much more, and in addition their field of social movement is more restricted. By the time they reach third form, the presence of larger structures almost doubles, and the number of those without friends is halved. The number of intimate circles of close friendship is also somewhat reduced. The characteristic condition of the students in the second form is reflected by the fact that the role of groups consisting of three to six members—recruited mainly of classmates—is the largest there. More than half the students belong to such groups. Figures regarding students in third form may express the "turning outward" from the family and from the school or a freer movement and orientation outside these limits.

It is interesting to note that the number of those who are without friends is smallest among the best and the worst pupils. (Outstanding, 2.5 per cent; good, 4.8 per cent; average, 7.1 per cent; bare pass, 8.6 per cent; failed, 3.4 per cent.) In the case of outstanding pupils this is accompanied by the most numerous presence of intimate-closed structures (30.4 per cent as against 21 to 23 per cent among the others), among students who have failed large, gang-like formations are more pronounced than in the other categories (25.7 per cent as against 15 to 18 per cent for the other students). These findings are easy to interpret in the light of practical educational experience. The attention of outstanding pupils is directed mainly towards those who have the same level of attitude and aspirations, and is therefore more limited.

The extensive and large groups of failed students, presumably organized outside the school, are explained by the feeling of acute failure at school.

Finding out whence the ties of friendship derived was considered most important in our survey. We have asked pupils to indicate the field of social contact in which their friendships originated. On the basis of the information obtained we established types which made the qualification and quantitative evaluation of the linkage orientation of the individuals possible. The various types can be easily surveyed in the table below.

Origin of friendship	Whole sample	Sex		School		Form		
		Boys	Girls	Grammar school	V.S.	First	Second	Third
Exclusively within the school	33.8	36.3	32.2	29.4	41.1	35.2	31.1	25.4
Exclusively outside the school	7.0	6.7	7.1	7.3	6.3	5.8	5.4	10.2
Within and outside equally	23.7	22.1	24.8	25.0	23.6	22.6	29.6	29.0
Overwhelmingly within the school	9.5	11.2	8.5	11.1	7.1	10.9	8.3	9.3
Overwhelmingly outside the school	20.7	18.0	22.6	21.3	19.5	20.2	20.1	21.4
Unusable answer	5.3	5.7	4.8	5.9	2.4	5.3	5.5	4.7

We find that, in general, the forging of links within the school dominates among secondary-school pupils in Budapest. 43.3 per cent of friendships originate exclusively or overwhelmingly in the school, and only 27.7 per cent exclusively or overwhelmingly outside the school. The nature of the student way of life and its structural character explain this completely (the volume of time spent together, the complex—institutionalized and occasional—surface contact, common interests, the large "supply" for the selection of friends, etc.).

It is, however, food for thought that more than one-quarter of the students establish their friendships exclusively or overwhelmingly outside school. And if we consider that the "half and half" group is also linked just as forcefully to contacts outside school as to those which originate at school, the tendency becomes even more significant. But in evaluation and interpretation we have to refrain here too from employing exaggeratedly categorical formulae.

There is no doubt that in strongly urbanized conditions it would be a complete illusion to entertain a picture of a school community as one that blends almost exclusively the social-amical relations of the students and is the single base for the formation and organization of their social links (i.e. as far as links with persons of the same age are concerned!). The school community cannot be imagined as a sort of closed, isolated structure within which contacts are sought almost exclusively. Today's school communities differ mainly in this social fact, and in the conclusions to be drawn from it, from the community-model established by Makarenko.

The grouping according to ages clearly indicates again that the ties to the school loosen as the years pass, and the role of the social world outside school and the establishing of friendships with non-schoolmates increases. With increasing age, secondary schools become more and more open, and cohesion is reduced. In the social orientation of students the importance of the social area between the family and the school increases gradually.

But this finding needs to be adjusted. The process is far from taking an identical course in all the categories formed according to marks obtained. It appears that this is the factor that plays the most important determinant role in the regulation of the phenomenon, while the ones shown in the table above produce only degrees.

In proportion to the deterioration of marks obtained, the school more and more "pushes" pupils and induces them to leave the framework in which they are unable to achieve a lasting positive evaluation of their personality. We have already noticed this tendency in the most different contexts, and can consequently consider it proven. We here meet the grave inner conflict of the "at school" form of existence and the one-sidedness of its dimensions of evaluation.

Only a radical extension of the latter can produce an educational solution; the school has to draw into its "official" system of evaluation all those dimensions (and the modes of activity carrying them) which do in fact exist in the world of the young, and make possible the limitation of the almost exclusive one-sidedness of appreciating only intellectual achievements. Otherwise we cannot hope that this relatively large section of pupils will ever become integrated organically into the community life of the school, and will accept its norms and patterns of evaluation. Nowadays, when the chances of higher study and the hopes for the future attached to them divide secondary-school pupils in any case, causing inner tensions and conflicts of interest among them, this side of the topic deserves special attention.

Institutional Community Links

How large is the group of students who are linked to the school and to their companions by institutional-official ties? The extent of the community relations which have become institutionalized in the school is a decisive question. We asked those covered by the survey whether they hold an office—and if yes, what office—in the youth organization. Our expectations were not too high, but the results were, even so, startling.

Offices held in the youth organization	Whole sample	Sex	
		Boys	Girls
Hold no office	60.3	69.7	53.8
Hold office in the basic unit (limited to the form)	23.5	19.2	25.8
Hold office on a school level	14.2	10.2	17.4
Hold office outside school	1.3	0.0	2.4
Unusable answer	0.7	0.9	0.6

The most unfavourable feature obviously is that a large group of secondary-school pupils—the overwhelming majority—hold no office at all in the school community.

In these circumstances, secondary-school organization and self-government have to struggle with serious difficulties. The relatively small number of office-holders also merge into the personally uninterested large passive bloc. Consequently, the ventures of this active group are also often surrounded by complacency. Without the extension of institutional community relations, and of actual and real rights and opportunities for self-government, we can hardly hope that the student communities of the secondary schools become more differentiated, and that the number of pupils who are in positions of "responsible dependence" and "responsible organizer" becomes wider.

The diminutive number of offices held outside school (in the case of boys, their total absence) indicates that the activities and tasks available outside school are scarce, the "public life" of schools is closed and inward-looking. In this respect the two

movements—in opposite directions—are especially conspicuous. While the links and scenes of activity of the students most decidedly move outside the school-walls, the direction of the movement of public life and organizational developments within the school do not express this trend sufficiently. The feminization of office-holders may be considered a peculiar symptom. The girls outstrip the boys in every aspect of holding community office. Besides other reasons (e.g. the higher number of girls at secondary school, their greater inclination to conformity, "reliability" and "orderliness", etc.) the feminization of the teaching profession certainly also plays a role here. Self-government in the secondary schools is built too much on the person of the teacher and direct inducement by him or her, and woman teachers, who are in the majority, find contact more easily and more naturally with girls. In secondary schools the holding of community office is closely correlated with marks obtained. (There are five possible marks in each subject.) This is what the figures show:

Office held in the youth organization	Average mark				
	Excellent	Good	Average	Pass	Failed
Holds no office	38.1	51.1	64.3	73.2	77.6
Holds office in the basic unit	42.0	29.9	20.2	15.5	9.0
Holds office on a school level	18.8	18.2	12.7	11.3	11.2
Holds office outside school	0.0	0.8	2.4	0.0	2.2
Unusable answer	1.1	0.0	0.4	0.0	0.0

The two opposite trends give a clear indication of the fact that the number of office-holders diminishes and the number of those without office increases in a direct ratio

to the deterioration of marks. We may be inclined to hold that this is in order, since in every effective community function high proficiency in studies is of course acceptable.

Yet, if we consider all that has been said before about "discrimination" at school against those who achieve low marks and about the narrowness of the scale of evaluation, we can only conclude that it is exactly organizational activity and self-government at school which provide the area where this group of pupils could assert themselves and achieve—at least partial—recognition.

We wished to ascertain the extent of participation in the various specialized groups of the school community by asking pupils what voluntary but institutional groups they were members of.

Membership in groups	Whole sample	Grammar school	Voc. School
	per cent		
No membership	16.0	16.1	15.8
Specialized group (science or practical)	34.2	41.2	22.6
Literary circle	2.1	1.3	3.4
Political debating circle	14.9	14.4	15.8
Arts group	4.0	5.4	3.1
Sports group	26.6	23.4	31.8
Other	18.8	16.3	22.8

(The percentages add up to more than 100 per cent, since the membership was not confined to one group.)

It is a welcome fact that the proportion of those who do not participate in any group at all, is very small. The outstanding role of specialized groups is characteristic of secondary schools, while the figures indicate that sports dominate in the technical secondary school. But all in all—perhaps with the exception of the specialized groups in the secondary schools—it cannot really be said of any form of association that it attracts masses of students.

Leaving aside those mentioned, each type of group comprises only a small part of the students. The sectional character of the various arts and literary groups is especially disquieting. The institutional forms of sport could also be wider. Groups in the "Other" category represent many kinds of special interests (technical—especi-

ally in the secondary schools, clubs, collectors, etc.), but these do not represent either trends of characteristic interests or larger groups of students.

We are certain that an increase in the variety of the forms of autonomous association and the extension of their fields of activity would have a beneficial effect on social conditions and community cohesion in secondary schools.

We are convinced that the structure and dynamism of the social-community relations arising in the inner world of the school are very much influenced by the methodical-organizational forms of teaching. And here we have to count to this very day with a great number of conservative elements—the predominance of verbal lecturing, the diminutive proportion of cooperative-active forms of work, tedium and passivity in the classroom, etc. The renewal and further development of teaching methods and of self-management in schools can only be imagined realistically together, with the two tiers supporting each other.

Our data have already indicated that the effect of the unfavourable factors is precipitated mainly in the third form. It is then that orientation outside school, and withdrawal from the norms and values of school, become intensified. This circumstance reflects also the fact that it is generally by the time they have reached third form that students (and their parents) know whether they will go on to higher education or not. By this time it has become obvious whether the marks suffice for this. The average and the bad students—seeing that the chances of higher education are nil—take less and less interest in their links with the school, are less and less inclined to well-behaved conformism, and naturally turn to activities in other directions.

The questions which were discussed are capable of solution only if the theoretical analyses are organically linked with a knowledge of the social basis and with a thorough investigation of the processes which occur in schools. The concrete sociological approach may enable us to form a sounder judgement of the situation and the future of the school communities, although the data so obtained can in no way be used to provide educational norms or objectives.

THE WORKERS' CHANGING LIFE
I. SOCIAL MOBILITY AND LIFESTYLE

by

MIKLÓS SZÁNTÓ

What are the workers like in Hungary, the workers who have, with the liberation of the country, grown from the oppressed proletariat of earlier times into the leading political force of socialist construction? What are they like, or, in other words, how do they live today? These are the questions which have been latent in the discussion, often an abstract discussion, about the working class. The Marxist idea "the class in itself" —regardless of whether it knows where it belongs and what it owes to society, and "the class for itself"— of which Attila József wrote that "it is iron-clad in the class struggle" still holds true today. But what are the proportions today, to what extent are the masses pervaded by a conscious sense of being workers, and on the other hand how many of them just live uncomprehending of the meaning of the term and why do they live in this way? The answers to these questions will contain few scientifically reliable facts, they will frequently be biassed by an over-generalization of personal observations, and consequently they may be illusory and disappointing.

Ferenc Erdei referred to these problems in one of his writings: "One should think over the fact that more than two decades after the beginning of our socialist industrialization we have more, and more reliable, data on agriculture and the peasantry than about industry and the working class"[1]. This in spite of the fact that by the beginning of the 1970's already 44.1 per cent of those employed worked in industry and in the building industry, and only 25.6 per cent in agriculture. Industrial workers constitute the biggest class in Hungarian society today, even numerically.

Sociologists usually agree that the working class is not a homogeneous

Miklós Szántó's essay as well as Ágnes Simonyi's article were first published in *Társadalmi Szemle*, the theoretical monthly of the Hungarian Socialist Workers' Party (July, 1973)

[1] Ferenc Erdei: *Város és vidéke*. (A town and its country). Szépirodalmi Kiadó, 1971. p. 133.

interests so require. The role of the foreign partner cannot go beyond contributing to recognizing jointly—in the course of examining the common tasks or objectives—that the given task cannot be carried out rationally with the existing economic organizational forms. It may also happen that a new organizational form turns out to be more advantageous for both parties than the existing one.

5. And finally let us not forget that efficient economic cooperation between East and West is necessary also in connection with the growth of the developing countries. I have outlined their expected position. It is evident that a world system consisting of contradictory and confronting elements, yet trying to achieve a relative equilibrium, will earn the confidence of only such countries the development progress and comparative political consolidation of which seem to be guaranteed. Otherwise we shall have to face regular and organized or amorphous and anarchic endeavours directed towards upsetting the equilibrium. This is why I think that in the present period, at a time of détente, we must apply intensive research energies to find out where and how we can jointly act to the benefit of developing countries. In other words: cooperation between the two blocs, between East and West, designed to maintain the world system in a state of equilibrium, and to promote the direct economic interests of the parties, must not act to the detriment of others and should be carried on to the benefit of the developing countries. If not, the equilibrium of the "world system" will become unsteady, and East-West relations will also suffer. At any rate a "world system" should be conceived as relying mainly on the responsibility and policies of the existing power centres, but also on serving the interests of countries the populations of which do not as yet live under conditions required, and made possible by twentieth-century developments. It is perhaps still possible today to act rationally in this respect, by tomorrow feelings, measures, passions and coercions might well accumulate to make this impossible.

It will have become clear from the foregoing that I regard East-West economic cooperation as a decisive component and precondition of the present world system and—after a successful and far-sighted solution of the fundamental bilateral problems—this cooperation will have to make an impact on the rest of the world. This is the only way in which certain threatening dangers can be averted by rational human action.

social unit, but is stratified. The various strata can be distinguished from one another in part on the basis of their way of life, in other words by the pattern of their essential and habitual activities, and the duration, time-balance and instruments of these activities.

A recent survey, in 1970, concerned itself with the structure of the week-end activities of the gainfully employed urban industrial workers. One of the analyses broke down the data by training and qualifications of manual workers, that is skilled, semi-skilled and unskilled groups. Because of the natural limitations of the method used, this present study, which relies on this investigation, cannot undertake to deal with many aspects of the questions which arise in connection with the style of life of workers, but can, on the other hand, make certain points.

My approach to defining the way, mode, or style of life was as "a specific structure of recurrent essential activities". (Other sociologists are also pretty close to this concept. Ágnes Losonczi, for instance, writes: "The style of life of people is based on an entire system of human activities. Apart from, or independent of, activity systems, it is impossible to examine any style of life."[2] Zsuzsa Ferge also starts from the premise that the style of life includes "activity carried on (or occurring) within a given framework, in other words it presupposes the goals for which the individual uses the framework available[3], the latter including the objective conditions and circumstances, personal conditions and social relations.)

The major growth of the Hungarian working class took place in the last twenty-five years or so, during a comparatively short period. The main source of its increase was the peasantry. The peasants who chose plants instead of their plots of land took the approach, the feelings, attitudes and customs of the villager to the factory with them. This antagonistic combination of the old mode of life and the new elements still exists. The new socialist working-class had to be "trained at an abbreviated course", to represent the future in the present as it was exercising power, and to get rid of some of the deeply engraved marks of the past. This was a difficult process.

The working-class style of life has altered in recent decades. The conditions and circumstances of living have changed, the living standard has gone up, the structure of consumption has become modified, and in consequence the means, the system of instruments, are now different. All this has been determinative in changing the frequency of different activities,

---

[2] Ágnes Losonczi: *Életmód és társadalmi változások* (Style of Life and Social Changes). Szociológia. 1972 No. 2, p. 175.

[3] Zsuzsa Ferge: *Társadalmunk rétegeződése* (The Stratification of our Society). Közgazdasági és Jogi Könyvkiadó p. 250.

their ranking and their duration. The institution of free Saturdays every other week in most of industry has changed the pattern of working hours established after the Liberation, and has increased the time at the disposal of the workers, giving them more time outside productive work.

MULTI-STEP MIGRATION

The special features of the present working-class life style cannot be understood without analysing the historical process of becoming workers. The present social structure in Hungary is a result of, and a station in, the changes of the recent past, especially of vigorous industrialization. The collectivization of agriculture—as a social change of major importance—itself speeded up the process of peasants changing into workers on a mass scale. What were these changes like? The majority turned into industrial workers and at the same time town dwellers through a "multi-step migration".[4]

Multi-step migration means in effect that tens of thousands of semi-skilled and unskilled workers accepted at first the transitory existence of living in a workers' hostel or in lodgings, or paying for no more than the use of a bed for a certain number of hours, in the hope of eventually being allocated a flat or building a home of their own in the cities. This took long years of strenuous effort. The new workers up from the village had to quickly master a great many things: to adjust themselves to conditions at their place of work, to get to know new people while away from the social ties of the old community—of the village and the family—which had both protected and restricted them. A feeling of loneliness and isolation, of being lost in the teeming city crowds, had to be overcome. Depending on the educational background, and the age at which the move took place on whether they came from a well-to-do or a landless family, and finally, on the luck or otherwise attending reception, there were countless individual variations, but with a familiar repetition of the basic patterns. The new life was built on the experiences of the old, utilizing and adapting these; renewal was based on preservation. There are many signs that passing over into the working class is a process—and a way of living—filled with tensions and conflicts.

4 The extent and frequency of commuting is still considerable showing that migration is still going on, largely since the cities have been unable to absorb and house these masses on the move. For reasons which cannot be discussed here, the infra-structure has not kept abreast with these rapid changes in occupation and location of employment.

OLD ATTITUDES IN A NEW SITUATION

The mass-scale of re-stratification had as a consequence that the peasants turning into workers took it for granted that the channels leading to the new life would be constantly open. The tensions between the new conditions, the industrial skills and the industrial human context on the one hand, and the earlier rhythm of life, the experiences of farm work, and the links of the village community on the other, keep recurring daily for many a long year, for the new situation has not yet bred the attitudes and behaviour it requires. The starting differences at entry into the working class between the sons and daughters of urban artisan or worker families, and people with a village background, are very great. The former have a much better chance of making a more advantageous occupational choice, and of getting into a more favourable trade, obtaining a better job.

Once we examine the structure according to qualifications, we find that half of the present workers, and within this one third of the skilled, more than half of the semi-skilled and more than two thirds of the unskilled workers are of peasant origin. The flow, as I said, depends on a multi-step process and hence is not closed, for a large percentage start as unskilled workers and become semi-skilled operators, possibly training to become skilled. Looking at the problem from the trade and occupational end we see that the proportion of workers with a rural background is very high in mining, in the foundries and in the building industry, in other words in those industries where performance requires more than average physical effort, where qualifications are also relatively easier to come by, and where there are a great many semi-skilled and unskilled workers.

Sociologists have attempted to examine the effect of the social position of the parents—including their financial and material position and the educational background of the father—on the present-life-style of workers. The past follows people for many generations, people who have grown up under sound conditions and in a healthy and well-established home in the city need not overcome the resistance of the new medium and so the same efforts on their part go further than those of others who start from a more difficult position. The latter have to do their utmost to accomplish what the former do easily. The burdens of the past play a part also in the time of adjustment and the cost of sacrifices it takes to drive down roots in the city and the factory, they determine with what school and vocational attainments the "changeling" embarks on the daily life of workers.

1971 figures show that of Hungary's gainfully employed (to be sure, the rate of development is fast) 38.7 per cent have not completed the eight grades of the compulsory general school, 42.2 per cent are general-school and 13.8 per cent secondary-school graduates. The vast majority of those with low schooling are commuters from the villages. The restraining force of the peasant past comes out in bold relief against the fact that some 85 to 90 per cent of the Budapest precision fitters and turners—who in their majority spring from the urban working class—have completed the first eight grades, whereas only 45 per cent of the foundry workers and smiths working in the capital, most of them are of peasant origin, have done so.

Just about every sociological work on the life of workers emphasizes the serious problem of unskilled workers and enumerates a long list of discouraging examples telling of the consequences of long-distance commuting. Both categories consist overwhelmingly of village people. The commuting worker who lives in a village is in the majority of cases doing double-duty. For him his rural residence is no "garden city" chosen for the sake of the fresh air in preference to the noisy and smoke-ridden "factory district", it is an agricultural place of work with a secondary occupation and an income to supplement his wages. The commuter is—both in fact and symbolically— on the move between the factory and agriculture, between the village and town, and he seems to have become arrested at the half-way mark. This is certainly a factor that has some bearing on his life style.

THE CHANGING RHYTHM OF MOBILITY

I cannot agree, however, with those who regard the multiple and long-term effects of mobility as some kind of destiny affecting the generations to come. Participation in the division of labour, the nature of the work performed, is basic and determinative in regard to one's life style. The length of time spent in production and the conditions of this engagement—for instance, the shifts worked—the intensity of work and one's attitude to work, one's identification or non-identification with the job to be done, the degree to which expectations in regard to work are fulfilled, the fatigue caused by work, the income derived from it, the possession of the skills and education required for coping with the tasks on the job, or the prestige of one's post, are all factors which influence one's activities outside work. In the final analysis it is one's place in the division of labour that determines one's way of life, that provides the setting and the scope of movement, which leads to the development of various types of life-styles—various even within the given setting. The place in the division of labour is only the final determinator. Great differences are possible within the strata structured according to the place filled in the division of labour. Two men may be working next to each other in the same factory, doing the same job and using the same means of production, and nonetheless their life-styles may be widely divergent. There are great differences in culture due to differences in family background, schooling, perhaps educational stimulation by worthwhile company, or simply the existence or absence of personal aptitudes or interests.

By the 1970's, the majority of the young members of the Hungarian working class were born in urban areas and are the children of workers. The present generation of older workers—now around 50—who have always been workers, lived the larger part of their adult life after the Liberation. But not even industrial workers who started their working life in industry, and spent their childhood in towns, all have the same life-style.

The development of socialist agriculture with large-scale cooperatives with subsidiary industrial workshop has increased the demand for skilled workers in the villages. For reasons inherent in production, for technical reasons and under the impact of demographic factors as well, mobility has slowed down. It has slowed down, but the village is still nonetheless, distinctly under the spell of the attraction of lighter work and defined working hours—which actually presuppose some regular leisure. The city has the appeal of its colourful variety, wider supply of different forms of entertainment and, last but not least, it has the lure of the freedom it offers from constant control by the family and village environment. At the same time a partially opposed effect is exerted by the large demand for manpower which also appears on the part of the agricultural enterprises. Likewise it acts as a repellent for young people who have recently moved from village to town that, as a regrettable behaviour pattern established during long years of manpower surplus, the difficulties of the process of adaptation are still often underestimated and the need for facilitating this process is still largely ignored. This is one reason why "migrating birds" and the "man without roots" are such frequent types among the new industrial working class.

In the first twenty years after the Liberation, practically all social strata were present in the majority of families and consequently socially heterogeneous families became so wide-spread as to be typical, in the course of the past ten years however the slowing down of mobility has contributed to a change and the newer sociological conditions both in the family and in urban society indicate a tendency toward greater social homogeneity.

The Economic Conditions

Now, starting with what we know about the characteristic features of mobility, let us examine the elements in various life-styles, and the trends in consumer demand and requirements. If we wish to sketch the present level of the Hungarian workers' economic position, we can say that, for the majority, requirements are satisfied at an intermediary level. Without overestimating the achievements of the past ten years, one could say that we have risen to a higher, qualitatively different, standard of consumption where the vast majority of the population are able to satisfy their basic requirements. This stage has been attained in a relatively short time despite the grave heritage of the past. What are the characteristic features of this stage?

1) Housing stands highest among the indices. We found in our survey that for 40 per cent of the urban workers housing remains a central problem despite the fact that recent years have brought considerable improvements in the situation.

2) The differences in income, sharp in the past, have become. mitigated. The differences have become smaller, and the levelling process has continued. The differences in content and quality are, however, there, chiefly in housing conditions, the consumption pattern and cultural requirements. There is still a relatively broad section of the population which, partly because of their low income level, or the irregularity of their incomes, where there is only one earner in the household for instance, because of the housing situation, or because of the low standard of requirements in other fields is still far from prosperity and spends almost the whole of its income on food.

3) As a rule, however, the sums spent on food are to make up a decreasing proportion of family expenditures.

4) The market has become saturated with durable consumer goods which were in such heavy demand in the 1950's such as cooking ranges, radios or motorcycles. Mass consumption has recently shifted to refrigerators, television sets, washing machines and cars. These offer different possibilities in the mode of life, and pose new problems and create a new situation. The question "how will we carry on, whither now?" has acquired added weight. The general rise in prosperity has accelerated, particularly in the last five years. Together with this the difference between those in an intermediary and unfavourable situation has increased, .leading to a sense of discouragement among families where life is tough. Unequal development is apparent not only between various strata, but also regionally. There are areas of the

country which have fallen behind the national average because of bad roads and the absence of public utilities.

5) Instalment-plan buying through credit and loans from the National Savings Bank is widely practiced.

6) The increase in cultural expenditure lags behind the increase in incomes. The cultural gap has widened between professional people and the workers, as well as between urban dwellers and villagers. With the mass spread of television the number of theatre and cinema tickets sold has decreased, and the number of books bought is increasing only slightly. Requirements concomitant with urbanization are fast growing, but cultural and human requirements, and the demand for education, are not growing proportionately despite the fact that the prices of cultural commodities have not gone up significantly. All cultural services are still relatively cheap in Hungary.

CHANGES AFTER THE REDUCTION OF WORKING HOURS

In the 1960's the length of working hours was pinpointed as one of the chief problems. As Marx argued in *Outlines of the Critique of Political Economy* a nation is truly rich if working hours are reduced from twelve to six. Wealth is not command over surplus working hours, but the time that remains at one's disposal, apart from the time that has to be expended by all individuals and society as a whole.

The Ninth Congress of the Hungarian Socialist Workers' Party dealt with the problem. Analyses showed that conditions had become ripe for reducing working hours in Hungary. The resolution of the Congress stated that weekly working hours in industry were to be reduced to 44 by the end of 1970. On this basis the Government gradually but steadily introduced free Saturdays every other week. Individual plants and companies have to make their own arrangements.

Our investigation has already been able to study and analyse the effects and consequences of the measure. Leisure during the working week has not changed as a result of the measure; it still remains scarce and scattered. Only at week-ends, when a lot of time is available in a single "block", is there ample room for activity. Data indicate that the transformation of the mode of life has started only very slowly.

There are three fairly distinct patterns of week-end activities among the workers:

1) The structure of activities remains what it was before the introduc-

tion of free Saturdays. The families in this group are not making anything of the improved opportunities, but enjoy the fact that they are not so much under pressure, that housework need not be done in such a hurry and with such a sense of strain. About 20 per cent of the industrial workers surveyed belong to this group, unskilled women workers, 37 per cent of whom still complain of an overload of work at home, being the most heavily represented.

2) Sixty per cent of working women in all categories of training or skill —and 40 per cent of the men—do the housework that has accumulated during the week on Saturday, leaving them one genuine day of rest, Sunday.

3) One quarter of the industrial workers, mostly the young and educated, enjoy a longer one-and-a-half or two-day week-end when they have Saturday off. Families in the higher income groups who posses a car or motorcycle belong to this category almost without exception.

There are four factors which are determinative in the utilization of the possibilities offered by free Saturdays: sex, age, cultural level, and car ownership. The utilization of leisure time depends largely on whether the families in question dispose of the means required for cultural activity. The big change is marked by the spread of car and week-end cottage ownership. In the case of families which have solved their housing problems, the acquisition of these means is under way or is planned next and determines their consumption patterns. The possibilities are, however, unequal, and the conditions of satisfying these requirements are different for various strata.

Although working hours were not reduced, and time resources did not alter, until the end of the 1960's, certain changes in the use of leisure became noticeable already early on in that decade. The available time resources were being re-adjusted. This was a change for which television was largely responsible. At the beginning of the '60's there were very few homes equipped with a TV set, its purchase was not feasible below a family income of less than 1,000–1,200 forints per capita. The advance in this sphere was exceptionally fast; instalment-plan buying and the increase in purchasing power have made it possible for people to give precedence to the purchase of TV sets ahead of just about every kind of household equipment in all areas of the country where TV reception is good. The appearance of this device changed the leisure activities of people, and to some extent their entire way of life. With the spread of TV, families changed their habits, and the proportion of time allotted to different activities altered. Life became transformed and adjusted to the set.

Early in the '60's the cinema was the most frequently used means of mass culture. People went to the movies once or twice a week, and spent about four or five hours a week there. By the end of the decade, visits to the cinema became much less frequent, and watching the telly became the most widely-practiced and most time-consuming activity of the masses. The average family devotes from two to four hours a day and 12 to 18 hours a week to this new pastime.[5]

Extra Work for Extra Money

Extra work and subsidiary activities are widely undertaken by a growing proportion of working people, especially married men with families, and among them above all those whose training and skills are widely sought after in some of the hard-to-secure trades and services. According to our survey 18 per cent of the men who are skilled workers take on regular or occasional subsidiary work to supplement their incomes. For two thirds this extra work is not of a regular nature but consists of odd jobs. Subsidiary money-earning activity is much more frequent for people in Budapest than for those living in the country. It is most probable, of course, that the actual proportion of those who take on extra work, especially in the form of odd jobs, is much higher than reflected in our data. That this is a "touchy" question is indicated by the fact that a relatively large proportion of the subjects abstained from answering it. Forty per cent of those answering the question indicated that the lowness of their income, 30 per cent that the interesting nature of the extra work available, and 25 per cent that a temporary shortage of money, motivated them in accepting subsidiary work. When they were questioned in greater detail, many of those who had given financial difficulties as their reason explained that they had wanted to purchase something and had to obtain the money needed through extra work.

Some sociologists argue that people whose working hours have been reduced do not regard leisure as something of "value", and that is why so many of them spend the extra hours regularly or occasionally in money-making activity. In my view it is wrong to regard this simply as a sign that people have no demand for free time or underestimate its value. It is probably the other way around. The wish to satisfy their rapidly increasing material requirements is a strong drive and they are often persuaded to give up their extra leisure in oder to acquire, through extra work the means for

5 The "housing-estate style of life", which manifests itself in just about the same way in every Hungarian town, is also connected with this new dominant role of television. This mode of life develops under the impact of the interaction of several factors. What is typical is that people go out a lot less and spend more of their leisure in their own homes.

spending week-end leisure under better cinrcumstances. Thus it is wrong to jump to the conclusion that this sudden spurt of interest in extra work deserves condemnation. One must not judge before one knows the full picture. The socio-economic factors which work for the increase in second jobs or other extra-job paying activities can be summarized on the basis of our survey as follows:

1) The distribution of participants according to occupation, sex, age and family status indicates that family-men between 25 to 50 prefer to take on subsidiary jobs in every category, and the ratio increases directly with the demand for the skill the man in question happens to have.

2) This demand is expressed in the fact that the wages paid for extra work are considerably higher, since the shortage of manpower keeps the level of wages high, especially in the field of services.

3) Consumer demands grow fast, purchasing power does not grow in proportion, and the tension developing between the two makes people do what they can to attain the level they regard as desirable by overtime, second jobs, and regular or occasional extra work.

Apart from the economic factors in a narrower sense, other subjective factors also play a part:

4) Extra work outside of one's job at the factories enterprises and companies is less regulated by discipline; usually the person performing it chooses the place and time of doing it himself.

5) The more "voluntary" nature of this work is moreover indicated by the fact that a relatively large number of people justify such subsidiary activity by saying it is more interesting.

CULTURE AND ADULT-EDUCATION

Extra leisure become an obvious value if it can be "turned to good account", if the means, like TV, radio, a car or a plot of land, exist for its utilization, or if one has at one's disposal sufficient "free" cash that can be spent on culture. It is of value if the free Saturday is available for a housewife to cope with accumulated housework, and for certain groups of people for engaging in paying subsidiary activities. The required and adequate quantity of means and of the income are relative and not absolute levels. There is no direct linear interrelationship between living standards and the frequency, meaningfulness and wealth of educational and cultural activities. Financial success is often combined with an absence of intellectual wants. The prices of cultural services are relatively low, books, cinema seats, etc.

are inexpensive. Thanks to the high state subsidies, even people in the low-income brackets can afford high-standard culture if they want it, if the demand is there, and its satisfaction has become one of the requirements of life, that is a habitual pattern of life. But a threshold does exist: a certain part of the income has to be available for allocation to this purpose, and some free hours are necessary. Without this spare time is a gift without any use. And this is not merely a matter of promoting culture, it is not only a shortcoming of education, nor simply a problem of cultural standards, but also a question of means, of institutions, a range of choice and the ability to choose all of them together and at the same time.

A significant proportion of working people still do not regard a gain in leisure as a rise in their living standards. They appreciate only changes that can be turned into cash, such as wage increases and price reductions.

A double trend is the most characteristic of the process of acculturation. With the general increase in schooling and specialized qualifications education is becoming more democratic and the differences between the different sections of the population are reduced. On the other hand, new inequalities are developing on new foundations, inequalities which are at cross-purposes with the above process. Educational differences are increasing between working women with small children and their husbands. A similar polarization can be observed between the urban workers and commuters from the village, and between the skilled and unskilled workers.

If apart from school attainments we also examine indices of culture in the family, the characteristics of their mode of life and the periods of time spent in various types of activity, and the educational level, it will be evident that the majority of Hungarian earners are gaining in culture. This is an achievement of which we have every reason to be proud. Still, a fairly large stratum cannot keep abreast of the majority and falls behind, with the gap continuing to widen. Although schools and all the vocational courses are wide open to the working masses, and millions avail themselves of the new opportunities, we should be aware of the fact, for instance, that some two million adults in Hungary have not completed to date the eight grades of general school.

The question is to what extent the various strata avail themselves of existing opportunities. Considering the requirements for the intensive development of the economy, one cannot be satisfied, particularly not if one examines the extent, depth and speed of the acculturation process. The general decrease in the demand for vocational courses, the drop-out rate at the workers' schools, and the large number of people who have not completed the eight grades of general school are all problems.

The level of vocational qualifications and skills of the labour force seems to become opposed to the concrete requirements of the places of employment. Throughout the country there is a national manpower shortage, and yet there is redundancy within the individual companies. It still holds that hanging on to redundant personnel seems "more economical" than rational technical development. There are many places where the management does not demand, and does not support, the training and further training of skilled workers, for they consider the vocational level of their personnel adequate for present requirements.

THE CRITERIA OF DIFFERENTIATION

Depending on what people spend money on, what activities they spend their time on and what these acquisitions and pastimes mean to them, what they choose of the opportunities and the value system that stimulates their decisions, a variety of life-styles develop, each characteristic of a stratum or group. The different strata of society are expressions of different life styles, but then these forms of behaviour act upon each other. Some consumption patterns and models of behaviour appear to other groups as examples worth following or deserving rejection. Consequently, the question is not simply what types of working class life appear today in our society, but also what is the direction of any change, and from where working people choose the desirable models for living.

We live in a society in transition, we are going ahead on the road of socialist construction toward an advanced socialist society. In this period of transition there are many shades blending into each other without distinct boundary lines—without any "pure" types. The ideals of life-styles are varied, periods of different evaluation systems follow on one another in quick succession. In the last twenty-eight years employment opportunities, and with them the values of different qualifications, changed practically at five- or seven-yearly intervals, incomes and material standards rose, and with these rises the consumption pattern became modified, the chances of restratification improved. The changes in life-style follow the economic, social and political changes more slowly, with many different transmissions, and transformed by a variety of effects.

We are at the stage of research: many attempts are being made to categorize in different types the life-styles of workers, but, for lack of sufficient experimental evidence, these still have not—and could not have—led to reliable results. We are aware of the fact that the patterns of life of Hungarian workers—the structure of the activities they regularly perform—are strongly differentiated, but at present we are as yet unable to define the criteria of the differentiation and cannot sketch the "types" on this basis.

Nonetheless, in order to suggest the historical changes, it would be worthwhile to examine—though not in detail—how the types of workers' life-styles—each of which was more or less typical of a stratum of workers—have altered, which of them continue to exist and with what modifications, or rather what new forms of attitudes and behaviour, and modes of life we see today. Instead of portraying strictly distinct types, I wish to indicate merely certain characteristics of some of the existing types, which generally blend into each other.

PATTERNS OF LIFE-STYLES

The late Péter Veres, the writer, a few years ago posed the question why the sort of educated worker committed to the movement and hungry for culture and improvement, has been less frequently seen since the victory of the working class. In an article that stimulated discussion, he wrote that the consciousness of "historical presence" and commitment to community service—features which used to be characteristic of the organized workers of Hungary—are no longer sufficiently prevalent. The life of the stratum of workers he speaks about in these words—a small section of society before the Liberation—was then a continuous "emergency situation", the movement gave them the only way of life and only venue of activity, and education was for them a weapon in the service of the movement and at the same time intellectual drill for the future.

Today the composition of those active in the movement is different; their life-styles are different and so are their possibilities of activity within the working class. The role of education as a means to an end has also altered for them: now they need differently structured knowledge, knowledge in which the emphasis has shifted to vocational and technical fields. The mass of workers who are consciously active are however much larger in number today than ever before in the course of Hungarian history.

Formerly, the urban skilled worker of working-class origin, often succeeding his father in the trade, the kind who loved his job and was a perfectionist in it, but stayed outside the movement, was a very valuable type of the Hungarian working class. His consciousness as a worker was based on his vocational skill and performance. This type is still present in Hungarian industry, in fact a large proportion of working group leaders and

4*

foremen belong to it, and the members of this stratum are there in the socialist brigades and among the work-place veterans. Their pattern of life is characterized by solid reliability, and a steady family background; they save money, they fit out their homes, and usually they want their children to rise to professional technical occupations. This stratum which can today no longer be sharply distinguished by its activities in the movement, is supplemented by skilled workers of peasant origin who, as a result of processes taking place in the past twenty years, make up very high numbers.

The people who have come up to town from a village long for security both at their places of work and in the urban environment, they have no "world-shaking" ambitions. In recent years they have gained a great deal materially, having satisfied their basic requirements, but the younger age-groups among them have difficult housing problems, perhaps even more so than other types of workers. They want to lay down roots, to gain a footing in the working class. Above the age of forty their style of life is conventional, often conservative. In the case of the men the extra-work activities are largely concentrated in the home. The life of working housewives with children is difficult in this group, after housework they are glad if they can manage some TV watching. Their children are generally semi-skilled and skilled workers who have graduated from primary school and—more recently—have often completed secondary school as well.

Obviously—for their presence derives from our present stage of development—there are still commuter-workers. The majority have a consistent ambition to "get settled", that is to get a satisfactory job close to their home or to become townspeople. Many of them are semi-skilled or un-skilled, their roots in the trade are not deep and they rarely develop a sense of identity with their work. "Wage-earner consciousness" is the most wide-spread among them, they work hard in the pursuit of money and the prestige of money is very high with them. Although the other types are also "setting up house" materially, the commuters are probably even more consumption oriented, they are obsessed with buying things, building homes, decorating their houses, and go in for such prosperity symbols as a heavy wrought iron front fence, etc. Long travel and farm work at home often cause special problems in their lives, they often drop out of education and cultural activities or life in the movement.

In the period before the Liberation a characteristic type was the industrial worker who regarded employment in a factory only a transitional phase and was constantly preparing to become "independent" to set up his own shop. In critical times he was likely to go bankrupt and to return to the factory. A similar mentality, though springing from very different socio-economic conditions, can still be observed among vocationally well-trained and chiefly young workers. Workers at the subsidiary industrial-type plants of the cooperatives and workers in the service industries often come from this group. A large percentage of people in jobs which are in great demand in the servicing industries, such as electricians, fitters and mechanics, and radio and television technicians, do repair and maintenance work for a wide circle of friends and acquaintances, many of them take on second jobs and entertain hopes of changing over to small-scale industry. Ostentatious purchases are frequent in this stratum, many of them like to follow the consumption and behaviour patterns they see among leading professional people, the pursuit of "status symbols."

The type of declassed workers—formerly independent artisans, office employees, etc.—has disappeared by now. There is, however, a type of worker today which deserves special attention, a type which did not slide down on the social scale but still considers himself or herself as "demoted". These are the young people who aspired to become graduates but did not make the grade at the university entrance examinations, found a job in industry and since then consider themselves passed over. One can read about young unskilled workers who will refuse skilled work for which they are qualified because that would be something final, the acknowledgement of the end of their ambitions. So they prefer to continue doing heavy manual work for the sake of the illusion of being in a transitional phase. An interesting subcategory is the worker from whom the job means only "earning money", and who prefers to put almost all his efforts into his extra-work hobby.

There are even today lumpen elements, "migrating birds", alcoholics and vagabonds. The group consists largely of unschooled rural young people who stay at workers' hostels. In a certain sense representatives of some trades enjoying a boom—chiefly in the building industry—men and women who make good money, but can make no effective use of their incomes, are of low education and culture and without ambitions, people who by-pass the opportunities inherent in their position, who stick in the mud, and get their fulfilment from drinking bouts and aping an attitude of "proletarian gentry", belong to this group.

Even this brief outline should make it clear that the changed living and behavioural patterns of workers show some very positive and also some negative elements which reflect subjective traits and aptitudes, and at the same time the effects of present social and economic conditions that are still partly rooted in the past.

*

There are many problems apart from the welcome facts of development. Further extensive and detailed research is needed, but the tasks are already evident. The Party has put the need to examine the position of the working class on the agenda and concrete measures have been taken to improve their living standards and to strengthen their leading role. The analytical studies and the resulting plans for the improvement of the school system and for raising the level of general culture will, no doubt, make their effects felt in the growth of self-awareness as a force in society. Obviously the sums "invested in people" have to be increased, the prestige of education and vocational qualifications have to be made greater, the sense of community has to be developed and the hegemony of the socialist system of values has to be ensured. This is, of course, not envisaged as some kind of wizardry, but is something that should be done by the logic of the matter as expressed in interests which have a compulsive force which workers recognize and grow to respect and which therefore motivate their activities. There is need to expand and enrich the range of choice and the ability to choose, or—to use Brecht's words—"the terrible temptation of the good."

II. HOW DO WORKERS LIVE?

Interviews with Twelve Workers

by

ÁGNES SIMONYI

The question formulated in the title comes up almost daily today. Realistic ideas, extreme views and illusions clash in discussions on various aspects of the problem. In fact there is little scientifically reliable information to provide a concrete and comprehensive answer today, as this is pointed out by Miklós Szántó in his The Workers' Changing Life on p. 38 of this issue.

It was considered a good idea to ask those concerned themselves, in order to supplement and make more plastic the available information and to raise additional ideas—though certainly not to provide the missing facts. Their responses do not, and cannot, offer a complete picture of the life of Hungarian workers today. Subjects were picked at random since there was no adequate scientific basis for a representative sample. Of course, what could be done was done to collect the answers from various types of people, from men and women, from young and old, those whose legal domicile is Budapest as well as from lodgers at workers' hostels, from skilled and semi-skilled workers, etc. and from those working in a number of different industries. One of the considerations governing selection was to interview in the first place members of the Hungarian Socialist Workers' Party, but not them alone. Questions referred above all to non-industrial activities, that is the extra-job activities, of workers and the conditions of these activities. The replies—of which twelve are here published—are from employees at the Csepel Iron and Metal Works, the Láng Engineering Works, the Taurus Rubber Company, the Budapest Hosiery Factory, the Budapest Housing Construction Enterprise, and the Contractors for Public Buildings.

*

Mrs. Gy. J., 41, machine knitter. She has been working at the Budapest Hosiery Factory since she was 15. Her husband is an electrician who works for a glass-trade cooperative. She has a daughter of 16 at secondary school who would like to become a teacher. The family was allotted a one-and-a half-room apartment at the Lágymányos housing estate in 1957. She and her husband make about the same amount of money, 6,000 forints a month between them.

I am in charge of a brigade, mine is the outstanding one of the factory, and in addition I am the workshop Party secretary. This means a lot of extra work, but I like doing it because I am glad to be able to do something for others. I joined the Party once again in 1971, I had been a member before 1956 as well, but when the Party was reorganized, I became pregnant, and later I could not do any voluntary work because of the baby. I am sorry about the lost years, otherwise I would be a Party veteran by now. My husband is not a Party member. Their shop is a small co-op, there things are not so well organized. I would like it better if he worked in large-scale industry, but he makes better money where he is.

I stay back at the factory after working hours almost every day I've got to attend conferences, or look after the brigade's business, and I am also Madame Chair of the Council of Socialist Brigade Leaders. Since last year, I regularly get invited to the meetings of the management council, which is very important since there I hear about all the problems of the factory as a whole, and I can give concrete replies to the women working with me, why the quality is poor, or why there is no yarn, and why the bonus is not as big as we would like it to be.

In addition I am still attending school, the seventh grade now. I feel a bit ashamed for doing schoolwork with a hoary head, nor do I know I shall manage, for the family are spoilt. Up to now I did not insist they help at home, but now the factory puts great stress on the socialist brigade leaders having at least completed the eight grades of General School. I read a lot, and I plunged into it all with great keenness, but am afraid of maths. The school takes up five hours a day, four days a week. When I am on the afternoon shift, I can't go, when I work at night, I give up some of my sleep, and when I am on the morning shift, I spend the whole afternoon at school. At times like that I do the cooking after school, otherwise in the afternoon, but I cook everyday, without fail. When I am on the afternoon shift, I can do a lot before going to work. Then I come to the factory rather tired, but otherwise I feel better knowing that everything is allright at home.

We women like to work alternating shifts even though it is more tiring. At least I can do the laundry and some ironing on Saturdays. I arrange my work at home, to give me some time to watch TV at nights. I am very fond of This Week, of Twenty Questions, of films and of Forum.

Sunday afternoons are free. About twice a month I meet my girl-friend, with whom I work in the knitting hall. She is the Party secretary of the local organization. We talk over the problems at the factory. Our husbands don't really like it. On Sunday afternoons we go to the cinema, take a walk or visit a museum. Once a month, when we can manage, we go to the theatre. I love to read, and am especially fond of serious books. I own the entire series of the Masterpieces of World Literature. Sometimes I think I would prefer never going anywhere, just reading. I read the papers, too.

Népszava (a daily), *Nők Lapja* (Women's Journal) and sometimes *Ország-Világ* and *Tükör* (weekly magazines).

For our summer holidays we usually go to Rumania, to my in-laws. There we go to see the sights and make excursions. We plan to do this again this year. Though right now my brigade won a six-day trip to the Soviet Union at a quiz about the country. I was there already last year with the Friendship Express. When I came home, I was really touched because my brigade proposed to work a Sunday shift without pay for Vietnam even though I had been away.

*

J. M. is 28. He started to work at the age of 14 at the Machine-Tool Plant of the Csepel Iron and Metal Works. Three years ago he graduated from the Engineering Industrial School, he makes 18.60, the highest possible hourly wage (17.80 + 0.80 technician's supplement). He has been a member of the Party since 1966. He lives with his mother and his step-father, still an active worker, at Csepel, in a room and kitchen dwelling already earmarked for demolition.

It is my definite intention to continue my studies. I have reached a certain point, and now I want to relax a little.

This should give me the opportunity to decide what I really want to do. I won't go to university, it is too late for that and it takes too much out of you. I would like to study languages or perhaps enrol in a technical college. Here in the factory I prefer to continue working as a manual worker. I did have the opportunity to become a technician, but I feel I don't have the proper professional knowledge as yet and I would not like to be a bad executive. At any rate it would hardly be wise to leave now. We are getting a lot of new machines, and the new technology is something that one ought to learn at the work-bench. When I completed technical secondary school, I could have become a coordinator or technician for 2,600 forints a month. In this way, I think, I am better off—not only financially, but I also feel I am contributing more. This gives you a certain sense of self-assurance, and you feel you can speak out if you don't like something.

My working-hours are from 6:30 a.m. to 3 p.m. Twice or three times a week there is something on at the factory, some kind of political or volunteer work. Then I get home only later. I belong to the Party Committee of the Machine-Tool Works and I joined the Workers' Militia last year as well.

By the time I get home, dinner is ready, I eat, and I read the paper— *Népszabadság*. I consider *Magyarország* the most valuable journal, and I usually also buy *Új Írás* and *Világosság*. I read what are called the fashionable books, most recently I read *Le Papillon*, and now I am reading *L'Étranger* and *La Chute*.

I give my mother a thousand forints a fortnight as my contribution to household expenses, and I spend the rest of my money on having fun and travel. I have been to Rumania, the Soviet Union, and Finland. This year I would like to go to Bulgaria. I own a motorbike, I use it for getting around Hungary. It will take something really serious to make me give up the way I live now, not owing an explanation for anything. That is something one will give up for a really meaningful relationship only. You need a financial and moral basis for marriage. I like being in love, but marriage is something different. There are a lot of bad examples which can often be traced back, of course, to financial causes. I won't marry for love, for that passes after a while. I have been keeping company with a girl. She is a meteorologist, she lives in my friend's place. I get a sense of satisfaction out of being accepted as an equal by a girl who has "a higher position in life" than me. Perhaps I will get married. I would like to live in a way that neither of us violates human freedom, that both of us respect each other's plans.

I like to visit clubs, the clubs of the Central Institute of Physics Research, the Ministry of Finance, and the Technical University. I try to meet people who have something new to tell me. I go along to the Workers' Reading Club of Csepel, where workers who write novels, short stories and poetry go.

When I have some free time, I draw from the model. I used to attend sketching clubs, but the various "-isms" get on my goat. One would like to be oneself and save oneself from bad impressions, and for this reason I am reluctant about these groups. What I'd like to say is starting to coalesce in my mind. But until I have enough to say, I don't want to grapple with the brush. If I could only paint the tension vibrating at the plant, that would be something, and I have not seen that done by any painter.

I love to roam over the city's streets. I stop when I like ad spend half-hours watching people, concentrating on their faces, on the way they walk. People would like something to happen to them, and I watch those who are waiting for something to happen.

*

Mrs. L. H. is 37, and a semi-skilled worker at the Budapest Hosiery Factory. She makes 2,000 forints, her husband, 2,300. They have two sons, 14 and 13, and they live in a two-room apartment at the Óbuda housing project.

We have arguments with my husband, chiefly on account of money. He has said what he wants, and I can clearly see what we can afford. There were times when we kept our money apart since he would not believe that so much would stretch only so far. To give an example: he would like to go away somewhere for our summer holydays every year. Of course, it would do the family a world of good, we could indeed do with it, but how can one manage? Last year he managed to get us fixed up for Bakonybél, that was cheap. There was no need to spend on extras as you do on the Balaton. Making sacrifices we can manage to go. I fight for every hundred forints, one must look after one's money. In the middle of the year we never go anywhere except for walks in the hills; that is the cheapest amusement. The Buda Hills are not far. Having an evening out and going to Pest costs a lot of money. We have no bus season tickets for we work close by, and the kids go only to school. When I go to the factory, I actually enjoy the fifteen-minute walk. On the other hand, I have a woman colleague who tells me off for saving on the tram fare.

My husband finds travel the best recreation. Using their premium from the Spirits Factory he and his friends have been to Rumania and Yugoslavia. Now I as well asked at my plant to be sent to Miskolc-Tapolca for my holidays since that is supposed to be good for people with thyroid trouble.

I was getting nervous on account of our financial worries and had some trouble with my thyroid. I was operated on in 1970 and was off sick for six weeks, but I should have had a rest for at least two years. But that was when our home was torn down, and here in the new flat we got instead, costs are even higher. I undertook to work at piece rates at the fine-hosiery plant. I make two thousand forints a month but certainly work for it. I use 99 per cent of my working hours, and I take on a lot of overtime as well. When the children start earning, I would like to go back to regular hourly wages. I consider myself at a disadvantage because other women's husbands often make more—sometimes by a whole thousand. And the children always come up with special requests because they want to keep up with the other kids.

I get up at a quarter to five in the morning and prepare mid-morning snacks for the children. When I get home, I am in a rush to get our evening meal cooked. Sometimes enough is left over for lunch next day, and that means some saving. There is always the laundry and house work, and it takes a lot out of me, and I get tired easily. You're under constant pressure. In the afternoons I sometimes manage to lie down for an hour, but then I find that the children are coming home.

When we have to buy something, we prefer to lay aside the money gradually, for the instalments kill us. Our TV set is fourteen years old, it should be replaced, but we could not manage five thousand forints in ten months. And the children ruin their shoes in a month, the older one is especially hard on his. I wear my things for a long time, and cannot afford to get tired of anything. I make my own dresses and I can fix the runs on my stockings.

I never got to the cinema, and my husband does not crave for it either. The children go sometimes. It's two years since we last went to the theatre, the trouble is that one has to look well-dressed to go. I often listen to the radio and am especially fond of radio plays. We should spend more time with friends, but it is difficult to go out and that too costs money. One of my fellow workers sometimes comes up for half an hour after work, or else I go to see her. It is difficult to find fellow workers who are in the same boat as we are in. One of the women who works with me talks about their car all the time. I am way behind in that too; the most I can say is that of a Sunday we were out in the hills, the sun shone and we played ball.

*

L. K., 39, ferro-concrete fitter, foreman. He has been working at the Budapest Housing Contractors since October last year. Before that he had been employed for ten years at a different enterprise in the building industry. He averages 4,500 forints a month and a separation allowance is added to that. His home is at Tiszapolgári, and his family consisting of Mrs. K., housewife, and a daughter of 13 and a son of 10, live there.

I have to work in Budapest. It is not for fun that one lives away from home, but at home one cannot make half as much, and there is nothing like the big city when it comes to employment opportunities.

When there is no overtime, I go home every week-end. In winter there is week-end overtime once a month, in the summer twice a month. We leave Friday afternoon and get back at dawn on Monday. We finish work at 5. We get to the hostel at about 6 or half past, have something to eat, a beer and watch TV. Once in a while we go to the cinema. I try to make do with 150 forints a week, but when we go out, even 300 forints are not enough. We live very simply here, there are eight of us in a dormitory, four from my group at work. I have friends here with whom I have worked for the last five years and who have come with me to this enterprise.

What I can't understand is how some women can go to work with two children. That means the man goes home and the women goes out. This way I know that the kids are allright and are not roaming the streets. And I have seen plenty of the things that go on at the offices. It is no good people telling me that a woman who is not like that will stay all right there, for there people tempt her, and for the first few times she may say no, but with the fourth or fifth who asks her she will go out. And once she stays at home, there is no temptation there. Of course, now people are in a rush to get some place, to acquire things, and the only thing most people are interested in is making a lot of money and buying a car. Of course, it would be nice for us, too, to buy some furniture, for one of our rooms stands empty, but the time will come. This way when I go home I know at least that my wife is waiting for me.

I have been a Party member since 1956. With us that has been a family tradition. My mother, my grand-father and even my grand-mother had all belonged to the Party. Poor people were happy after 1945 because things started to get better. At home a lot of the people who are now at the top were just leaving the Party when I joined.

My gang is a socialist brigade, and we have already won all kinds of certificates. We buy one paper every day, the *Népszabadság* or the *Esti Hírlap*. We discuss the problems on the job, and politics. We don't go to the theatre, for that is too expensive for us, and for that matter it can't hold my attention. On the other hand I like plays on the radio. We always go to Wednesday's game, and when I am at home then I see our own district team play. That is my fun at home, too.

*

B. V., 21, is a working girl from Pilisvörösvár. She has been with the Budapest Hosiery Factory for less than a year.

This is my fourth place of employment. At one I stayed for less than two months. I worked in the weaving industry as a semi-skilled girl, only 6-hours a day on two machines. Then I went to the Elzett factory, there again only for a 6-hour day. Then in the timber industry as a messenger. There I had to do all kinds of things—stamping labels and packaging, reception of goods, averaging 1,800 forints. I started to study typing and shorthand, but stopped. I have a good job, there are many who have to work under more difficult conditions.

I get up at 4:30 in the morning and get in by six o'clock. Sometimes I go home, sometimes I stay here. My friends are here at Óbuda, for I have been coming in to Óbuda for the last four years to work. We go to the cinema and dancing. The last bus home leaves at a quarter past eleven, so that we either have to go to an earlier performance, or else, I sleep here in town at a girlfriend's place.

I give the money I earn to my mother, but I get everything I need. In fact it goes further this way, for I could not make it stretch so well. There are five of us children at home, my mother is a charwoman, my father a miner, but he has retired. The seven of us together make about 9,000 forints. We have our own home, and just now we are building a bathroom to it. Perhaps I shall stick to Vörösvár, for it is not far from Budapest; we are just as much part of the scene as people in the city, we know how things are in Pest.

I am not keen of marriage. The way things are I am free and can do what I want to.

*

E. K., 35. Her first, and until now, only place of employment has been the Taurus Rubber Company. She has been there since 1953. She is a full-time work-group leader at the camping-goods plant of the Palma Factory. She has been a Party member since 1967. With various supplements and bonuses her monthly pay rises as high as 2,800–3,000 forints. She lives at Csömör, which is accessible by the Gödöllő line of the Budapest suburban railways, with her mother and a daughter of 13 whom she has raised alone.

I did not want to get married, after all the quarrels this seemed the better way. One sees so many unhappy marriages that it's better not to risk it. My daughter never suffered any disadvantage for being raised by me alone. Of course, there is no telling what she heard or did not hear, in school. One thing is certain, there is less personal attention in school than there used to be even for us. Fortunately I have three brothers and they spend some time with her. I do not miss having no husband, I am busy and do a lot of volunteer work.

I am a Party worker, and still do work for the Young Communist League. As socialist brigade leader, I go to the brigade leaders' conferences. Once a month I have to organize a collective visit to a museum. I never go to the cinema other than with the brigade, and go to the theatre only twice or three times a year.

Often it is the distance that stops me going to the theatre or cinema. The fact is that I would not get home before midnight, and I have to get up at 4 in the morning. At Csömör there is absolutely no amusement. But then I had plenty of fun earlier. From 1953 on I was a folk-dancer in the Béla Bartók Dance Ensemble. I started dancing as a Young Pioneer. We travelled the country with the Ensemble, and often went to the theatre, to cinemas and dancing. I was in the group until 1960, when my daughter was born. Then I quit. I started an amateur group in the village as volunteer work. Since then it has been disbanded, the girls and many of the boys too, got married. Lack of support from the village was always a problem. There

was no one to sponsor it, and there was always a shortage of halls, and when
we did get one, it was cold.

I have just had a house built. My older brother who is an architect
designed it to cost about 100,000 forints. Out of this, I am just finishing
repayment on a 10,000 forint company loan. In addition I got 55,000 forints
from the National Savings Bank. Two years ago I got a bigger profit share,
10,000 forints, and started building in the spring. We tore down the old
house and sold the material. By autumn the new house was ready.

When I am on morning shift, I work until two in the afternoon. Until
about 3 or 3:30 there is always something to do in the factory. On the
suburban train I read or crochet, and get home by 6. I spend an hour every
day with my daughter, then something to eat and by the time I look at the
clock again it is 8. Perhaps I watch TV, but more often than not I am glad
to get to bed, for I have to get up at 4. On Saturdays and Sundays I do the
laundry, iron, and clean the house. During the working year I don't mind
not having any rest, but I am usually particular about my two-week annual
holyday. In 1968 I went to Moscow, the trade union arranged the trip.
And last year, as a reward for my volunteer work, I was given the chance
to go to the GDR for next to nothing. In other years I spend my holidays
at Lake Balaton, or Lillafüred, at trade-union resorts.

Apart from the family I have no social life. My girl friend lives a long
way away, when we meet in the tram or the suburban train, we chat for
ten or fifteen minutes. My brothers usually visit us with their families.
For the time being I have no thoughts of marriage, I would not want to
sacrifice either myself, or the family. Perhaps in ten years. It is very difficult
to find the sort of man who understands everything, and accepts one as
a human being, work, family and all.

*

F. K. is a mechanic, a foreman at the Taurus Rubber Company. He is 43, and the father
of three grown-up children. Only the two younger ones, a boy in his late teens and a daughter
just about to get married, live with him and his wife in a two-and-a-half room apartment
with all mod. cons. in Buda. The whole family are working, Mrs. K. is a cashier at a grocery
store, the daughter also works for the grocery chain, and the son is a journeyman mechanic.

I do shift work. When I work in the morning, I get up at 4. After work
there are always things to be done. I am a member of the Cordatic Factory
Party Committee, the Trade Union Committee and the Shop Committee,
and I am organizing secretary of the local Party cell. All this adds up to
a few hours of extra work every day. If there is nothing on, I get home by

4 in the afternoon. My wife and the children all do shift work, so it is only every fourth or fifth week that we are all together. I get myself a meal, wash the dishes, and watch TV until those on the afternoon shift come home, and then go to sleep. The TV is turned off by the rest of the family.

I don't like morning shifts, I have no leisure then. When I work afternoon, I get up at 9, I tidy up, have something to eat and I'm off. I like night shifts, especially in summer. I have my angler's retreat on the Danube; I have rented it for the last five years from the Angling Association, and then I can rest there during the day. The air is good, and I like to bask in the sun. I have some fruit trees, and read the papers there, *Népszabadság*, *Esti Hírlap*; and *Magyar Horgász* (The Anglers' Journal). We spend the weekends on the Danube whenever possible. Three of us share a plot there with my younger sister and with a friend, a chemical engineer. They are the friends whom we have at our house and go to visit. I don't mix socially with my work-mates. At autumn week-ends I often have to be on duty at the factory. True, such overtime means extra forints, and at home I would just watch TV.

We spend our summer holidays on the Danube as well. The children went to the GDR last year, the trip was arranged by the IBUSZ Travel Agency. I have never been outside the country, and my wife hasn't been abroad either. I had enough of travel within Hungary. I qualified as a skilled worker at Cegléd, and until January 1956 I served as a professional soldier. It kept me very busy and I had to travel to the country every week. I barely arrived home and often had to be off on duty right away.

That is probably why I long for tranquility. I think one can rest best away from everyone. There is very little leisure, and one spends that doing something monotonous that makes no sense, but one feels that one is resting.

*

K. V., is 21, he comes from Nagyhegyes in the county of Hajdú-Bihar. He is single and came to Budapest to work six years ago. He has been a navvy for the last three years with the Public Buildings Construction Company. He earns 2,500 forints a month and lives in a workers' hostel.

At home there were eleven of us including my parents, and so there was always plenty of work to be done. And I was nothing special in my studies.

I send the money I earn home, or take it home when I feel like it because commuting is no fun. I get on the train at midnight, and arrive home at 6 in the morning. In the morning I help around the garden, doing whatever needs to be done, occasionally in the cooperative as well. When I stick about at the hostel, and there are several of us here, we drink beer, although it is against the rules, but still one does bring in those two or three bottles. When the TV programme happens to be entertaining—cabarets, thrillers, adventure films or war films—we watch. Sometimes I visit my cousins in the Sixth District. I have the time and the inclination to read, but the damnable thing is that the "lights" can't take it. Otherwise I have no problem with my eyes, but I just can't read for longer than ten minutes. Then they go dim.

I am courting a girl in the County of Szolnok, and alternately go home, or visit my girl. She works at the refrigerating-machines factory at Jász-berény, her village is 11 kilometres from there. Pest is a mere 90 kilometres from her home. I plan to get married in September and would stay with her parents. The bus will take me to work in the morning and home at night. One and a half hours of commuting all told.

I don't see much sense in acquiring a skill. If they look down on me, let them, for a man with a special trade is no better than me. For me to push hard, to study, to finish secondary school would cost my parents money. And where does a lad who takes all that trouble get to? There is some tradesman's work I can do all the same. I can handle a carpenter's tools, or a stone-masons's, and do what an electrician does. Skilled workers do not make any more money than I do.

*

F. Cs., 31, works as a navvy for the Budapest Housing Construction Enterprise. He is single, and earns about 2,500 forints a month.

I live at the Szobránc Street hostel. There are ten of us in a room; it is a pretty crowded place, you can't do anything there. I only go home at night to sleep, at 7 or 8. I come from Etyek, near Debrecen, I have worked in a good many places. Laying parquetry is my trade. I worked at home, too, but there was not enough money in it. I spent eleven years at Tatabánya, laying parquetry there. One could earn good money laying parquetry, but you had to put down acres to do that, down on your knees all day long. My knees had to be pumped twice, so I quit. I used to work as a roofer, too. But why learn a trade when even the skilled prefer to work as navvies, for there is more money in it.

I go home every week, and my mother lays aside the money if there is any left. When I am at home, there is always some work to be done around the house, the fence needs fixing, or something else. My mother is 75, and lives alone. I am her youngest son, someone has got to be with her. I wouldn't think of getting married while she is alive, for I won't have anyone say something nasty about her. And then I would not take anyone to live in a one-room-kitchen flat with my mother. I have had a bit to do with women, and this way there is at least no need for a divorce. As a matter of fact this money is not enough for marriage.

There are ten of us brothers and sisters, four of us in Budapest. Once or twice a week I go to my sister's or sister-in-law's house to watch TV, for at the hostel there are too many around to enjoy it.

At home there might be some work at the cooperative farm, but they won't take me in, for I am too far from the "hearth", and haven't got "god-father", am only a "step-child". Here at the company I have some friends, we like to drink a glass of beer or two and talk. I bring food from home, for I cannot afford to go to restaurants, although now and then one does. I rarely go to the cinema, only once a month, I like good films, those with fighting.

*

F. K., 43 is a pipe-fitter at the Láng Engineering Works, earning 15 forints an hour. His wife and elder daughter both work at the Láng Factory, each of them in the store. His younger daughter is now working after having finished a business secondary school, but plans to continue her studies. Their total income is 7,000 forints. For the past three years they have lived in a two-room flat built by the National Savings Bank which they own, but have not paid for yet.

We get up at 4:30 and get to work at 5:30. We get home at about 3:30. We shop and cook. The trouble is that we love to eat. Three thousand forints or more goes on food. I love to cook, and I would be a cook if I could chose again. We never eat at the works canteen. Then comes washing-up, and after that the wife is off to the bathroom. We wash everything at home, I would be ashamed to take it to the laundry. If you can walk that far, you can wash it. It's not hard work, sometimes I do it, sometimes she does it, you just throw in the detergent, and there you are.

The family spending is my wife's business, when I need money I get it from her. Every month we lay aside 100 forints each, that is all we manage. I never think of a car, you can't dream of a car with our kind of money. The husband's pay must be at least 5,000 forints to get one. The family are on to me to get new furniture. It is really not bad, but it is not "modern". And what is wrong with it? It's dark, and now the fashion is light. They want me to spend 18,000 to have light-toned furniture! Is it big enough for me? It is. Then it'll do. I am all for having an electric hair-dryer and electric massaging machine, everything that makes for comfort! But to have light-toned furniture! I am willing to put my money on rebuilding the bathroom, the bath-tub is too small, and I like to have a good stretch in the tub.

We rarely go to the cinema—twice a month that's all. Our fun is the telly. It is like the fifth member of the family. Whether the programme is good or bad, it's turned on. When it was out of order I just looked and looked, wondering what was wrong, for it seemed as if someone were missing from the family. The wife reads much more than me. I would like to be read to. I have glasses, but after four or five pages I get tired, and after fifteen I fall asleep. When it comes to politics, well I will look at a programme on the telly but I won't read the paper for it.

Sunday afternoon we go down-town window-shopping, unless something good is on the telly. Sundays we go for walks but not long ones, just take the bus up onto Liberty Hill and then walk down to Moscow Square. When the weather is good we go bathing.

Those who work close to me are good friends of mine, but we don't go to each other's houses. I don't mind if they come to see us, but I refuse to sit about formally in someone else's house. We visit each other with my brother-in-law, he is a tanner at the Leather Factory, and his wife an office worker. They have two daughters about as old as ours. I call regularly on my mother who has been living alone at Újpest for a year now. We try to go away somewhere for our summer holidays every year. If it falls through, there is always bathing near here.

We are home-bodies, and perhaps too introverted. Plenty of families have not taken so much trouble with the kids, and they grew up just the same, but for us their well being was always a source of worry.

*

A. H. is 29, and an engine fitter at the Láng Engineering Works. He has been married for four years and has a daughter of two. His wife works at the same factory. He gets 13 forints an hour, and the two of them collect about 4,000 forints a month. They live in a sublet basement room at Rákospalota, an outer suburb and, as he says, their lodgings are tolerable in winter, for the room can be heated, but is cold and damp in the summer. Up to now they managed to put aside 50,000 forints with a view to buying a home.

We are trying to save money, so we don't go anywhere. Of course, on account of the baby we could not have gone out much anyway. After not going for several years, we just saw a film for the first time when the baby was home with my mother-in-law for part of the winter. Our only hobby is going for walks, and that is good for the baby too. When we are at home, one of us takes care of the little one, and the other one prepares the "feed". I work from 6 in the morning to 2 in the afternoon, and then take the baby home from the crèche. We take the evening meal home from the factory canteen. The fact is that at home it is impossible for us to cook, for three families are using the same sink. We heat the food, the washing-up water and the water for the bath all on just one electric plate. Now we shall soon leave these lodgings, and hope to get a room-and-kitchen place at Dunakeszi. True, it will cost more—for our basement I paid 15,000 forints in advance for three years—but at least the baby will have a chance to move about. Now when I lift her out of the cot, she falls either against the oil stove or the electric cooker.

They called me into the Marxist school, but I won't go, for I have no chance to do my home-work. I have to turn off the light at half past seven, and we can listen to the radio only until 7:30, we must be quiet on account of the baby. Unfortunately the plays are always after eight, and the cabaret programme has also been shifted from Saturday to Monday night. On the tram one sometimes gets a chance to read. I read *Esti Hírlap*, and also buy *Ezermester* (Jack of All Trades). Here at the factory I get *Universum* and the *Turbine*. It is a shame I know, but I could count the books I have read on the fingers of one hand.

When we have free Saturdays we spend Sundays at my mother's in Buda. We sleep there, and get breakfast, dinner and supper, and that means a saving of about 200 to 300 forints. My in-laws also occasionally send us sausages and ham, and apples and grapes.

I have been a Party member for the last four years and have done confidential work for the last three. I could not have joined directly, for first I had to prove myself. By now I am appreciated, and my hourly wages rise fast, but still a lot of people like to say I know nothing of life. They are older people from the old regime and they don't like someone like me. What's more, they don't stick to the rules. A young man sees that this or that rule or regulation is expedient, but the old are stubborn and won't listen to reason. The trouble is that all forums and organizations become ineffective, for we just talk but nothing changes. For instance, someone is late, they speak to him, but nothing happens.

I would like to grow on the job. One must not be ready to accept money instead of opportunities. I could go to the building industry, or do something else for more money, but that takes a lot out of one. I would like to improve in what I am doing. Of course, it is good to have money, for I cannot go to the market with my ideas instead of cash. True, we are

finding solutions for the problems every day and at the same time think of
the future, too. Man is like a pile driven in the ground, the more he is hit
and hammered, the surer he stands.

*

S. L. is 41, and an electrical fitter. He is work-group leader at the electric repair shop of
the Cordatic Factory of the Taurus Rubber Company. His wife works at the Beloyannis
Factory. They have a son of 12 and they live with the grand-parents. They just recently
moved from Nagytétény in the outskirts of Budapest to a new flat at a Budapest housing
estate. He earns 3,000 forints, she 1,500, and the old folks get a pension of 1,080 forints.

I am permanently on the morning shift, get up at 4:30, get in by half
past five and work until quarter to 2. When I get through, there are things
like trade-union work, seminars, Civilian Defence, or some kind of conference. I am Shop Committee secretary, a member of the Trade Union
Council, and on the Trade Union Economic Committee. The latter was
formed this year and deals with the problems of the factory. I have just written a paper about the state of the equipment and what should be done to
preserve it. I have had several innovations accepted. As Shop Committee
Secretary I have a lot of work to do also, for there are more than four
hundred trade union members under me.

I was a Party member, joining in 1947. In 1956 I was working at the
Ganz. After the Counter-Revolution I said to a few men who used to be
Party members and were doing office work, let's join, but they said as far
as they were concerned the answer was "never". Then when, early in 1957,
the Party organizers visited the factory, they all suddenly decided to join.
That made me decide not to join myself.

In 1958 I went to work for a cooperative. I put up with it for four years.
The one advantage was that I had the chance to travel all over the country.
I worked a lot with people, at mines and in factories. I became a versatile
man, and I still benefit from this. I am an electrician when that is needed,
I am a mechanic, or fitter or painter as required.

I came to Taurus after reading an ad in the paper. I did not know anyone
here, but I had grown sick and tired of the cooperative with all the former
self-employed petty capitalists and army officers. I hesitated for a long time,
but then I joined the trade union movement as a steward. An election put
me into the Shop Committee. I made up my mind never to accept any
extra volunteer work, but then finally I did after all join the Party in 1970.

At home I am the quarter-master general, I do the shopping. I still shop
at the Big Market Hall, for I got used to it in the old days when I went

home to Nagytétény. There are the butchers I know, and the vegetables and eggs are also cheaper there, so it is worth the detour.

We have to pay a lot for the new flat and our expenses are higher. We save a little on travelling by tram, from Nagytétény we had to take the bus. We walk a bit, too, and we need that, at Nagytétény we got used to moving about and the air was always fresh by the Danube. There we had a chance to keep animals; we had rabbits and I wake up four or five times because of the dryness of the air or the noise. There one heard only the ships passing by at night, and one was able to fish. But there we had only a single room for a three generation family. I thought that once we coped with the housing situation, one could spend some time studying. But TV takes the books out of your hand. I still read travel books. One has to brush up what one knows. I have a lot of books at home, sometimes it takes three starts, but in the end I read them all.

As a rule, we have our meal at 4:30, or 5:00. Then I have to spend some time with the boy, I deal with the trade-union business for which I did not have enough time here in the factory. Whenever I have to write up something I do it at home, and I read *Népszava*, for that is the trade-union paper. I also read *Figyelő* which raises a number of problems and *Villamosság*, a monthly on electricity. The radio is always turned on at five in the morning. In the telly I look at the films and the scientific programmes. I like to go to the movies, but preferably without missing anything good on the telly. We usually look for a good film in the papers, preferably not a love story, but an adventure film that is suitable for the boy. I don't like the threatre, but my wife and our son sometimes go to afternoon performances. I am used to comfort, and I prefer staying at home. Last year my wife's brigade got a season ticket to the Opera, and we did go fairly regularly, though sometimes I went only for my wife's sake, and managed to think out an innovation while the music was on.

I am sorry that I have not studied and have not gone to technical secondary school. It was easier to go visiting in the villages and do canvassing there or to organize rural schools. I liked that better than studying. And yet if I had done it then, I might have got further by now. I have given up further education. I can always acquire the knowledge that is wanted in life. Our son, I hope, will do differently! So I try to be strict with him, for unless he does his maths now, he won't get anywhere. It is not enough to count the money you make.

*

These twelve straightforward and frank statements do not, and cannot, provide sufficient foundation for drawing far-reaching conclusions. They cannot, because those interviewed were only from a narrow group, and the problems touched on were only in a limited field. Nonetheless these answers confirm realistic views on the life-style of Hungarian workers. Above all they affirm the fact—obvious even without sociological research—that the objective living and housing conditions and material standards of Hungarian workers improved considerably in the last quarter century, and especially in the past ten years. Today people worry about problems—for instance, the acquisition of certain consumers' durables—which in the past did not concern people living in their restricted circumstances. Of course, some partially unsolved grave problems still exist. Such are the state of some of the workers' hostels and the housing situation.

As to the subjective factors in the approach to life—parallel to the improvement in living standards—it is certainly a welcome sign that most of the workers assess their position and opportunities realistically, try to utilize their advantages constructively, and know what they want and how to go about it. There are at the same time people who still think in vague and obscure terms and who do not quite know what to do with themselves—and this applies in the first place to what they do in their leisure.

Another important fact is—and this has also been confirmed by the interviews published— that owing to significant differences in both the objectives and subjective aspects of development, the life-style of Hungarian workers is widely differentiated. This is something that has to be kept in view in all further research on the life-style of workers, and considered also when it comes to taking measures that affect the way of life, or when political and educational work is planned.

JÚLIA SZALAI

DIVISION OF LABOUR WITHIN THE FAMILY

Since the earliest times man was born into family communities and lived through certain determinant periods of his life of lesser or greater impórtance in family communities. What does the attribute "of determinant importance" mean in this case? It means that the family is one of the most important educating communities which directly conveys to the individual social norms and values, aims and the means to reach the latter; thus, the time a person has spent within a family considerably influences the development of a social being as a member of the "great society of mankind". Hence the norm and value system man has primarily acquired in the family is not a matter of indifference from the point of view of either the individual's adjustment to society or of his admittance to society. For this reason society, in some way or other, always controls the family as such and what it teaches. However, the measure, form and content of control considerably changed in the course of history. Its development was always in the closest possible connection with the problems of social equality: the question of supervision always cropped up as a subquestion of social equality for social relations determine its content and aim in the first place. It would go beyond the limits of this paper to give even a rough outline of this close connection, an analysis would have to describe a number of concrete social facts, deal with real social

relations and situations and follow the history of problems of equality and control. Therefore—without aiming at completeness —I have attempted to outline only why there is in my view a close, and, from the point of view of control, a primarily determinant connection between equality and social supervision.

In the first place it has to be taken into account that today's civilized "modern" societies are loose societies inasmuch as the closed corporate production function of the family as well as the vitally important role the family played in safeguarding the survival of society has practically ceased. It should be pointed out that problems of keeping the family as such under control and the possibility of conflicts between the individual and society emerged and obtained a definite character in modern societies for the first time, apart from incidental and exceptional occasions. This means that the great majority become members of the social division of labour in a wider sense—beyond the framework of the family division of labour. Accordingly they become members of new communities, creators and vehicles of new norms, values and objectives, and convey the new system of norms in one way or other to the family, in many cases of course with considerable distortions and generational devïations. The possibility of a new kind of control differing from or maybe even opposed to that of the family comes into being through an at least partial secession from the family. What has all this to do with problems of social equality? The fact is that in the division of labour the position of individuals is not equal nor are the "advantages" and "disadvantages" such as: income, prestige, possibility and degree of identification with work, chances to take part in management and direction etc. for all these are closely connected with the individual's position in the division of labour. Closely connected with the aforesaid is the fact that the consciousness of their social position i.e. the evaluation of their situation and, in this context, their expectations and norms, objectives and intentions related to change are not equal either. It follows that the content of the internal control as developed in the family—transmitted by individuals and determined by material factors and factors of consciousness —is also divergent. At the same time, the structure of management, guidance and institutions—which developed at an earlier stage in the evolution of the division of labour and became an all embracing system in line with the unfolding of capitalism— represents the given state of affairs for them. The division of power and participation in the developing system of institutions and organizations which proclaim social norms, objectives and expectations in today's differentiated society—more or less definitely—but systematically becomes the monopoly of certain social classes and sections; this, of course, does not mean that their activity is exempt from every kind of social control; it only means that on the basis of existing power relations they enjoy a relatively higher autonomy in their activities and decisions than other sections of society and classes and are able to make their interests effective even if the latter put up resistance. "Official" social control—embodied by the introduction of measures, setting up and running organizations etc.—is dictated and induced by this power and directing system. Since the chances to make one's way in life are

not equal for all members of society, the ability to establish control in the above sense as well as the control as such and, consequently, the effect of check kept on families, is not equal either from the point of view of individuals and their communities.

Now let us consider from the point of view of the family division of labour in what form social differences appear in narrow and relatively closed family communities and what social control means in relation to the community?

In the first place it is necessary to clarify forms of exercising control over families. Basic types of control that can be easily discerned are:

a) An extreme case is that of a family which forms a closed autonomous community within society; since society cannot directly control family activities, the values and objectives the family imparted to the individual can only be set against real social expectations after the individual has left the family. It frequently follows that the individual has to put up with a number of unsuccessful experiences when he becomes integrated into the social division of labour and society wastes much useless energy in order to rectify what the individual has brought from home. ("Ex post" form of control).

b) Another extreme case is when direct channels for exercising control over the family are available and, as a result, the process of adjustment to society goes off smoothly for both the individual and society ("Ex ante" form of control).

These two forms of control appeared and clashed as the outcome of a long historic process. Today our main task is to consciously select the method by means of which "ex post" control-elements can be eliminated and substituted by previous control. In other words: if the ideal society is conceived as one which ensures equality for its members, the necessity of post-control diminishes and conditions of previous control are increasingly given the more progress is made towards this goal; this, however, means increased socialization of the family. It is not mere chance that Plato and Sir Thomas More, who both concerned themselves with Utopian societies imagined the education of children as a social commitment. What then does the concept: socialization of the family mean in a differentiated society? The main point is that society realized control by taking over a considerable part of the activities of family life and so-to-speak absorbs the family. In this way society creates both the material and the ideal conditions of "ex ante" control and by so doing narrows down the field where it is necessary to exert "ex post" control. This concept includes—in the widest sense of the word—the ideals of society, its objectives of differing temporal duration as well as all the means and ways enabling it to reach the aforesaid. Of course, this kind of investigation takes place from a particular aspect, the aspect of the family and the division of labour in the family, generally speaking only, the expectations, decisions and activities of society in respect to the family are closely connected with other kinds of social processes and activities. Hence, the present situation and development in Hungary of the division of labour in families will be analysed on the basis of the dimensions of socialization. The family controlled by various conflicting forms within a mobile society of pluralistic values and "sub-cultures" is at the extreme pole of the historically realized dimension. The other pole, conceived as an ideal one, is represented (in contrast to the former one) by the "ex ante" controlled community which integrated with and became absorbed by society. The central question (consisting of a number of subquestions) is:

Where is the place of the Hungarian family of today between these two poles, to what extent does the division of labour within the family correspond to social expectations and what need is there if any for subsequent control? There are two approaches to the problem through concrete analysis, one of which is family-centred whereas the other is society-centred. The first is interested in the effective formation of the division of labour in the family and can be divided into two spheres:

a) Division of tasks deriving from childbirth and education of children incumbent on parents. In this sphere of family activities "plus" charges fall to the lot of women for biological and psychological reasons.

b) Caring for the family was in the course of history also mainly the task of women. To what extent does this hold good in our days? This question is important for it is the beginning and end of the disadvantageous situation of women as against men. This investigation is therefore closely connected with problems of emancipation and social equality and is the transition to the social-centred approach.

The latter is expected to give an answer regarding society's expectations in respect to the family, the extent to which society has provided for conditions in order to fulfil these expectations and—provided that those conditions are given—the ideas of the members of society—of fathers and husbands, mothers and wives—do meet expectations on the family and on the division of labour.

The shaping of decisions

The first group of questions of the family-centred investigation of the division of labour is related to the education of children in the family, how parents divide these tasks between themselves, how much time do they spend on their children and under what conditions etc. The present study relies on Hungarian data of the international time-balance investigation of 1965–66. The time-balance included industrial towns with a population ranging from 40,000 to 200,000, sufficiently diversified industry (i.e. the population does not engage in a single traditional industry only) with at least 30 per cent of the inhabitants working in industry and a maximum 25 per cent in agriculture; the town had to be the centre of the region, meaning that a part of the population of the nearby settlements commuted to town every day and worked in industry. The outer boundary of the town—which was still included in the sample—was drawn where the number of commuters did not exceed five per cent of the population. For these reasons Győr was chosen in Hungary.

The persons questioned were asked to record on a school time-table-like questionnaire how they had spent their days, what time different activities took and certain other aspects e.g. who was present, who helped them and what secondary activity did the person questioned perform besides— say—did he or she listen to the radio while cooking? In Hungary the survey was supplemented by a questionnaire the aim of which was to obtain information on activities in the family and at home. One of the main points of the supplementary questionnaire was to show the division of work at home, that is, research was done into the content and extent of housework.

This study therefore relied on data provided by two closely connected investigations. Since then, however, new questions also arose in respect to which neither of the surveys gave an explicit answer, although it would have been highly important and interesting to clear up the problems enumerated below, from both a theoretical and a practical point of view.

One of the problems is, for example, whether the husband's or the wife's decision counts in the division of labour at home, the decision of which of the spouses does the shaping of the character in the distribution of activities mainly depend; to what extent do income, dwelling etc. determine the shaping of decisions in the division of labour; what is the influence of the urban or rural character of the place of residence in the case of identical incomes, that is, does

it further development tending towards equality, or that towards the preservation of traditions in the division of labour.

The emancipation of women taken as a complex question against the background of production, services, network of social institutions and organizations, and where— within this complex system—the place of the "subsystem" of inequalities in the family is situated in reality etc. is a further set of problems. All this requires detailed investigations, for example, a comparison between men and women in respect to skill, scope of activity, employment, incomes, social prestige of work in the sphere of production or from the viewpoint of laws, statutory provisions and decrees; moreover, differences according to the place of residence ought to be investigated with special regard to the disadvantageous situation of women as against men.

Education of Children

The first group of questions in the family-centred division of labour is concerned with the education of children in the family circle, how do parents divide these tasks, how much time do they spend on their children, under what circumstances and so on.

Education in general and particularly that of children plays a highly important role in the realization of the ideal "ex ante" control. Society is aware of this as shown by a number of measures of social policy, for example, by the development of the crèche and kindergarden system. The many problems that emerged in this respect are well known. The capacity of these institutions is insufficient but even if the needed material and personnel conditions could be provided for, another thought provoking problem— particularly important from the viewpoint of the present subject—arises: the expectations of socialist society towards the family manifested themselves most directly by expectations in respect to women. The economic requirements of industrialization made it an absolute necessity to draw women into the orbit of production, yet the demand to establish equal rights for women was an explicit social aim embodied by a number of measures and institutions whose purpose was to ease the situation of women and mothers. One of these measures was the crèche-kindergarden system. However, this system was only instituted for women and mothers who are employed; this shows to a certain degree that the system was mainly established to serve working women. The other objective: the social education of children, that is, preliminary control and providing "equal chances" can only be a partial objective at best. The situation is somewhat different in the case of schools. The primary school—called general school in Hungary—is, in fact, "general" for it is compulsory for all and, therefore one of the basic conditions of socialized education had been fulfilled. Reforms of the educational system—particularly in the four lower forms—brought about a number of positive changes in respect to the second basic condition i.e. the content of the curriculum which was expanded; there are new educational appliances, illustrated primers reminiscent of story-books and in addition new subjects such as environmental studies. However, the third basic condition, namely, sound teaching and really good teachers are still lacking in some cases.

All this goes to say that the role of the family is almost exclusive in the education and care of children before they are admitted to school and almost equals it during school years. This is emphasized by the fact that school—because of the gap between kindergarden and school, and school and family and because of peculiarities of the Hungarian school system—exerts "ex post" control where the conduct of children as developed by the family is supervised. What does the development of the mode of life of children depend on? Obviously on the parents who

educated them. Their ideas, however, are closely connected with their mentality, system of values and norms. The orientation of values of adults is a function of their position in the division of labour. This therefore is the most decisive dimension from the point of view of which the division of labour in the family and the problems of the education of children will be examined.

In addition, it also has to be taken into account that education to a large extent depends on the extent and intensity of care parents devote to the education of their children. This is determined by two fundamental factors, one of which is the composition of the family, the number and age of children representing a minimum time and intensity demand while the other factor is the maximum time parents can spend on their children. Differences are of course far greater in the case of women, dependent on whether they are housewives or in employment and it is certain that this factor highly deviates not only in respect to the length of time but also as regards the content and structure of time parents can devote to their children. (See Table 1.)

The time-span ranges from 20 minutes to 3.5 hours. Differences of social position are not differentiating factors, however, the fact whether mothers go to work or not is of considerable influence as regards the time spent with children. Unfortunately, the fact that mothers stay at home the whole day does not mean that parents spend a longer time together more intensily on their children, because the mother's extended time is compensated for by the "liberation" of the father from education. Mothers who are "only housewives" spend 1.2–1.8 times as much time on their children, on the other hand, husbands of women not in employment spend only half the time on their children as husbands of women who are employed. The latter type of family life is more harmonious from the point of view of time spent with children since father and mother play their proportionate part in

TABLE 1

Time spent on children on weekdays on the average (minutes)

	In clerical and professional employment				Manual workers			
	husband	wife	husband	wife	husband	wife	husband	wife
	wife employed		wife not employed		wife employed		wife not employed	
Families with children on the average	45	57	19	105	42	70	22	84
Families where the smallest child is under a year old	34	214	27	—	51	181	24	179
Size of sample	5	4	3	—	19	15	6	5

education. In families with a baby, fathers have to take a greater share in the education of the older children and by devoting—say—only a few minutes more to the children they compensate a part of the mother's time while she looked after the baby. (See Table 2.)

More than half of the time of women is taken up by "domestic chores" (dressing, washing, care of sick children etc.). The husbands position is just the opposite. The latter are concerned with education in the narrower sense of the word, in every group. The determinant factor of the pattern of activity of husbands is here also whether their wives are earners or stay at home and devote themselves to the household and the family. This means—seen from another angle—that fathers stick to a greater degree to education at the expense of other kinds of housework.

TABLE 2

Time distribution of parents' activity with children
(in per cent)

	Clerical and professional				Manual workers			
	husband	wife	husband	wife	husband	wife	husband	wife
	wife in employment		wife not in employment		wife in employment		wife not in employment	
Care of children	35.9	60.8	24.4	48.6	39.7	86.4	24.1	64.0
Education (playing, reading etc.)	64.1	39.2	75.6	51.4	60.3	31.6	75.9	36.0

It is interesting too, how parents divide their time between the above mentioned two kinds of activities. Table 3 shows that there are considerable differences also according to the place occupied in the social division of labour, although differentiation according to whether women are in employment continues.

Parents doing clerical or professional work set greater store on education particularly if the mother stays at home and attends to the children and does the housework in addition. In families of manual workers physical care comes first. It should be added that differentiation according to activities is of no importance from the point of view of the development of children. In the case of small children physical care and games, going for a walk, etc. are of equal importance. The aim of this differentiation is to characterize the attitude of parents and to learn what they take upon themselves and what they consider more and what less important. More detailed analyses show that parents doing clerical work devote more time to the intellectual-bodily development of their children (playing, walking outdoors, telling stories etc.) and it can be assumed that they look after their children more efficiently and with a higher compe-

tence. Unfortunately—and in this primarily lies the effect of the post-control of the school—school education does not decrease the disadvantages resulting therefrom to the detriment of children of manual workers, on the contrary, it increases the latter's handicap as is shown by differences in average school achievements.

A further breakdown of the pattern of activities shows that women have far more definite ideas in respect to what has to be done with their children than husbands do. This provides an explanation for the fact that there is a closer relationship between the ideas of mothers than between those of fathers as regards the distribution of time spent on education, order of importance and time expended on certain activities. There are, of course, differences between women also which depend more on the section of society they belong to and less on the differences between the categories of those in employment and those not in employment.

Thorough analysis of the time husbands dispose of has led to the same results: differences are more considerable according to whether or not their wives are in employment whereas they are slighter if the question is examined from the point of view of the social division of labour.

TABLE 3

Division of activities of the time both parents spend on their children

	Professional and clerical				Manual workers			
	wife in employment		wife not in employment		wife in employment		wife not in employment	
	min.	per cent	min.	per cent	min.	per cent	min.	per cent
Physical care of children	50	48.9	45	36.5	60	54.0	47	44.0
Education	52	51.1	79	63.5	51	46.0	59	56.0
Total	102	100.0	124	100.0	111	100.0	106	100.0

Finally, if the pattern of activity of husbands and wives is compared it appears —in conformity with the above—that there are more differing features than similarities. The degree of deviation is the slightest in the group of professional people, particularly if both parents are in employment. The difference between the two structures culminates at the other pole i.e. where the wife of a manual worker is a housewife.

To sum up matters it can be said that women are in fact burdened with a "plus charge" due to childbirth and education and, in addition, to a greater degree than could be justified, by the fact of *motherhood*. This is particularly so in the case of housewives whose position is in many respects disadvantageous anyway.

Neither the number nor the standard of Hungarian children's welfare institutions provides a suitable basis for implementing socialized education and discontinuing "ex post" control. The most important measure taken in recent years as regards the care of mothers and children was the introduction of the child-welfare allowance. The latter means that mothers can choose, after maternity leave expires, whether or not they want to take up their earlier job at unchanged conditions and let a crèche, a grandmother etc. look after their baby, or stay at home and draw the allowance, which amounts to 600 Ft a month, for three years. The alternative offered as well as the appreciation expressed in respect to childbirth and motherhood are positive features. It eases—in the short run—social tensions which mainly affect manual workers, and diminishes to a certain degree the many burdens of young mothers such as going to work and in addition looking after a home and baby.

Housework

The other aspect of this piece of research concerns housework in the narrower sense of the word, that is the division of activities in providing for the family as a whole. Throughout history this was a typical woman's job. It has been pointed out earlier why this question is of particular significance in socialist society whose declared aim is to establish social equality. Accordingly, and in harmony with values as proclaimed by the new social order, certain commodities were put on the market and services introduced with the object of facilitating the situation of mothers and wives; a considerable part of them were explicitly intended to take over tasks which otherwise have to be done in the home. However, as with children's welfare institutions, in this case too the drawback is that services and commodities are of low standard, their quantity is insufficient and there are no institutions providing complex services from cooking to washing. Another problem—the effects of which are not known yet—is that a considerable part of services are performed by women, that is, "housewives" do housework when in employment. There are "technical" problems, social aims are not clear either.

It has been briefly outlined above that society should take over the larger part of domestic activities by providing services and granting social allotments, for this is the most suitable way to ensure equal chances in housework in a differentiated society. This, however, can only be effective if society tries to ensure that all its members are given an opportunity to take equal advantage of services and allotments, for only in this way is it possible to keep a check on at least a part of earlier inequalities and tensions. A precondition is that recourse to services etc. should mean an unequivocally positive alternative for every family. In other words: it should not just be a paying proposition for certain people but be available to all members of society irrespective of their income. The following data show that there are many problems:

TABLE 4
Domestic appliances per hundred households

	Head of the family			
	Executives and professionals	Other clerical	Skilled or semi-skilled worker	Unskilled worker
Sewing machine	44	45	42	37
Washing machine	71	59	55	28
Vacuum cleaner	55	35	17	5
Floor-polisher	15	5	2	—
Electric or gas boiler	20	13	5	1
Refrigerator	25	13	7	1

TABLE 5
Average per capita costs a year (forint)

	Head of the family			
	Executives and professionals	Other clerical	Skilled or semi-skilled worker	Unskilled worker
Cleaning and washing	164	83	29	17

TABLE 6
Average time spent on housework in families with children (minutes)

	In clerical employment						Manual workers					
	hus-band	wife	total	hus-band	wife	total	hus-band	wife	total	hus-band	wife	total
	wife in employment			wife not in employment			wife in employment			wife not in employment		
Time spent on house-work	67	178	245	54	355	409	93	222	315	88	386	474

The considerable differences are not only due to differences in incomes but probably to deviating traditions, a different order of values, leaning towards conservatism or the new as well. This had to be mentioned in advance otherwise the length and structure of time devoted to housework and the division of labour between husband and wife could not be appropriately analysed, for the main point of the question at issue is the time and energy saving of family members. A clear picture could be best obtained if the hours and minutes saved owing to various domestic appliances could be taken into account. Failing this, only their assumed effect can be indicated.

It appears from analyses of the time spent on housework that the minimum is one hour and the maximum 6.5 hours (on the average per group); in every group therefore more time is spent on housework than on education. In this respect, however, two points of view have to be taken into account; first, work done for the family as a whole includes cooking, washing, cleaning etc. for the children, too, the time requirement of which appears here; hence, earlier data can be considered as time exclusively spent on children. Secondly, in view of today's housing conditions and degree of mechanization the time needed for housework is more definite and generally longer than the time required to look after children.

The division of housework shows that there are signicant differences between husband and wife as well as between social groups. It is worth while noting that in this case the tendency of the division of labour is precisely the opposite to earlier experience: here the primary differences arise from the fact whether women are in employment or housewives whereas differences according to the place occupied in the division of labour are only of a secondary importance. In the case of husbands the latter is the dominant factor. It should, however, be added that time-data for husbands—according to which manual workers help their wives half an hour more a day—are contrary to everyday experience and data from other sources as well. This is attributable to the fact that here the concept "housework" was interpreted in a wide sense and includes work done around the house. To this manual workers contribute to a far greater degree than clerks or professional men. If housework isinterpreted in the narrower classical sense the participation of husbands appears as the opposite.

Table 7 shows that the division of labour between husband and wife is far less uniform in respect to the family as a whole than regarding the care of children; this is a negative phenomenon, for the contrary could be justified by certain activities and their time requirement which only the mother can perform. It appears that women in so-

TABLE 7
Time distribution of husband and wife according to different activities (in per cent)

Activity	Professional and clerical				Manual workers			
	husband	wife	husband	wife	husband	wife	husband	wife
	wife in employment		wife not in employment		wife in employment		wife not in employment	
Housework	27	73	13	87	30	70	19	81
Education of children	44	56	15	85	37	63	21	79

5

TABLE 8

Time distribution between housework and education of children
(those in employment only) (per cent)

	Professional and clerical		Manual workers	
	husband	wife	husband	wife
Housework	60	76	69	76
Education of children	40	24	31	24

ciety primarily do the work of housewives and not that of mothers while men are ready to take over a relatively greater part of the education of children. The division between the two groups of activity of the time spent at home corroborates the aforesaid.

The table only contains data for earners since the aim is to clear up how time is divided between the two important kinds of activity after husband and wife have come home from their place of work where they have spent about the same time.

In Hungarian society today housework is therefore divided in a traditional way which is disadvantageous to women and prejudices their emancipation. It seems that while preliminary control (socialization) is a definite social aim in certain spheres of education, similar endeavours cannot be found in housework.

If the only one working is the head of the family, child care allowances are not available to family members. This means that Hungarian society grants even certain remedies to working women only which creates, in addition to earlier inequalities, a new kind of differentiation between women at work and those who work at home; this difference will become the more glaring the more women take up employment. This is a far-reaching problem requiring much complex research.

Detailed analyses of the different patterns of activity look for an answer to the question: to what extent does housework

and the division of time spent on housework follow the traditional pattern and what changes have the earlier mentioned factors (household appliances, services, housing conditions and women entering employment) brought about. In other words: is the division of labour of complementary or competitive character within the mentioned disproportions in the time schedule? Complementary here means the traditional type of division of labour, that is, certain kinds of activities are only done by husbands and others by wives; in a division of work of competitive character spouses perform about equal work of all sorts. First, however, it has to be cleared up what is to be understood by traditional (complementary) division of housework. In the course of history—provided that there was a division of housework at all—the latter relied on the difference of physical strength between men and women. Men performed strenuous work while women did easier work mainly in the house. Sometimes a differentiation was made between work around and inside the house; these notions were related in practices to social facts enhancing the characteristically disadvantageous position of women: slight participation in matters of the outside world, complete exclusion from taking part in politics, and in close connection with these, their lesser knowledge. Hence, men were able to point to higher intellectual qualities and mental superiority in addition to biological arguments embodied by greater physical strength. What has been called earlier complementary division of labour seldom appeared in a pure form. Modifications of it generally brought about heavier burdens for women who had to take over classical man's jobs. This was furthered and became justified by technical development as a result of which less and less strength and the kind of skill men have was needed. The question now arises: is there a reversed shouldering of work, do men perform traditional women's jobs and to what extent?

As a first approach to an answer, housework was divided into two groups; on the basis of this breakdown it could be established whether the work of the husband or of the wife brings about the disintegration of the complementary division of labour. (See Table 9.)

At first glance it is striking that in every group of manual workers, work requiring great muscular strength plays a far more important role in the pattern of activities than in the case of those doing clerical work.

TABLE 9

Division of labour between husband and wife (per cent)

Housework	Professional and clerical				Manual workers			
	husband	wife	husband	wife	husband	wife	husband	wife
	wife in employment		wife not in employment		wife in employment		wife not in employment	
Work around the house requiring physical strength	65	4	74	17	69	12	91	29
Easier housework	35	96	26	83	31	88	9	71

This fact is closely connected with housing conditions which differ from class to class in addition to the earlier mentioned conditions of mechanization and availability of services. Sociological research has shown that the proportion of those living in state-owned flats decreases progressing downwards from those who hold leading posts (50 per cent) to unskilled workers (23 per cent). The composition of those who live in one-family houses is reversed. The proportion of unskilled workers living in the latter is 48.8 per cent whereas the ratio of members of the professions and of executives is 13.3 and 17.8 per cent. It takes a long time to equip a family house completely and in the meantime those who live there have to carry out activities requiring considerable

physical strength, from which those in state-owned flats are exempt. There is generally running water in the latter whereas in a considerable proportion of one-family houses those who live there have to carry water from the well.

This table however, does not answer the question whether the disintegration of the division of complementary work helps competitive work to flourish or if it points to a third type in the division of activities. This problem can be analysed in different ways. We have to investigate to what extent the help of men eases the burdens of women and decreases the drawbacks deriving from domestic chores of married women who have a job although housework requires the full time and energy of a person. The share of husbands in housework was, therefore, examined, as well as the effect it exerts on the schedule of women. This can be gauged by comparing the weight of the most and/or least time-requiring activities with the total time spent on housework in every group. The aim is to express as a percentage the maximum-minimum time requirement in the housework schedule; the index of the proportionate division of labour is the difference between the maximum and the minimum percentage.

TABLE 10

Share of activities in different groups (per cent)

	Professional and clerical				Manual workers			
	husband	wife	husband	wife	husband	wife	husband	wife
	wife in employment		wife not in employment		wife in employment		wife not in employment	
a%—b%*	30	50	44	44	34	46	55	40

* a%—activities requiring maximum time; b%—percentage of activities requiring minimum time.

According to Table 10 the sharing out depends in the first place on the employment of the wife and—if both husband and wife are working—on the section of society they belong to, but in the second place only. Men in families where the spouses are professional people work according to the most uniform schedule while deviations range up to a considerable 50 per cent in the case of women of the same families. A similar tendency appears in the case of working-class families if both are working. At the same time, the pattern of activity of a housewife is more uniform than that of her working husband. The fact therefore that husbands take part in housework to a higher degree considerably modifies the time-table of women; with more time on their hands and exempt from any duties, they can devote themselves to a higher degree to traditional female work (cooking, ironing, washing, patching up clothes etc.). The more uniform schedule of housewives goes together with heavier work which requires bodily strength: in this case the husband lends a helping hand to a lesser degree only, and spends most of his other time on traditional men's jobs such as gardening, digging, hoeing, wood-cutting etc. This is therefore a new, third type of division of labour between spouses in the case of working women: husbands take over all sorts of housework as a result of which their pattern of activity becomes more proportionate and harmonious; accordingly, wives are charged with less housework and their schedule assumes a more complementary character in a positive sense. The division of labour between husband and wife in housework follows the above mentioned pattern which relies on the historical lack of equal rights of women.

Finally, if housework is broken down by components a clearer picture shows interesting results: husbands and wives evaluate the order of importance of housework differently; wives stress the importance of certain activities husbands attach less importance to, and vice-versa.

If the weight of a day's housework is investigated seperately in the case of men and women it appears that the ideas of husbands in respect to their participation in housework differ to a far greater degree than in the order of importance in the education of children. It should be added that these divergences cannot be explained unequivocally either by the employment of wives or by the fact of belonging to a certain social class. This points to the fact that husbands take a hand in housework far more sporadically than in education. More intensive participation in domestic chores is a less important and more dispensable item of their schedule than occupation with their children; in the latter field they give relatively more and steady help to their wives. In the case of wives, the situation is reversed. The graphs representing the division of time women spent on housework practically coincide or run parallel; in all groups the same activities are at the top and at the bottom, in order of importance. Accordingly, women have far more definite and rigid views in respect to care expended on the family as a whole than on the time-requirement and importance of the education of children. All this corroborates what was said earlier, that women are housewives in the first place and mothers only in the second place.

Finally the question arises: do the members of society find it "natural" that spouses divide work to so slight an extent? Women are charged with many burdens while men shoulder far fewer: disproportions in the division of labour are even more striking in housework than in the education of children. If one or another of the partners has a guilty "social conscience", endeavours to change matters could be carried out more easily. In other words: to what extent are families worried because of the unequal division of labour? What are the expectations of spouses in regard to themselves and to each other in respect to housework? Spontaneous and characteristic answers can be obtained if family members are asked about their views regarding their participation in housework and the answers are set against available facts. The latter are taken from the time-balance investigation while opinions represent answers given to the following questions: "In your view, how much time do you and your wife (husband) spend on housework?" (Table 11.)

The opined time-data reflect in every case ideas and intentions and it appears that the answers are section-specific and depend with equal force on the employment of the wife and on the actually performed hours and minutes spent on work. Women in every group thought that they have spent more time on housework than corresponded to

TABLE 11

Data of time spent on housework in families with children on the average (in minutes)

Opinion of		Professional and clerical				Manual workers			
		about husband		about wife		about husband		about wife	
		presumed	factual	presumed	factual	presumed	factual	presumed	factual
		data		data		data		data	
wife working	husband	78	67	276	178	66	93	288	222
	wife	78	67	282	178	72	93	294	222
wife at home	husband	42	54	432	355	54	88	438	386
	wife	48	54	456	355	36	88	432	386

facts. This points to two effects. First, a considerable part of the work is tedious and burdensome and is at the bottom of the scale of social appreciation. From this point of view therefore women find continuous repetitive work trying. On the other hand, it is known from complaints by men and women that the lack of a "cosy family nest" causes serious conflicts. Therefore, women —first of all housewives—believe that the prestige of housework is best furthered at least in the family circle, if the family is provided for to perfection and for this reason they spend their whole day, one might say almost all their time, on housework. Women at work also often compound with their conscience by declaring that their work is not at the expense of housework and try therefore to increase the time ratio of housework to the detriment of their "leisure time". In order to decide which of the two effects dominates, the statement of husbands on the help given must also be taken into account.

Manual workers—and their wives even more so—believe that "housekeeping is a woman's job". Women declare that the participation of men in housework amounts to half an hour although it is in fact one and a half hours. "Self justification" in respect to lending a hand in housework is mainly stressed by manual workers. Those in professional or clerical employment, both of whom are working, find this kind of activity most burdensome; in view of both partners the husband ought to take part in housework more intensively.

It appears therefore that precisely those families are willing to eliminate disproportions and broaden the basis of the division of labour where the question has been solved for the most part and that there is but very slight hope of liquidating the disadvantageous situation of women out of their own resources where the division of labour causes the greatest problems at present.

The sum and substance of the study is that not much can be expected from "natural" development in the distribution of work in the family, nor even a partial solution of the problems of inequality. It is necessary that society contributes to such an extent to housework which would really enable progress towards the realization of social ideals which have been earlier referred to as the only possibility to keep a preliminary check on the family in a differentiated society.

KÁROLY VARGA

LEISURE AND DIVORCE
Marital Cohesion in the Time-Budget

No other social institution is enshrouded in such mystic haze as the family. Scientific research, inevitably, strips it of illusions and secularizes it. Professor René König, the well-known family sociologist, by way of illustration frequently cites the idyllic picture of the Holy Family as represented by religious tradition and the fancy of painters to contrast it with the way it is rendered verisimilar by historical-sociological research. The Flight to Egypt, for example, is visualized by the free play of pious imagination as the Blessed Virgin Mary sitting on a donkey with the Child Jesus in her lap, with a few bundles behind her. The donkey is being led by St. Joseph who—in some versions—also carries a few bundles. However, persons well-informed on the contemporary patriarchal family system would depict Joseph sitting on the donkey, Mary walking a few steps behind him carrying the child on her back together with all the bundles on her shoulder and in her hands.

The family, as one of the most complex functional units of the social order, is highly esteemed in any traditional view of the world. In traditional society, all production is family production, politics—to a certain extent—cover family policy and in the social hierarchical system, the family finds a situation for the young ones.

The stressing of the idyllic picture of the Holy Family was a reaction to the general social mobility which followed in the wake of industrialization, and which shook the traditional institutional forms of the family and of matrimony. Social differentiation removed more and more of its functions, and by so doing, from a functional viewpoint stripped the family to its essentials. The foundations of the build-up of the social-cultural personality continued to be laid by the nuclear family circle, the intimate group, but it was no longer adequate that only the family should start off the young ones in well-proved careers within the social hierarchy. The function of assigning roles, a function of fundamental importance, was assumed by schools and universities which decided on the basis of objective standards each young person's station in life. A previously manifested disposition in a certain occupation or profession was the decisive yardstick in allocating jobs.

There is no doubt that the family, deprived of its secondary functions, became more vulnerable to the fluctuations of social mobility. The dense and entangled texture of interests which, concealing the disorders, brought about the failure of its main functions, no longer exists.

However, the feeling of a "family crisis" produced unrest not only among the devotees of religious and traditional views of the world but also among sociologists who, though observing the phenomenon closely,

did not become aware of any further connections. The disintegration of the family, that is, the abandoning of earlier complex social functions, was mistaken for its disorganization, that is, its internal decomposition. Other sociologists, however, pointed out that the two processes can be quite independet and that the disintegrated family —the peculiar group of intimates who were content with starting the socio-cultural build-up of descendants—can find a new stability. Moreover, some sociologists started a counter-attack voicing the opinion—supported by research—that the drawback of the family is its traditional over-organization. In particular, the negative effect which the firmly controlled German family exerts on psychical health was emphasized, and direct relations were sought between their educational ideal and the authoritarian fascism.

The sociologist is concerned with the questions of the disintegration and mutilation of the family, and with the breaking up of marriage from the aspect of an observer and analyser; whereas the social politician considers it from the viewpoint of a healer, reformer and protector of social hygiene. The decisive role in this depends on value judgements. Is a high divorce rate advantageous or disadvantageous? The sociologist is restricted to observations and analyses such as "the divorce rate is low in times of war and economic depression whereas it rises when there is a boom and social optimism prevails." Further: "in cultures characterized by higher matrimonial mobility, children set a higher store on the company of peer groups, and adults on that of colleagues and friends. On the other hand, in cultures characterized by a more stable marital system, family orientation is fostered by the young and the old alike, opening up new channels to a number of social-psychological phenomena of which the uninitiated do not even guess the origins." In the American society, which is known for its high divorce rate, children—according to McClelland's data—feel the need to become popular among their friends, whereas in the West German society, where the divorce rate is low, the patriarchal educational ideal develops an abstract sense of duty in children. Their problem is: "What is the proper thing to do?" and "what is bad form?" on the basis of idealistic moral precepts, in contrast to the USA where the question is: "What does everybody else do; on the basis of which common and mutual form of behaviour could I best fit in with others?"

Sociologists performing these analyses usually find that their results do not necessarily underpin the formation of value judgements. The social politician and social philosopher synthesize several aspects and, therefore, quite frequently take over the torch when the sociologist fails.

It is to be hoped that this preface has served to avoid some confusions and misunderstandings. This is a professional sociological study, and so it is not concerned with synthesizing and evaluating empirical results. If, therefore, investigations show that—under certain conditions—marriages are disorganized as families change from the patriarchal-authoritarian pattern to egalitarianism, I do not intend to classify this empirical relationship according to any moral or ideological principle. That is not my line, and there are others better versed in that field.

The Range of this Investigation and the Antecedents of the Subject

This study is one of the subjects of the international time-balance investigation co-ordinated by the European Co-ordination Centre for Research and Documentation in Social Sciences in Vienna. Twenty-one research institutes from twelve countries took part in an examination, guided by the Hungarian project-director Sándor Szalai. The investigators interviewed about 30,000 people in one or more medium-sized industrial towns in different countries, from the non-agricultural population of active age.

The model towns were: in Bulgaria—Kazanlik, and eleven neighbourhood villages; in Czechoslovakia—Olomouc, and one representative sample chosen from 90 villages near Olomouc; in France, six towns—Arras, Besançon, Dunkerque, Chalon-sur-Saône, Epinal and Metz; in the GDR—Hoyerswerda and its neighbourhood; in West Germany —Osnabrück (but in West Germany a comprehensive national sample was taken in addition); in Hungary—Győr, and one representative sample chosen from 74 villages in the neighbourhood of Győr, in Poland—Toruń and its neighbourhood; in Peru—Lima and its neighbourhood; in the Soviet Union—Pskov; and in the United States—Jackson, Mich., and a complete urban representative survey; and in Yugoslavia—Maribor, and six villages, and Kragujevac together with two neighbouring villages. In Belgium—a comprehensive national sample was taken.

The interview recorded precisely every minute detail of a day in the life of the person interviewed, who first completed a questionnaire received earlier and then drafted a report of a day with the assistance of the interviewer: what he or she did from one minute to the next, what else at the same time, with whom or in the presence of whom and where? 150,000 punched cards containing the bulk of information were processed by seven computers in Moscow, Cologne, Prague, Paris, Warsaw, Brussels and Ann Arbor, Mich. The first results of this comprehensive research were presented by the international work-group at the Evian World Congress of Sociologists, and aroused much interest. Subsequently, studies of the various separate subjects were elaborated, and the present paper presents the essentials of one such study.

In the first phase of the research work, when the computer was producing the first numerical results, I was in Cologne and made the startling observation which prompted me to write this article. Why do husband and wife spend together two hours more daily in Osnabrück than in Győr? This is a significant difference in view that the statistical samples amount to about three thousand people, a fact which excludes the possibility of coincidence. I started to collect the odd-looking data relevant to this question. Two lines of inquiry intrigued me and aroused my interest from two points of view. In his family-sociological lectures, Professor König criticized fiercely the anachronistic over-organization in West German families; on the other hand, Pál Lőcsei's article published in *Kortárs* stressed that the numbers of those separated and not legally divorced were high (in addition to the high number of *de jure* divorced couples) which confirmed earlier information about the trend of broken marriages in Hungary. Two different worlds, two sets of complaints to illustrate the interesting figures: how much of their time do working husbands spend with their wives?

In Osnabrück the average was 4.3 hours, only slightly less than with their fellow-workers (4.9 hours).

In Győr 2.2 hours, scarcely amounting to one-third of the time spent with their fellow-workers (7.1 hours).

And how much of their time do working women spend with their husbands?

In Osnabrück 4.4 hours, that is, about twice as much time they spend with their colleagues (2.6 hours).

In Győr 2.0 hours, i.e. precisely one-third of the time spent with their colleagues (6.0 hours).

Now, before dealing with the question seriously, one could jokingly say that, on the above basis, the relative weight of the presence of husbands as compared to that of colleagues is six times less in Győr than in Osnabrück, so the image of husbands would be six times dimmer in the minds of their wives as compared to that of their colleagues.

However, even stranger connections manifest themselves. If a working man gets married, the bridegroom's stag party on the eve of his wedding means that he embarks on a new way of life in Osnabrück; but not in Győr. From then on, a German bridegroom decreases the time spent with his colleagues by almost one and a half hours, whereas a Hungarian one by only 0.2 hour, that is, twelve minutes. This shows that the conjugal state is more significant and respected in Osnabrück than in Győr, and that from the fact of matrimony more efficient independent variables can be deduced in Germany than in Hungary. (For the time being, we ignore the other differences, since they will partly reappear in the comparisons of eleven countries.)

These differences set one thinking. To what extent does the shorter working time in Osnabrück, or the higher rate of TV viewing account for them? Obviously, it does not explain everything for, as we have seen, the question does not refer to the time spent with the family, but with the wife. Once we decided to go more fully into the problem, that is, to delve deeper into the latent variables such as whether the couple watched television or talked when together, then we were obliged to include comparison data from other countries too. Once this decision was reached, the character of the research work changed fundamentally. Until then it was a descriptive investigation. Certain questions, such as family orientation in a country (and as a matter of curiosity in some other country as well) remained in the foreground. But from then on, it turned into hypothesis-testing research: instead of characterizing the examined units—countries, or more precisely, the population of the sample towns—the interest centred on interconnections, and on the theoretical importance of the latter. We had to look up the results of earlier research on the correlation of joint spare-time activities and marital cohesion.

Before dealing with the three theoretical questions which constitute our main subject, two problems must be cleared up. First: how are we going to establish correlations between the time-budget data of any town, and the rate of divorce in the country as a whole in order to demonstrate that there is a relationship between cohesion and/or degree of broken marriages and relevant time-budget variables? Data of a single town, on the one hand, and national data, on the other: can any conclusion be drawn from them? Secondly: how are we going to draw conclusions from the divorce rates of the single countries in view of Pál Lőcsei's research mentioned earlier according to which the number of broken marriages not included in statistics assumes huge proportions. Besides, there are countries where it is easier, while in others it is more difficult to obtain a divorce. When all is said and done how can divorces provide an index of broken marriages?

Fortunately, we were not the first to encounter such difficulties. As regards the first question, M. Pinard pointed out that with the progress of industrialization, the economic-social conditions in one country tend to be equalized, thus the same factors influence marriage and divorces in every part of the same country. As a result, differences in marriage and divorce rates gradually disappear between the regions of the country, while the differences between various countries increase. This is the so-called "*intra*cultural homogeneity—*inter*cultural heterogeneity" formula known from international comparisons. This means that a country's carefully chosen sample can represent the entity—provided it is a sufficiently large sample—naturally, for a comparison with a similarly chosen sample elsewhere. If the samples included in the comparison were not standardized from any important social-economic aspect, the average in either sample would be distorted by the predominance of women, in another sample by that of youth, in the third, by university graduates, in the fourth, by villagers. Our sample towns are exemplary in this respect and were included in the comparison considering even the most subtle points, for instance, childless couples were not compared to families with children,

and occasionally the non-agricultural population in a town was compared according to their status.

Regarding the second question, that is, to what extent, if at all, do divorce rates reflect the actual disorganization of family life, W. Goode, a well-known authority in the field, has established four groups of phenomena characterizing matrimonial instability and disorganization, in addition to the dissolution of marriages by one of the partners (this category includes, besides legal divorce, marital separation and desertion). Of these the one called the "empty shell" family concerns us; it refers to the case when husband and wife shoulder a number of duties but repudiate providing emotional support for each other. The problem is in short, why do such marriages break up in some cases and why don't they dissolve in others? According to Goode, in countries where it is easy to obtain a divorce, the number of broken marriages is by and large congruent with the divorce rate *even in the lower social classes*. This manifests itself mainly in countries above a certain level of industrialization; on the other hand, in countries where divorce is rendered more difficult, the actual dissolution of marriages and the rate of divorce are only congruent *in the upper socio-economic strata*, while the divorce rate is below the number of broken marriages in the lower classes. In other words: in every country owing to frustrations and other burdens, more marriages are broken in the lower social classes than in the upper ones, but this fact is reflected by the divorce rate only in industrially developed countries. In less industrialized countries, although the decomposition of family lives is likewise more common in the lower than in the upper strata, the divorce rate is higher in the upper than in the lower classes. This is partly due to the poor being less able to afford the expenses than the rich, and partly to their shrinking from complicated legal proceedings. Goode proves his theory by a number of examples, among others by that of Hungary.

We can support his statements by time-budget data in six other countries, as well as the four countries which Goode, too, has analysed (USA, Belgium, Yugoslavia, Hungary). A significant correlation could be observed between spending time in a way which points to disorganization and the divorce rate in every stratum in highly industrialized countries, whereas this correlation manifests itself only in the upper classes in less industrialized countries. For instance, there is no such characteristic relationship between the time spent away from the spouse and the divorce rate in the lower strata. However this is a subject for another study. What interests us here is the fact that the relationship between the actual disorganization of marriages and its expression in the divorce rate is no longer uncontrolled or obscure, for it can be taken into account precisely and occasionally its effect can be kept constant.

Home Orientation and Marital Cohesion

We have tried to find a relationship between the time a husband and wife spend together and marital cohesion, studying couples in Osnabrück and Győr independently from *where* they were together. Now we are going to correlate the time spent at home with divorce rates in eleven countries. Fortunately, abundant literature is available on this problem. From Scheuch's investigations it appears that the soundness of family life goes together with leisure time spent at home. Goode's famous research into the world of divorcees shows that according to a fourth of divorced women, the main reason of their broken marriages was the disinterest of the husband in the home, the children and the wife. The examinations of family problems carried out by Brim classify 25 types of marital complaints according to their frequency of occurrence. The complaint "the husband spends too little time with his family" came second. In Brim's examina-

tion factor analysis was also applied. Thus he found out which family problems are coupled to other problems, and moreover, which problem can be traced back to deeper-rooted factors, and what kind. Accordingly, the second type of complaint is particularly sensitive to the "husband-wife relation," that is, to the family as intimate group. In this case the path leads from Goode's "empty shell" family (repudiation of emotional support) to extra-marital relations. The latter clearly emerges from Klinger's analysis according to which "the time spent away from the home" as a cause of divorce, is related in 39 per cent of the cases to the secondary cause of divorces, namely, "love-affair with a third party at the place of work or elsewhere."

Now let us examine more closely some time-budget data concerning time spent at home. If the eleven investigated countries are classified according to how many minutes of their leisure time the working, married men, fathers of family, have spent at home it appears that Peru (82.4 minutes on the average) Yugoslavia (67.2) and Belgium (50.1) stand first, whereas the GDR (26.3 minutes on the average), the USA (22.4) and Hungary (20.3) stand last. (The category "leisure time" in the code-system of the multinational time-budget project includes activities other than work, such as conversation, entertaining guests and resting, but does not include such matters as self-education, reading, watching TV or listening to the radio.) If the eleven countries are classified according to the crude divorce rate (i.e. per thousand inhabitants) and/or net divorce rate (i.e. per thousand marriages), then two of the three countries classified in the first place, Peru and Belgium, are, again at the top of the table and the GDR the USA and Hungary at the bottom though with the slight difference that Hungary and the USA change places. The following table shows the classification according to the leisure time spent at home and the two kinds of divorce rate.

Table I

*Order of the leisure time spent at home of working married men
and divorce rates in eleven countries*

Countries	Order of		
	leisure time spent at home	divorces per 1,000 inhabitants	divorces per 1,000 marriages
Peru	1	1	1
Yugoslavia	2	7	6
Belgium	3	2	2
France	4	3	3
Poland	5	4	5
West Germany	6	5	4
Bulgaria	7	6	7
Czechoslovakia	8	8	8
GDR	9	9	9
USA	10	11	11
Hungary	11	10	10

(If the rank-correlation is calculated between the order of leisure time spent at home and the order of the two divorce rates, value tau = 0.78 is obtained in both cases which in view of the long line is significant at p = 0.00019 level, showing that the possibility of incidental parallelism in the classification is infinitesimal.)

The Hungarian reader might be struck by the last and last but one position Hungary occupies and will, therefore, understand that the author, too, was puzzled by the differences between the data for Hungary and West Germany which ranks near the middle of the list.

Now, if holidays (bank holidays) are examined it appears that although there still is a considerable relationship between a husband's leisure time spent at home and the cohesion of marriages, it is not so significant as on working days. This is easily understandable. Moreover, Scheuch's precise data also show that on week-ends, leisure time spent with the family, but not at home, is more important.

The same connection is of less importance in the case of childless families; this, too, is understandable, as it is a less laudable phenomenon for a newly-wed husband to stay at home.

Interesting results are obtained if reading, education and pastimes related to mass communication are included in the leisure time category (i.e. the time that remains after bread-winning, housework, looking after the children and the psychological necessities such as sleeping, eating, washing, etc.). It appears that the length of this leisure time category taken in a wider, more inclusive sense does not correlate with family cohesion. It seems that neither a husband buried in his newspaper nor husband and wife watching a crime-play on television are pillars of conjugal stability.

The wife—particularly if there are children—spends so much time at home anyway that no significant correlations could be established between the time a wife spends at home and marital cohesion.

In this way one becomes aware of the somewhat disillusioning fact that one of the buttresses on which the stability of marriages rests is a stay-at-home way of life. Watching television may keep couples at home, but it does not prevent the dissolution of marriage. Viewing the question from another aspect, it can be said that few doomed marriages can be prolonged along with a retired mode of life unless there is a TV set at home.

It seems that of pastimes at home, talking to the spouse (either as primary activity, or a secondary one during meals) stabilizes marriage most effectively. Conversations in the evening hours are, according to Scheuch's examinations, very important in uniting married couples. The husband tells of the wrong he had suffered from his boss, the wife gossips, they express their indignation and are scandalized together, co-ordinating their personal systems of values without necessarily noticing. Through conversations in the evening, they are able to turn into a common family affair those parts of their lives which are absorbed by their separate professions or matters of work, which are otherwise alien to the other. This is all that would need to be said on the subject of home-orientation and marital cohesion if there wouldn't be a marked correlation—a very striking one—between the two. It is peculiar that as a result of lengthy data collecting, coding and processing, countries were ranged in a certain order regarding a time-budget variable whereafter it appeared that the order coincides exactly with the order of divorce rates in the countries listed. One is inclined to think that a third variable, for example, the level of industrialization, produces an effect which inconspicuously influences both the rates of staying at home and of divorce. And is the order obtained not after all reminiscent of some other order?

In similar cases—in comparisons of various countries on different levels of technical-economical development, where the quality to be compared is related to the dimensions of the traditional against the modern way of life—the suspicious variable is the index of *societal differentiation* which, devised following R. Marsh's system, includes the proportion of the non-agricultural earning population of any country and the energy consumption per head. Marsh calculated this index in respect to 114 nations including, of course, the eleven countries whose time-budget data were analysed. On this basis Peru, Bulgaria, Yugoslavia and Hungary are characterized by low value indices, Poland, France, the GDR and Czechoslovakia by medium value indices, and West Germany, Belgium and the USA by high value indices. Now, if similarly to Table I, a new order of disorganized marriages is established either in the order of indices deriving from the time-budget

data or in the order of indices produced from the national divorce rates, it will come as a surprise that the rank order of societal differentiation has no significant connection with either of the above rank orders.

Hence, one cannot say that industrialization brings about more leisure time and that more of it is being spent at home. It is true that the absolute length of leisure time increases with the growth of industrialization, but there are data to show that the working husbands studied spent an increasingly smaller part of their longer spare time at home. Thus, leisure time spent at home does not alter much with the degree of industrialization. Neither do divorce rates conform to the level of industrialization in the countries included in the comparison. (In other scales of value, it may well be the other way round, but it would be an oversimplification if marital disorganization—in spite of the distortions by intermediate variables such as countries where it is easy or difficult to obtain divorce—were simply be considered with a function of industrialization.)

This negative result, however, should not be ruled out, for it might be incorporated in some more high-grade interconnection. The fact that lower and higher divorce rates occur both at lower and higher levels of industrialization means that divorce as such is not characteristic of some types of society, but that it is a general human phenomenon. Husbands spending more or less of their leisure time at home is a phenomenon manifesting itself *with similar irregularity* in developed and underdeveloped societies (*irregularity* means, in this case, non-alignment with the level of industrialization). This statement is referred to in Marsh's system as "universal generalization."

Let us survey the *relationship* between home orientation and marital stability, taken separately in the more or the less industrialized countries. It appears that the correlation is slight in less industrialized countries, and high in the more industrialized. Thus, the statement on the relationship of the two variables is by no means a universal generalization. Accordingly, it is not a general human phenomenon that the time spent absent from home leads certainly—or at least very probably—to the disorganization of marriages, for it is characteristic only of more highly industrialized societies. In Marsh's system this observation is called *contingency generalization*. In the following we shall show examples of both universal and contingency generalizations. The analyses are based on the results of time-budget research covering two continents.

Authority Structure of the Family and Marital Cohesion

The traditional family is patriarchal, the realm of the "pater familias" and husband. The not-necessarily-bearded-and-old patriarch glanced round the circle of his subjects, content or offended. He was always surrounded by the whole family. On the other hand, in the modern, egalitarian family husband and wife live opposite, as it were, to each other and see it written on the other's face what each expects and whether he or she is quite serious about it. Intricate research has established precisely that in modern egalitarian families, compared to traditional ones, the husband and wife spend more time in each other's company than together with the whole family. According to Scheuch's empirical thesis, in authoritarian families leisure time is family-oriented, whereas in egalitarian families it is rather partner oriented.

Such data provides opportunity for working out the two family types in time-budget variables: the leisure time spent with the spouse is simply divided by the leisure time spent with the family. In the case of a high quotient, the family is a more egalitarian family type than in that of a low quotient. In order to prove the practicability and validity of our data, the calculation could be performed also in relation to a special leisure activity, conversation, taken either as a primary activity or a secondary one, e.g. during evening meals. For this purpose the time spent by the couple in talking is divided by the time during which the whole family took part in the conversation. In this case, too, higher quotients point to egalitarian families and lower quotients to authoritarian ones.

Once the two family types had been established by time-budget indices, the only thing left is to find out which is more stable and/or unstable. First, however, I must stress that the Hungarian families rank among the traditional authoritarian families, especially from the aspect of conversation rather than from their arrangement of their entire leisure time.

There is a positive correlation between the divorce rate and both indices of egalitarianism. The more egalitarian a family, the more prone it is, *ceteris paribus*, to dissolution. (The probability of a nil-hypothesis—i.e. considering the result merely accidental—was measured on the basis of the conversation index $p = 0.008$, i.e. it is less than one per cent.)

If the countries under observation are grouped according to family egalitarianism, the question arises whether there is a higher correlation between egalitarianism and dissolution in the authoritarian or in the egalitarian groups? Does the dissolution of marriages show an accelerating or a slackening tendency as egalitarianism gains ground? Well, the tendency is accelerating in respect to the countries under observation. Borrowing a phrase from Levinger, a well-known authority in the sociology of divorce, one could say that a gradual breaking up in the power-joints of a family does not lead noticeably to dissolution, for it is compensated by the internal forces of attraction it releases. It is more convenient to live in an egalitarian marriage than in an authoritarian one. However, a further loosening of the power structure, or in the words of Goode who expresses the same idea from a somewhat different angle: "the slackening of the forces upholding the framework" drives this process at a faster rate towards a yet unknown dissolution rate, or more precisely, towards a still unknown marital mobility level, or divorce and re-marriage rate. According to both Levinger and Goode, the decisive cohesive force is not the attraction of marital happiness, but an external, more or less compulsory cohesion.

However, it is not quite as simple as that. It is obvious that partners in egalitarian families will not put up with marital problems for as long a time as in authoritarian ones. But it should be taken into account that marital discord, which occurs in any type of family, is decreased not increased where the communication between partners is manifold, animated and interesting. Thus, the higher conversation rate between couples, previously used as the index of egalitarianism, is not at the same time an index of discord and dissolution. This would be a gross misapprehension. The egalitarian and authoritarian family types could also have been produced by means of other indices (as it had been developped in fact out of the time-budget on the basis of Scheuch's hypothesis using the rate of the extent couples go into company together). Conversations in the evening —mentioned earlier to connection with home orientation—help to stabilize family life if the daytime experiences are exchanged in a cosy atmosphere and attitudes to them can be co-ordinated. This is the very criterion met by the conversation model of egalitarian families. On the basis of the literature of the subject we accept the hypothesis that the extent of conversation between husband and wife is better suited to point ahead to marital cohesion in egalitarian family type societies than in those of authoritarian family types. The time-budget data resulting from the compound operations performed on the computer at Cologne University substantiate this hypothesis with some refinements. In France, Czechoslovakia, Yugoslavia, Bul-

garia, Hungary and Peru there is no significant correlation between the extent of daily conversation between husband and wife and the divorce rate, while in the USA, in the two Germanies, Poland and Belgium the correlation is significant on a level of $p = 0.025$.

Now, what does this correlation mean as regards social differentiation? Earlier it was thought that divorce rate and home orientation, taken separately, do not follow societal differentiation. However, the closeness of the two correlates with the level of industrialization and urbanization to an extent already perceptible. It seems that family egalitarianism is even more closely bound to industrialization. First, it can be observed that the more industrialized and differentiated a society is, the more frequently the form of family labelled "the egalitarian family type" occurs. (The possibility of a nil-hypothesis is no higher here than it was in the case of the first index: leisure time spent with the spouse per leisure time spent with the whole family: $p = 0.001$, and the second index: conversation with the spouse per conversation with the whole family: $p = 0.002$.)

It seems that not only egalitarianism itself, but also the effect it exerts on the dissolution of marriage is in close relation to the differentiation index. The egalitarianism indices show a close relationship to divorce rates only in industrially developed societies, while there is no such correlation in less industrialized ones. Hungary is a case in point, as in Hungary a non-egalitarian family type goes together with a very high divorce rate.

Thus, our observations regarding the authority structure of the family could be inserted in Marsh's model in such a way that both the individual variables and their relations fall within the scope of the contingency generalization. In other words: the more frequent occurrence of equality between husband and wife, and the fact that egalitarianism facilitates the dissolution of marriage are neither of them general human phenomena, for they both depend on the level of industrialization.

"Conjunctive Affiliation" or "Sexual Heterogeneity?"

Guided by the literature of the subject we could be sure of the results of our investigations to this point. We knew what could be expected from home orientation and from egalitarianism regarding marital cohesion. Now, however, we come to hypotheses which—put into operation in time-budget terms—reveal contradictions. The first peculiar term in the above heading denotes (in Ackerman's theory) the phenomenon in which the social relations of husband and wife, their fitting into their social backgrounds—this "affiliation"—joins rather than separates them. Such a conjunctive affiliation comes from the sub-culture being common, offering common value judgements, from belonging to the same social stratum or having come from the same village, even from distant branches of a large family, and so on. In our time-budget data, the common circle of friends is such a conjunctive affiliation: whether husband and wife go out to attend amusements together or separately and, in general, to what extent they pursue together those leisure activities which involve others. On the basis of Ackerman's theory it could be assumed that leisure time activities involving other persons point toward marital cohesion the more husband and wife enjoy them together, whereas it is a factor of dissolution in proportion to how often it separates them. After all, the same company of friends tend to identical standards of value; a consensus is usually reached in disputed matters, until problems uniting those who belong to the same group of friends become more frequent while the ones which separate them become rarer. Two separate groups of friends represent two separate worlds.

The counter-hypothesis to this was formulated by Young. In cultures where husband and wife seek their amusement separately, groups are sexually homogeneous. They are at any rate far more homogeneous than groups consisting of couples (married couples). The sexual heterogeneity of groups made up of married couples is a trying test of the stability of a marriage. Each partner of another married couple, is an active participant—one also could say "a player"—in one and the same interaction system, becoming immediate sexual objects at the same time, says Young, who then attempts a detailed analysis of the atmosphere of sexually heterogeneous social groups. The aim often is to reach some excitement and another man is often more gallant than a husband who, more or less conspicuously, may pay attentions to other women.

It is clear that the two hypotheses are irreconcilably opposed so that we must try to decide: which of the two is confirmed more clearly by our time-budget data? Does the amount of leisure time spent with the spouse outside the home, in entertainment, dining out, etc. show a positive or a negative correlation with the divorce rates? We found the correlation a positive one! The attempted conjunctive affiliation proved a weaker variable than sexual heterogeneity in terms of the time budget.

However, conjunctive affiliation is a more highly reliable structural determinant of divorce rates than would enable us to accept the fact that its influence was not perceptible from analysing time-budget data. Ackerman pointed out that if it cannot be applied in a concrete case, probably a wrong index was chosen, for the concept itself is certainly correct. Hence, another approach must be attempted. The theorem of conjunctive affiliation holds that husband and wife, but particularly the latter, have to break with their earlier forms of behaviour through which they had been integrated into their pre-material social texture, give up their former groups of friends, neglect, or better still forget their previous acquaintance. That is, they must radically break with *disjunctive* affiliations, otherwise the marriage continues to be unsteady. Ackerman also proves that divorce rates are lower in cultures where disengagement of husband and wife, particularly of the latter, from their former environment is possible, than in those where there are no institutions or customs to facilitate disengagement.

Well, disengagement can also be processed by time-budget variables, a similar phenomenon was mentioned in the first part of our study, referring to the consequences of a bridegroom's farewell party in West Germany and in Hungary. We can now systematically control what at the beginning had only been surmised, in the correlation of the two countries. The two precisely defined variables chosen for this purpose are: (1) The quotient of the time married and/or not married working men and women spend with their colleagues, (2) the quotient of percentages of the married and not married population attending adult education. Those kinds of quotient indices are already known from studies of equality. In this case they express—each separately in its own dimension—the extent to which the system of pre-marital social relations and interactions continues after marriage.

Since disengagement of women is particularly important, let us examine how far the quotient of women correlates with the divorce rate.

Table II

The order of two index quotients of unmarried and married working women and of the divorce rates in nine countries

Countries[1]	Order of		
	Frequency Divorce per 1,000 inhabitants	Quotients before and after marriages	
		of the time spent with colleagues	of attendance at continuative education
USA	1	1	2
Hungary	2	4.5	2
Czechoslovakia	3	2	3
Yugoslavia	4	4.5	1
Bulgaria	5	3	8
West Germany	6	8	5
Poland	7	6	6
France	8	9	9
Belgium	9	9	9
		$\text{tau} = 0.67$ $p = 0.006$	$\text{tau} = 0.33$ $p = 0.11$

[1] Data were available from only nine countries, as the above comparison did not figure in the computing programme covering eleven countries. The basic data were worked out from a preliminary report submitted to the Evian Congress, which only included the nine countries listed above.

The figures of this table agree with the hypothesis. The "post per prior" quotients follow fairly regularly the divorce rates in each dimension. Thus, the extent of disengagement from the earlier social group has some kind of connection with the stability of marriage. The probability of the contrary is shown by the fairly low p values at the bottom of the table.

The Hungarian data deviates on the two dimensions and does not illustrate well the regularity already noted. Measured against the time spent with colleagues from work, the high divorce rate in Hungary goes together with a medium disengagement rate, whereas measured in the dimension of adult education it goes together with an expressedly high disengagement rate. Regarding colleagues Hungary does not contribute to the correlation between disengagement from the pre-marital social circle and the stability of marriages. Regarding adult education, Hungary outright contradicts the expected correlation, more than any other country. Of the three interrelations investigated here—interconnections between divorce rates on the one hand, and home orientation, family equality and conjunctive affiliation on the other—the Hungarian data show "regular pattern" only in the first one, while in the other two, they are more or less irregular. However, regarding the Hungarian type of broken marriages we have obtained some highly probable information indicating the more and the less important factors responsible for divorces. Egalitarianism has not yet developed in Hungarian families to an extent where it could explain the extraordinarily high divorce rate. Social affiliation following marriage also changes a significant amount, as it appeared from the two available indices.

The third interrelation, the first one discussed, is the negative correlation between the divorce rate and leisure time spent at home. In this respect the Hungarian time-budget data are correct. It appeared that Hungary was placed second among eleven countries in frequency of divorce, and first in the brevity of the leisure time husbands spend at home. This variable proved so watertight that it appears to compensate the shortcoming of the two other pre-estimating time-budget variables. In view of this, it is difficult to repudiate the assumption that the unusually high divorce rate in Hungary is closely related to the deficiency of home orientation, that is, that Hungarians—and naturally, husbands first and foremost—are not too fond of staying at home. This could be broken down into further factors: for example, it is rather obvious that housing conditions may be responsible for this, but our present data does not provide an answer to how this idea could be processed further. This belongs to another kind of sociological investigation.

Returning to our original train of thought, one question still remains to be answered: is there a relationship between the disjunctive affiliation and/or the liquidation of the conjunctive affiliation and social differentiation, that is, the level of industrialization? The answer is negative. At any level of industrialization there are disjunctive affiliations both destroyed and such, as remain intact, in all countries investigated. On the basis of Marsh's model it can be said that disengagement from the pre-marital environment and the positive effect this exerts on the stability of marriage is a general human phenomenon, independent from the level of industrialization.

However, there is one more question. Both indices adopted for treating the subject of affiliation—being together with colleagues and/or attending adult education before and after marriage—reach outside the merely private sphere and join in the system of social institutions, in production, and public education. Thus, regarding these indices, an individual is less affected by another individual, and far more by the specific institutional structure of his country of residence; his behaviour cannot be considered as independent from the system of production and the educational organization of his country.

Six of the eleven countries investigated are socialist countries and five are capitalist countries, that is, the eleven countries belong to two different social systems. Does the phenomenon that life is organized rather around productive and educational state institutions in the socialist countries than in capitalist countries appear in the time-budget data? As an answer to the question, the order of the quotients in Table II can be rearranged simply according to whether they are socialist or non-socialist countries. The average of the quotients in both dimensions, to both men and women, is higher in the socialist than in the non-socialist countries. Marriage does not entail such a great break in a person's relation with social institutions in either of the two dimensions mentioned above. The point, here, is not simply the level of industrializa-

tion and such related phenomena as for example shorter working hours, for it was demonstrated that the index of societal differentiation does not show any kind of correlation with the disengagement from colleagues and school, after marriage. No. The point is the differing ways in which the social and private spheres intertwine, which can be felt in Bulgaria which is less industrialized as well as in Czechoslovakia which is highly industrialized.

However, it would not be easy to prove a correlation between the latter phenomenon and divorce rates. It is true that in Eastern Europe the diverco rate is higher than in Western Europe. However, it is highest in the USA. Hence, the relation between divorce and social systems continues to be an unsolved question which will be the subject of much more comprehensive, difficult and interesting research.

MIHÁLY GERGELY

SUICIDE IN HUNGARY

Hungary heads the list

According to a W.H.O. report, a thousand people a day commit suicide, and at least as many fail in their attempts. In most European countries, and in North America, suicide is among the top five-ten causes of death.

Yearly averages of suicides per 100,000 population, 1961–63

Hungary	33.9
Finland	29.0
Austria	28.3
Czechoslovakia	28.2
Japan	24.7
Denmark	24.2
German Fed. Rep.	24.1
Switzerland	23.3
Sweden	21.7
France	20.7
Australia	19.6
United States	15.6
Britain and Wales	15.1
New Zealand	13.0
Poland	12.8
Scotland	11.7
Canada	11.1
Israel	10.4
Holland	9.1
Italy	1.1

W.H.O. statistics published in November 1968 on the suicide wave in the world's industrially advanced countries indicate that, according to surveys, in eight of these countries suicide takes third place, following heart ailments and cancer, as the cause of death in the 15–45 age group. Death by choice has now become a fundamental problem of public health. It is most acute, as the W.H.O. statistics show, in the German Federal Republic, Finland, Austria, Czechoslovakia, Switzerland, Canada, Denmark, Hungary and Sweden.

W.H.O. data show that suicide is also posing an increasingly dangerous threat in the developing countries. Of the 17 countries of Africa, Latin America and Asia, it is among the top ten causes of death in ten of them.

In Hungary over 3,000 suicides a year have been registered in recent times (1968), and therefore over 3 per cent of all deaths were due to suicide. There have been more deaths by suicide than from tuberculosis. Of the 50 killers listed in the international "Causes of Death," there are only four or five which appear more frequently than suicide.

Glancing at the past, and taking a look at the national suicide statistics for the late part of the last century, we learn that in this respect there has been little change in the countries of Europe. The suicide rate in Hungary for the same area as the present was pretty high as far back as 1897: 21 suicides per 100,000 population. By 1910 the figure had risen to 27. At that time this ratio was higher than many other country in the world. And Hungary has been among the countries with the highest suicide rates ever since.

In so far as attempted suicide is concerned, the figures, according to a the "Suicide Trends in Hungary" issued by the Hungarian Central Statistical Office, ran as follows: 1963–9, 439; 1964–10, 952; 1965–10, 745, 1966–12, 569 and 1967–14, 983.

Statistics of suicide

Figures published by the Central Statistical Office in 162 copies, for official use, entitled "Suicide Trends in Hungary 1966–67," show the present suicide situation to be as follows.

". . . Reports of suicides can be controlled through demographic statistics, and their full validity can be proved," write the authors, discussing the accuracy of these figures. "Only part of the attempted suicides, however, are brought to the attention of the authorities, and one can only make assumptions on the proportion of the attempts brought to light out of the whole. We assume that in the years under review 70 per cent of all suicide attempts in Budapest came to light, and only 50 per cent of those outside Budapest."

"In the past 70 years," writes "Suicide Trends in Hungary," "the suicide rate in Hungary has been consistently high. In 1897 the figure over the present area of the country was already over 20 to the 100,000, and only dropped below this twice in the twentieth century, though there have been considerable fluctuations, rising well over this mark, during this period. The number of suicides was highest in 1932, reaching 35.1 per 100,000, and between 1930 and 1937 it was over 30 to the 100,000, each year. It was lowest in 1954, with 17.7 to the 100,000, but the whole 1946–1958 period showed that only once, in 1952, did the rate go above 25 per 100,000. A noticeable rise took place in 1959, and for the following three years, until in 1962 the suicide index fluctuated between 25–26 per 100,000. Another upswing began in 1963, and by 1967 the suicide rate was as high as 30.8 per 100,000 again."

All in all, the suicide trends in Hungary went from 1,463 or 21.2 per 100,000 in 1897, with fluctuations in between, to 3,150 or 30.8 per 100,000 in 1967.

Causes of death

Major causes of death were included in the demographic statistics in the *Hungarian Statistical Pocket Book, 1969.*

Cause of death	1967 deaths	
	Number	per 10,000
Arteriosclerosis and coronary ailments	26,428	25.9
Malignant tumours, including lymphatic tumours	20.609	20.2
All arterial injuries affecting the central nervous system	16,235	15.9
All other accidents	3,287	3.2
Suicide and *self-inflicted injuries*	3,200	3.2
Respiratory tuberculosis	2,274	2.2
Hypertension accompanied by coronary ailments	2,186	2.1

The Minutes of the Meeting of the Hungarian Society of Paediatricians, with the participation of the Hungarian Psychological Scientific Society, held on February 16–17, 1967, dealing with problems of puberty, published by the Hungarian Society of Paediatricians in 1967, contains a lecture by Dr. István Körmendy (Health Department of the executive committee of the Budapest Municipal Council) entitled "Social Problems Connected with the Protection of the Health of Adolescents."

". . . Leading causes of death in Budapest, averaged over 1961–1965, give the following trends:

Infancy: premature birth, deformity, injury at birth, pneumonia

1–4 years: pneumonia, accident, deformity, tumour

5–10 years: accident, tumour, deformity, pneumonia

10–14 years: accident, tumour, *suicide*, pneumonia

15–19 years: *suicide*, accident, tumour, cardio-vascular disorder.

". . . Turning to suicide, we find that this cause of death, which, as we have seen, takes a high priority, begins to make a serious appearance between the ages of 10 and 14, and is the most common cause of death between the ages of 15 and 19. While in most European countries the number of fatal suicide attempts in the 10–14 age group is at most one per 100,000, in Hungary it is three times this figure. According to W.H.O. statistics, in contrast to a suicide mortality rate of 4–6 per 100,000 in the 15–19 year age groups in the German Federal Republic it was 9.6, in Switzerland 10.8, in Austria 11.7, in Czechoslovakia 12.1 and in Hungary was 17 per 100,000."

The indifference of society

There is no other social phenomenon as obscure and mystifying, explained in so contradictory a manner and as neglected as the problem of suicide. Until very recently the subject was practically never broached in print, with the result that there was little possibility of accepting, rejecting or indeed assessing any kind of assertion on the subject.

The book which is even today recognized as the authoritative work on the question is Emile Durkheim's *Suicide—A Sociological Study*. It was written seventy years ago, and a Hungarian translation only appeared in 1967. Out of mere curiosity I asked a number of doctors who are directly concerned with suicide cases about it, and reluctantly came to the conclusion that by no means all of them had read even this basic book on the subject, or, if they had opened it, had not progressed beyond the halfway mark.

In my investigations on this subject I was able to ask various personalities a number of questions designed to reveal the extent to which people in important positions, town and county leaders, doctors and political figures, were aware of the problem of suicide in their own areas of authority. The result was depressing. And they were not alone in displaying ignorance.

Suicide as an alarming social phenomenon is one of our most disturbing demographic problems. It is a peculiar epidemic which "executes" 3,000 persons a year in Hungary, secretly, apparently with no means of prevention, yet it is completely and totally ignored in public thinking, and is never publicly mentioned. Before 1945 the newspapers used to publish sensational reports of a number of suicides every day. After 1945 the subject swifty disappeared from the press, and statistical summaries were excluded from national statistical publications. Statistics on suicide only reappeared in 1957, and in 1958 the Central Statistical Office, in conjunction with one of the police departments and the health authorities, began a regular survey and study of suicides and attempted suicides.

It was in fact no more than six years ago, in 1964, that the first study on the subject giving detailed information was published by the Central Statistical Office. This study dealt with suicides occurring between 1959–1963. Since then occasional references to suicides—though still not enough—once again appear in the press. Articles on the subject take the form of short reviews of publications by the Central Statistical Office, quotations from foreign publications, and five or ten-line reports in the news columns dealing with particularly tragic instances.

A comparison of the two forms of violent death appearing in the 1969 *Statistical Pocket Book* show:

Form of death	Number of deaths			Death ratio per 10,000 population		
	1938	1950	1967	1938	1950	1967
Suicide	2,684	2,074	3,200	2.9	2.2	3.1
Other violent death (murder)	402	266	192	0.4	0.3	0.2

Difficulties of investigation

In the course of the months I was collecting material for this study I visited Csongrád County, which for some time has been at the head of the county lists for suicide statistics. Following an extremely valuable day and a half spent at the Neurology and Psychiatry Clinic in Szeged, thanks to the kind help afforded by the first assistant professor, Dr. János Szilárd. I made an attempt to visit one of the city's hospitals. I waited patiently and politely until the chief physician had finished with all the patients waiting in front of his door, and I entered his room as the last one in the line. I introduced myself politely, showed my Writers' Association membership card, and my letter from the magazine *Kortárs*, commissioning the article. The letter requested the staff of the county and city health departments to give me all available assistance, and was countersigned and sealed by the relevant department head in the Ministry of Health. He studied the signature for several moments (his assistant had already informed him of my request), then returned it, and our short but illuminating talk began. He cited his Hippocratic Oath which he could not break,. and the regulations which made it impossible for him to reply to my questions, to talk of his experiences, or even to show me over his department, since he was not even permitted to show me his instruments. He was very polite, but he showed me the door within five minutes.

This discouraging meeting, and another somewhat similar experience following close on its heels, convinced me that the subject still remains embedded in the mind as something difficult and delicate, which it is advisable to avoid. Very probably the Szeged chief physician would not have got rid of me if he had not been afraid of trouble and complications for voicing his opinions.

Its classification as a "delicate issue" is no doubt the major reason why so amazingly little medical, or sociological work on suicide has been published in Hungary during the past twenty years.

Motives for suicide

Anyone studying the motives for suicide can easily see the complexity of a single case of suicide. In the vast majority of cases the reason finally appearing in the statistics is not the sole nor indeed the most important factor, but simply the last link in the chain. It is simply the last straw, the last drop of water which makes the brimming cup run over at last, when self-control is finally thrown overboard. This is why outsiders are so perplexed and amazed when they hear of certain individual cases since the motive given explains very little, and appears quite incommensurate with the effect.

In most cases the reason is given in a note left behind by the suicide, or a verbal statement should he survive the attempt. This reason is accepted without qualification and without any further investigation into possible motives, for lack of time and opportunity, as well as for back of a professional staff capable of undertaking the work. And it is this motive which appears on the hospital sheet, in the statistical reports.

In evaluating this information, we must take at least two basic facts into consideration. In the first place the "successful" suicide is no longer in full possession of his judgement at the time of writing a farewell note, or perhaps eyplaining his action in his dying words. Most play out their fatally tragic role under such a power of suggestion that their every gesture is exaggerated, their every attitude a false pose, in keeping with the extraordinary, strange role they have assumed. The would-be suicide recovering from his unsuccessful attempt is in a similar psychological and psychic condition, and everything he says is influenced by the peculiar role he has adopted, which he cannot refrain from playing to the end. Another factor to be considered in determining the self-evaluation of his motives is the diminished intellectual power of a person gradually regaining his senses after days of unconsciousness.

In the second place there is the lesson I learned in the course of collecting this information, which can only be mentioned *en passant* both because it is too complicated a subject to discuss here, and because the majority of suicide cases have too little self-knowledge. They misunderstand their own physical and intellectual qualifications and possibilities, and are consequently unable to escape the impasse in which they find themselves. It is therefore necessary to maintain considerable reservations in accepting the reason for his suicide given by such a person.

Below is a breakdown of suicides and attempted suicides according to probable reasons.

	1935–1939	1959–1963
	Average of years per 100,000 population	
Illness, mental, emotional disease	23.0	19.0
Family conflict	21.1	39.3
Unhappy love affair	13.1	10.3
Drunkenness, Alcoholism	2.5	5.1
Financial difficulties, housing troubles	20.1	3.7
Committing a crime	2.1	2.0
Other and unknown	18.1	20.0

The third volume issued by the Central Statistical Office, covering 1966–1967, examines the reasons for attempted suicide in greater detail.

Number of attempted suicides, classified according to probable reasons, for men and women

10*

Number of attempted suicides

1965–1967

Probable reason for attempted suicide	1965			1966			1967		
	men	women	total	men	women	total	men	women	total
Nervous and mental disease	424	723	1,147	676	1,174	1,850	754	1,504	2,258
Other diseases:	192	270	462	225	379	634	295	353	648
i.e. coronary and vascular	39	74	113	70	116	186	63	87	150
tumour	8	17	25	10	19	29	15	30	45
contagious disease	30	27	57	30	23	53	41	34	75
illness—precise ailment unknown	102	144	246	129	206	335	157	191	348
disability	13	8	21	16	15	31	19	11	30
Family conflict	1,328	3,542	4,870	1,283	3,684	4,967	1,635	4,572	6,107
i.e. with spouse	915	2,123	3,038	962	2,541	3,503	1,102	2,796	3,898
with parent, child	199	777	976	235	835	1,070	190	795	985
other relative	56	245	301	57	242	299	70	165	235
Family conflict, details unknown	158	397	555	29	66	95	273	816	1,089
Blow by fate	42	94	135	33	92	125	52	85	137
Poor school marks	46	163	209	90	210	300	98	315	413
Disciplinary action at school	16	31	47	23	41	64	35	76	111
Unhappiness, disillusionment over love affair	289	668	977	285	831	1,116	510	1,241	1,751
Financial difficulties	95	140	235	48	98	146	43	120	163
Alcoholism	131	16	147	571	216	787	358	78	436
Drunkenness	216	34	250	139	62	201	420	235	655
Commission of a crime	64	57	121	51	31	82	77	40	117
Old age	19	45	64	15	57	72	13	46	59
Abandonment	42	83	125	36	117	153	60	223	283
Shame over pregnancy	—	59	59	—	110	110	—	94	94
Housing problem	54	124	178	23	84	107	19	66	85
Difficulties at place of work	122	204	326	70	136	206	74	155	229
Other	100	323	423	182	380	562	391	918	1,309
Unknown	287	673	960	357	730	1,087	8	20	28
Total	3,466	7,269	10,735	4,137	8,432	12,569	4,842	10,141	14,983

A careful study of this table will allow several conclusions to be drawn and a number of generalizations to be made.

Suicide due to illness, particularly nervous and mental illness, shows a rapid, large-scale rise. This is a characteristic of the swift pace of modern living.

The low proportion of suicides due to direct financial difficulties is worth noting, particularly if it is remembered that in the years 1935–38 (previous table) the figure was 20.1 as compared to today's 3.7 per 100,000. This figure alone reveals a great deal about changes in social life.

The number of suicides due to alcoholism and drunkenness is high. This will be discussed in detail later, and here it is only necessary to register the disturbing fact.

Suicide figures on account of poor school marks and disciplinary action at school are also high.

The information on difficulties at place of work as a cause of suicide does not, in my opinion, present a realistic picture of the situation. My personal experience leads me to believe that difficulties at work, including undermining activities by one's colleagues, intrigues, uncontrolled ambition and the unpleasantness in the atmosphere of the workplace which ensues upset people to a far larger extent than the figures suggest.

And finally the reason which gives the most food for thought: family conflict. Of all known attempted suicides in the past three years (that is, the ones appearing in statistical summaries) over 40 per cent were due to family conflict and an unbearable unhappy atmosphere within the family. Even within these figures the degree of conflict between husband and wife is frightening. The family unit has changed so much in the last forty years that considerable upheaval was inevitable. The large number of women in gainful employment, with money of their own, has changed the relations between the two sexes, ending the prerogatives of the husband as the sole wage-earner as it has ended the complete financial subordination of the wife. It has

given her opportunities for independent existence, and this is one of the essential conditions for equality. As a result the divorce rate has shot up, for marriages which had been unhappy became terminable, and the wife was no longer at her husband's disposal in the old way. (Hungary, incidentally, tops the international divorce statistics.) But the improvement in living conditions has not been followed by a similar change in ways of thinking, which is why most people find themselves incapable of solving their family conflicts.

A few case histories

J. K. is a secretary. The manager of the company was 58 years old, but an active man in good physical condition. His former secretary married, and he took care that her successor was equal to her in looks, for he was attracted to beautiful, slightly plump young women. The new secretary, however, repulsed his advances. She loved her fiancé, and was unattracted to her employer. The manager, nevertheless, continued to besiege her, and threatened her with dismissal if she did not yield-way. The secretary was afraid to tell her jealous fiancé, but her nerves gave way, and in desperation she took a large overdose of sleeping pills. After her recovery, a lawyer friend offered to accompany her to the manager's flat, where she presented a letter she had received from him, containing the address and a note saying that he was expecting her to visit him alone on that date. They calmly turned the blackmail tables on the startled manager: if he did not immediately stop pursuing the secretary, they would report the whole affair, and of course they would not forget to include the incriminating letter. The manager formally promised everything, and they returned the compromising letter. — A few days later he had the secretary transferred. (Budapest, December 1968)

Kati M. was an industrial apprentice 15

years old. She was unconscious when the ambulance brought her in. She had swallowed a large dose of barbiturates because her boy friend had cut a date for the second time. She thought this would be a good way to frighten him.

A 40-year-old artist lived a disorderly family life, and was beginning to be a failure. As a result he jumped from a fourth-floor window one day. His left leg and right arm were broken in a number of places, and his shoulder bone fractured. When, following a four-hour operation, the man regained consciousness, it was night. There was no nurse in the ward, and the other patients were asleep. As soon as he was properly aware of his surroundings, and of himself, he dragged himself with unbelievable willpower to the open balcony. This second jump, from the sixth floor, was fatal. (Budapest, May 1969)

G. B. was Jewish, he had been deported and survived Auschwitz. His wife, three children and all his relatives died in the Auschwitz ovens. After he returned home he tried to begin again, to forget. He remarried. His little shop provided a reasonable existence. He married a Christian woman, who was incapable of understanding his memories, and the nightmares of his horrible past, which appeared with increasing frequency, first in his dreams, then his waking hours, in the form of fears and apparitions, as fears that it could all happen again. If a friend or neighbour rang the bell, when he thought he heard the tramp of boots and the barked commands, he screamed, "They're coming for me again! They're here already! Don't open the door!" The wife simply made sarcastic remarks, trying to lessen her husband's propensity for "play acting," which is what she believed his ever-increasingly serious psychic disease to be. Relations between the couple deteriorated, and finally only the flat, and financial dependence on each other, kept them together. In the end, at the age of sixty-seven, in the course of a hallucinatory attack, the man hanged himself. (Western Hungary, November 1968)

Á. M. is a 15-year-old girl, who took two kinds of sleeping pills. A year and a half earlier her stepfather, through a mixture of flattery and threats, persuaded her to have sexual intercourse with him. The girl protested the first few times, but curiosity and sexual desire overcame her qualms. Her mother knew nothing of the relationship, and this deepened the emotional crisis in the young girl. In the note she left behind she only wrote: "I discovered that I'm in the way no matter what... I'd like you two, at least, to be happy!" The doctors saved the girl's life, and cured her of the pneumonia, a complication which followed the attempt. (Budapest, February 1969)

Mrs. M. L., age 48, chose death for a peculiar reason. She lived in one of the Budapest suburbs. For about a year she had been jealous of her 53-year-old husband, for he desired her less and less frequently. Finally, a neighbour told her what was happening. She had known many kinds of shame, but she still could not believe it, but finally she caught him in the tiny garden chickenhouse, indulging in sexual perversions with their beautiful white hen. The woman decided to kill herself rather than continue living with the shame. She took a large dose of drugs, but was saved. (Budapest, February 1969)

A 40-year-old theatre director, a woman with a degree in the Humanities, found her flat completely empty on returning home from a week's stay in the countryside. Her husband, also a university graduate, with whom she had lived for fourteen years, had taken away the furniture of the two rooms in her absence, and had moved in with a girl of twenty-five. Since the woman had suspected nothing, it took her completely by surprise, and she collapsed. She must have taken a tremendous dose of drugs, to judge from the empty bottles found on the scene. She lay unconscious for two weeks, and then died. (Budapest, December 1968)

A. L. is a secretary, 19 years old. Her fiancé went into the army, and one Saturday evening she went out dancing alone. She was a pretty, desirable girl, and she spent most of the evening dancing with two boys, who offered to see her home at the end. On the way they invited her to an espresso for a coffee, which was followed by gin, and wine. The next she knew was waking up the following morning in a strange apartment, lying in bed between the two men. She promptly went into hysterics, screaming and protesting that she had been a virgin, that she had been keeping herself for her fiancé. The boys managed to quiet her down, and then they asked her to leave. A. L. walked along the street, completely broken, hanging her head. Suddenly she saw an unopened bottle of Trioxazine (a strong barbiturate) lying on the pavement. She went into an espresso, and unnoticed, swallowed all twenty tablets. She remained sitting there until she lost consciousness. The fact that she had really lost her virginity on that night was confirmed by medical examination. (Budapest, December 1968)

Mrs. P. is 47 years old. Her husband, a doctor, had died two years earlier from a coronary thrombosis. She had lost her mother four months before, and her only child, a son of twenty-three, had gassed himself the day before and had died. She took an overdose of sleeping pills. Her stomach was pumped out in time, and she survived. (Budapest, December 1968)

L. G. was only thirteen years old when he was admitted to the hospital, after an attempted suicide. He was physically underdeveloped and skinny, but extremely intelligent, with a bright face, lively eyes, and his well-composed replies indicated that he deserved a different fate from life. His reason: no one loved him, not even his mother. His father had died three years earlier, his mother had remarried. He could not go near his stepfather, for he frequently beat him. Not for bad work at school, for the boy was a good pupil and never absent, and in fact loved school and was successful there. He loved his mother, and could not understand

why she had turned against him and had joined forces with a stranger. He turned on the gas oven in the kitchen, then opened the two doors leading into the room, took out his history book, and sat down at the table to study it and wait for death. Fortunately the neighbours smelt the gas seepage in time, and saved the unconscious child. (Budapest, November 1969)

Z. N. was a reviser for a book publisher, 37 years old. He was unsuccessful in his work, and his conscience was tortured by a memory from the war years. He persuaded his wife to join him in committing suicide. One day, without any drama, he started off toward the balcony, and put a leg over the railing. He then stepped back, and called his wife to come too. Then he looked down from the fifth floor, to make sure there was no one on the pavement to be injured and threw himself over. His wife did not follow him. (Budapest, August 1968)

G. Z., a Protestant minister, was facing court proceedings for acts of homosexuality with young boys. In his shame and fear, he took an overdose of sleeping pills, then tied himself to a heavy armchair, and turned on the gas. The smell of gas was noticed, and he was taken to hospital and his life was saved. He was afterwards found guilty by the court. (Miskolc, April 1969)

S. H. is a girl of 19. She was very much in love with a black university student, and they found it hard to bear the amazement and contumely they met, combined with the unswerving opposition of the desperate parents. The girl was driven to a state of emotional exhaustion, and tried to commit suicide. She survived. (Szeged, 1968)

Farewell notes

The most moving form of human testimony is the farewell note of a suicide. It is more dramatic than the last message of a condemned man.

"Don't ask what happened to me. I have

a despising husband who despises me and who has condemned me to death by starvation! I won't let him condemn me, I'll go myself! Dear Ilonka, Jani, Pali, I loved you so dearly, please forgive me! With love and kisses, *Anni*."

*

"Dearest One, Don't be angry with me for being a nuisance but I can't stand living any longer. I love you very much and I always will love you and I'm doing this because of you. I only ask one thing, when I am dead, write to my mother and write her the truth about why I did it. I had seven abortions because you wanted me to and to make you happy. The time when you said you would marry me is coming closer, you promised me that too and now you are walking out on me because there is only a month to go, because there are witnesses that you would only marry me in August... I'm doing this because of you, I can't stand living without you. Good bye, Pirike."

P. S. "If you want to know, I poisoned myself, I can be found on the bench. If I don't succeed in dying you'll be very sorry, so let me die."

*

"My dear Panni, Don't make a to-do, don't scream, or make a scene. It's not the thing to do. You'll have a letter! They'll give it to you discreetly! With love, Father. Please love Pisti and Juckó... I loved you, above all else, I hope you loved me as well...

The carpenter has taken away most of his tools.

I was a Protestant. The 13th psalm, 'I will sing unto the Lord'..."

*

"Dear Joli and Klári, I'm saying good-bye to you with this letter, and good-bye to life too. It's impossible to live under family conditions like this. I had planned out a beautiful life for myself. In the sixth class I still wanted to be an engineer. In the

seventh class I refused to answer the teacher, though I knew the answer. I spoiled my marks just to revenge myself for my father's cruelty. Always studying, never being allowed to do anything else, I can't stand it. He woke me up at five o'clock every morning, so that I could in the morning too... In school Daddy told them that I ran away from home because of a slap. Let's start by saying that it was three slaps, not one. I keep noticing, more and more, that he lies. If one bottle of Tardyl isn't enough, I don't know what I'll do... Sincerely, Zsuzsi, Budapest, April 14, 1969."

*

"Klára, I hope that now you'll live in peace. You are free to love everyone who bothers to ask for your love. That's your element. To repeat your words—'It's my nature to do it'. You don't have to notify anyone, and don't make any kind of scene either before or after my cremation. I don't need a grave for my ashes... If despite this you play the suffering wife, and even organize a funeral, and show up there, I only hope that you'll live for a very very long time, and suffer a whole lot, so that you'll feel something of what I've already lived through... Tell Pisti whatever you want to, when he's big enough he'll find out why things had to be this way. Jancsi."

*

"In life I was everything to you only not your wife your Bitch Slut Whore I kept sons-of-bitches I never took care of my family I wasn't a devoted mother. I didn't cook I didn't wash I didn't clean the house you all ran around dirty and ragged I didn't bother with anything, I didn't do anything only spent all the money and never gave you anything to eat. That's what you say I didn't give a damn about you I didn't satisfy your sexual feelings either, because I belonged to someone else, said you... It hurts to leave my children who I suffered for..."

*

"Dearest Miklós, In saying good-bye I can only say, work, and if you can, study, keep studying! Take care of yourself, because people are rotten to the core, take it from me! Think of me with love, I wasn't bad. Maybe later you'll find it out. Give this letter to Marika and Jutka. A million hugs and kisses, Mom."

*

"I don't know where I put my identity card; I've put out the birth certificate. Much success in life, be a big 'football man' and *Get Back at Them!* As though you were your father! Love Mom."

*

"I didn't want to turn the gas on because that woman would smell it and she'd say it was her I wanted to poison. Because she wouldn't stop at anything. I hope she doesn't have a minute of peace, that's my last wish, if there's a God then she'll get it all back, but I hope the others do too. Kisses, Mom.

"It hurt that yesterday you didn't do what I asked you to."

*

"My sweet Teri, Only Baldy knows why I had to die. Maybe you can get it out of him. Bye, Ida."

The times in which we live

There are a number of factors to be taken into account. From 1914 onwards in Europe and North America, and in Asia and Africa since the beginning of the Second World War, all generations have been war generations, born prior to, during or after the great world wars, being either soldiers, war wives, widows, children who have experienced the sufferings of war, or children of revolutionaries and counter-revolutionaries, and all today living under the nightmare of thermonuclear war.

Added to this are the social revolutions which began after the Second World War. The suffering which followed, the disillusionment, the destruction of religious and traditional beliefs in the great upheavals of science and progress.

This is the social background to suicide. To me it is incomprehensible that even today there are reputable people, well-educated, with professional experience, who still claim that suicide is the tragedy of the individual, that is, that the community, society can do nothing.

Why in the first place?

Most of the reasons given above apply to Hungary as to other European countries— war, revolution, the decline of religion, the change of social systems.

Only the rate of suicide remains comparatively unchanged, it is the only social phenomenon which remains the same. In fact, despite expectations which in all other territories were fulfilled, the situation has if anything worsened.

Statistics seem to prove the research theory that the main determining factors are the special national characteristics of the individual countries and their peoples, which would mean that each and every country has its own stable, barely changing suicide rate. But so far there has been no final and conclusive proof of it. Nonetheless, the behaviour, thoughts and deeds of people living in the same community, large or small, contain surprisingly many similarities, or identical characteristics, which seem to indicate that the people of larger communities, villages, cities and countries have special, individual characters, and it seems obvious that in a study of the apparently mysterious suicide statistics this factor must be taken into consideration.

The general make-up and the physiological and psychological condition of the individual of course also has a great deal to do with it, his abilities, opportunities and family circumstances, and his own inner life.

It is consequently an over-simplification to attribute the deed to a single reason.

Suicide and alcoholism

Between 1963–64, 34.1 per cent of male suicides and 5.8 per cent of female suicides were found to be alcoholics or under the influence of alcohol.

The quantity of liquor sold in thousands of grocery stores, liquor stores, restaurants, espressos and buffets is steadily increasing, and consumption is growing at a tremendous rate. (In 1960 the total value of alcoholic beverages sold in shops and restaurants was 7.5, by 1968 it was 13.1 thousand million forints, that is, the per capita consumption of alcoholic beverages in Hungary, including infants, came to 1,300 forints last year. This means that an average family of four spent 5,200 forints on liquor, according to the data in the latest *Statistical Pocket Book*.) Until this trend is changed, no substantial improvement can be expected. Anti-alcohol propaganda, detoxication stations and detoxication cures in themselves are illusionary. As long as liquor shops, anxious to overfulfil their sales plans (which is the basis for bonuses), are allowed to operate at the entrances to factories, enterprises, or in their immediate vicinity all propaganda measures to reduce drinking are hypocritical, inacceptable and ineffective.

Example

Another aspect of suicide is the force of example. The effect of suicides in the family, among relatives, or friends, is often visible in the next attempt.

What happens to the suicide?

Nothing can be done for the successful suicide.

Those who are still alive when the suicide attempt is discovered, are taken to hospital. They are taken in by private car, taxi, or in the majority of cases, by ambulance. But where to? This is the most disturbing factor, for even those who could be saved through modern medical intervention cannot be taken to suitably equipped hospitals, for departments of this kind can only be found in Budapest and Miskolc. In the other towns, counties and districts of the country, suicide cases are taken in in whichever hospital happens to be on the emergency list, and this is often the third of fourth hospital to be visited.

What can society do for them?

Firstly, we must speak and write on the subject in the natural tone it deserves, and discuss the problem and its possible solutions.

Secondly, we need articles in newspapers and magazines, and studies on the question. This social epidemic must become a part of our public thinking and our social consciousness. We have to change the present position in which not only does the average person have no idea of the question, but neither do highly-qualified people in responsible positions.

A research group of experts should be set up, including doctors, psychologists, sociologists, economists, writers and journalists.

There are statistical surveys which show that between 40 and 60 per cent of those preparing to commit suicide indicate their intentions in some way or other. They betray themselves in subconscious appeals for help, and it is therefore possible, if we only pay a little attention, to be aware of it. Another indication is that 30–40 per cent of people preparing to commit suicide visit doctors, or neurologists, prior to committing the act. These doctors should look for the revealing symptoms. Often the patients state their intentions openly and threaten suicide, and we should not ignore their words.

Some form of "Good Samaritan" committees should be set up in the villages, districts and towns.

A special telephone service for suicides could also be established in the larger towns. Such services have been operating with good results in large cities in a number of countries.

A larger number of suicides could be saved if we organized intensive care departments, at least in every county seat, as the first step. The experiences of the Budapest Korányi Hospital, and the Miskolc Toxicology Intensive Care Department could be used. The Miskolc example shows that this department can be organized on a modern level, and the total costs are not more than one million forints. Each one of these district intensive care departments should be served by at least one psychologist and one assistant, who would have the task of helping the attempted suicides to find their way back into the community. And as a second step, intensive toxicology departments should be established in a number of the local district hospitals.

Without post-hospital care, we cannot hope to lower the number of suicide cases. This care should in fact begin during hospitalization, and the psychologist attached to the department could begin it. This would involve talks with the family, with co-workers, the heads of the patient's place of work, and if necessary, with the Council authorities, to see where they could help.

*

I am neither a doctor nor a psychologist, I am only one of the many who has twice been tempted by the enticement of voluntary death. This is the reason why I understand and sympathize with those who succumb to the enticement. I would like to be able to save as many of them as possible. *

* The full text of this essay was published in the literary review *Kortárs*, November and December 1969.

IMPACT OF THE NEW CHILD CARE ALLOWANCES

by

EGON SZABADY

In the past fifteen years Hungarian demographers have given a great deal of attention to the investigation of fertility trends. This was largely due to the peculiar tendencies in fertility rates in Hungary in the years following the Second World War, when fertility rates continued to decrease—a tendency which had been characteristic of all European countries in the interwar period. In the early 1950s, in the wake of the war, a temporary increase occurred in Hungary, but this was followed by a decrease in births up to 1962, when the birth-rate reached its lowest point. For some years the rate stagnated at around 13 per thousand births, and in 1966 it began to rise, the upward tendency continuing into the late 1960s.

From its early beginnings Hungarian demographical research has also undertaken the investigation of economic, social and socio-psychological factors in fertility trends. Profound economic and social changes took place in Hungary after the Second World War, and these changes also affected the birth-rate. There was, for instance, an enormous increase in social mobility as compared with the preceding decades, and this not only brought about vertical changes attaining a new stratum but—due to the size of the movement—also transformed the different strata themselves, setting new ideals and norms of behaviour for those belonging to it; the number of gainfully employed married women increased suddenly; the educational level of the women of economically productive age also rose; as a result of internal migration, the number of the rural population constantly decreased and urbanization just as constantly increased. These changes are, of course, not only characteristic of Hungary, but in this country the transformation was compressed into a comparatively short period of time.

Hungarian demographers did not limit themselves to the traditional methods of fertility study, that is, the analysis of the fertility data in censuses and vital statistics, but, based on questionnaires among the population, also investigated the concepts and practices of family planning, as well as the social and political factors which affected such ideas. The first specific fertility and family planning survey took place in 1958–1960,[1] and later—in 1965–1966—another similar survey was carried out by the Hungarian Demographic Research Institute. In the period between the two surveys in 1960 and 1964, the Institute and the Central Statistical Office collected information among women in hospital for induced abortion or childbirth —this survey was repeated in 1968—and Hungarian demographers also carried out a careful analysis of the fertility data in the 1960 census and the 1963 micro-census. The 1970 population census provided a great deal more information on the development of fertility than the previous censuses. For the fourteen-years-old and older female population—i.e. for 25 per cent of the population listed in the census, figures are available on the number of children born, children living with the mother, children living separately from the mother, and children deceased. The main data on the total number of children born as well as the history of the marriage(s) of the mother are known, and will be analysed in a short time.

From the demographical point of view, the most important conclusion derived from the 1965–1966 fertility, family planning and birth control survey[2] was that at the time of the survey young married people in Hungary were planning to have so small a number of children as to endanger the

---

[1] *A termékenységi, családtervezési és születésszabályozási vizsgálat fontosabb adatai* (Major Data of the Fertility, Family, Planning and Birth Control Survey). Central Statistical Office, Budapest, 1963.

[2] The 1965–1966 Hungarian survey formed part of an international comparative survey series initiated by the IPPF's Commission for Europe. The plans of the survey were worked out by Hungarian demographers commissioned by IPPF, and it was in Hungary that the programme was first carried out, after co-ordination with the countries concerned, thus providing a basis for surveys in other countries.

Several publications have dealt with the programme, the methodological and organizational problems and the major results of this survey; the present study is intended to deal only with the findings relevant to the selective role of social factors.

The publications on the 1965–1966 fertility, family planning and birth control survey are the following:

E. Szabady: "Tervezet a nemzetközi összehasonlító születésszabályozási és családtervezési vizsgálatra" (A Programme for the International Comparative Birth Control and Family Planning Survey). *Statisztikai Szemle*, 1965, No. 8–9, pp. 898–901.

E. Szabady–Dr. A. Klinger: "Az 1965–66. évi termékenységi, családtervezési és születésszabályozási vizsgálat" (The 1965–66 Hungarian Study on Fertility, Family Planning and Birth Control). *Demográfia*, 1966, No. 2, pp. 136–161.

E. Szabady: "A családtervezési vizsgálatok egyes kérdései" (Some Problems of Family Planning Surveys). *Demográfia*, 1967, No. 2, pp. 219–237.

E. Szabady: "Családtervezési trendek: a magyar vizsgálat" (Family Planning Trends: The Hungarian Study). *Demográfia*, 1968, No. 3–4, pp. 333–346.

E. Szabady: "Hungarian Fertility and Family Planning Studies. Social Demography and Medical Responsibility." Proceedings of the Sixth Conference of the International Planned Parenthood Federation, Europe and Near East Region, held in Budapest, September 1969, pp. 12–13.

maintenance of the present level of the population. From the sociological point of view, on the other hand, the results of the investigation, which explain this attitude, are important. The young married couples interviewed gave the following three factors as the main reason for resorting to contraception: (1) a recently born child, (2) housing problems, and (3) material difficulties in the early stage of married life, partly due to the problems of setting up a home for the new family. Of the young married couples using contraceptive measures 63 per cent in the first and second year of marriage, and 54 per cent in the second to fourth year of marriage gave these reasons. In the course of married life, the importance of the three factors gradually diminishes.

There were comparatively few who, when asked about their reason for using contraceptive measures, declared that the mother was inhibited from giving birth to more children because of the difficulties of bringing up the child. Even among the economically active women there were only 2 per cent who gave this reason for the use of contraceptive measures; of the inactive women less than 0.5 per cent gave this reason. In the case of economically active women this low percentage is surprising, since here caring for, providing for and raising the child inevitably increases the burden laid on the women.[3]

Gainful activities obviously put a strain on women to an extent that must in fact be one of the main factors in family planning, even if the fact does not appear from the subjective replies of economically active women.

The figures of the 1965–1966 survey relating to total desired live-births clearly indicate the role of economic employment in family planning by women.[4] According to these figures, in that space of time desired live-births per 100 economically active women interviewed totalled 201, whereas for 100 economically inactive women the total was 245: the planned fertility of the inactive women was thus some 20 per cent higher than that of women gainfully employed. The difference between active and employed women, and inactive women showed itself also by socio-economic groups: it was highest in the case of those employed in non-agricultural manual work compared to the inactive wives of non-agricultural manual workers who did not go out to work, and lowest in the case of those engaged in manual work in agriculture and the inactive wives in this group.

---

3 For the problems of gainfully employed mothers in Hungary, see E. Szabady: "Gainful Occupation and Motherhood—The Position of Women in Hungary". *The New Hungarian Quarterly*, 1963, No. 34, pp. 51–63.

4 Desired live-birth = children born + further birth planned.

Desired live-births per 100 women

Socio-economic group	Economically active	Economically inactive
Agricultural manual workers	255	257
Non-agricultural manual workers	200	243
Non-manual workers	175	206

Not only did the economically active women plan a smaller family, they also gave birth to less children at the time of the survey and in previous years. In 1949, for example, in the case of the non-agricultural stratum the fertility-rate of economically active women was only one-third of that of the others, and although the difference diminished in subsequent years, in 1960 the birth-rate among economically inactive women exceeded that of economically active women by 68 per cent. Even in 1965–1966, the birth-rate among dependent women was still higher. Then, in 1967, a significant change came about with the introduction of the allowance for child care.

The allowance for child care was instituted by the Hungarian government at the beginning of 1967. Under the government decree introducing the system, economically active mothers are free to choose whether they will continue to work or will ask for leave without pay, during which period they receive an allowance of 600 forints monthly until their child reaches the age of three.

The introduction of this measure, novel in character even by international standards, was prompted by policy considerations of demography and public health. The aim of demographic policy is to increase the number of births. The public health aspect of the measure was based on the realization of the fact that the morbidity rate was much higher among the infants of economically active mothers placed in nurseries, than among infants nursed at home. The majority of economically active mothers, moreover, could not even make use of the nurseries, since the nurseries were unable to admit more than 10 per cent even of the children born in low birth-rate years. The need for nursery places was several times higher. Most working women were thus obliged to leave the child in someone's care over the day, generally a person who usually just minded the child and fed it the food prepared in advance; the majority of tasks connected with child care was left to the working mother to carry out after working hours. Obviously this double burden had a bad effect on the working standard of many mothers, and this fact, as well as the inevitable frequent absence from work of mothers with a small child, was also detrimental to production. In addition, while many a mother with a small child made great efforts both to carry out her work and to care for her child, an untapped supply of female labour was coming to the fore in various settlements. All these factors, as well as labour policy itself, had their place in the decision to allow the temporary interruption of the employment of normally economically active young mothers.

The effects of this measure—primarily one of family policy—were followed up by the Demographic Research Institute from the beginning of the child care allowance system with the aid of a collection of figures giving complete coverage and now, on the basis of two years' experience, it is already possible to evaluate the results. The information acquired has made it possible to draw an inference on the demographical efficiency of the allowance system and to examine the social factors influencing the young mother in her decision whether to avail herself of the allowance and give up work temporarily or not.

The experience of the first two years shows that the allowance system is more popular than expected. In both years, about two-thirds of the economically active young mothers availed themselves of this opportunity. At the time when the Demographic Research Institute closed the collection of information for the second year, more than 100,000 mothers with small children were already staying at home, taking advantage of the allowance; their number amounted to 144,000 at the beginning of 1970 and to 167,000 at the beginning of 1971. According to the latest available figures in September 1971, 175,000 women were already on child care leave, which means that about 10 per cent of economically active women had stopped working.

In these two years, taking advantage of the allowance for child care varied by social strata. It was primarily the employed women engaged in manual work who made use of it. Nearly two-thirds of the female manual workers took advantage of the allowance, whereas in the case of non-manual workers the rate was already significantly lower in the first year (58 per cent) and decreased further in the course of the next year (to 45 per cent). In the case of co-operative farm members the rate was somewhere between those of the two other strata, and here its use increased in the second year as against the first year (from 60.5 per cent to 65 per cent).

The differences in the rate of use reflect the degree, which varies according to social stratum, of the dilemma facing the economically active young mother when she has to decide whether to consider caring for her child as her principal task over three years and to accept the drawbacks of interrupting her work and career, social connections and, last but not least, financial situation, or to continue working with caring for the child as an additional burden. The majority of women engaged in manual work choose to stay at home: in their case, a two or three years' interruption does not mean a major break in their career and the nursing allowance of 600 forints monthly amounts to at least half their former monthly earnings. Where non-manual workers are concerned, for those engaged in clerical work the position is similar; those, on the other hand, whose occupation demands higher qualifications, a sense of vocation, and with higher earnings, will be more reluctant to interrupt their career, and in their case the rate is therefore lower. The specific choice of the non-manual stratum with higher qualification can be clearly seen by the data broken down according to the level of schooling: those with only elementary, i.e. general school education made use of the allowance at the rate of 72 to 73 per cent in both years; for those with secondary school education it was 60 to 61 per cent; and of the university graduates only 30 per cent temporarily gave up their job.

The type of occupation and educational attainments itself also shows in the proportion of women giving up the allowance before its expiry (i.e. before the child has reached the age of three years) and returning to their former job. According to figures collected in the first two years, 18 per cent of those drawing an allowance renounced it before its expiry; in the case of non-manual occupations the proportion was nearly double (27 per cent as against 14 per cent). The rate of discontinuance was lowest in the case of co-operative farm workers, where it did not even reach 10 per cent. Analysis of the data according to educational attainment shows that there is a direct relationship between the rate of discontinuance and the mother's educational level: in the case of those with general education the rate was 15 per cent, with secondary schooling 25 per cent, and of university graduates 46 per cent. It is clear that those with a higher qualification are not only reluctant to make use of the allowance, but also give it up at an earlier date to return to their career as soon as possible.

The Demographic Research Institute has analysed the rate of use and its changes according to a number of other factors, such as the husband's occupation, income, educational attainment, the age of the non-manual mother, the duration of the marriage, the number of mother's live-births and live-born children, the type of settlement in which she resides and in which she works, or her type of employment. None of these factors, however, made the same differences as the educational attainment and occupation of the non-manual women. The other factors at most completed and coloured the overall picture, leading to the conclusion that it is primarily the young newly married, and especially the manual workers, who are interested in the child care allowance.

In 1967, the year the allowance for child care was introduced, the birth-rate rose by 8 per cent, followed by a further 4 per cent rise in 1968, whereas in 1969 it stagnated essentially on the 1968 level. From the middle of 1970 to the middle of 1971 a slight decrease occured. By the second half-year of 1971 the number of births was practically stabilized on the 1969 level. The fact that after a consistently low level for years, a comparatively significant rise occurred simultaneously with the introduction of the allowance for child care obviously raises the idea of a causal relationship.

The detailed analysis of the data reveals the fact that the increase in birth-rate varied by social stratum. The greatest difference, however, shows itself between economically active women and dependent women: whereas the birth-rate among the former increased, that of the latter continued to decline.

Up to 1966, we repeat, the birth-rate among housewives or dependant women, despite the tendency to decline, exceeded that among gainfully employed women. The change came about in 1967, when the birth-rate among gainfully employed women rose significantly, while that of house-wives declined, and this tendency continued in 1968. In 1969–1970 the birth-rate among gainfully employed women was still higher than that of housewives, but as compared to 1968 it shows a certain decrease in the last two years. The declining trend in the birth rate among housewives continues.

On a detailed analysis of the data it appears that the 1967 and 1968 increase occurred among the women working in non-agricultural branches, and here also a slight decrease can be observed in 1969–1970. Within the group of economically active women, a significant rise, or in the last two years, a fall, manifested itself primarily in the stratum where the use of the child care allowance was highest, i.e. among women doing manual work, where the birth-rate by and large reached the level of women engaged in non-manual work.

It should be pointed out that the difference in the birth-rate among economically active and dependent women can be attributed in the main to the different age distribution of the two female groupings. In point of fact, the age pattern among the dependents is older. In the age bracket which is most important in terms of fertility—that of women below 30 years as also with those belonging to the same age-group, the rate among economically active women is higher.

*Birth rate trends among economically active and dependent women
according to social stratum*

Socio-economic stratum and economic activity	Number of live-births per 1,000 women of 15–49 years						
	1960	1963	1966	1967	1968	1969	1970
Agricultural (gainfully employed and housewives together)	63	50	53	54	51	48	47
Non-agricultural (gainfully employed and housewives together) of which	63	56	55	59	61	61	59
gainfully employed of which	48	50	51	60	67	66	64
manual worker	45	48	49	60	66	65	64
non-manual worker	54	53	55	60	68	68	66
housewife of which	78	64	62	7	40	49	44
wife of manual worker	87	73	73	68	60	59	3
wife of non-manual worker	42	31	25	21	17	17	19

The average birth-rate among the female agricultural population has again decreased in the second year of the child care allowance. The low birth-rate among the agricultural population is, however, exclusively due to the aging of the female agricultural population, to the increased growth of the age-groups above 30 and 40 years. Even is present-day Hungary the birth-rate is highest among women of the agricultural population who are below 24 years of age, and also within certain higher age-groups the birth-rate among women engaged in agriculture is higher than among women of the corresponding age, engaged in non-manual work.

Also related to differences in the age pattern is the higher birth-rate among non-manual workers than among manual workers: with a standardized age distribution, the birth-rate of manual workers becomes higher. A particularly significant increase in the birth-rate can be found among women under 30 years of age engaged in manual work; and it is also in the age-groups under 30 that the birth-rate among women engaged in non-manual work shows the greatest increase.

The figures, consequently, clearly show that the introduction of the child care allowance played a significant role in the movement of the birth-rate in 1967 and 1968. And in fact, the increase in the birth-rate occurred precisely

Age-standardized birth-rates by social stratum

Social stratum	live-births among 1,000 women of 15–49 years		
	1960	1968	1970
Agricultural	59	64	63
Non-agricultural of which	59	58	56
manual	66	64	61
non manual worker	44	47	48

in those strata where greatest advantage was taken of the allowance. The change or stability of trends up to 1966 in the various groups making up the population primarily reflects the degree to which they made use of the allowance and the extent to which it affected their demographical behaviour. The fact that, for example, in the case of the agricultural population the birth-rate trend did not change is certainly due to the conditions attached to the allowance, which exclude a section of the women engaged in agricultural work from its benefits. For one condition of the allowance is either one year of continuous employment, which is not the case with many seasonal agricultural workers, or—in the case of co-operative farm workers—120 days of participation in the collective work. A number of co-operative farm workers working on their private plots, too, and having been already pregnant over the major part of the period in question, do not meet this condition.

The effect, therefore, of the introduction of the allowance for child care was to produce a comparatively sudden change in the birth-rates characterizing the different social strata. It is too early at present to determine whether these changes are only due to the fact that women have their first and second children at an earlier age, but even if this were the case for the present, the fact is still favourable in terms of the actual increase in the birth-rate. Postponing the birth of the first child does, as a matter of fact, involve the danger that finally no first or further children are born; conversely, it may be assumed that the birth of the first and second child increases the chance of further children.

Under the effect of the child care allowance the birth-rates of the different social strata have come essentially nearer to one another. In fact, this is a continuation of earlier trends, which can be observed in the results of the mobility investigations carried out by the Demographic Research Institute. This research project, which described the inter-generation and intrageneration mobility of men between 1938 and 1962–64 on a nation-wide basis, also provided data for an analysis of the interrelations between social strata, mobility and fertility.[5]

The figures on the number of children of the men show that the average number of children of those interviewed in the first half ot the 1960s varied according to social stratum· in the younger age-groups, however, the differences were considerably smaller than in the older ones. For whereas in Hungarian towns (with the exception of Budapest), for men of 60 years and over, only 1.5 children had been born to men of professional status, 2.0 to other non-manual workers, 2.7 to non-agricultural manual workers and 3.3 to agricultural workers, in the case of men of 20 to 29 years the corresponding figures were 0.7, 0.7, 0.9 and 0.0.

Average number of children in the main social strata, by age-group

Age-group (years)	Urban			
	Professional status	Other non-manual workers	Non-agricultural manual workers	Agricultural workers
20–29 years	0.7	0.7	0.9	0.9
30–39 years	1.4	1.5	1.8	1.8
40–49 years	1.8	1.8	2.1	2.2
50–59 years	2.3	1.7	2.2	3.1
60 years and over	1.5	2.0	2.7	3.3

Age-group (years)	Rural			
	Professional status	Other non-manual workers	Non-agricultural manual workers	Agricultural manual workers
20–29 years	1.0	0.9	1.2	1.4
30–39 years	1.6	1.7	2.0	2.2
40–49 years	2.0	2.2	2.6	2.5
50–59 years	2.0	2.4	2.9	2.9
60 years and over	2.6	3.5	3.3	3.4

5 *Társadalmi átrétegeződés Magyarországon* (Social Re-stratification in Hungary). Publications of the Demographic Research Institute. Budapest, 1970.

The trend is less marked with the Budapest men interviewed. Men of professional status in the higher age-groups have more, and in the lower less, children than other non-manual workers. This may in part reflect the general tendency observed in economically advanced countries in recent years, namely that, in contrast with earlier periods, it is not the stratum with the highest income and level of schooling that has the lowest number of children, but the lower income group, composed mainly of medium-level employees and clerical workers with 8 to 12 years of schooling.[6] The effect of the introduction of the child care allowance is to act against this tendency since, as pointed out above, the allowance has become popular mainly with those with a secondary school education, whereas it has only slightly affected those with higher qualifications.

One of the most important final conclusions of the mobility investigation was that social mobility—from peasantry to working class and non-manual workers, from working class to non-manual workers and within the latter group from the employee group to the professional class—has led to a decreased fertility in the sense that the mobile persons and families have in most cases adopted the concept of the family prevalent in the new environment and adapted their family planning to the ideal of the new stratum, i.e. a lower number of children. Those of working class and peasant background, or former manual workers and peasants, who have moved into the professional or other non-manual stratum, as well as those of peasant background and the former peasants who have moved into the working class in provincial towns and in villages, have completely adopted the lower fertility principles corresponding to the new social environment.[7] With the decrease of the differences in the birth-rate between various social strata, future movements of the population as envisaged at present are not likely to cause further essential changes in fertility trends. As a matter of fact, from the mobility investigations of the Demographic Research Institute it has become clear that the fact of movement itself does not—apart from the difference in fertility between the original stratum and the later recipient stratum—lead to a decrease in fertility. Those moving, therefore, will not have to make increased sacrifices in terms of reducing the number of their children in order to pass into another social stratum.

The introduction of the child care allowance marks an important phase in Hungarian demographic policy, and, further developed, it may, together

---

[6] G. Z. Johnson: *Differential Fertility in European Countries. Demographic and Economic Change in Developed Countries.* Princeton, 1960, pp. 36–72.

[7] The only exception found was in the Budapest working class, where those with peasant background had a somewhat higher number of children than those of working-class background.

with other measures of family policy, contribute to the solution of the Hungarian demographic situation. It may also claim international interest among the sociologists and demographers engaged in the problems of fertility, since its effects can be observed under almost unique "laboratory" conditions in the extensive survey of the Demographic Research Institute.[8] The results achieved up to the present still fail to provide an answer to a great number of questions, but it can be assumed that the data of surveys to be carried out in the next years will contribute to the solution of further problems.

[8] *Gyermekgondozási segély* (Allowance for Child Care). Periodical Statistical Publications, Vol. 147. Central Statistical Office, 1969/3.

Gyermekgondozási segély (Allowance for Child Care). Publications of the Demographic Research Institute, Budapest, 1970.

For an evaluation of the significance of the allowance see E. Szabady: "A gyermekgondozási segély társadalmi és demográfiai jelentősége" (The Social and Demographic Significance of the Allowance for Child Care). *Társadalmi Szemle*, 1969, Vol. XXIV, No. 7-8, pp. 99–105.

EGON SZABADY

POPULATION CHANGES IN HUNGARY IN THE LAST TWENTY YEARS

In the course of the twenty years that have passed since the liberation of Hungary, considerable changes have occurred in the demographic situation. The socio-economic transformation which has taken place has had its effects on the composition of the population, and these changes have in turn produced further consequences. Developments in the country in the two decades since the liberation in 1945 have not proceeded in a steady, uniform flow, and variations have correspondingly made themselves felt in population structure and trends. It is therefore difficult to present a comprehensive picture of demographic developments in Hungary since the end of the Second World War in a short survey such as this. We can only pick out the main features which characterize this period and compare them with population development between the two world wars.

1. POPULATION STRUCTURE

At the time of the liberation in 1945, the population of Hungary—estimating the losses during the Second World War at 420,000, was somewhat under 9 million. Twenty years later the population was more than 10 million: at the end of 1964, to be precise, it was 10,135,000, i.e., it increased by 1.1 million in two decades.

The approximate increase of 13 per cent over the last 20 years—disregarding for the moment the catastrophic demographic losses of the Second World War—was less than that in the twenty years following the First World War, since between 1920 and 1940 the population of Hungary increased by 1.25 million, or 17 per cent. The lesser rate of increase was caused partly by the drop in the rate of natural growth, owing to a reduction in the birth rate, and partly by various losses through migration.

Population growth was far from uniform in the course of the twenty years under investigation. The rate of increase was relatively higher between 1948 and 1950, when it approached 1 per cent annually. From then on the natural rate of increase began to fall, with the exception of a temporary increase between 1952 and 1955, when it attained its highest level, 1 to 1.2 per cent, since the liberation. In 1956—owing to the large illegal emigration—there was an actual decrease in the population, and from 1957 on the trend towards a gradual fall in the rate of increase continued. The figures have only been stabilized in the last three years (1962–1964), and that at the lowest level so far, an annual 0.3 per cent.

It was only in the first years after the Second World War that the natural reproduction rate of the population ran parallel to developments after the First World War, when the rate was also 10 to 11 per thousand. But in the earlier period the relatively high rate persisted some time longer, in fact for seven years, whereas after the Second World War it persisted for only three years. In both cases the rate of natural reproduction began to fall after this initial improvement—the decline was only temporarily interrupted by the rise in the rate of increase of 1953–1954, due to administrative measures against abortion—and the declining rate of increase has been considerably greater than it was in the inter-war period.

Birth Rate

The extent and the trends of natural growth rates of the population since libera-

| Date | Population | Population growth | | | | Population growth (in percentages) [a] | | | |
		Years	Increase or decrease (total)	Natural reproduction	Migratory balance	Increase or decrease (total)	Natural repro- duction	Migra- tory balance	Average [b] annual increase or decrease
31.12.1920 [c]	7,986,875	—	—	—	—	—	—	—	—
31.12.1925	8,341,562	1921–1925	354,687	388,130	-33,443	4.5	4.9	-0.4	0.87
31.12.1930 [c]	8,685,109	1926–1930	343,547	383,708	-40,161	4.1	4.6	-0.5	0.81
31.12.1935	9,014,733	1931–1935	329,624	292,164	37,360	3.8	3.4	0.4	0.75
31.1.1941 [c]	9,316,074	1936–1941	301,341	267,883	33,458	3.4	3.0	0.4	0.65
1.1.1949 [c]	9,204,799	1941–1948	-111,275	332,547	-443,822 [e]	-1.2	3.6	-4.8	-0.15
1.1.1955	9,766,600	1949–1954	561,801	543,933	17,868	6.1	5.9	0.2	0.99
1.1.1960 [c]	9,961,044	1955–1959	194,444	372,589	-178,145	2.0	3.8	-1.8	0.40
1.1.1965 [d]	10,135,000	—	—	—	—	—	—	—	—

a) In relation to the population at the beginning of the period.
b) Geometrical average.
c) Census data.
d) Population calculated on the basis of the final figures of the census of 1.1.1960.
e) Including non-registered deaths.

Trend of the principal vital statistics
(per thousand persons)

Years (average)	Live births	Deaths	Natural increase	Live births	Deaths	Natural increase
1921–1925	240,129	162,503	77,626	29.4	19.9	9.5
1926–1930	221,594	144,853	76,741	26.0	17.0	9.0
1931–1935	198,025	139,592	58,433	22.4	15.8	6.6
1936–1940	182,444	128,867	53,577	19.9	14.1	5.8
1941–1945	181,503	152,901	28,602	19.4	16.4	3.0
1946–1950	186,861	114,284	72,577	20.4	12.5	7.9
1951–1955	203,434	106,800	96,634	21.2	11.1	10.1
1956–1960	163,219	102,230	60,989	16.5	10.3	6.2
1961	140,365	96,410	43,955	14.0	9.6	4.4
1962	130,053	108,273	21,780	12.9	10.8	2.1
1963	132,335	99,871	32,464	13.1	9.9	3.2
1964[a]	131,899	100,594	31,305	13.0	9.9	3.1

a) *Provisional data*

tion have been determined primarily through changes in the birth rate. Developments in the number of live births were almost completely parallel to that of the natural growth of the population. In the years following the Second World War the gross reproduction rate did not increase immediately (in 1945–1946 it was under 19 per thousand). This was very different from the position after the First World War, when, compensating for the half a million births or so that failed to materialize owing to the War—the birth rate shot up considerably and increased by 27 to 32 per thousand between 1919 and 1926. Such a compensatory process was not noticeable after the Second World War, since essentially there had been no decline in the number of births. After the first two years, the birth rate increased to a small extent (it was 21 per thousand between 1947 and 1950), and then fell again (1951–1952: 20 per thousand). Partly due to measures against abortion, the crude birth rate increased again in 1953 to 22, and to 23 in 1954. From 1955 there was a considerable annual fall in the birth rate, due in part to the fact that abortion had been legalized In

1962 the birth rate fell to 13 per thousand and it has since remained around this level.

The decline in the number of births over the last nine years—a considerable drop even by international standards—is similar to that which occurred in the period after the First World War. Following the compensatory increase, the numbers fell in the late 'twenties and especially in the 'thirties, only a little less than the similar fall experienced in the second half of the 'fifties and in the 'sixties, for the average birth rate of the years 1936–1940 was 32 per cent lower than that of 1921–1925, and that of 1961–1964 35 per cent lower than that of 1946–1950.

The decrease in the number of births can also be seen in the number of children per married woman. At the beginning of 1963 the figure was an average of 229 children per 100 married women, 28 less than the 1949 figures. After the First World War, between 1920 and 1949, the decline in the number of the children born was much greater, i.e., 105 per 100 married women. The decline in the birth rate has been less in the post-liberation period than between the wars.

Mortality Rate

Throughout the last twenty years, the mortality rate has fallen considerably, with the exception of the deaths caused by the 'flu epidemics of 1953, 1959 and 1962. The rate of reduction was, however, far from even: after the exceedingly high figures of the three post-war years, the mortality rate fell in 1948 to 11.6 per thousand, and fell to the lowest level which has been achieved, 9.6, in 1961.

The lowering of the death rate can be seen—better than by the crude death rates—by the standardized death rates, which eliminate the effect of changes in distribution according to the age composition of the population. In terms of the age composition of the population before the First World War, the crude mortality rate would be around 6 to 7. Standardized to the age distribution of 1910, mortality fell between 1938 and 1963 to less than half, 47 per thousand, which is considerably better than the decrease following the First World War, since in 1938 the standardized death rate was 58 per thousand, as compared with 1911. This considerable improvement in the mortality rate after liberation is all the more noteworthy, as it becomes increasingly difficult to reduce still further a death rate which is already on a low level.

Expectation of Life

The decrease in the death rate increases expectation of life at birth. According to the latest mortality tables (1959–1960), expectation of life for males is now over 65, and for females nearly 70, that is, an increase of 10 to 12 years over twenty years ago. The expectation of life for males increased, however, by 14, and for females by 15 years in the corresponding twenty years period after the First World War, i.e., it was greater than the increase after the Second World War. This indicates a certain slackening in the decline of the mortality rate.

Mortality Distribution by Ages

Decreases in the death rate differed in the various age groups. The death rate for infants fell between 1940–41 and 1963 by two-thirds, for those under five by almost three-quarters and for those between five and nine years by four-fifths; the drop in the death rate for the higher age groups was considerably less: the mortality rate for those 70 years old and over improved by roughly one-fifth, and for those in the oldest age group (85 and over) by only one-seventh. Nor have even these improvements been uniform. The mortality rate of infants and children—apart from small fluctuations—fell steadily throughout the twenty-years period, but the figures for the old show certain periods of increase, followed in recent years by practically no changes.

These same differences in the decrease in the death rate can equally be seen in the period following on the First World War, when the decrease in infant and child mortality was most pronounced, although far less than the decrease after 1945. In the twenty-year period after 1945 the death rate dropped by 36 per cent for infants under one year, and 63 per cent for all children under five, while that of the old remained nearly unchanged (the figures for the group of the 85's and over showed only a 4 per cent increase at the end of the period over the beginning).

Cause of Death

Considerable changes have occurred in the mortality figures classified according to the cause of death. Contagious diseases, which in 1941 accounted for a crude death rate of 179 per 100,000, have lost their former importance over the last twenty years. In 1963 the crude death through contagious diseases had fallen to 32 per 100,000 or less than one-fifth of the former figure. Breaking down the overall figure, death from tuberculosis fell by 82 per cent, as compared to the 49 per cent decrease in the twenty years following the First World War, and all the contagious diseases together by 60 per cent. In addition to these successes, there have been outstanding improvements in the mortality rates for pneumonia and gastric and intestinal catarrh (primarily due to the introduction of new drugs and therapeutic measures, and their success in controlling infant and child mortality), which fell respectively to 13 per cent and 16 per cent of the 1941 mortality rate. In the corresponding earlier period, between 1920 and 1941, the fall in these two causes of deaths (to 64 per cent, and 26 per cent respectively), which was already considerable, was none the less much smaller in extent.

At the same time, deaths due to tumours, arterio-sclerosis and other heart and circulatory diseases continued to increase in the period following the Second World War. But the rate of increase was no greater than the rate after the First World War. It is worth noting, however, that accident fatalities, which had remained stationary between the two wars, rose considerably in the twenty years following the Second World War. In 1963 the mortality rate from accidents amounted to 38 per cent more per 100,000 persons than in 1941. The suicide rate also remained high.

Infant Mortality

The improvement in the infant mortality rate has played an important part in the decrease in the general level of mortality. The crude death rate for infants under one year was gradually reduced after the considerable increase in the figures for 1945; in 1948 it was already under 100 per thousand lower than at any previous period. In the early 'fifties the figures remained stationary, but by then they had fallen to half the pre-liberation rate. From 1958 there was an acceleration in the rate of decrease; and

in 1961 only 44 infants out of a thousand died during their first year. In 1962 the figures temporarily rose (to 48 per thousand), to be followed by further improvement, and in 1964 the most favourable rate to date was attained (40 per thousand). In the twenty years after the Second World War the level of infant mortality has in fact fallen by over 66 per cent, as against the 40 per cent reduction in the twenty years after the First World War.

This decrease was largely due to the improved treatment of acquired diseases (pneumonia, gastritis, contagious diseases, etc.). The mortality rate from congenital defects, however, has remained unchanged, as can be seen from the fact that deaths on the first day after birth have remained unchanged, and the number of those dying within the first six days has hardly declined at all. On the other hand, deaths from the first to fifth months dropped to one-quarter, and from the sixth to eleventh months to one-sixth.

Distribution Changes According to Age Groups

The twofold consequences of natural changes in the population can be observed in the distribution according to age groups. Owing to the fall in the birth rate, the percentage of children (under 15) in the total population has fallen: in 1964 it was 24 per cent, as against 26 per cent in 1941. The population indeed increased by 8 per cent, but there has been scarcely any increase in the actual number of children between 1941 and 1964. Owing to the improved mortality rate, the number of the old (60 years and over) is increasing. In 1964 they were more than 1.5 million, or 15 per cent of the population. This represents an increase of more than half a million (53 per cent) over 1941. After the First World War, between 1920 and 1941, the older age group had increased, but only by 280,000, or 39 per cent.

Population age-structure by major age groups (in percentages)

Date	Total population	0—14	15—39	40—59	60—
31.12.1920	100	30.6	41.3	19.1	9.0
31.12.1925	100	29.0	42.0	19.7	9.3
31.12.1930	100	27.5	42.6	20.1	9.8
31.12.1935	100	28.4	40.5	21.0	10.1
31.1.1941	100	26.0	40.6	22.7	10.7
1.1.1949	100	24.9	38.8	24.7	11.6
1.1.1955	100	25.8	35.9	25.8	12.5
1.1.1960	100	25.4	36.8	24.0	13.8
1.1.1961	100	25.2	36.5	24.2	14.1
1.1.1962	100	25.0	36.2	24.3	14.5
1.1.1963	100	24.6	36.1	24.5	14.8
1.1.1964	100	24.1	36.1	24.6	15.2

Marriage Rate

The increased number of marriages is a very significant demographic trend of the twenty years since the Second World War. Throughout this whole period the marriage rate has been higher than in the corresponding period after the First World War.

What is extraordinary in this marriage rate as compared to the past, or to other countries, is that following the post-war rise, the number of marriages did not decline, the high marriage rate continuing for twelve years. Until 1957—with the exception of three years—it was above 10 per thousand, and for four years it even exceeded 11 per thousand. During this particular period after the Second World War the marriage rate was consistently higher than in any year after 1923. It then began to fall, and in 1962 there were only 8.1 marriages per thousand. After this, the lowest level, a small rise followed; in 1963 the marriage rate was 8.6 per thousand.

This high marriage rate can primarily be explained by an increased "disposition to marry." The changes in socio-economic conditions, the greater financial security of the young, improved opportunities for work, and, not least, the economic emancipation of women, increased the number of marriages contracted at a younger age. Before 1945 only one-fifth to one quarter of the men who got married were under twenty-five, as opposed to almost half of them in 1963, while among the women those under twenty increased from under 30 per cent to 33 per cent to 35 per cent during the same period. The trend towards marriage at a younger age stopped in the 'sixties, and the number of marriages contracted under twenty-five even decreased, although still considerably exceeding the rate before the Second World War.

Divorce and Re-marriage

Another factor contributing to this increase has been the growing number of second or more marriages. Before 1945 one of the parties in 18 to 19 per cent of all marriages was widowed or divorced; in recent years this proportion has risen to more than 28 per cent.

This is largely due to a considerable increase in the number of divorces. After the end of the Second World War the number of divorces per thousand marriages, which

Breakdown of adult population (from 15 years upward) by sex and personal status (in percentages)

Date	Total population	Unmarried	Married	Widowed	Divorced
Men					
31.12.1920	100	34.7	60.3	4.6	0.4
31.12.1930	100	34.1	61.2	4.1	0.6
31.1.1941	100	32.5	62.5	4.2	0.8
1.1.1949	100	30.6	64.5	4.0	0.9
1.1.1960	100	23.7	71.5	3.4	1.4
1.1.1961	100	23.4	71.8	3.4	1.4
1.1.1962	100	23.4	71.7	3.4	1.5
1.1.1963	100	23.6	71.5	3.3	1.6
1.1.1964	100	23.7	71.3	3.3	1.7
Women					
31.12.1920	100	27.3	56.8	15.2	0.7
31.12.1930	100	26.4	57.8	14.6	1.2
31.1.1941	100	24.7	59.3	14.6	1.4
1.1.1949	100	22.7	59.1	16.6	1.6
1.1.1960	100	17.3	64.4	15.7	2.6
1.1.1961	100	17.0	64.7	15.6	2.7
1.1.1962	100	16.8	64.8	15.6	2.8
1.1.1963	100	17.0	64.6	15.5	2.9
1.1.1964	100	17.0	64.5	15.4	3.1

by international comparison was high even in the inter-war years (in the last years before the Second World War it fluctuated at just under 3 per thousand), rose continuously until 1959, when it approached 9 per thousand. In the 'sixties the divorce rate has been roughly stationary on a somewhat lower level: there are now 7 divorces annually per thousand marriages.

These changes have considerably altered the distribution of the population by personal status. The number of married persons has increased beyond all previous figures. Seventy-one per cent of all males and 65 per cent of all females over 15 are married. Between 1941 and 1964 the number of men and women living in the marriage state increased by 24 per cent, even though the percentage had already increased consider-

ably between 1920 and 1941 (by 29 per cent). The number of divorced persons has also increased to a considerable extent, although the growth rate has been smaller (at 138 per cent) than between the two wars (166 per cent).

Reproduction Rate

The most effective way of showing the present position is through the reproduction indices. Due to the large decrease in the number of births, the pure reproduction index has tended to fall since 1958 and indicates a fall in the population in the future; according to the data of the 'sixties, these indices are between 0.8 and 0.9. The fall in this index has, however, been less than that of the rate of live births, on account of the considerable improvement in the mortality rate, and within this of the infant and child mortality rate. Between 1940–1941 and 1963 the net reproduction index fell by 16 per cent, exactly to the same extent as in the twenty years after the First World War.

II. Social Changes

The most significant changes in population distribution have occurred directly as a result of the socio-economic transformation of the country. The victory of the socialist system of production, which brought with it speedy industrialization and an extensive increase in the number of those gainfully employed, has produced fundamental changes in the population statistics.

Working Population

In the first place, there has been a profound change in the ratio of working to dependent population. While the total population increased by 8 per cent between 1941 and 1963, the number of those gainfully employed rose by 24 per cent. And during that period, the number of dependents per 100 wage earners dropped from 107 to 81.

The increase in the number of the inactive working population* exceeded the rate of increase in those gainfully employed, due to both extensions in the scope of the pension scheme and the ageing of the population. During this period it more than trebled and in 1963 approached 8 per cent of the population.

The ratio of the active working population, which fell somewhat between 1960 and 1963 owing to the socialist transformation of agriculture, was 48 per cent to 46 per cent in 1941. The increase between 1941 and 1963 amounted to 11 per cent. But if the reduced numbers in employment caused by the Second World War are taken into account, the increase has in fact been greater; compared to 1949 (when the number of persons in work was 140,000 lower than in 1941) the increase was 15 per cent.

The growth in the number of those gainfully employed is largely due to the increased number of women gainfully employed. The number of women in gainful employment increased by 69 per cent between 1941 and 1963; in the inter-war period it only increased by 11 per cent. In 1963, 38 per cent of all persons in gainful employment or with pensions were women, as against 28 per cent

* Those not in gainful employment but in receipt of an income, in the overwhelming majority those in receipt of state pensions.

Population distribution by employment
(in percentages)

Date	Total population	Gainfully employed			Dependents	Dependents per 100 persons in work
		Active	Inactive	Total		
31.12.1920	100	45.7	1.3	47.0	53.0	113
31.12.1930	100	44.0	2.0	46.0	54.0	117
31.1.1941	100	46.1	2.2	48.3	51.7	107
1.1.1949	100	45.1	2.8	47.9	52.1	109
1.1.1960	100	48.9	4.4	53.3	46.7	87
1.1.1963	100	47.5	7.7	55.2	44.8	81

in 1941. And while 26 women out of 100 earned their living in 1941, this figure had risen to 41 by 1963, while the ratio of men earning their living did not change (71 per cent). More than half of the women between the ages of 15 and 54 are today gainfully employed (54 per cent in 1963).

Economic Distribution of Working Population

The economic transformation of the country is also reflected in the distribution of the working population according to the different branches of the economy. The industrialization which is a concomitant of the socialist system of production and the change-over to large-scale agricultural production led to a considerable reduction in the number and proportion of the population engaged in agriculture. There was hardly a trace of such a trend in the period between 1920 and 1941, when the number of those employed in agriculture even slightly increased, and the percentage only fell from 58 to 50 per cent. Nor, at the beginning of the period following on the Second World War, was any trend towards a re-division of labour as yet visible; on the contrary, the percentage of those employed in agriculture increased on account of the agrarian reform, and amounted to 53 per cent of the working population. But with the beginning of the five-year plans industrialization led to a considerable reduction of those employed in agriculture; between 1949 and 1960 their number fell from 2.2 million to 1.87 million, and their percentage of the working population to 38 per cent. This process continued in the early 'sixties, as a result of the socialist transformation of agriculture, but was largely due to formerly independent farmers—and consequently classified as part of the working population—reaching the age of retirement and becoming pensioners of the agricultural cooperatives. By the beginning of 1963 the number of those employed in agriculture had fallen to 1,566,000, and their proportion to 33 per cent.

The other side of the coin in the process of transformation is the large-scale increase in the number of those employed in secondary industry. The number of those employed in secondary industry, including the building trades, had already risen in the inter-war period (by 57 per cent between 1920 and 1949), but this increase was intensified in the period after 1949: by 1963 their number had increased—from 963,000 to 1,810,000 —by 88 per cent and today accounts for nearly one-third of all of the working population.

The number and percentage of those employed in transport and in the public services also increased considerably. In 1963, 6 per cent of all persons in employment were employed in transport and almost 8 per cent in the public services. Through the extension of the pensions scheme, those members of the working population who had retired or no longer worked formed a not inconsiderable group within the whole. In 1963 they amounted to 14 per cent of all those gainfully employed as against 6 per cent in 1949. Their number, which doubled between 1920 and 1941, rose to even more between 1949 and 1963.

As a consequence of the socio-economic transformation of the country, the distribution of the working population according to occupation also changed. In the first place, the socialist transformation of agriculture brought to an end the significant place in the statistics occupied by the self-employed or auxiliary earners in the family, although in 1941, 41 per cent and in 1949, 54 per cent of the working population fell within this category. In 1963 this group consisted of just over 200,000 persons, amounting to no more than 4 per cent of the total. During the same period a new social stratum had emerged, that of members of producers' cooperatives. In 1963 they exceeded 1,000,000 and indeed represented more than 20 per cent of the working population. As a corollary of industrialization, the number and the proportion of those in employment has

Structure of the working population according to branches of the economy

Date	Working population	Agri-culture	Industry, including the build-ing trades	Transport and com-munica-tions	Trade	Miscel-laneous
31.12.1920	3,652,489	2,128,008	639,588	113,465	202,877	568,551
31.12.1930	3,822,121	2,030,844	825,984	107,968	252,190	605,135
31.1.1941	4,297,407	2,164,975	1,005,348	139,768	282,941	704,375
1.1.1949	4,154,543	2,196,185	963,493	164,927	219,990	609,948
1.1.1960	4,876,232	1,872,730	1,682,233	296,321	308,441	716,507
1.1.1963	4,790,050	1,566,400	1,809,700	314,400	324,950	774,600

Structure of the working population according to branches of the economy (in percentages)

Date	Working population	Agri-culture	Industry, including the build-ing trades	Transport and communi-cations	Trade	Miscel-laneous
31.12.1920	100	58.3	17.5	3.1	5.5	15.6
31.12.1930	100	53.2	21.6	2.8	6.6	15.8
31.1.1941	100	50,4	23.4	3.2	6.6	16.4
1.1.1949	100	52.8	23.2	4.0	5.3	14.7
1.1.1960	100	38.4	34.5	6.1	6.3	14.7
1.1.1963	100	32.7	37.8	6.5	6.8	16.2

grown steadily. In 1949, 2,000,000 persons or 46 per cent belonged to this category, and in 1963 already 3.35 million or 70 per cent of the whole working population. This increase has far surpassed the increase between 1920 and 1941, when the number of workers and employees had grown by no more than 17 per cent.

The effect of changed opportunities for work is also shown by the shift in the types of occupation. In 1963 nearly one-fifth of all employees and cooperative members were professional and clerical workers and four-fifths manual workers. In 1941 the percentage of professional and clerical workers among those in employment was only 12 per cent. In the earlier period, between 1920 and 1941, the number of professional and clerical workers increased by just over one-third; between 1941 and 1963 it increased by 300 per cent. At present the ratio is 24 professional or clerical workers to every 100 manual workers, as against 13 in 1941.

Urbanization

This occupational-social transformation took place concurrently with the process of urbanization. Between 1949 and 1963 the urban population increased by 25 per cent, while the village population remained essentially unchanged. Today 42 per cent of the population live in towns. The trend to urbanization had already emerged before the Second World War. In the twenty inter-war years—the figures being based on present-day administrative classifications—the urban population increased by 26 per cent, almost

Territorial distribution of the population

(in percentages)

Date	Total population	Budapest	Other towns	Villages
31.12.1920	100	15.4	19.9	64.7
31.12.1930	100	16.6	19.7	63.7
31.1.1941	100	18.4	19.9	61.7
1.1.1949	100	17.3	19.3	63.4
1.1.1960	100	18.1	21.6	60.3
1.1.1961	100	18.4	22.3	59.3
1.1.1962	100	18.7	22.6	58.7
1.1.1963	100	18.9	22.9	58.2
1.1.1964	100	19.0	23.2	57.8

the same rate as after the Second World War. During that period, however, there was also an increase of 11 per cent in the village population.

The present increase in the urban population has been due to large-scale internal migration from the village to the town. Between 1949 and 1963 the urban population of the towns increased by the addition of 550,000 persons from the villages, or 16 per cent of their 1949 population. This increase due to migration occurred mainly in the new socialist towns and in Budapest. Today the population of Budapest approximates 2 millions, more than 230,000 of whom migrated to the capital since 1949.

Education

As a result of the cultural revolution accompanying the social transformation, there has been a considerable improvement in the level of education. Following the transformation of the school system, between 1941 and 1963 the number of those who had completed the eight classes of primary education increased by 180 per cent, those who completed their secondary education by 168 per cent, and those who graduated from a university or other institution of higher education by 110 per cent. In the earlier

comparative period the increase in the educational level was far below this rate: between 1920 and 1941 the number of those who completed the eighth class of primary education had only increased by 66 per cent, and the number of those who had graduated from a university or institution of higher education had only risen by 25 per cent.

At the beginning of 1963, 20 per cent of the population of seven years and over had ended their formal education with full completion of the eight classes of primary education; in 1941 only 7 per cent had managed to achieve this. The percentages of those who had completed secondary school increased in the twenty years after the Second World War from 2 to 5.8 per cent, and of those who had graduated from an institution of higher learning from 1.1 to 2 per cent.

The results of educational progress look even more impressive if we investigate the education of the population of different ages. At the present time over 38 per cent of the total population of 15 years and over have completed at least the eight classes of primary education (as against 15 per cent in 1941), and 10 per cent of the population 18 years old and over have completed secondary school (as against 4 per cent in 1941).

The improvement in the level of education is especially striking where women are concerned. Feminine education has been un- der a considerable disability as compared to masculine education. While masculine edu- cation still enjoys certain advantages, the disparity is much less; the number of women enjoying the benefits of higher education has increased at a faster rate than the number of men; between 1941 and 1963 the number of women graduating from institutions of higher education quadrupled, while that of the men "only" doubled; in 1963 there was a 500 per cent increase in the number of

women who completed their secondary edu- cation over the figures for 1941 (for men the increase was 100 per cent).

This short survey is designed to show the more important demographic changes which have taken place since the Second World War. Its limited objective has been to present a coherent historical sketch of the demo- graphic processes and changes which have taken place in the population structure as a result of the socio-economic transformation of the last twenty years.

Educational levels of the population (in percentages)

Date	10 years and over. No schooling	15 years and over. Completed at least 8 classes of primary education	18 years and over. Taken secondary school leaving exam	25 years and over. Taken university degree or higher diploma
Males				
31.12.1920	10.3 a)	12.7	—	3.3
31.12.1930	7.4 b)	14.1	—	3.3
31.1.1941	5.2	16.1	7.0	2.8
1.1.1949	4.1	21.9	8.1	3.1
1.1.1960	2.6	34.5	11.6	4.5
1.1.1963	2.0	40.8	12.7	4.8
Females				
31.12.1920	15.3 a)	9.8	—	0.2
31.12.1930	11.1 b)	11.8	—	0.3
31.1.1941	7.5	14.1	1.6	0.4
1.1.1949	5.5	19.5	3.3	0.5
1.1.1960	3.7	31.3	6.3	1.1
1.1.1963	2.9	35.9	7.6	1.3
		Total		
31.12.1920	12.9 a)	11.2	—	1.7
31.12.1930	9.3 b)	12.9	—	1.7
31.1.1941	6.4	15.1	4.2	1.6
1.1.1949	4.8	20.6	5.5	1.7
1.1.1960	3.2	32.8	8.8	2.7
1.1.1963	2.5	38.2	10.0	2.9

a) *In these years, of 12 years and over.*
b) *Excluding those who have not gone to school but are literate.*

MIKLÓS SZÁNTÓ

THE HUNGARIAN DIASPORA

I recently received a letter from Andor Mészáros, a sculptor of Hungarian origin, now living in Melbourne, Australia. "Someone", he wrote, "who was called Sándor Barna at home and is called Stanley Brown, within a week of his arrival has not only never been a good Hungarian but will never make a good Australian either. Every culture, like every individual creation, consists of two parts. It has a local value and an eternal human, international quality. For ourselves we can enjoy the Hungarianness of our culture, and for Australia we have distilled the eternal human quality of our culture, and what is more, for Australia's benefit. Those Australians who have come to understand the universal values of Hungarian culture have usually become interested in the typically Hungarian values as well."

Behind these lines can be perceived deep inner changes in the nature of Hungarian emigrant life; the outlines of a new patriotism appear, which no longer shuts itself up in national ghettos in the host countries, is not inconsistent with the interests of these countries, and at the same time accepts that the thousand-year-old history of Hungary did not end in 1945. The emigrant is a patriot when he is a vital link between the Hungarian people building anew on the old foundations and the peoples of the receiving countries.

The author of this article is the editor of the fortnightly *Magyar Hírek*, which keeps Hungarians abroad in touch with events in Hungary. This article, first published in the Budapest Catholic monthly *Vigilia*, deals with the approximately million and a half Hungarians who emigrated from Hungary before or after the war and are now living in Western Europe and on other continents, and does not refer to the Hungarian communities long-settled on the territories of neighbouring countries.

A long road had to be travelled, the polar ice cap of the Cold War had to be cracked by the "Gulf stream" of relations hips which altered direction some fifteen years ago.

What essentially was the earlier spirit of the emigrant? Ferenc Molnár, in a sketch written in New York some time ago, described the Hungarian emingrant as a sick man. "It begins by him feeling himself to be a tourist. As a mature man he escaped from somewhere to Paris or London or Rio de Janeiro or New York. He either liked the town or he didn't and he felt like a tourist. Then the months passed. And then the years. The tourist has not gone home. The tourist has got stuck. The tourist has become an emigrant. From a healthy man he has turned into a sick man. He has not noticed it yet, but others have already deduced it from his increasingly uncontrollable nerves, the great quantity and the small quality of his complaints, the rapid development of his hypercritical faculties, the steady decrease in his desire to meet his compatriots and his ever worsening English, because unconsciously he has given up the useless struggle in middle age with a foreign language. The emigrant does not yet notice any of this. He merely observes that he cannot sleep without sleeping pills. This happens to some earlier and to others later. To single men earlier. To family men later. To the well-to-do later. To the poor earlier. Children do not catch it: emigration is not a childhood complaint."

The fate of the emigrant is a hard one, and defences are needed. One way of dealing with stress is to take offence, to blame others. Where offended people meet quarrels easily arise. One of the most frequent topics of conversation in Hungarian emigrant circles —often called the Hungarian sickness—is the inability to get along with one another.

Groups seem to form in accordance with the date of emigration, and each group, organization and club is a stronghold at everlasting war with the others.

Another group of the offended is not angry with the world: they suffer from the wounds of real and assumed offences received in the homeland. They attempt to justify the fact they are made emigrants by conditions at home. The intensity of this justification increases in a direct ratio with the individual's feeling of uncertainty and the tension of adaptation.

Adaptation is not a one-sided process; the other side of it is being accepted. A Belgian scholar—Beda Claes—published a sociological study in 1962 in which, through the answers given in various questionnaires, he analysed the problems which arise when Belgians marry foreigners. Forty-one per cent of those questioned considered the marriage of a Belgian woman with a foreigner as undesirable. Twenty-seven per cent approved of it, on certain conditions: that it was a genuine love-match, that the man adapted successfully to Belgian life, broke with his old background and was a confirmed Catholic. Only 7 per cent regarded mixed marriages as natural without any further provisos, the remainder were cautious, non-committal, and expressed no opinion. A number of studies of the process of adaptation by young Hungarians after 1956 were made in various countries, and there was near unanimity that the incidence of psychological disorders was very high among them.

The rapidity with which an emigrant adapts depends on whether he is successful or not, on his family life, as for example in the case of mixed marriages, and the changes rung on these factors: the wife accepts him but the relations do not, or the whole family accepts him as an exception; they accept him, but not his culture and customs, and urge him to renounce a part of his personality, to break entirely with his previous life.

The Causes of Emigration

Emigration is in itself a peculiar break. With it something ends and something begins. Life has dramatic turning-points when everything comes to a concentrated head: the greater or smaller contradictions on the different levels of daily life mature into a conflict, the thousand small wounds inflame and bleed. The man—or indeed woman—refuses to continue his own history, bursts the banks in which his life previously flowed; the resolutions sharpen to a decision, and life moves into new channels. The emigrant renounces something, the attraction of the opposite becomes overwhelming, and the moment indelibly burns its mark into the soul.

It must be remembered a man's life is not only political. At the time of great historical events every political happening is mixed with the worries of private life, with family and personal interests. At the time of the great wave of emigration from Hungary, before the First World War, the life of millions was carried on in a long ten-year situation of conflict, when the spectre of starvation faced people with the need for some sort of decision. Basically, the situation was the same between the two World Wars. In 1945 the end of the Second World War found hundreds of thousands of Hungarians in various parts of Europe, thrown up there by the tides of war and faced with the question: where and how will they continue the civil life from which they were forcibly uprooted?

It would be a grave mistake to give stereotyped answers on the causes of emigration, of the moment of decision. The points of departure, the decisions, the angers of conflict, may be various, but the force which gives sufficient and effective energy to lift a man from the land of his fathers, and to transport him to alien soil also helps him to provide him with the reserve energy he needs to withstand the first, almost inevitable tribulations. It stops him running away, it drives him to face all the difficulties and survive them. The emotion, the concentrated strength is so great that its memory, as if petrified, is sharply preserved through the years to come. It plays a part in the process of putting down roots, it determines the colour, temperature, and often even the time-scale of adaptation, but above all it organizes—on an emotional level—the emigrant's relationship with the homeland he has left.

Even those Hungarians who left Hungary a mere fifteen years ago, most of them quite young, and who have visited Hungary regularly each year since 1965—those therefore who keep in step, as it were, with the homeland, who know and understand current Hungarian difficulties and problems—in their more intimate moments lay bare those few weeks which are the natural barrier between the here and the there. That period was a second beginning in their lives, a historic break, beginning a new calendar. They often say that at that time, at a certain point, the old film of their life broke, only to start unrolling again, reorganized, in a different time and place. There is a sort of no-man's-land between the two points. The old roots no longer hold them, the new roots have not yet grown.

A full break, however, is impossible: most emigrants have a dual tie. The first great exhibition of Hungarian artists living abroad was held in Budapest in August 1970. One especially fine piece of work admired by the visitors was the statue by Andor Mészáros, entitled *The Emigrant*. One of the frequent themes of classical mythology was two-faced Janus, one face looking back to the past, one face looking forward to the future. It is interesting that Mészáros worked the back of the figure in the utmost detail, the sad face full of intelligence, while the whole front of the figure is amorphous and expressionless.

The situation of emigrants was transformed by the move of the Hungarian Government when it declared an amnesty, and so made and makes it possible for emigrants to visit their homeland even if they left without passports and contrary to Hungarian law. The opportunity to make regular visits has significantly alleviated the homesickness felt by emigrants. It has altered the relationship between various groups of emigrants, and placed on a new foundation both the ties linking them with their homeland and the conditions which have rooted them and nourished them in the soil of the host countries.

Hungarians in the West

The majority of Hungarians in the West live in the USA. The 1960 census indicated that 770,000 Hungarians live there, if we take the following criteria: those who have come from Hungary themselves, those who have at least one Hungarian parent, those whose mother tongue is Hungarian, and finally those who regard themselves as Hungarians. (This figure does not include the children of Hungarian parents who were themselves born in America, i.e. the third generation, some of whom have remained in Hungarian areas and in regular contact with their grandparents, probably speak Hungarian, and are aware of their origins.)

There were significant settlements of Hungarians in Canada even before 1945. According to the various estimates there are today 90,000–100,000 Hungarians living in Canada. In South America the largest Hungarian settlement before the war was in Brazil. Today it totals approximately 60,000. In the Argentine there were about 10,000 Hungarians before the War, who were joined by another 4,000–5,000 later. Among the other South American states Venezuela and Uruguay have fairly large Hungarian groups; according to my estimate Hungarians total approximately 15,000 in the middle and southern parts of South America.

Outside Europe there are also a large

number of Hungarians living in Australia: approximately 35,000. There are also Hungarians living—generally in small groups—in many parts of Africa and Asia. In this area the largest group whose mother tongue is Hungarian lives in Israel.

In the period before the Second World War the only part of Europe to have a fairly significant number of Hungarians living there was France. Various estimates gave them as some 40,000 people; today perhaps 50,000 Hungarians live in France. Between the two World Wars many Hungarians worked in Germany. Their number today probably exceeds 50,000. In England there are something like 20,000–25,000 Hungarians, 15,000 in Belgium and about 10,000 in Switzerland, the Netherlands, Italy and Sweden respectively. In the rest of Europe there are much smaller groups of Hungarians.

On the American continent there are about 1,000,000, in Australia 35,000, in Africa and Asia—mostly in Israel—185,000.

These 1,500,000 individuals are Hungarian as regards their country of origin, language and culture, but it would be a mistake to assume that the emigrants are a homogeneous group, divided from each other and from their homeland only by geographical frontiers. The Hungarian emigration is differentiated, and highly structured mass.

The Structure of Emigrant Communities

The "million and a half staggering out to America", as Attila József described them, went there as temporary workers. They were not emigrants in the classic sense of the word. The First World War cut off the way home, and the selfish and short-sighted policy of the Horthy régime afterwards turned them into permanent settlers over there, and they thus became emigrants. What could these greatly suffering people have

against present-day Hungary? But we can take a nearer example. A few years ago in Middlesborough, England, the members of a small Hungarian club—mostly 1956 arrivals—organized a concert with the participation of artists from Hungary. The mayor of the town came and so did a well-known correspondent of an important London newspaper to be spending the week-end in the town. "Are these people émigrés who escaped from socialist Hungary?" the journalist asked me. "Then how's it possible that almost all of them have visited their homeland in the last year or two? And how's it possible that entertainers come from Budapest to entertain them? I don't understand the whole thing: one either is an émigré or one is not."

The subsequent conversation lasted till dawn, and it was not because of language difficulties that my companion experienced such difficulty in understanding the situation. It may indeed appear odd to those with only a superficial knowledge of the situation. The Hungarians there—by then British subjects, who had put down roots in England and were respected there—had fled from Hungary, and had asked for and been given political asylum as such. However, most of them left Hungary motivated by an urge for adventure, they wanted to see the world, or start their tangled family lives anew. Only a very small number of them were enemies of socialism. Many of them, even if they had feelings of political antagonism, were not hostile to the system but to the political line of Stalinism—it was the way power was used, a way in itself alien to socialism, which roused their hostility. The Hungary of today understands the motives that drove them and has made it possible to normalize relations with them. The 1965 amnesty gave it a legal form. Nearly 90 per cent of the Hungarians living in that small English town have visited Hungary in recent years, and there are many who come every year. The Hungarian body concerned—the World Federation of Hungarians—helps their clubs with books, records and by sending artists and entertainers. Are these Hungarians émigrés from present-day Hungary? János Kádár made the point clear in a lecture he gave, when he referred to the small number of professional émigrés whose livelihood is in unceasing anti-Hungarian activity: there are those who live in emigration and there are those who live on emigration.

Diaspora

Gyula Illyés, in several of his articles, uses the term *diaspora* to define all kinds of emigrant Hungarians.

The dates or periods in history which dictate the groupings of the Hungarians in the West have already been indicated. The date of each diaspora means a great deal. It characterizes and explains the circumstances of departure, the types of social classes and strata, the degree of difficulty encountered in adaptation, and the nature of the relationship with the homeland.

The large-scale emigration before the First World War was mostly composed of poor peasants. The receiving country was primarily the USA, and the Hungarians worked in industry there, mostly as unskilled or manual labour. Their aim was to save up a relatively large sum in a few years to enable them to return to Hungary and buy land there. They lived in ethnic ghettos, cut off from the people of the host country and its social organizations, culture and language. This situation only changed between the two World Wars. In those years emigration became more difficult, long economic crises shook the world, there was heavy unemployment, and the US frontiers were largely closed. The emigrants of this period left Hungary for Canada and South America if they were agricultural workers and to European countries, such as France or Belgium, if they were workers, primarily miners. Thus the goal of emigration changed,

as did the receiving country and in part the class from which they came.

In the years which precede the Second World War, in the terrible years of fascist hate and terror, a very valuable, talented section of the Hungarian intelligentsia had to leave, in part because of Jewish origin and in part for political reasons. They included Leó Szilárd, the atomic physicist, the Nobel Prize winners Eugene P. Wigner, and Dennis Gabor together with many writers, artists and musicians, among them Béla Bartók. Most of them went to the USA. Many took leading parts in the antifascist movements. Many fighters—and martyrs—of the European resistance movements came from the ranks of the progressive Hungarian emigrants.

At the end of the war and after there were large, widespread movements—in both directions—through the fragmented fronts, then the lines froze as the Cold War began. Anti-communist organizations were formed in the West from among the members of the former Nazi army and the Hungarian regiments allied to them. The USA, Canada and many other countries stopped the free entry of immigrants. The USA continued the system of quotas.

When the war ended the soldiers and the adolescent members of the paralimitary fascist youth organization remained organized in units and retreated into Germany and under the command and influence of officers, whose sympathies were mostly fascist. The retreating army was followed by the leading officials of the Horthy administration often fleeing together with their families; in some towns and villages all the officials left, especially where they believed their own panic-mongering rumours and obeyed the order to leave with the army. With them and behind them came gangs of bloodstained Hungarian Nazi criminals, "the Arrow Cross", threatening and forcing on even those who in the meantime had realized the senselessness of escape.

When the guns stopped thousands started

out to look for their lost families. Many of them, once they had found them—or not—returned home. Others were caught up by the prevalent fever and together with them, or alone, continued their way into the world. Between 1945 and 1947 many Jewish Hungarians who had lived through the death camps left the country. Their families, wives and children had died in the course of the catastrophe and their wounds were so deep they could no longer continue their lives in their old home. They preferred to abandon their past completely and to attempt to start a new life somewhere else. The different fronts and opened frontiers saw the coming and going of hundreds of thousands from East to West and West to East. It took years before the waves of this tempest-driven sea of people subsided. The front-line run through Hungary for a year. Valuable properties were destroyed, factories and livestock were taken away, towns were devastated by bombs and artillery fire. The country was quite literally in ruins. The people were in rags, hunger, and inflation crippled the country. There were many who simply did not believe it could be rebuilt in any acceptable time. Thousands of these people of little faith pulled up stakes and left.

As always in Hungarian history, the emigration was countered by a movement in the opposite direction. From the Soviet Union, from the various countries of Europe and even from far distant continents came flocking those progressive Hungarians of the socialist faith who wanted to be present and take part in the building of a socialist Hungary.

By 1948 the early coalition period had ended and the power of the working class became irrevocably victorious.

Between 1947 and 1956 many members of the former ruling classes and many right-wing politicians left the country and involved themselves in the life of Hungarian communities abroad. All this was helped by the growing Cold War. Criminals, smugglers and racketeers also smuggled themselves over the borders in great numbers. All those who left were aware that they would be unable to continue their old, familiar way of life in the conditions of the new Hungary. The serious errors of the Rákosi régime made their effects felt in those years. Many valuable people, scientists, technologists, artists and skilled workers and peasants, attached to their country, left Hungary during the difficult years because they felt outraged. Many also left who otherwise had no trouble with the régime but were frightened by changes which they did not understand.

In 1956, 200,000 people left the country. (Of these about 50,000 have returned.) This large-scale defection was due to a combination of the political mistakes of the fifties and the ruthless use made of them by external and internal enemies, the general mass confusion and the crisis of confidence.

People still defect in our day; occasionally those who leave the country on a holiday fail to return. They usually travel on the invitation of relatives, are mostly young, in the professions, or skilled workers. Most of them do not regard themselves as emigrants, and play no political role abroad. Irrespective of why they left, however, their going is still a loss and they injure the state in that the skills they acquired at home—at great cost to the country—are employed for the benefit of foreign countries.

The Second and the Third Generation

In addition to the first generation of emigrants who left their homeland, we have to consider the second generation, born in the host countries, and in many cases a third generation too. But we cannot use the term emigration in connection with such second and third generations. The fact of Hungarian origin is, however, important, and in many cases the families do not hide but rather keep alive the consciousness of their connection with their country of origin.

When the American policy of the "melting pot" was at its height, when it was planned to assimilate immigrants as quickly as possible, it was general for the second generation of Hungarians to leave the Hungarian settlements and marry into native American families. This process was helped by a score of historical reasons. In both the world wars Hungary, alas, fought on the side opposing the major host countries, and consequently many felt that a Hungarian name which emphasized their Hungarian origin might make them suspicious to their neighbours and hinder their careers. Those physicians and lawyers of the second generation whose interest was to retain their Hungarian clients stayed on at the settlements and married into the Hungarian families living there. Those who retained their religious ties or played a part in Hungarian organizations also stayed, retaining their language and continuing to regard themselves as Hungarians. (As a rule children in families where both parents or the mother is Hungarian tend to speak Hungarian and are more aware of their origins.)

The second generation is still burdened with a number of inhibitions due to the fact that their parents were immigrants. Their consciousness of being Hungarian is a factor of their good or bad relationship with their parents and of whether they live with their parents or not. Another is whether they get on in life. A number of sociological studies of emigrant life draw attention to the fact that the conflict of generations is exceptionally strong. Two different world views, two sets of customs and habits collide. The conflict of the generations is typical of our age. Emigrant life, however, with its special ambience, multiplies the conflicts. For most families throughout the world the mother tongue is the natural means of communication between parents and children. The language you learn at your mother's knee is the language of the country. But where the parents are immigrants there is a difference between the children's original mother tongue

and the language acquired in kindergartens and schools. Parents and children have different cultures, and the child is often the parents' bridge to their surroundings. He acts as interpreter and transmits the strange new customs. At the same time it is difficult to bridge the gap between fathers and their sons which is almost inevitable in the circumstances. How much disappointment lies hidden behind the usually embarrassed answers when one asks if the child can speak Hungarian. How many times one has heard it said, sometimes indifferently, sometimes aggressively: "He understands everything, but always answers in English." There is no problem if there is mutual tolerance, if parents and children agree in their judgement on the opportunities offered by the world, and if their image of the homeland leads to a pleased acceptance of their origins on the part of the children.

A well-known Australian woman artist of Hungarian origin once said somethig to me that came from the depths of her being and was a great pain to her: "My husband is a cultivated and witty man. One of the great sorrows of my life is that our children will never know how witty, how full of ideas and cultured their father is, because in English he only speaks the language of business and everyday life. He is only witty in Hungarian —and the children don't speak Hungarian."

The difficulties become unbridgeable if the old people surround themselves with the painted props of a long dead world, locking themselves away from the modern trends of the host country, when they see the new Hungary through the misty glasses of the past, and come into conflict with their children on both these counts, since the children are not tied to the past and are attracted to the future. Then they break away from the sad fathers, and throw off their own Hungarianness as an outworn dress.

There are certain features in many of those who left in 1956 which resemble the earlier behaviour of the second generation. This diaspora consisted largely of men. It scattered, married into the families of the host countries, and we have often heard the complaint that their children do not learn Hungarian. After the first few difficult years this group kept itself aloof from Hungarian organizations or church congregations, and many of them did not read Hungarian newspapers or books.

Today there is an appreciable renewal of ethnic communities in the leading countries of the western world. The old-style, forced assimilation only produced superficial results. The ethnic group continued to exist, the problems became merely marginal, but —as the events of our days show—they assume an important role in times of conflict and crisis. As the newer generation comes of age it has a renewed interest in the past of their families. Many accept their European identity and the young people of the Hungarian ethnic group are no exception. Experience shows that the second generation also goes to see Hungarian films and reads the magazines published in two languages. They may not read and write Hungarian very well, but many of them have a good command of the spoken language. The third generation exhibits a livelier, freer interest in Hungary. They are not burdened by the many inhibitions of their fathers and grandfathers. As a number of American and Canadian universities accept Hungarian as a second foreign language, many of them have an interest in renewing their command of the language they learned from their grandparents and spoke well as little children.

And what are their political attitudes? The bulk of those who emigrated up to the Second World War represented progressive political ideas, and were organized in left-wing organizations. This was the main reason why for years thousands of them were refused citizenship by the official circles of the host countries. During the war the Hungarians belonging to the progressive organizations fought against fascism and as an acknowledgement of this fact the majority received their citizenship papers after the war. The progressive Hungarians who remained in the West after the Liberation in 1945 lived through a period of great difficulty. They were growing old, they suffered from the atmosphere of the Cold War, the political mistakes committed at home and the changes in Hungary, which they often could not understand. Their numbers and influence have decreased. At the same time the émigré circles who opposed Socialist Hungary have also grown old. The right wing of the political émigrés is broken into fractions and is slowly disintegrating. Because of the advances of the forces of peace and the achievements of the socialist countries, among them the Hungarian People's Republic, the emigrants antagonistic to Hungary are rapidly losing ground, and their disintegration now seems inevitable.

The great majority of Hungarians abroad are not antagonistic to modern Hungary. They are friendly, but they are not a homogeneous group either. They are broken into many groups, varying according to the date of emigration, their position and their academic qualifications. The people who belong to this majority may be members of religious, cultural or sports organizations or unconnected with any outside organizations. One must be careful not to categorize these people along exclusively political lines. There are, for example, those who support socialism yet are far from a Marxist ideology.

The politically neutral majority very largely approves of the manifestations of cultural-intellectual life in Hungary and is even willing to help, if help is needed. This becomes especially clear in the course of certain campaigns which engage their sympathies: large masses were active in helping the victims of the recent floods, in the training of Hungarian athletes for the Olympics, or in the question of preserving their mother tongue. In 1970, 120,000 Hungarians visited their homeland. They came from all the corners of the earth, and this is not including the Hungarians who came for a visit from the neighbouring countries, i.e. Rumania, Czechoslovakia and Yugoslavia. The bulk of those visiting their relatives here belong to this politically neutral group friendly to Hungary. Most of them have come more than once in recent years and remain in constant touch with their relatives. They have learnt of the successes, problems and troubles in the building of socialism, they keep pace with the contemporary realities of Hungarian life. (That is, their information is up-to-date, not that they necessarily agree or identify with Hungary politically.) At any rate, as an effect of visiting their homeland, the friendly majority widen their horizons appreciably.

The bulk of today's émigrés, those who left in the last twenty to twenty-five years, came from different strata, with different goals and different equipment from their predecessors. And there is something else. Circumstances have altered radically in the host countries during the past sixty to seventy years as well. The Hungarian districts, the ethnic ghettos of New York, Cleveland, Detroit and Sao Paulo, have largely disintegrated. Living in a closed community in those days also meant that Hungarians mostly married other Hungarians. The emigrants of today enjoy different opportunities, by virtue of their knowledge of the language, their skills and their schooling. The attitude of the ruling circles in the host countries has also changed towards immigrants. They are anxious to create a united nation from the diverse immigrants. They do not lose sight of the pitfalls, and they are aware that it is the second generation that is important, whose children grow up with the national consciousness of their new country in their hearts.

For the second and third generation the word homeland means something quite different from its meaning for their fathers and grandfathers. The "old country" does not mean to them the glorified world, the immediacy of the sensations of childhood and youth that it means to their parents or grandparents, but a far off country which

perhaps they only know of from the tales of their mother or grandmother.

The basic economic-technological processes which irresistably drive our world ahead, and the accelerating pace which characterizes them, also affect the picture. They have an influence on the situation of emigrants and on their relationship with their homeland. In the first place is the shrinking of distances, the revolution of communications. The previous generation was divided from the homeland by time and broad oceans. To exchange letters was often a matter of months. In our age communication by post, by telephone, in person or through intermediaries has speeded up and multiplied. Visits between relatives are eased and helped by the new migration of tourism which moves hundreds of millions every year. Travel has become a matter of course, an everyday necessity. Thus relatives living beyond the frontiers have become almost neighbours. Telecommunications provide a flood of information, and the Hungarian living at the furthest corner of the earth can come across news of Hungary daily, direct or indirect, and acquaint himself with the creations of Hungarian culture. Contacts between nations in the fields of commerce, diplomacy and culture increase. Agreements multiply. Today national exhibitions are everyday events, there are film weeks each year, there are Hungarian books in the bookshops, sports events take place, folk ensembles give concerts, the concert halls and radios provide a chance to hear Hungarian music. This reaches everyone, but has a different impact on those living in different countries.

Nor can the second and third generation evade this impact. They feel everything Hungarian to be connected with themselves and relive again and again all that they have learned from their parents about being Hungarian and life in Hungary before they emigrated.

Religious organizations are another significant force binding emigrants to Hungary.

In the main their thinking is up-to-date, they perceive that contact with Hungary is of mutual value. They organize a great many group visits to Hungary—sometimes led by the priests themselves—and their experience of Hungary often radically alters the political moods of their members, and the opinions which they previously held about contacts with Hungary.

With regard to the Hungarian language, the present situation is the result of a long process of development. The present stage might be symbolized by the Budapest "Mother Tongue Conference" which was held in 1970. The young people who left in 1956, and who are most closely in touch with their families at home, are themselves mostly family men today, and it is now or never that the children being born in their families will learn Hungarian. The bulk of the first generation which left Hungary after 1945 has reached retirement age, and in these families the grandchildren have already arrived. The second generation works practically day and night, and the care of the third wave, the grandchildren, devolves on the grandparents, the majority of whom want their grandchildren to be conscious of their Hungarianness. This is shown by the fact that the evergrowing army of emigrants who come home for a visit often bring their children with them to learn a little Hungarian. This year the World Federation of Hungarians received very many letters from families all over the world asking about ways of sending their children over for special summer holidays. Everyone knows that children very soon perfect their knowledge of a language in the company of fellows of their own age, and certainly the children enjoy themselves here.

From all corners of the world where there are Hungarians in larger groups there was a demand, letters were received, emphatic queries were voiced by visitors, all urging some form of organization for this purpose. Steps could and should have been taken earlier, indeed, there may very well have been some negligence, but the "Mother Tongue Conference" was the first time all the conditions were propitious for a discussion on methods of teaching, and maintaining and developing the knowledge of Hungarian language and literature by Hungarians living abroad. The Conference assessed the present position, and discussed the various forms of organization which at this decisive moment could provide effective help for teachers of Hungarian to those living in the West. We can now help their work with language books, records, tapes and many other means.

The final statement of the "Mother Tongue Conference" emphasized that in its frank, open, debating atmosphere different opinions and points of views freely confronted one another. Friends of the Hungarian language have joined together from all over the world; the preparatory committee includes experts both from Hungary and abroad, essentially they represent the Hungarians of five continents. It has become clear that the preservation of their knowledge of the Hungarian language is the task of the Hungarians living abroad, and no one can do that for them, but it has also become clear that they can only carry out this task with help from Hungary —without that every attempt is bound to fail.

Some of those who took part in the "Mother Tongue Conference" were the victims of a series of attacks by extreme right-wing Hungarian organizations after their return home. But the majority of Hungarian emigrants did not join in these attacks. They clearly realized that the betterment in international relations, the atmosphere of improving economic and cultural contacts make these Cold War actions out of date. The attitude which flaunts its Hungarianness in words but is helpless in deeds, which in practice has done nothing to help the next generations living abroad to preserve their knowledge of Hungarian and their consciousness of their Hungarian origins, is both negative and arid.

The "Mother Tongue Conference" marks a new stage of development following and running parallel to the other forms of contact, family, semi-official, spontaneous and organized. If debate and co-operation for mutually valued goals is the essence of a dialogue, then the "Mother Tongue Conference" proved a real dialogue. At the closing session of the Conference Professor Denis Sinor* of Bloomington (Indiana, U.S.A.) summed up the historical situation in which a dialogue is both possible and necessary. He said: "Hungary is a socialist state. No one here wants to change this fact. It would be ridiculous for those living abroad to want to change it. I think that it is very important that when we speak to our compatriots living abroad we should interpret the Hungarian reality objectively. It is not necessary to be a socialist abroad, where we live, in order to be able to interpret the Hungarian system of government in an objective and sympathetic light. This is vital for both sides. We either remain in contact with socialist Hungary or lose contact with Hungary. It is as simple as that! But looking at it from the other side: the homeland either accepts that we live the way we live or it loses us. There is no other solution!"

Hungarian consciousness is something wider, more complex than the ability to speak Hungarian. "There is an interesting change everywhere in the world in the concept of belonging to a nation," wrote Gyula Illyés in an article in Magyar Hírek, the journal of the World Federation of Hungarians. "Someone who speaks good Hungarian is not on that account necessarily a good Hungarian, but someone may be a good Hungarian even if he cannot speak the language well. This is a surprising and new phenomenon. To be a patriot, to belong to a nation, is not as limited as it was fifty or a hundred years ago. Kölcsey's saying: 'The nation lives in its language' is not valid in the same way as it was then. The nation no longer lives only in its language. It lives beyond it, too, and even without it. There is national sentiment without the national language. There was in the past too. Széchenyi and Eötvös, the great figures of the Reform generation, were good Hungarians first, and only then learned to speak Hungarian well. The frontier of belonging to a nation is wider than the frontier of a language. Let us preserve our language abroad too, for our children as well, but let us not be dismayed if circumstances prevent us from preserving it, and let us not condemn those who failed to preserve it. They are not renegades because of that. Belonging to a community is these days becoming a matter of choice, like joining a party, religion or movement."

In its aim of ensuring a well-adjusted future for Hungarian emigrants and ameliorating the stresses that exist amongst them, the Hungarian Government is anxious to help in their peaceful adaptation in the host countries. It accepts the existing situation. This is expressed in law by the fact that the state accepts and recognizes the dual citizenship of the émigrés, and has no desire to trouble the lives of those of our compatriots who have put down roots abroad and established themselves there. The evidence for this lies in the many measures it has taken to build on a basis of settled relationships and mutual sympathy, which equally correspond to the interests of the Hungarians living in all parts of the world.

* See Denis Sinor's essay: "Teaching Hungary". The N.H.Q. No. 42.

CONTRIBUTORS

ACZÉL, György (b. 1917). Member, Political Committee of the Hungarian Socialist Workers' Party; Deputy Prime Minister.

BIRÓ, József (b. 1921). Minister for Foreign Trade. Since 1967 member of the Central Committee of the Hungarian Socialist Workers' Party.

BOGNÁR, József (b. 1917). Economist, Member of Parliament, Professor at Karl Marx University of Economics, Budapest. Heads the Research Institute on World Economy, Hungarian Academy of Sciences. President, World Federation of Hungarians. Minister of Trade, 1949–1956; President, Institute for Cultural Relations, 1965–1969.

BOLDIZSÁR, Iván (b. 1912). Novelist and playwright. Editor, *The New Hungarian Quarterly*. President, Hungarian P.E.N. Center.

FOCK, Jenő (b. 1916). Member, Political Committee of the Hungarian Socialist Workers' Party, Member of Parliament. Deputy Minister for Mining and Machine Production, 1952–1957; First Secretary, then Deputy General Secretary, National Council of Trade Unions, 1955–1957; member first of the Central and later of the Political Committee of the Hungarian Socialist Workers' Party, 1957; Secretary to the Central Committee of the Hungarian Socialist Workers' Party, 1957–1961; Prime Minister, 1967–1975.

GERGELY, Mihály (b. 1921). Novelist and journalist.

KÁDÁR, János (b. 1912). First Secretary, Hungarian Socialist Workers' Party since 1956.

KEMENES, Egon (b. 1924). Economist. Senior staff member, Institute of World Economy, Hungarian Academy of Sciences.

KEMÉNY, István (b. 1925). Sociologist. Staff member, National Széchényi Library.

KÖPECZI, Béla (b. 1922). Historian and literary historian. Deputy Secretary General, Hungarian Academy of Sciences. Professor of French, Eötvös Lóránd University, Budapest.

LAKOS, Sándor (b. 1921). Economist and social scientist. Before becoming Director of the Institute for the Social Sciences of the Central Committee, Hungarian Socialist Workers' Party, was Dean of the Party's Political Academy and also taught social science at the Budapest Technical University.

LUKÁCS, György (1885–1971). Eminent Hungarian Marxist philosopher.

ORTUTAY, Gyula (b. 1910). Ethnographer. Director of the Institute of Ethnography, Hungarian Academy of Sciences. Minister of Public Instruction, 1947–1950; Rector, Eötvös Lóránd University, Budapest, 1957–1963. Member of Parliament; member, Presidential Council of the Hungarian People's Republic.

PATAKI, Ferenc (1928–1974). Psychologist and educator. Headed social psychology group at Psychological Research Institute, Hungarian Academy of Sciences.

PUJA, Frigyes (b. 1921). Minister for Foreign Affairs. Held various posts after the war before becoming Minister to Sweden (1953–1955), and later to Austria (1955–1959). First Deputy Minister for Foreign Affairs, 1968–1973.

RÉNYI, Péter (b. 1920). Journalist specializing in cultural affairs. Deputy editor, *Népszabadság*, central daily of the Hungarian Socialist Workers' Party.

SIMONYI, Ágnes. Journalist. At present editor at the foreign language service of Hungarian Radio.

SZABADY, Egon (b. 1917). Demographer. Vice-President, Hungarian Central Bureau of Statistics; head of the Institute of Demography, Hungarian Academy of Sciences; editor, *Demografia*.

SZALAI, Júlia. Sociologist. Graduated in economics from Karl Marx University, Budapest.

SZALAI, Sándor (b. 1912). Sociologist. Member, Hungarian Academy of Sciences. Advisor to the Academy's Research Group for the Organization of Sciences. Deputy Director of Research, UNITAR, New York, 1966–1972.

SZÁNTÓ, Miklós (b. 1916). Sociologist and journalist. Fellow, Institute of Sociology, Hungarian Academy of Sciences. Member, Praesidium of the World Federation of Hungarians. Editor of *Magyar Hírek,* bi-monthly newspaper for Hungarians living abroad.

VARGA, Károly (b. 1930). Sociologist. Fellow, Institute of Sociology, Hungarian Academy of Sciences.